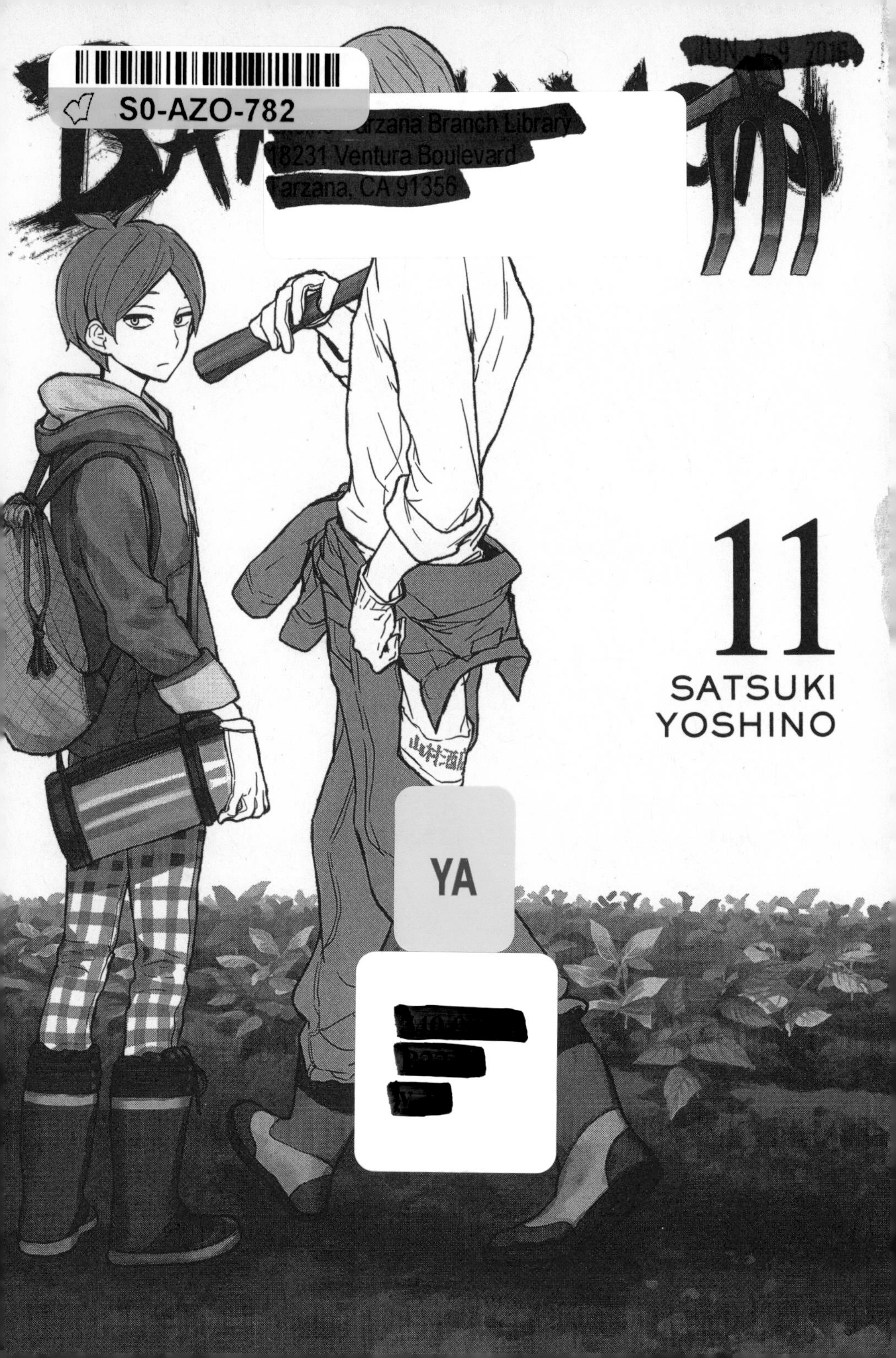
11
SATSUKI
YOSHINO

Contents

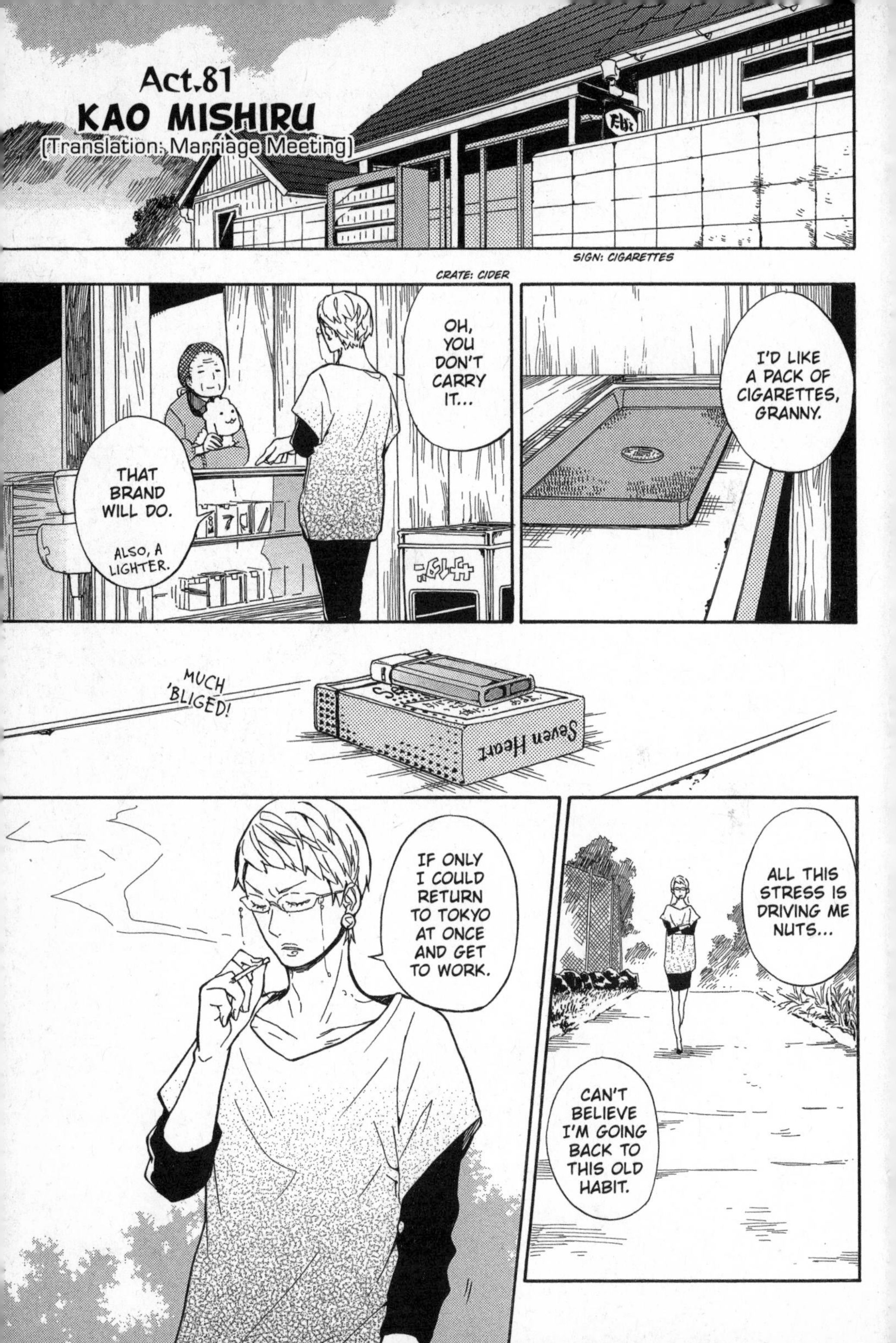
Act.81
KAO MISHIRU
(Translation: Marriage Meeting)
SIGN: CIGARETTES
I'D LIKE A PACK OF CIGARETTES, GRANNY.
OH, YOU DON'T CARRY IT...
THAT BRAND WILL DO.
ALSO, A LIGHTER.
CRATE: CIDER
MUCH 'BLIGED!
Seven Heart
ALL THIS STRESS IS DRIVING ME NUTS...
CAN'T BELIEVE I'M GOING BACK TO THIS OLD HABIT.
IF ONLY I COULD RETURN TO TOKYO AT ONCE AND GET TO WORK.

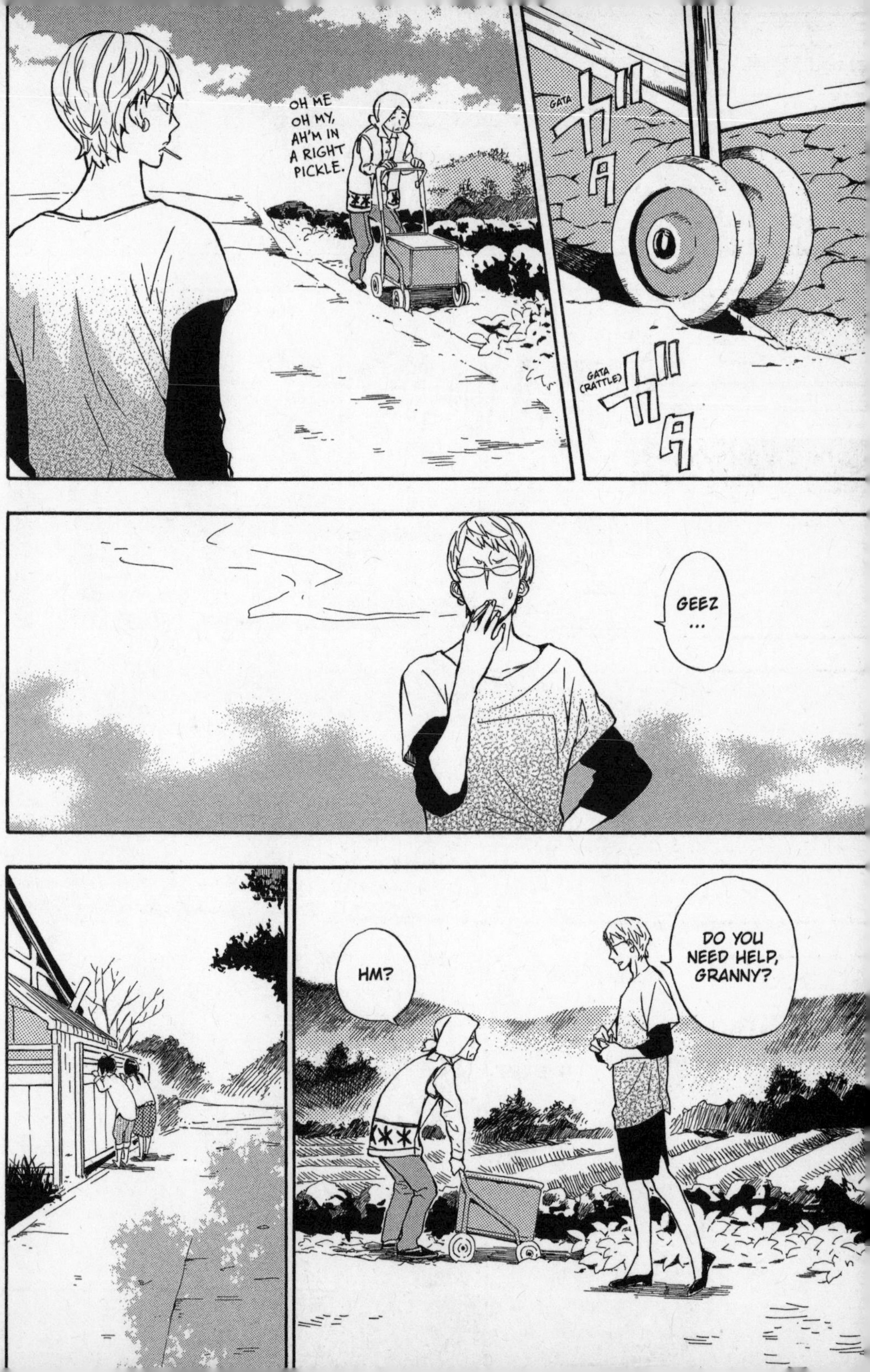
GATA
GATA (RATTLE)
OH ME OH MY, AH'M IN A RIGHT PICKLE.
GEEZ ...
DO YOU NEED HELP, GRANNY?
HM?

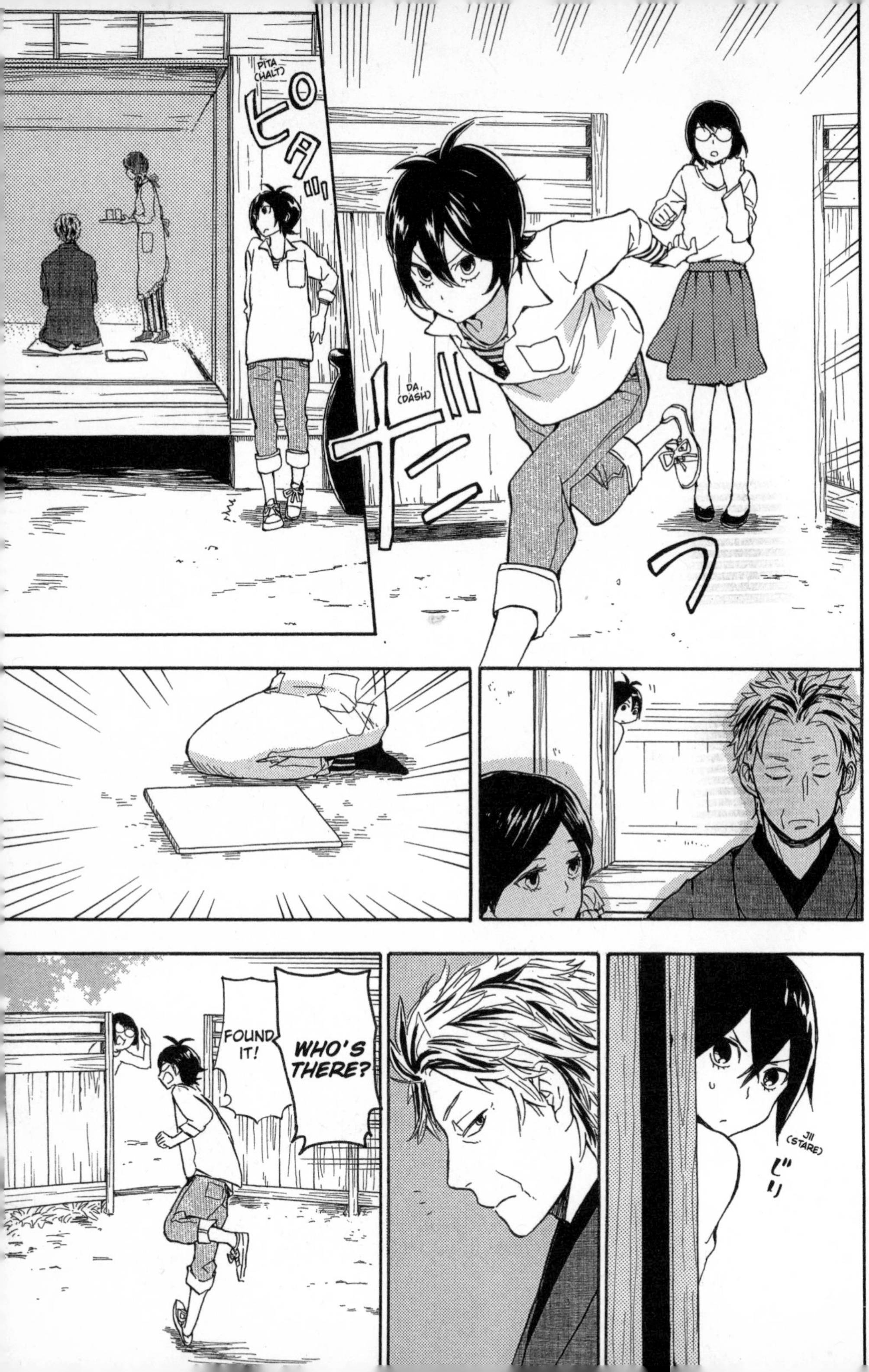
DA (DASH)
ダッ
PITA (HALT)
ピタ
JII (STARE)
WHO'S THERE?
FOUND IT!

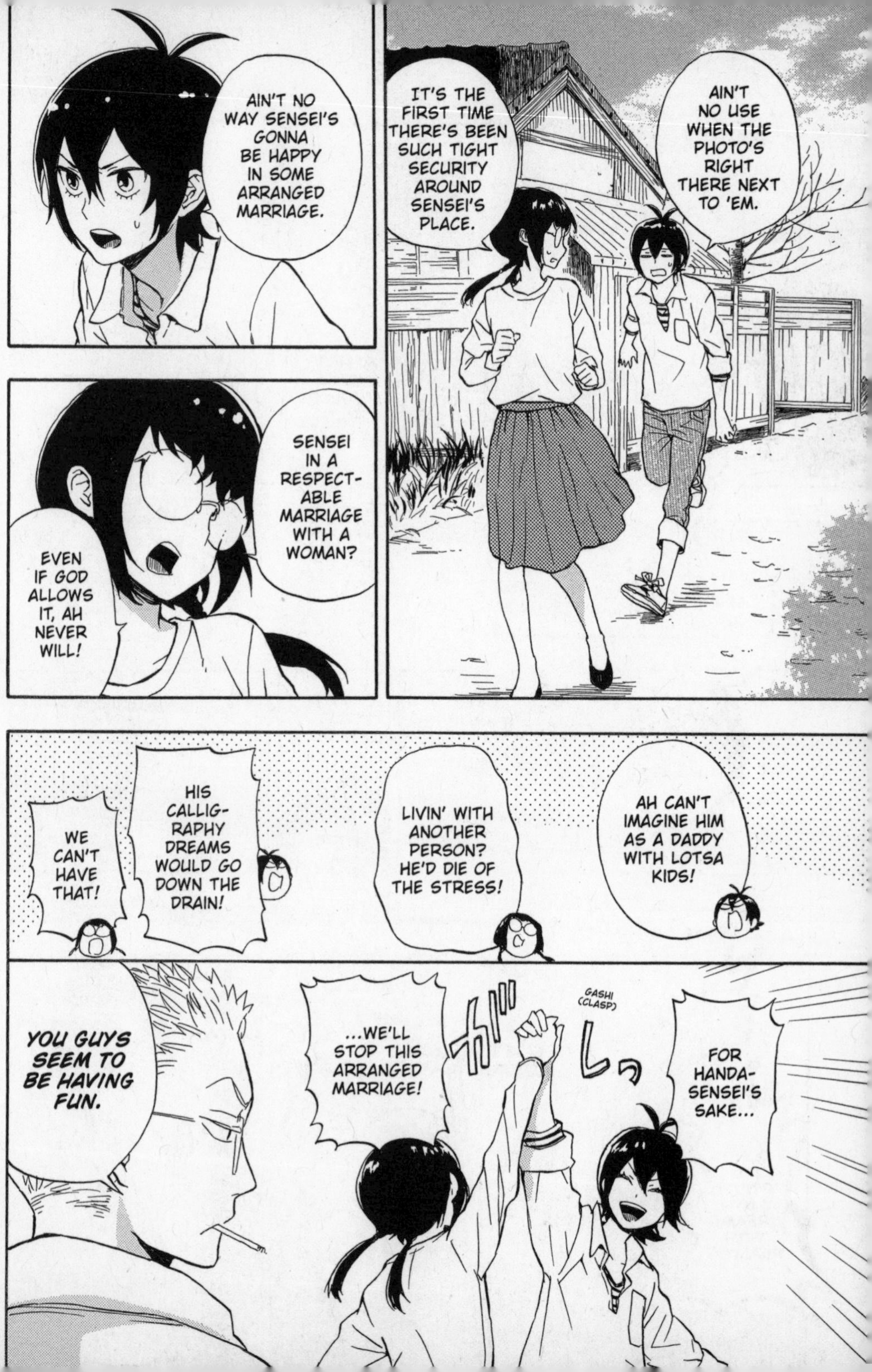
AIN'T NO USE WHEN THE PHOTO'S RIGHT THERE NEXT TO 'EM.
IT'S THE FIRST TIME THERE'S BEEN SUCH TIGHT SECURITY AROUND SENSEI'S PLACE.
AIN'T NO WAY SENSEI'S GONNA BE HAPPY IN SOME ARRANGED MARRIAGE.
SENSEI IN A RESPECT-ABLE MARRIAGE WITH A WOMAN?
EVEN IF GOD ALLOWS IT, AH NEVER WILL!
AH CAN'T IMAGINE HIM AS A DADDY WITH LOTSA KIDS!
LIVIN' WITH ANOTHER PERSON? HE'D DIE OF THE STRESS!
HIS CALLIG-RAPHY DREAMS WOULD GO DOWN THE DRAIN!
WE CAN'T HAVE THAT!
FOR HANDA-SENSEI'S SAKE...
GASHI (CLASP)
...WE'LL STOP THIS ARRANGED MARRIAGE!
YOU GUYS SEEM TO BE HAVING FUN.

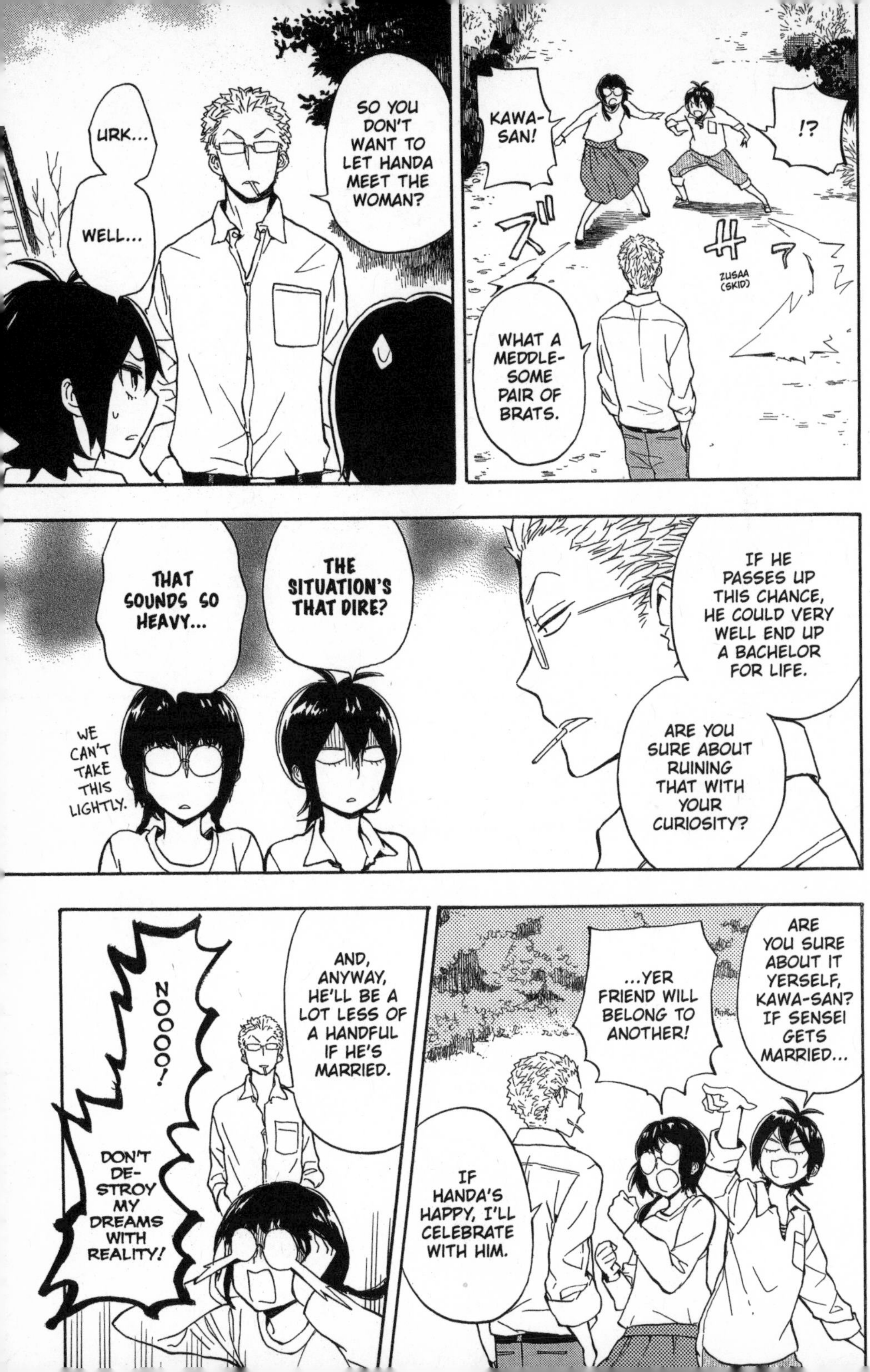
!?
KAWA-SAN!
ズザァ
ZUSAA (SKID)
WHAT A MEDDLE-SOME PAIR OF BRATS.
SO YOU DON'T WANT TO LET HANDA MEET THE WOMAN?
URK...
WELL...
IF HE PASSES UP THIS CHANCE, HE COULD VERY WELL END UP A BACHELOR FOR LIFE.
ARE YOU SURE ABOUT RUINING THAT WITH YOUR CURIOSITY?
THE SITUATION'S THAT DIRE?
THAT SOUNDS SO HEAVY...
WE CAN'T TAKE THIS LIGHTLY.
ARE YOU SURE ABOUT IT YERSELF, KAWA-SAN? IF SENSEI GETS MARRIED...
...YER FRIEND WILL BELONG TO ANOTHER!
IF HANDA'S HAPPY, I'LL CELEBRATE WITH HIM.
AND, ANYWAY, HE'LL BE A LOT LESS OF A HANDFUL IF HE'S MARRIED.
NOOOO!
DON'T DE-STROY MY DREAMS WITH REALITY!

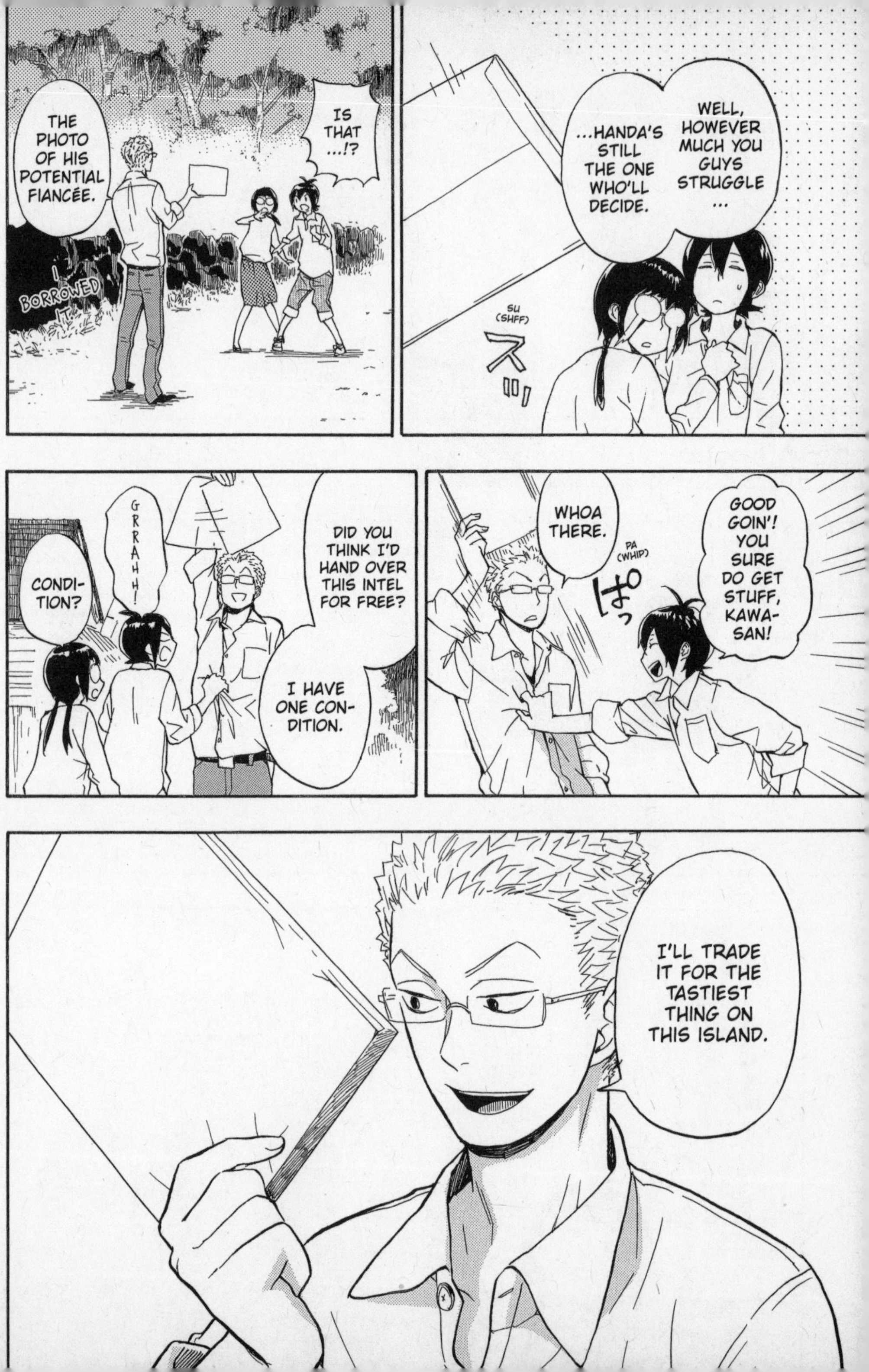
WELL, HOWEVER MUCH YOU GUYS STRUGGLE...
...HANDA'S STILL THE ONE WHO'LL DECIDE.
SU (SHFF)
ス
IS THAT ...!?
THE PHOTO OF HIS POTENTIAL FIANCÉE.
I BORROWED IT.
GOOD GOIN'! YOU SURE DO GET STUFF, KAWA-SAN!
PA (WHIP)
ぱっ
WHOA THERE.
DID YOU THINK I'D HAND OVER THIS INTEL FOR FREE?
GRRAHH!
I HAVE ONE CONDITION.
CONDITION?
I'LL TRADE IT FOR THE TASTIEST THING ON THIS ISLAND.

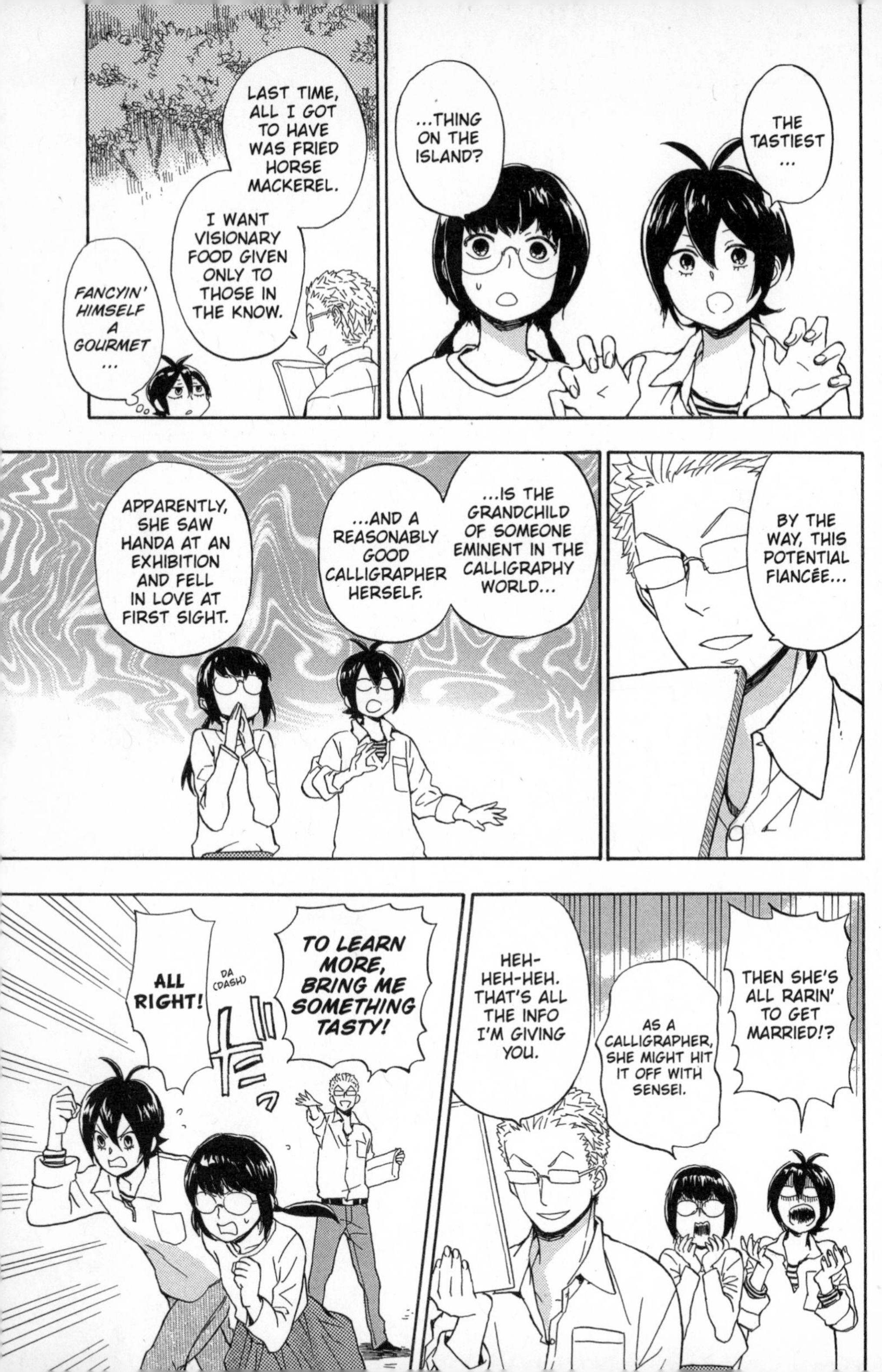
THE TASTIEST...
...THING ON THE ISLAND?
LAST TIME, ALL I GOT TO HAVE WAS FRIED HORSE MACKEREL.
I WANT VISIONARY FOOD GIVEN ONLY TO THOSE IN THE KNOW.
FANCYIN' HIMSELF A GOURMET...
BY THE WAY, THIS POTENTIAL FIANCÉE...
...IS THE GRANDCHILD OF SOMEONE EMINENT IN THE CALLIGRAPHY WORLD...
...AND A REASONABLY GOOD CALLIGRAPHER HERSELF.
APPARENTLY, SHE SAW HANDA AT AN EXHIBITION AND FELL IN LOVE AT FIRST SIGHT.
THEN SHE'S ALL RARIN' TO GET MARRIED!?
AS A CALLIGRAPHER, SHE MIGHT HIT IT OFF WITH SENSEI.
HEH-HEH-HEH. THAT'S ALL THE INFO I'M GIVING YOU.
TO LEARN MORE, BRING ME SOMETHING TASTY!
DA (DASH)
ALL RIGHT!

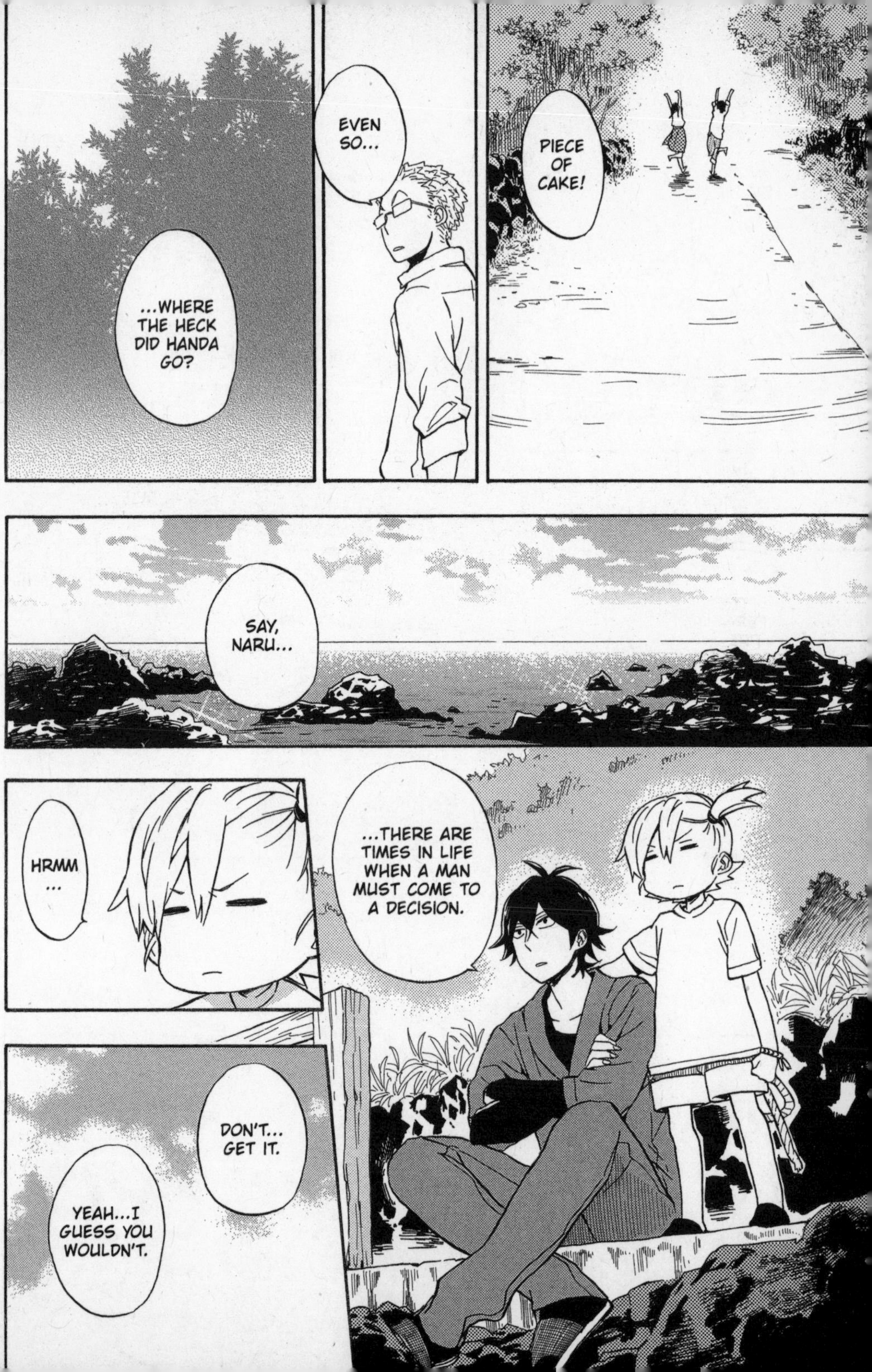
PIECE OF CAKE!
EVEN SO...
...WHERE THE HECK DID HANDA GO?
SAY, NARU...
...THERE ARE TIMES IN LIFE WHEN A MAN MUST COME TO A DECISION.
HRMM ...
DON'T... GET IT.
YEAH...I GUESS YOU WOULDN'T.

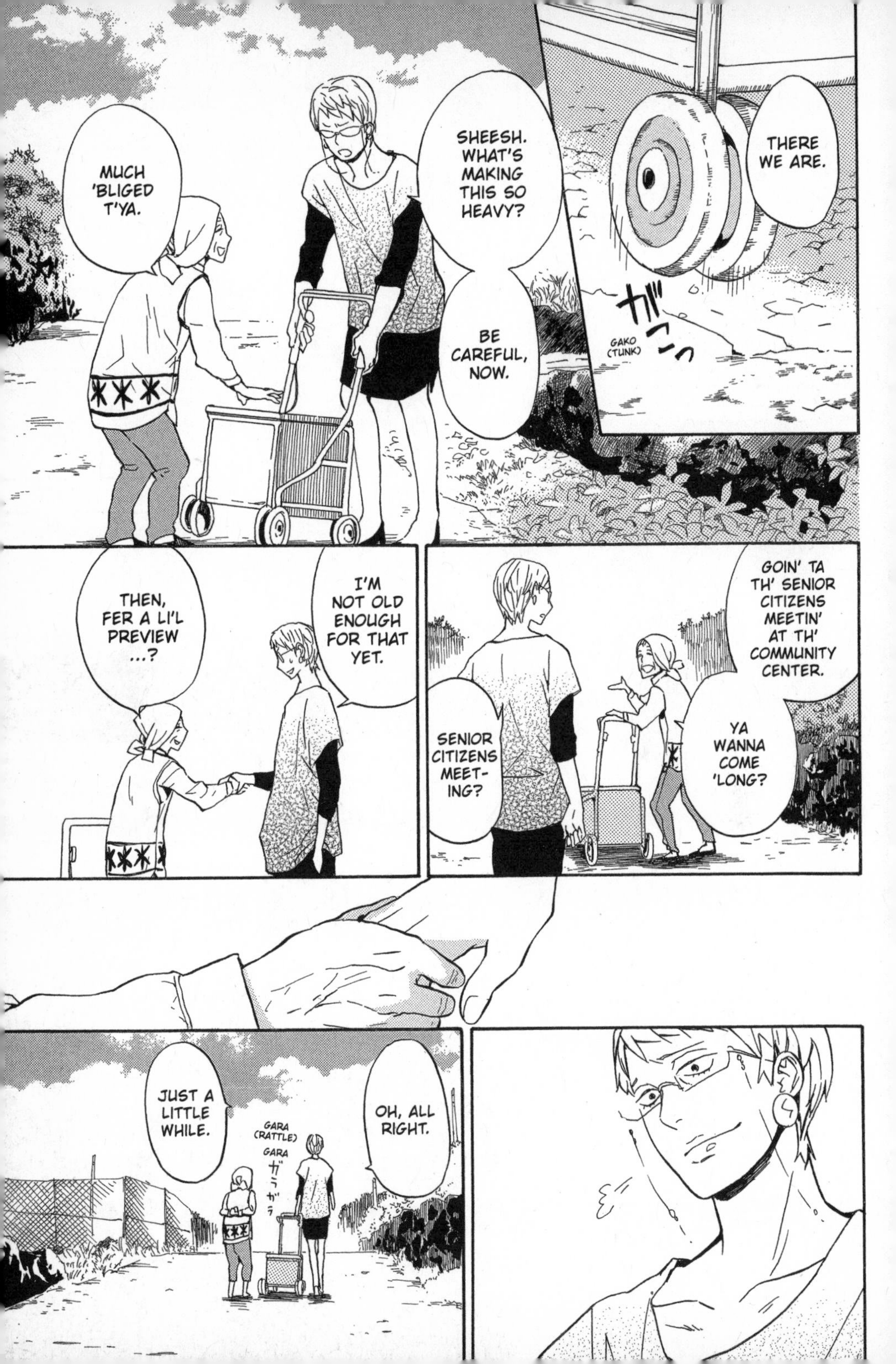
THERE WE ARE.
ガコッ
GAKO (TUNK)
SHEESH. WHAT'S MAKING THIS SO HEAVY?
BE CAREFUL, NOW.
MUCH 'BLIGED T'YA.
GOIN' TA TH' SENIOR CITIZENS MEETIN' AT TH' COMMUNITY CENTER.
YA WANNA COME 'LONG?
SENIOR CITIZENS MEET-ING?
I'M NOT OLD ENOUGH FOR THAT YET.
THEN, FER A LI'L PREVIEW ...?
OH, ALL RIGHT.
ガラガラ
GARA (RATTLE) GARA
JUST A LITTLE WHILE.

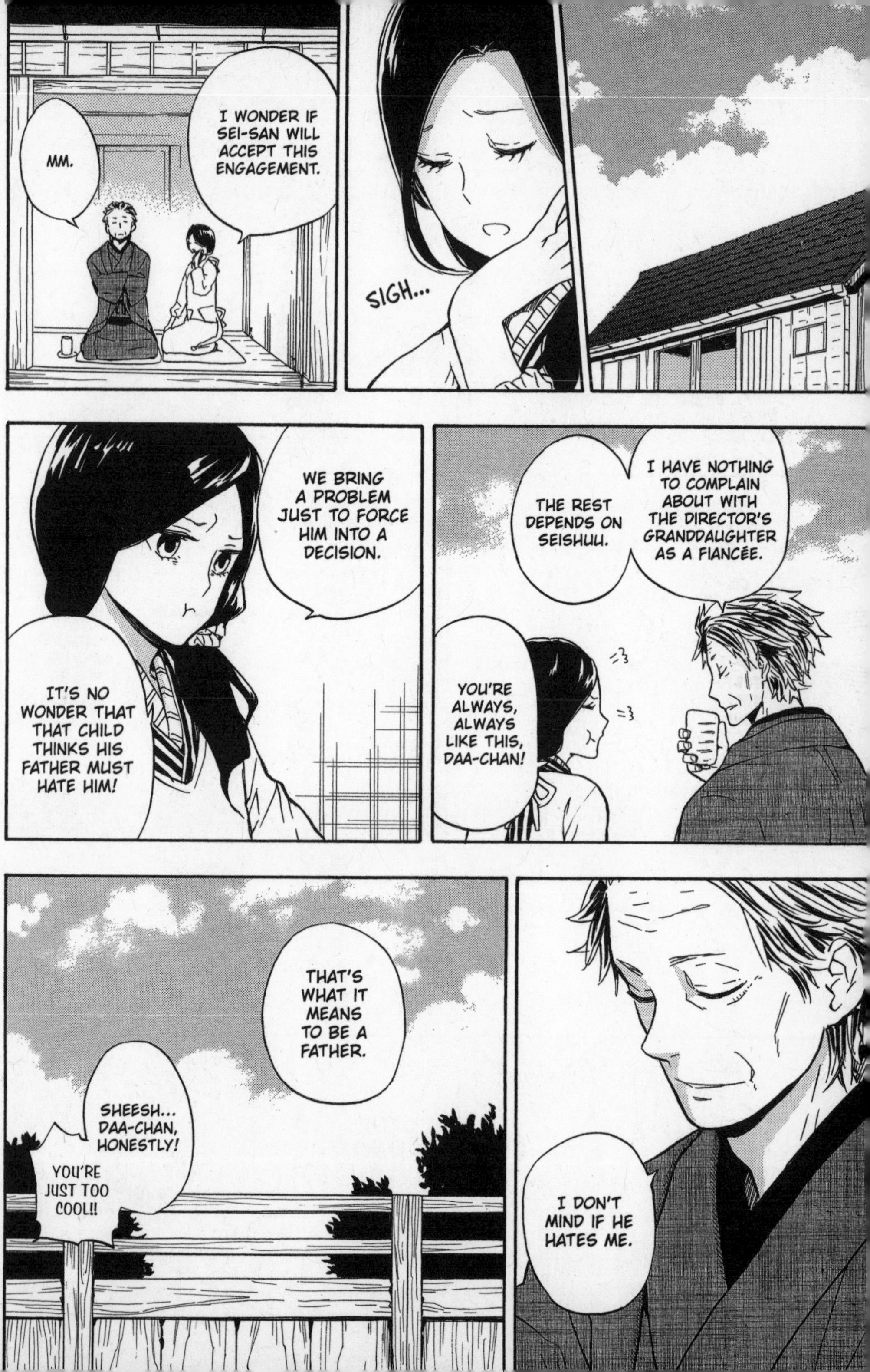
SIGH...
I WONDER IF SEI-SAN WILL ACCEPT THIS ENGAGEMENT.
MM.
I HAVE NOTHING TO COMPLAIN ABOUT WITH THE DIRECTOR'S GRANDDAUGHTER AS A FIANCÉE.
THE REST DEPENDS ON SEISHUU.
YOU'RE ALWAYS, ALWAYS LIKE THIS, DAA-CHAN!
WE BRING A PROBLEM JUST TO FORCE HIM INTO A DECISION.
IT'S NO WONDER THAT THAT CHILD THINKS HIS FATHER MUST HATE HIM!
I DON'T MIND IF HE HATES ME.
THAT'S WHAT IT MEANS TO BE A FATHER.
SHEESH... DAA-CHAN, HONESTLY!
YOU'RE JUST TOO COOL!!

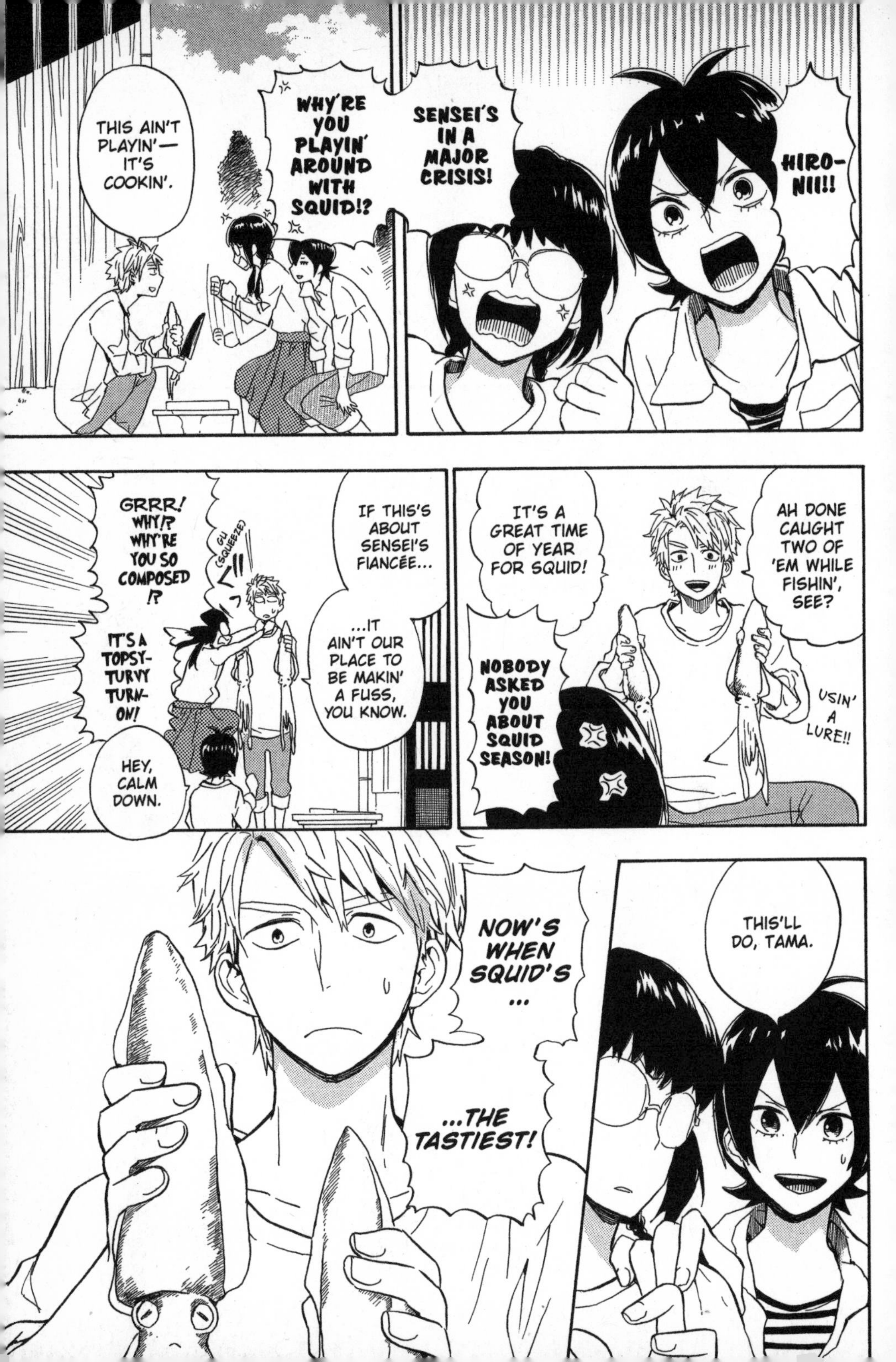
HIRO-NII!!
SENSEI'S IN A MAJOR CRISIS!
WHY'RE YOU PLAYIN' AROUND WITH SQUID!?
THIS AIN'T PLAYIN'— IT'S COOKIN'.
AH DONE CAUGHT TWO OF 'EM WHILE FISHIN', SEE?
USIN' A LURE!!
IT'S A GREAT TIME OF YEAR FOR SQUID!
NOBODY ASKED YOU ABOUT SQUID SEASON!
IF THIS'S ABOUT SENSEI'S FIANCÉE...
...IT AIN'T OUR PLACE TO BE MAKIN' A FUSS, YOU KNOW.
GU (SQUEEZE)
GRRR! WHY!? WHY'RE YOU SO COMPOSED!?
IT'S A TOPSY-TURVY TURN-ON!
HEY, CALM DOWN.
THIS'LL DO, TAMA.
NOW'S WHEN SQUID'S ...
...THE TASTIEST!

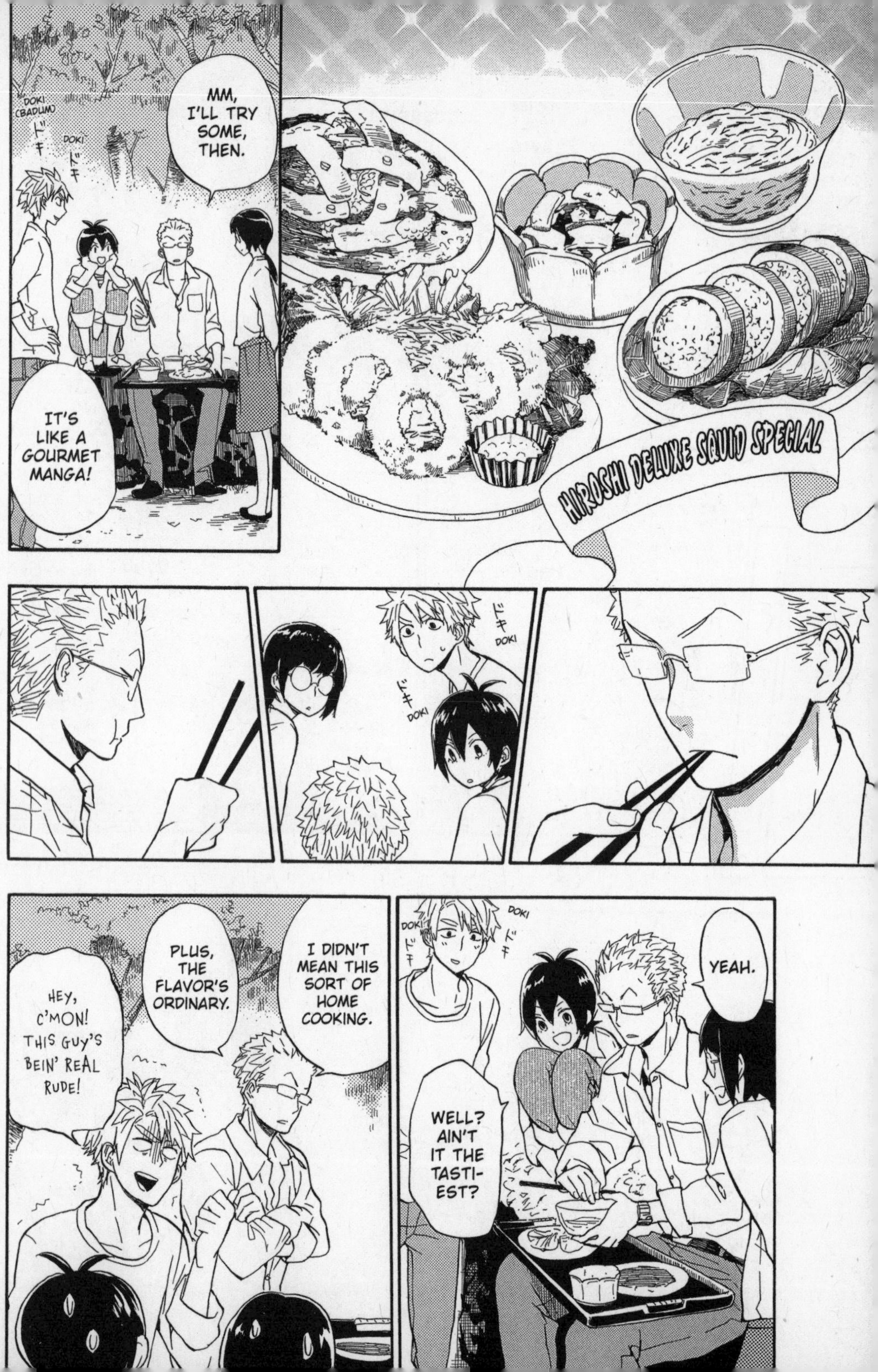
HIROSHI DELUXE SQUID SPECIAL
MM, I'LL TRY SOME, THEN.
DOKI (BADUM) ドキ
DOKI ドキ
IT'S LIKE A GOURMET MANGA!
ドキ DOKI
ドキ DOKI
YEAH.
DOKI ドキ
DOKI ドキ
WELL? AIN'T IT THE TASTI-EST?
I DIDN'T MEAN THIS SORT OF HOME COOKING.
PLUS, THE FLAVOR'S ORDINARY.
HEY, C'MON! THIS GUY'S BEIN' REAL RUDE!

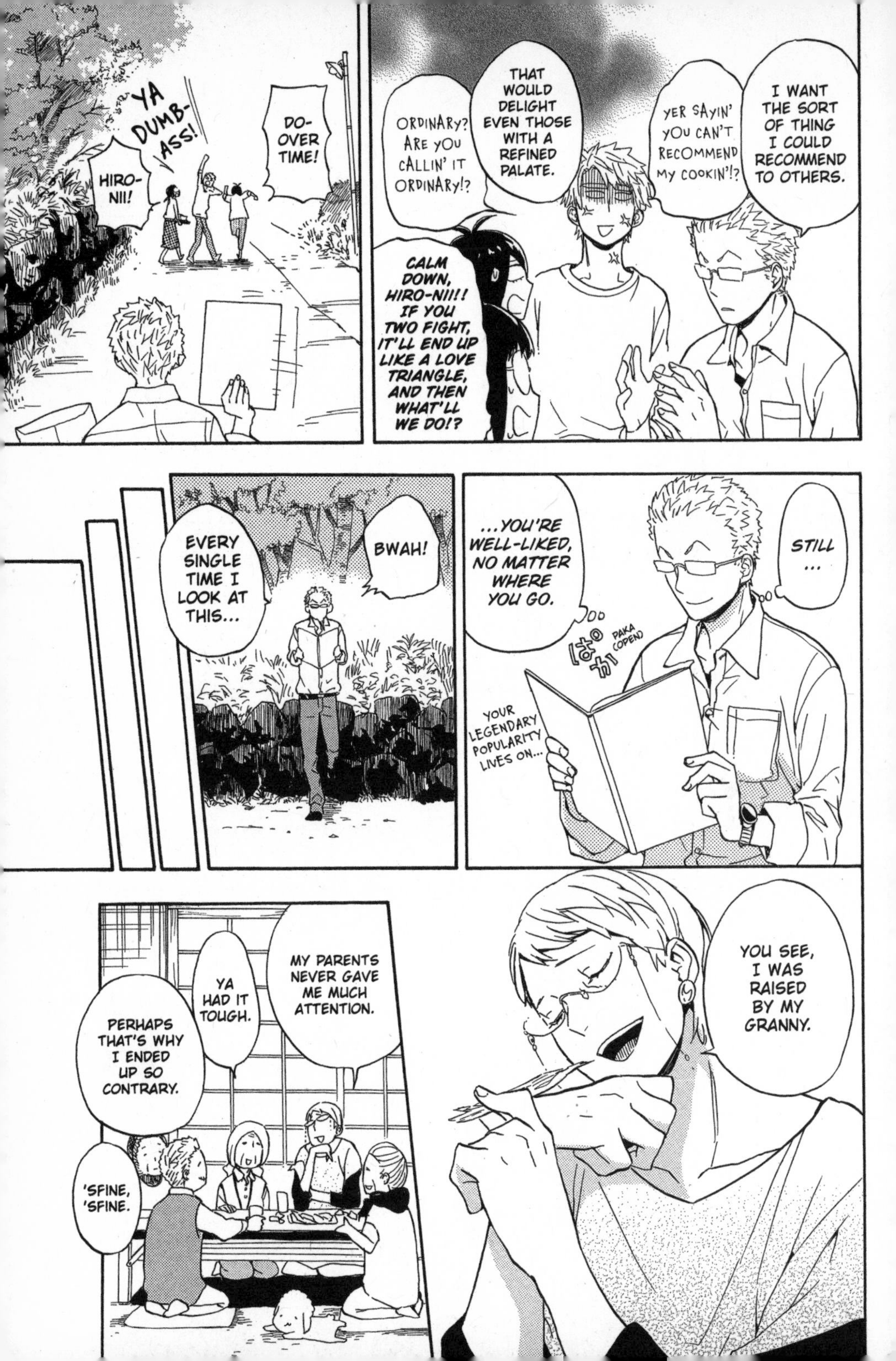
I WANT THE SORT OF THING I COULD RECOMMEND TO OTHERS.
YER SAYIN' YOU CAN'T RECOMMEND MY COOKIN'!?
THAT WOULD DELIGHT EVEN THOSE WITH A REFINED PALATE.
ORDINARY? ARE YOU CALLIN' IT ORDINARY!?
CALM DOWN, HIRO-NII!! IF YOU TWO FIGHT, IT'LL END UP LIKE A LOVE TRIANGLE, AND THEN WHAT'LL WE DO!?
DO-OVER TIME!
YA DUMB-ASS!
HIRO-NII!
STILL...
...YOU'RE WELL-LIKED, NO MATTER WHERE YOU GO.
ぱか
PAKA OPEN
YOUR LEGENDARY POPULARITY LIVES ON...
BWAH!
EVERY SINGLE TIME I LOOK AT THIS...
YOU SEE, I WAS RAISED BY MY GRANNY.
MY PARENTS NEVER GAVE ME MUCH ATTENTION.
YA HAD IT TOUGH.
PERHAPS THAT'S WHY I ENDED UP SO CONTRARY.
'SFINE, 'SFINE.

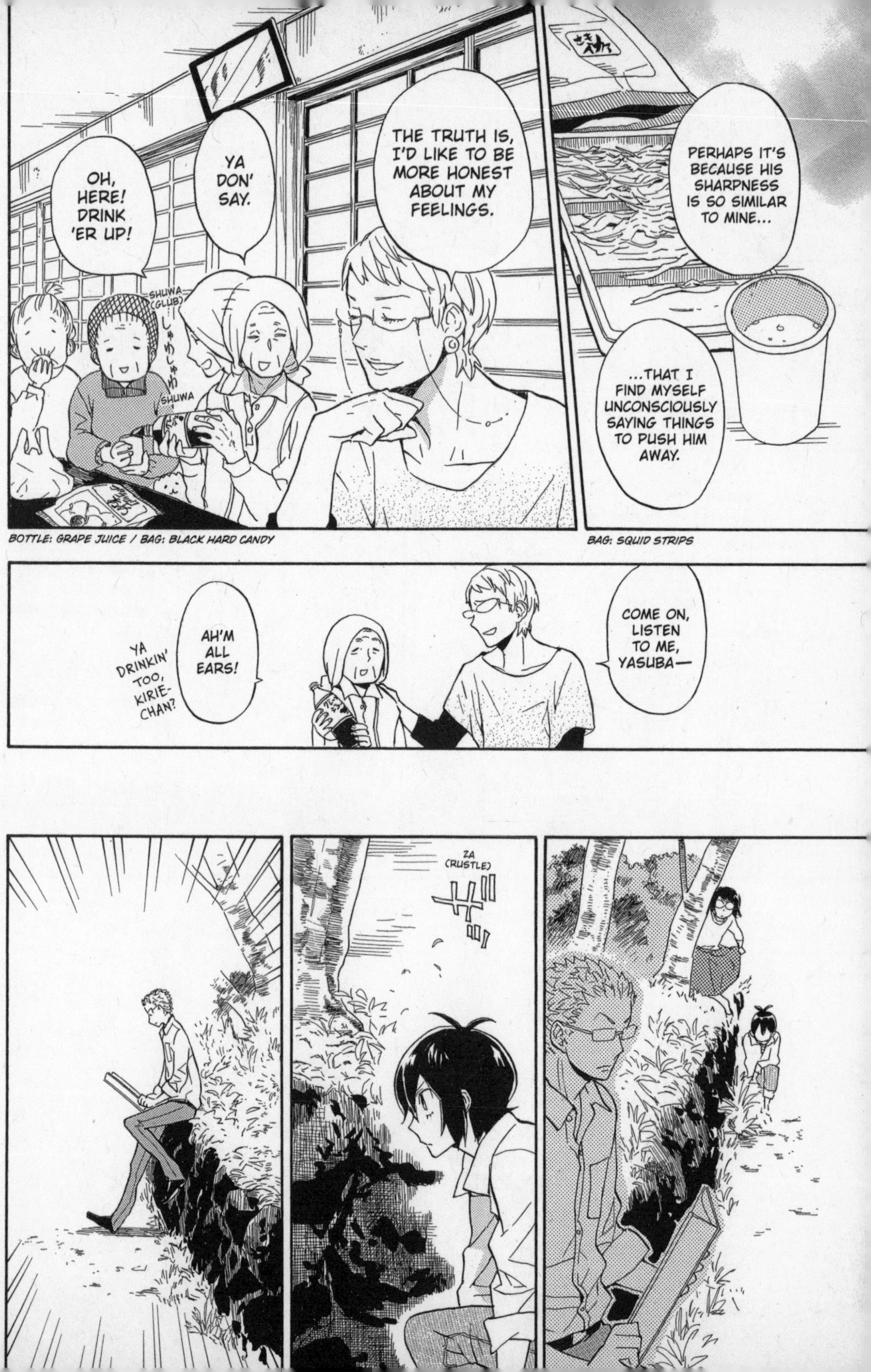
PERHAPS IT'S BECAUSE HIS SHARPNESS IS SO SIMILAR TO MINE...
...THAT I FIND MYSELF UNCONSCIOUSLY SAYING THINGS TO PUSH HIM AWAY.
BAG: SQUID STRIPS
THE TRUTH IS, I'D LIKE TO BE MORE HONEST ABOUT MY FEELINGS.
YA DON' SAY.
OH, HERE! DRINK 'ER UP!
SHUWA (GLUB)
しゅわしゅわ
SHUWA
BOTTLE: GRAPE JUICE / BAG: BLACK HARD CANDY
COME ON, LISTEN TO ME, YASUBA—
AH'M ALL EARS!
YA DRINKIN' TOO, KIRIE-CHAN?
ZA (RUSTLE)

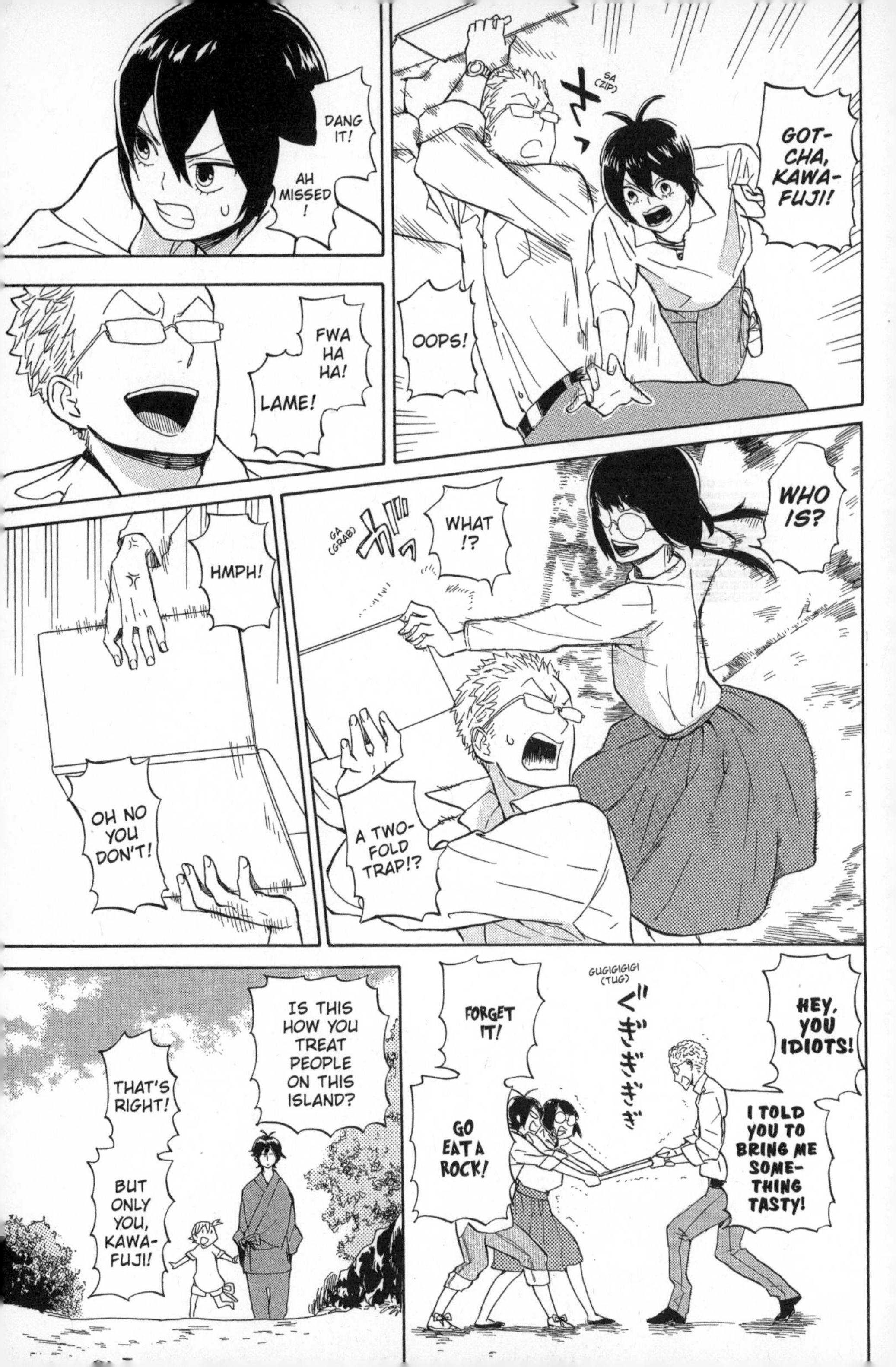
SA (ZIP)
GOT-CHA, KAWA-FUJI!
OOPS!
DANG IT!
AH MISSED!
FWA HA HA!
LAME!
WHO IS?
WHAT !?
GA (GRAB)
A TWO-FOLD TRAP!?
HMPH!
OH NO YOU DON'T!
HEY, YOU IDIOTS!
I TOLD YOU TO BRING ME SOME-THING TASTY!
GUGIGIGIGI (TUG)
FORGET IT!
GO EAT A ROCK!
IS THIS HOW YOU TREAT PEOPLE ON THIS ISLAND?
THAT'S RIGHT!
BUT ONLY YOU, KAWA-FUJI!

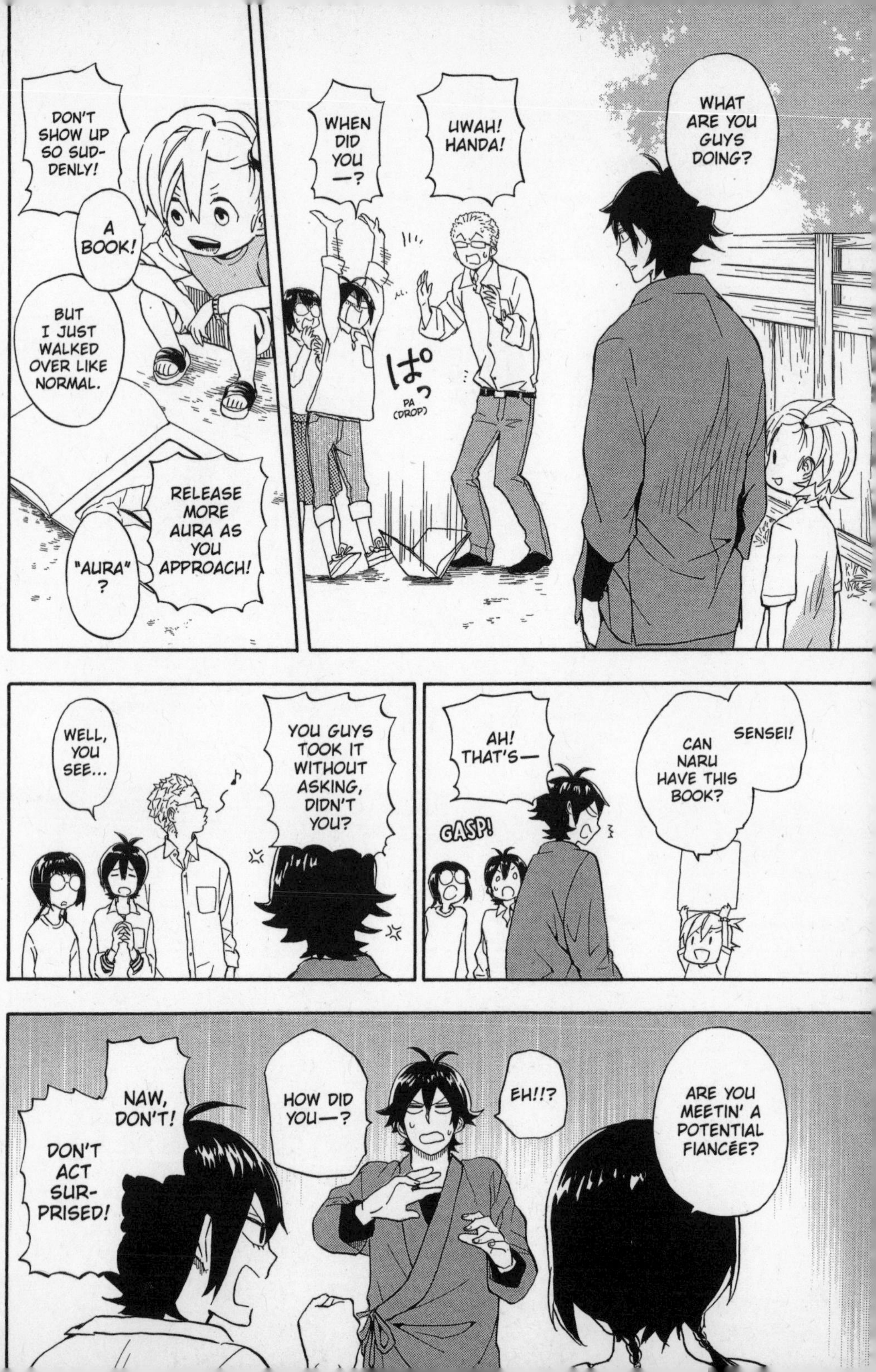
WHAT ARE YOU GUYS DOING?
UWAH! HANDA!
WHEN DID YOU—?
ぱっ
PA (DROP)
DON'T SHOW UP SO SUD-DENLY!
A BOOK!
BUT I JUST WALKED OVER LIKE NORMAL.
RELEASE MORE AURA AS YOU APPROACH!
"AURA"?
SENSEI!
CAN NARU HAVE THIS BOOK?
AH! THAT'S—
GASP!
YOU GUYS TOOK IT WITHOUT ASKING, DIDN'T YOU?
WELL, YOU SEE...
ARE YOU MEETIN' A POTENTIAL FIANCÉE?
EH!!?
HOW DID YOU—?
NAW, DON'T!
DON'T ACT SUR-PRISED!

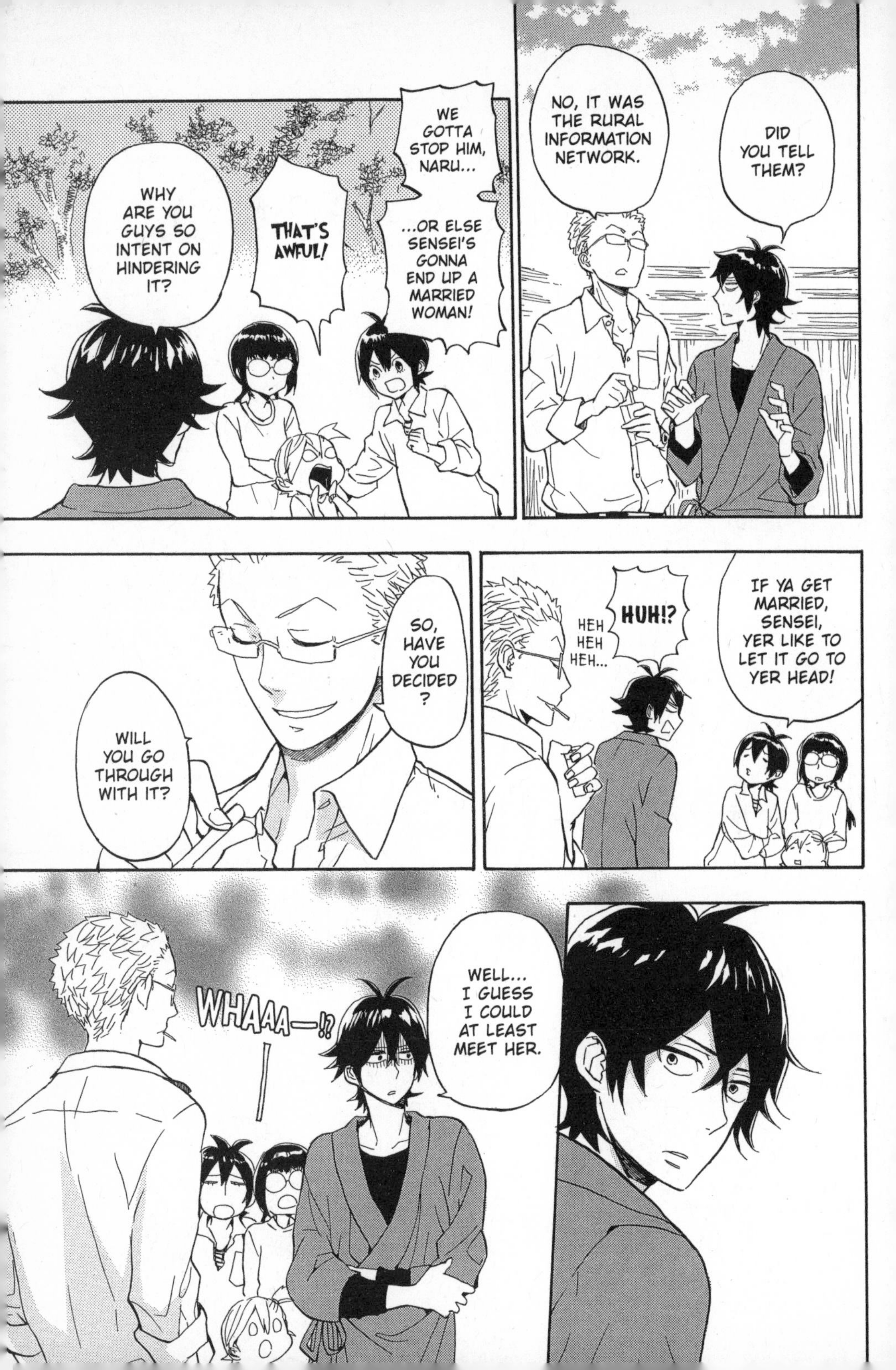
DID YOU TELL THEM?
NO, IT WAS THE RURAL INFORMATION NETWORK.
WE GOTTA STOP HIM, NARU...
...OR ELSE SENSEI'S GONNA END UP A MARRIED WOMAN!
THAT'S AWFUL!
WHY ARE YOU GUYS SO INTENT ON HINDERING IT?
IF YA GET MARRIED, SENSEI, YER LIKE TO LET IT GO TO YER HEAD!
HUH!?
HEH HEH HEH...
SO, HAVE YOU DECIDED?
WILL YOU GO THROUGH WITH IT?
WELL... I GUESS I COULD AT LEAST MEET HER.
WHAAA—!?

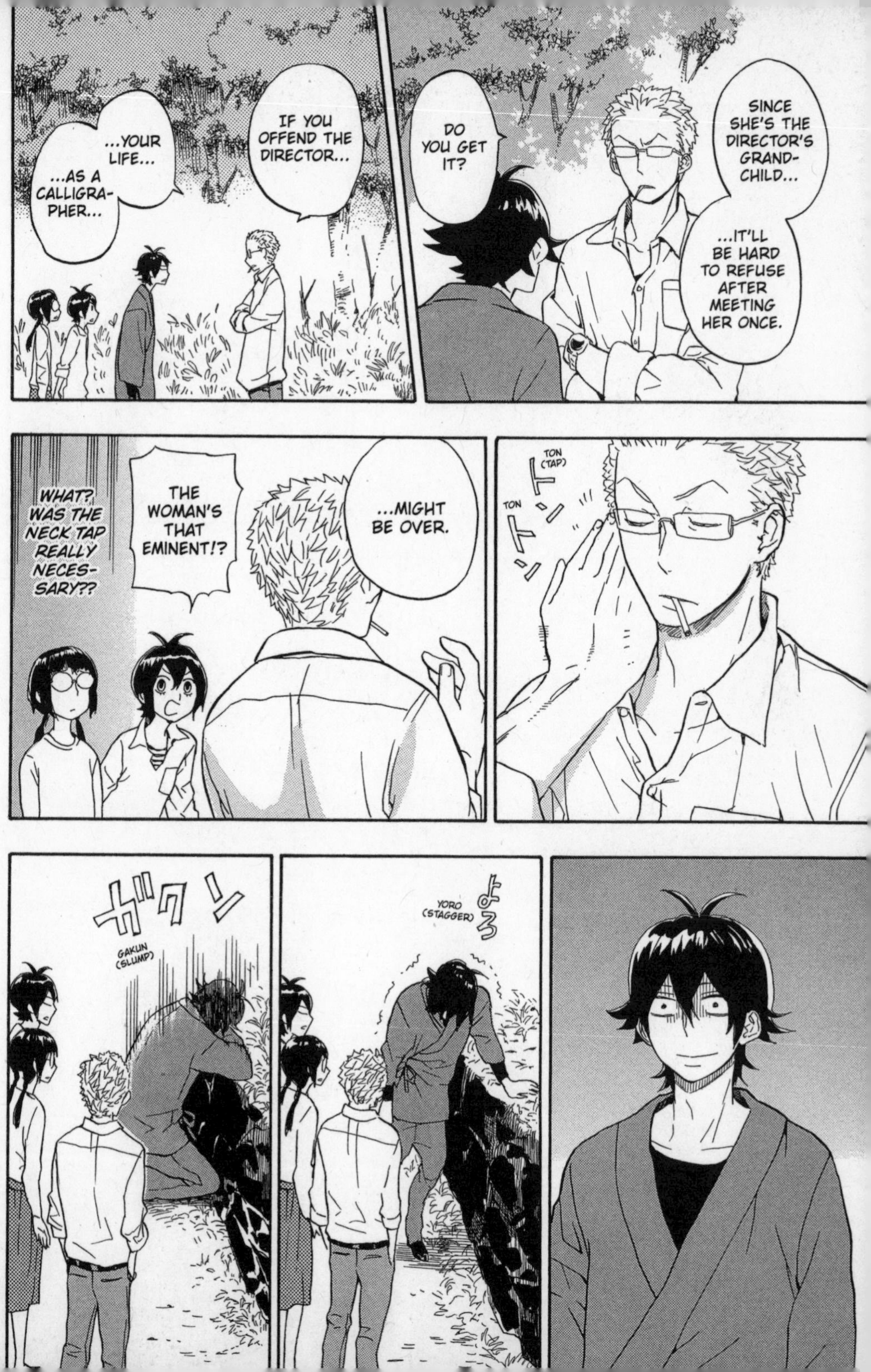
SINCE SHE'S THE DIRECTOR'S GRAND-CHILD...
...IT'LL BE HARD TO REFUSE AFTER MEETING HER ONCE.
DO YOU GET IT?
IF YOU OFFEND THE DIRECTOR...
...YOUR LIFE...
...AS A CALLIGRAPHER...
トン
TON (TAP)
トン
TON
...MIGHT BE OVER.
THE WOMAN'S THAT EMINENT!?
WHAT? WAS THE NECK TAP REALLY NECES-SARY??
よろ
YORO (STAGGER)
ガクン
GAKUN (SLUMP)

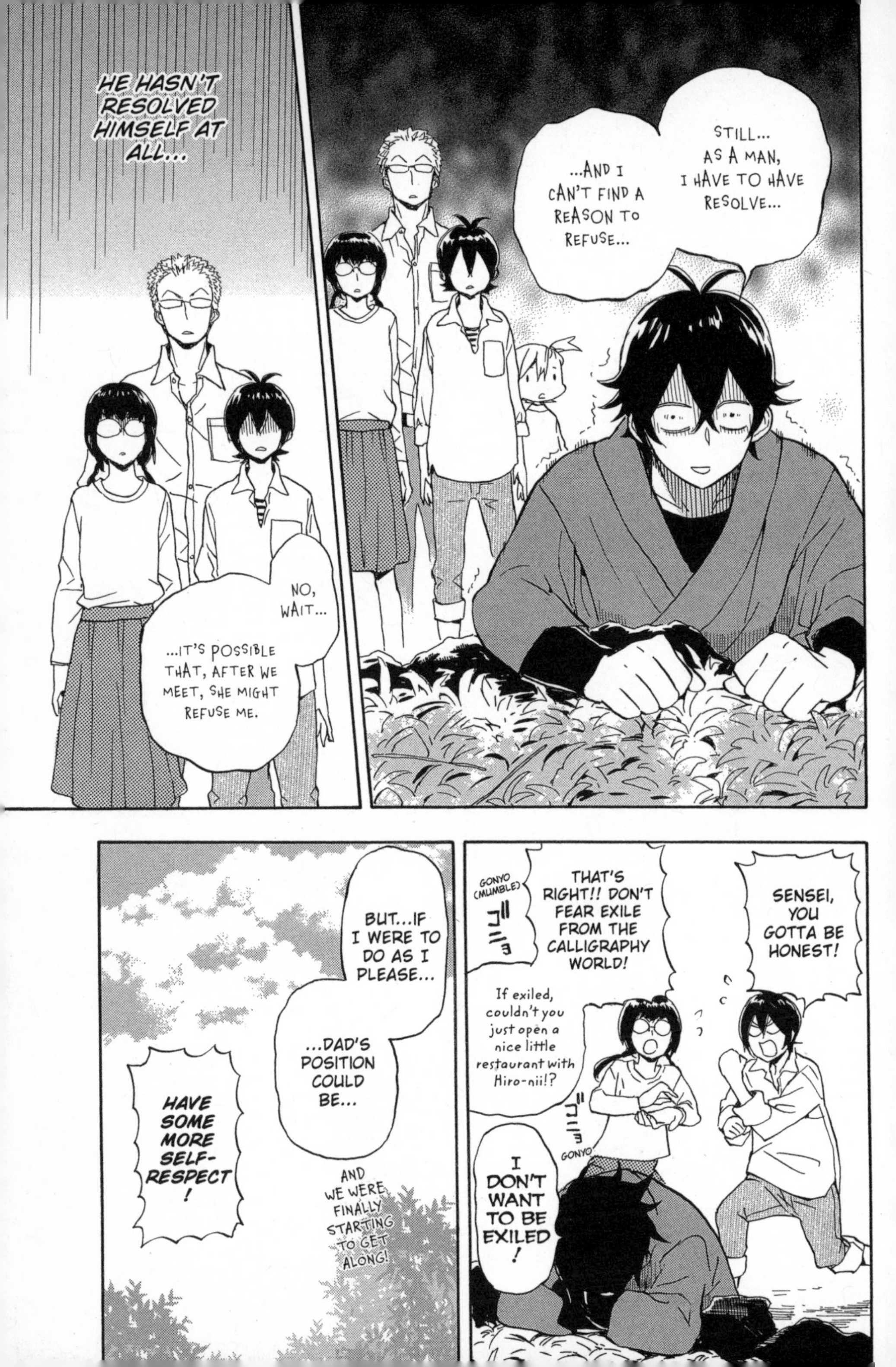
STILL... AS A MAN, I HAVE TO HAVE RESOLVE...
...AND I CAN'T FIND A REASON TO REFUSE...
NO, WAIT...
...IT'S POSSIBLE THAT, AFTER WE MEET, SHE MIGHT REFUSE ME.
HE HASN'T RESOLVED HIMSELF AT ALL...
SENSEI, YOU GOTTA BE HONEST!
THAT'S RIGHT!! DON'T FEAR EXILE FROM THE CALLIGRAPHY WORLD!
GONYO (MUMBLE)
ゴニョ
If exiled, couldn't you just open a nice little restaurant with Hiro-nii!?
ゴニョ
GONYO
I DON'T WANT TO BE EXILED!
BUT...IF I WERE TO DO AS I PLEASE...
...DAD'S POSITION COULD BE...
AND WE WERE FINALLY STARTING TO GET ALONG!
HAVE SOME MORE SELF-RESPECT!

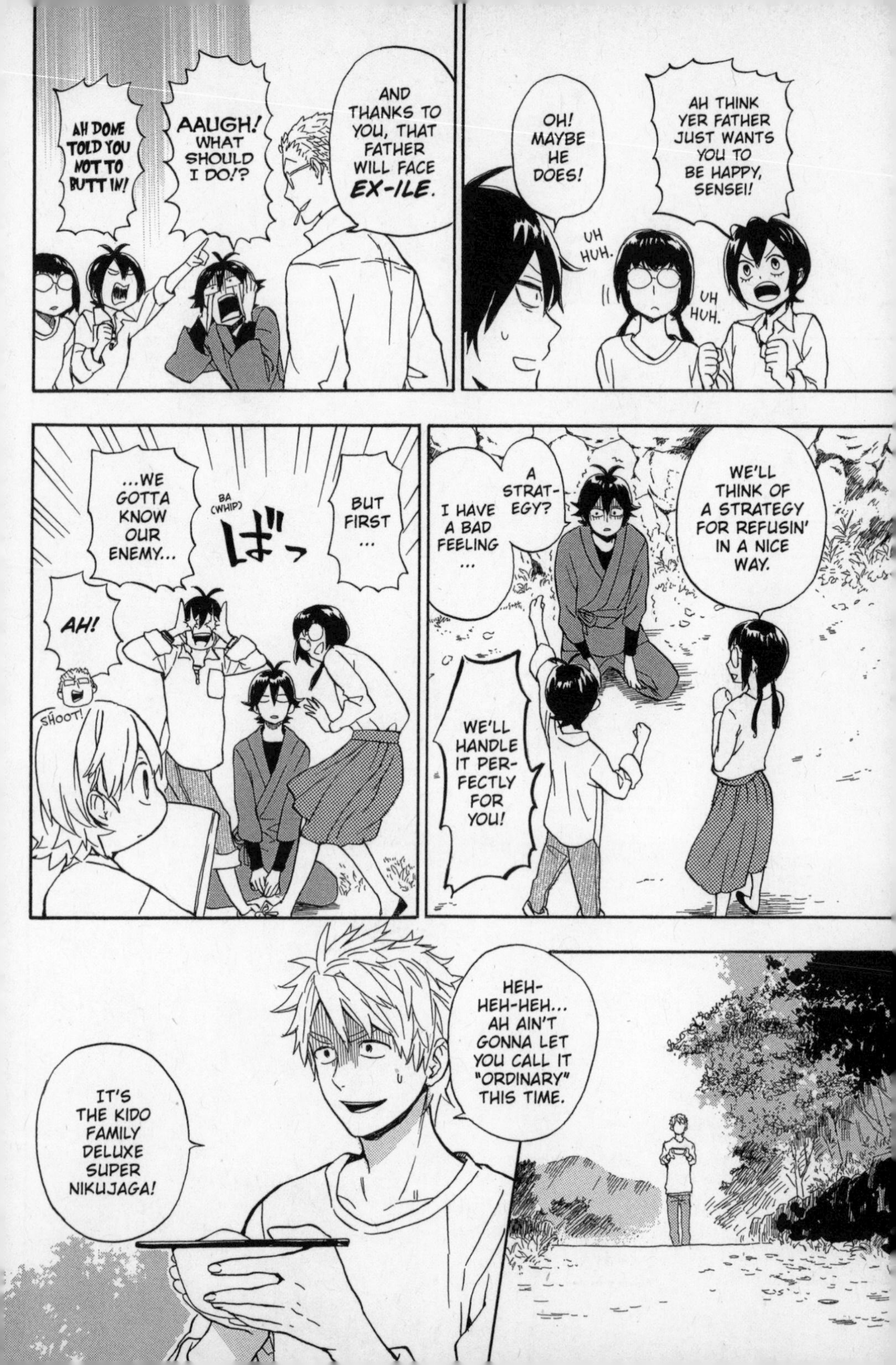
AH THINK YER FATHER JUST WANTS YOU TO BE HAPPY, SENSEI!
UH HUH.
UH HUH.
OH! MAYBE HE DOES!
AND THANKS TO YOU, THAT FATHER WILL FACE EX-ILE.
AAUGH! WHAT SHOULD I DO!?
AH DONE TOLD YOU NOT TO BUTT IN!
WE'LL THINK OF A STRATEGY FOR REFUSIN' IN A NICE WAY.
A STRAT-EGY?
I HAVE A BAD FEELING ...
WE'LL HANDLE IT PERFECTLY FOR YOU!
BUT FIRST ...
BA (WHIP)
ばっ
...WE GOTTA KNOW OUR ENEMY...
AH!
SHOOT!
HEH-HEH-HEH... AH AIN'T GONNA LET YOU CALL IT "ORDINARY" THIS TIME.
IT'S THE KIDO FAMILY DELUXE SUPER NIKUJAGA!

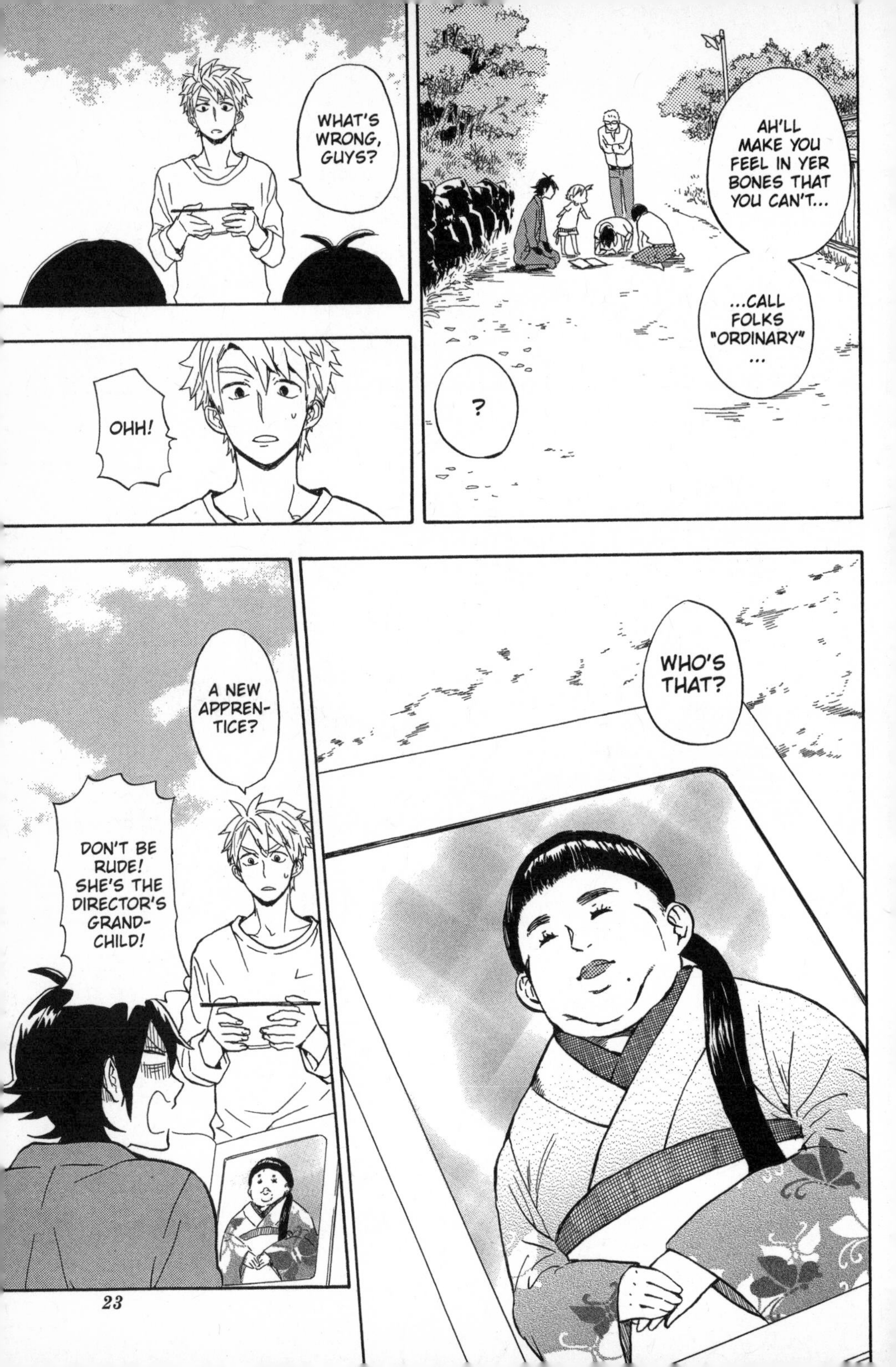
AH'LL MAKE YOU FEEL IN YER BONES THAT YOU CAN'T...
...CALL FOLKS "ORDINARY"...
?
WHAT'S WRONG, GUYS?
OHH!
WHO'S THAT?
A NEW APPREN-TICE?
DON'T BE RUDE! SHE'S THE DIRECTOR'S GRAND-CHILD!

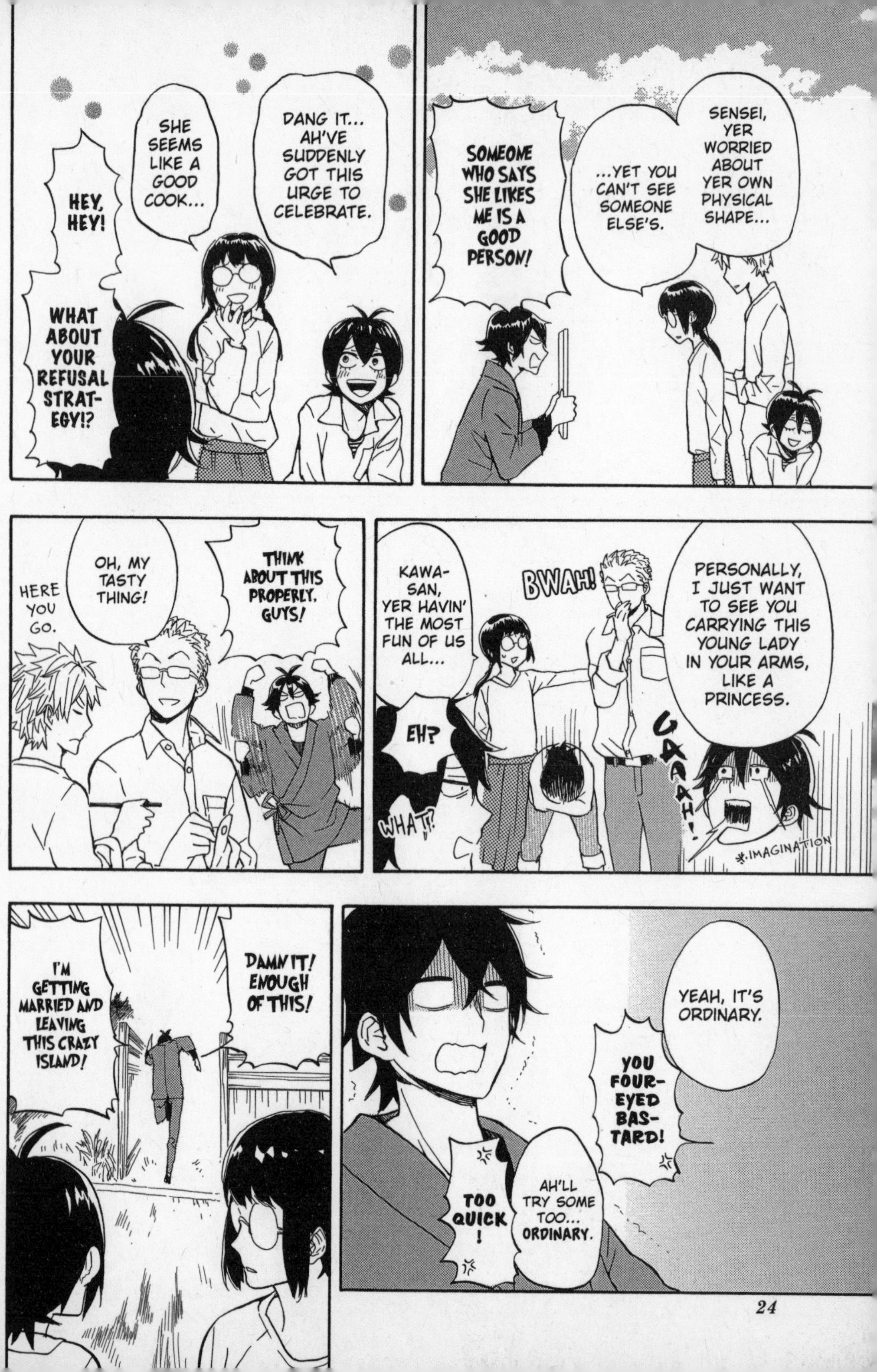
SENSEI, YER WORRIED ABOUT YER OWN PHYSICAL SHAPE...
...YET YOU CAN'T SEE SOMEONE ELSE'S.
SOMEONE WHO SAYS SHE LIKES ME IS A GOOD PERSON!
DANG IT... AH'VE SUDDENLY GOT THIS URGE TO CELEBRATE.
SHE SEEMS LIKE A GOOD COOK...
HEY, HEY!
WHAT ABOUT YOUR REFUSAL STRAT-EGY!?
PERSONALLY, I JUST WANT TO SEE YOU CARRYING THIS YOUNG LADY IN YOUR ARMS, LIKE A PRINCESS.
BWAH!
KAWA-SAN, YER HAVIN' THE MOST FUN OF US ALL...
UAAAH!
EH?
WHAT!?
*IMAGINATION
THINK ABOUT THIS PROPERLY, GUYS!
OH, MY TASTY THING!
HERE YOU GO.
YEAH, IT'S ORDINARY.
YOU FOUR-EYED BAS-TARD!
AH'LL TRY SOME TOO... ORDINARY.
TOO QUICK!
DAMN IT! ENOUGH OF THIS!
I'M GETTING MARRIED AND LEAVING THIS CRAZY ISLAND!

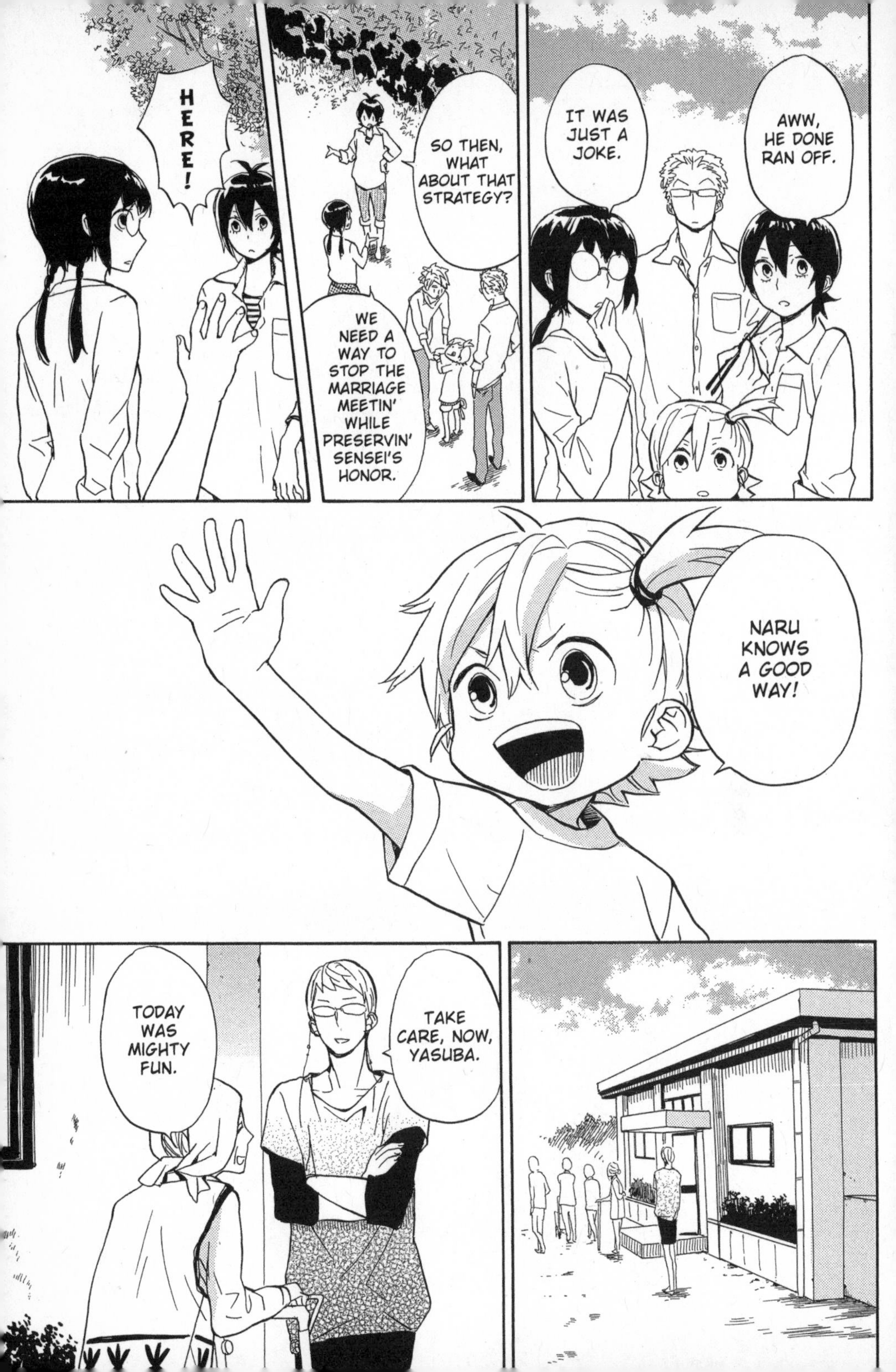
AWW, HE DONE RAN OFF.
IT WAS JUST A JOKE.
SO THEN, WHAT ABOUT THAT STRATEGY?
WE NEED A WAY TO STOP THE MARRIAGE MEETIN' WHILE PRESERVIN' SENSEI'S HONOR.
HERE!
NARU KNOWS A GOOD WAY!
TAKE CARE, NOW, YASUBA.
TODAY WAS MIGHTY FUN.

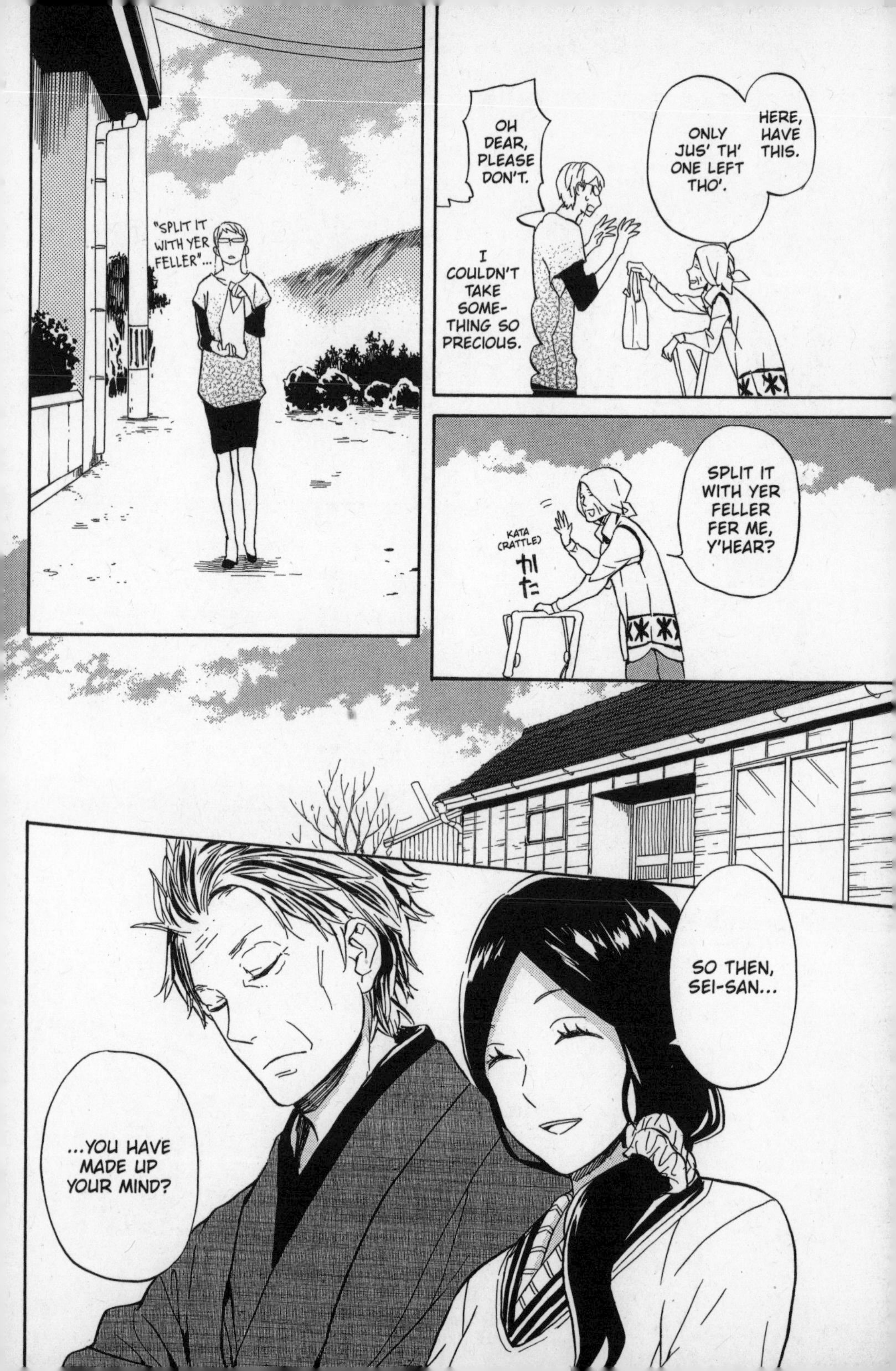
HERE, HAVE THIS.
ONLY JUS' TH' ONE LEFT THO'.
OH DEAR, PLEASE DON'T.
I COULDN'T TAKE SOMETHING SO PRECIOUS.
SPLIT IT WITH YER FELLER FER ME, Y'HEAR?
KATA (RATTLE)
かた
"SPLIT IT WITH YER FELLER"...
SO THEN, SEI-SAN...
...YOU HAVE MADE UP YOUR MIND?

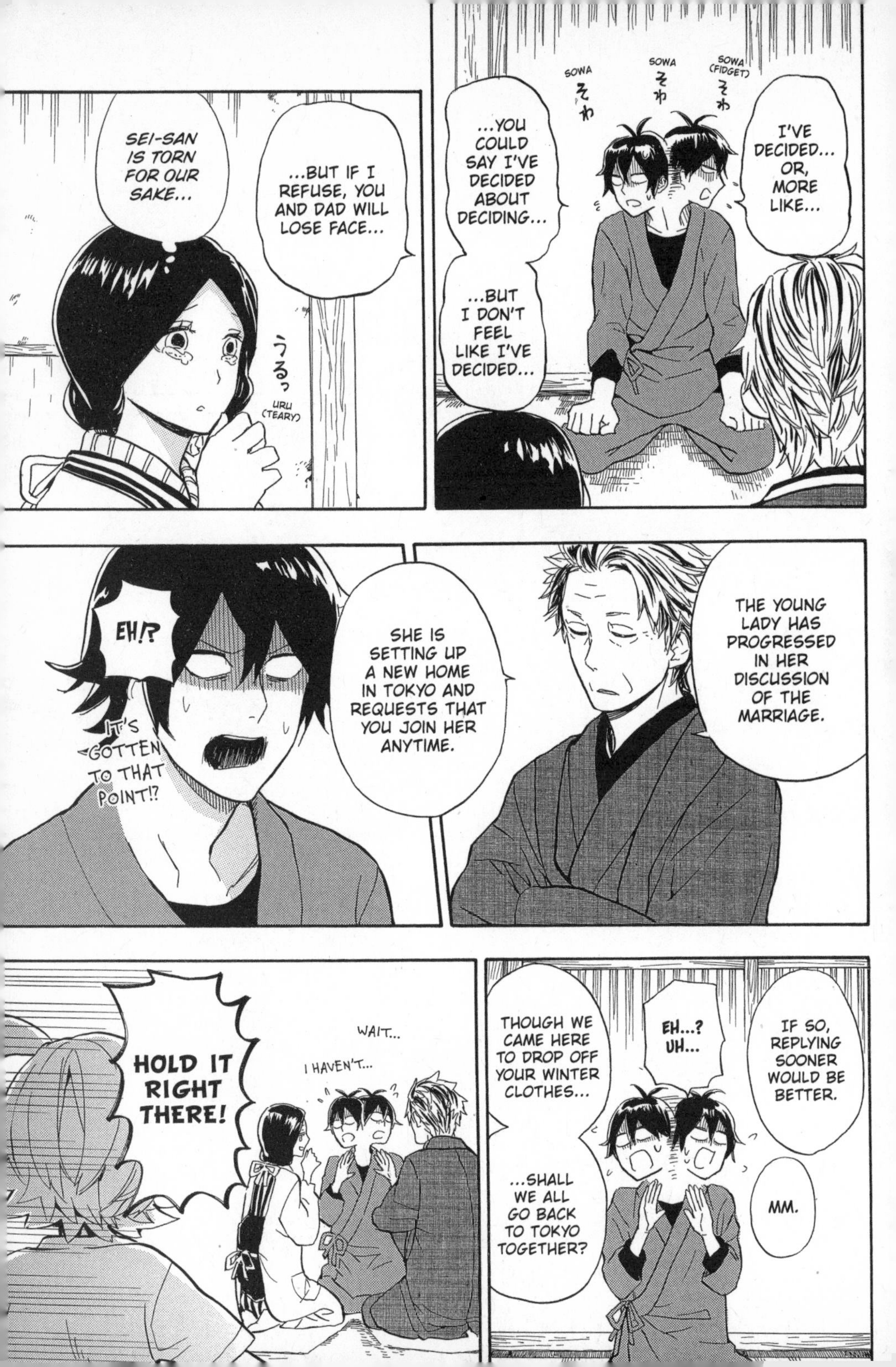
I'VE DECIDED... OR, MORE LIKE...
そわ SOWA (FIDGET)
そわ SOWA
そわ SOWA
...YOU COULD SAY I'VE DECIDED ABOUT DECIDING...
...BUT I DON'T FEEL LIKE I'VE DECIDED...
...BUT IF I REFUSE, YOU AND DAD WILL LOSE FACE...
SEI-SAN IS TORN FOR OUR SAKE...
うるっ URU (TEARY)
THE YOUNG LADY HAS PROGRESSED IN HER DISCUSSION OF THE MARRIAGE.
SHE IS SETTING UP A NEW HOME IN TOKYO AND REQUESTS THAT YOU JOIN HER ANYTIME.
EH!?
IT'S GOTTEN TO THAT POINT!?
IF SO, REPLYING SOONER WOULD BE BETTER.
EH...? UH...
MM.
THOUGH WE CAME HERE TO DROP OFF YOUR WINTER CLOTHES...
...SHALL WE ALL GO BACK TO TOKYO TOGETHER?
WAIT...
I HAVEN'T...
HOLD IT RIGHT THERE!

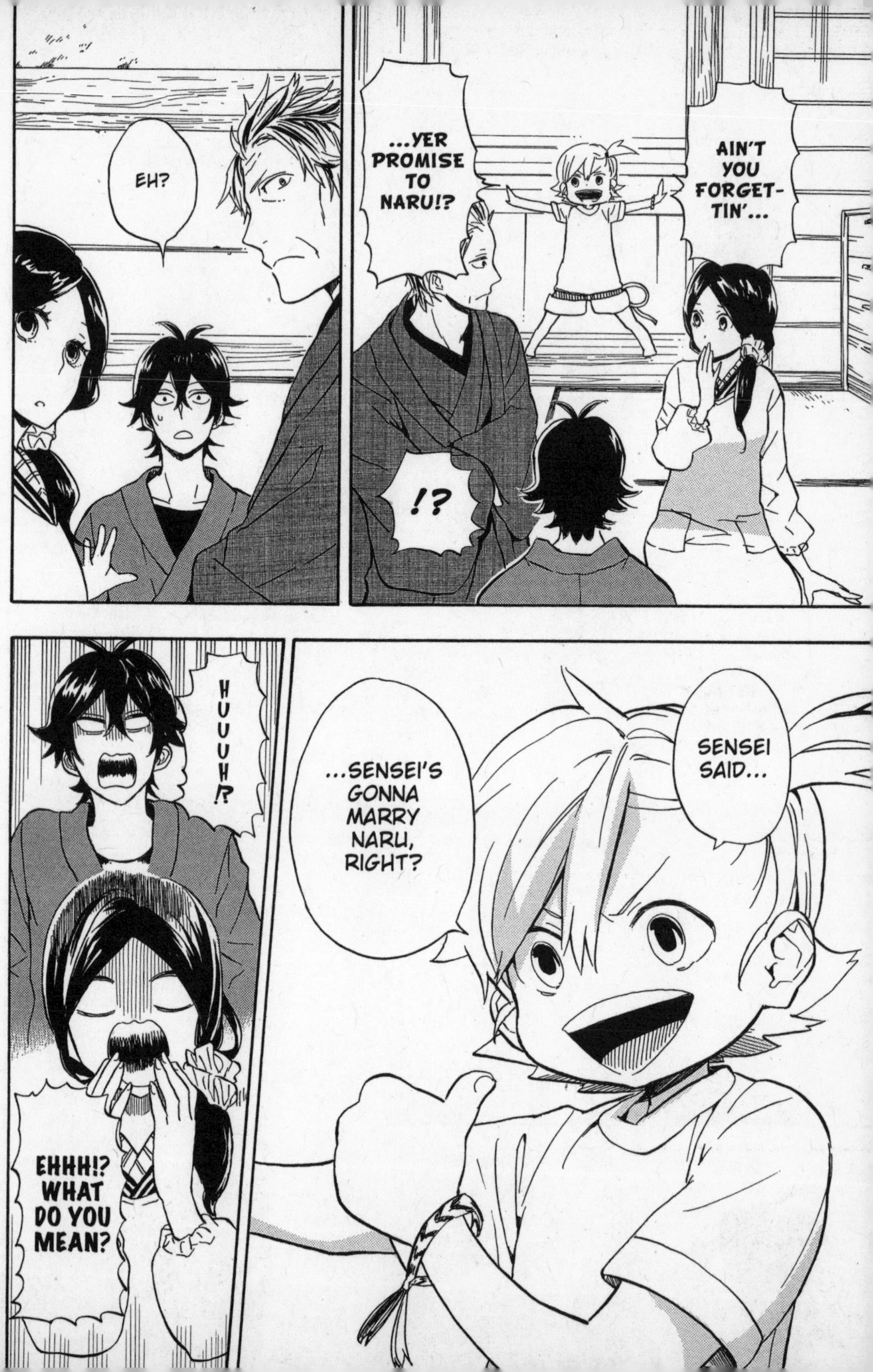
AIN'T YOU FORGET-TIN'...
...YER PROMISE TO NARU!?
!?
EH?
SENSEI SAID...
...SENSEI'S GONNA MARRY NARU, RIGHT?
HUUUH!?
EHHH!? WHAT DO YOU MEAN?

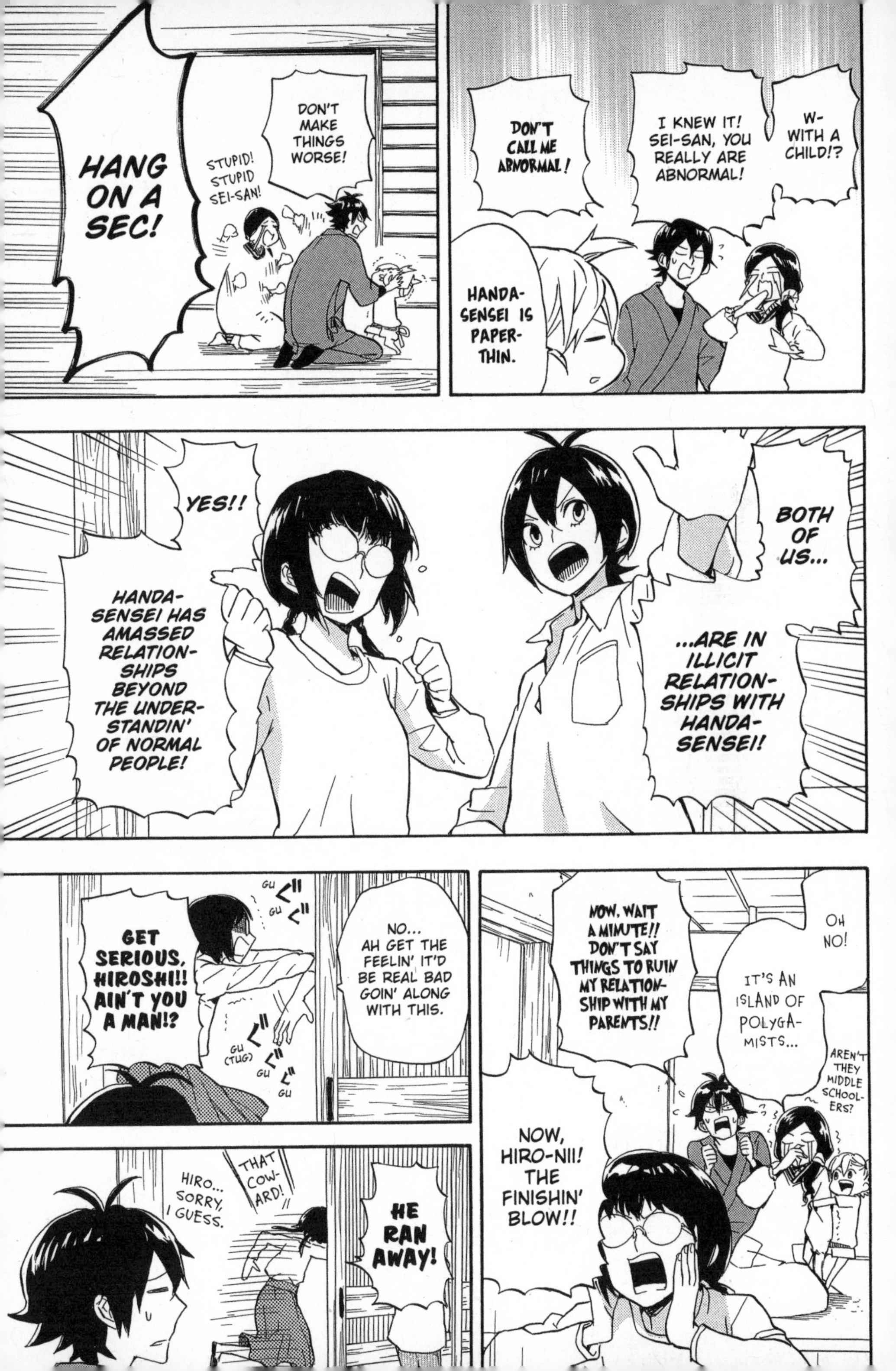
W-
WITH A
CHILD!?
I KNEW IT!
SEI-SAN, YOU
REALLY ARE
ABNORMAL!
DON'T
CALL ME
ABNORMAL!
HANDA-
SENSEI IS
PAPER-
THIN.
DON'T
MAKE
THINGS
WORSE!
STUPID!
STUPID
SEI-SAN!
HANG
ON A
SEC!
BOTH
OF
US...
...ARE IN
ILLICIT
RELATION-
SHIPS WITH
HANDA-
SENSEI!
YES!!
HANDA-
SENSEI HAS
AMASSED
RELATION-
SHIPS
BEYOND
THE UNDER-
STANDIN'
OF NORMAL
PEOPLE!
OH
NO!
IT'S AN
ISLAND OF
POLYGA-
MISTS...
AREN'T
THEY
MIDDLE
SCHOOL-
ERS?
NOW, WAIT
A MINUTE!!
DON'T SAY
THINGS TO RUIN
MY RELATION-
SHIP WITH MY
PARENTS!!
NOW,
HIRO-NII!
THE
FINISHIN'
BLOW!!
NO...
AH GET THE
FEELIN' IT'D
BE REAL BAD
GOIN' ALONG
WITH THIS.
GU
GU
GET
SERIOUS,
HIROSHI!!
AIN'T YOU
A MAN!?
GU
(TUG)
GU
GU
HE
RAN
AWAY!
THAT
COW-
ARD!
HIRO...
SORRY,
I GUESS.

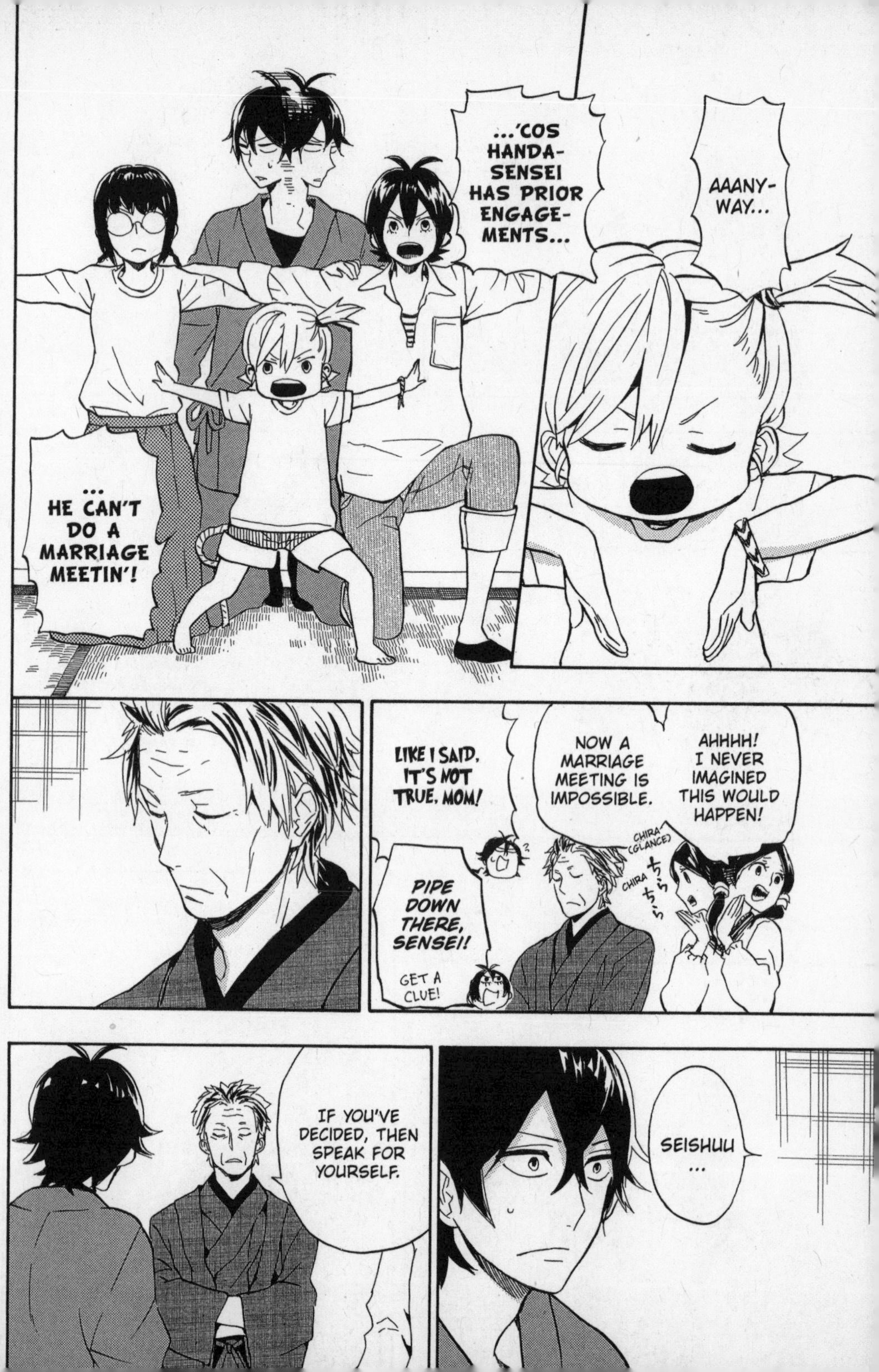
AAANY-WAY...
...'COS HANDA-SENSEI HAS PRIOR ENGAGE-MENTS...
... HE CAN'T DO A MARRIAGE MEETIN'!
AHHHH! I NEVER IMAGINED THIS WOULD HAPPEN!
NOW A MARRIAGE MEETING IS IMPOSSIBLE.
LIKE I SAID. IT'S NOT TRUE, MOM!
CHIRA (GLANCE)
CHIRA
ちら ちら
PIPE DOWN THERE, SENSEI!
GET A CLUE!
SEISHUU ...
IF YOU'VE DECIDED, THEN SPEAK FOR YOURSELF.

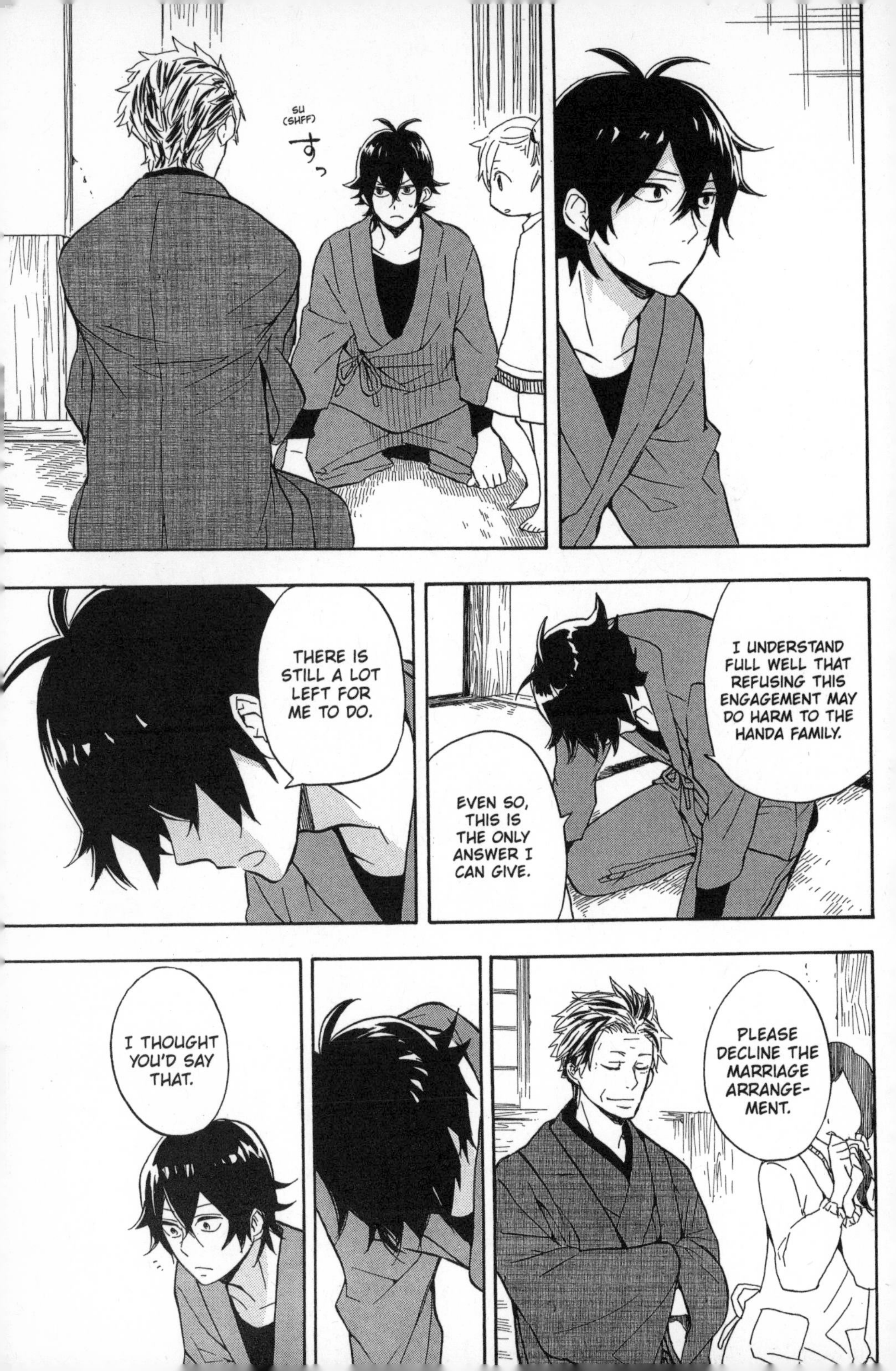
SU (SHFF)
すっ
I UNDERSTAND FULL WELL THAT REFUSING THIS ENGAGEMENT MAY DO HARM TO THE HANDA FAMILY.
EVEN SO, THIS IS THE ONLY ANSWER I CAN GIVE.
THERE IS STILL A LOT LEFT FOR ME TO DO.
PLEASE DECLINE THE MARRIAGE ARRANGE-MENT.
I THOUGHT YOU'D SAY THAT.

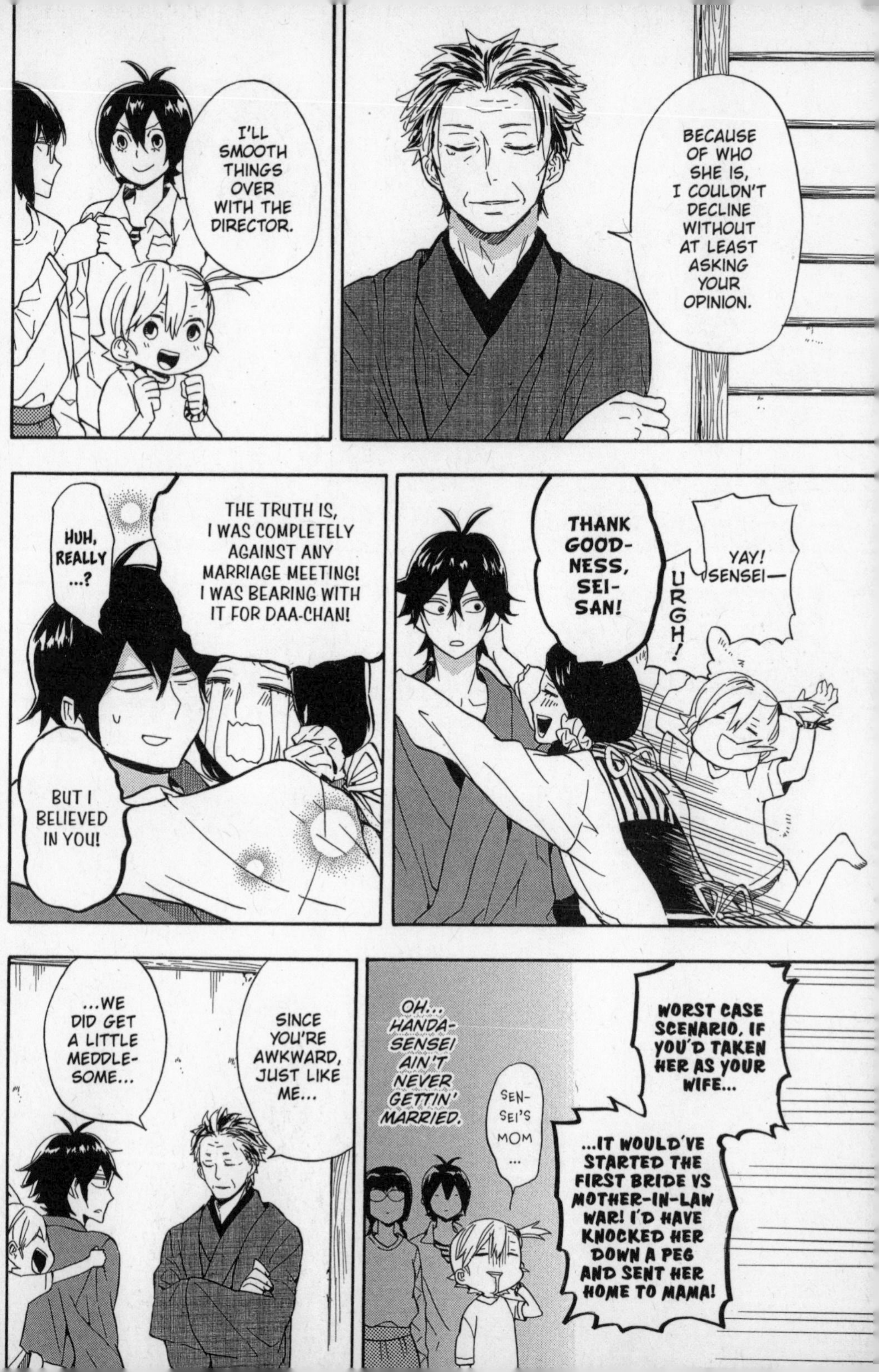
BECAUSE OF WHO SHE IS, I COULDN'T DECLINE WITHOUT AT LEAST ASKING YOUR OPINION.
I'LL SMOOTH THINGS OVER WITH THE DIRECTOR.
YAY! SENSEI—
THANK GOODNESS, SEI-SAN!
URGH!
THE TRUTH IS, I WAS COMPLETELY AGAINST ANY MARRIAGE MEETING! I WAS BEARING WITH IT FOR DAA-CHAN!
HUH, REALLY ...?
BUT I BELIEVED IN YOU!
WORST CASE SCENARIO, IF YOU'D TAKEN HER AS YOUR WIFE...
...IT WOULD'VE STARTED THE FIRST BRIDE VS MOTHER-IN-LAW WAR! I'D HAVE KNOCKED HER DOWN A PEG AND SENT HER HOME TO MAMA!
SEN-SEI'S MOM ...
OH... HANDA-SENSEI AIN'T NEVER GETTIN' MARRIED.
SINCE YOU'RE AWKWARD, JUST LIKE ME...
...WE DID GET A LITTLE MEDDLE-SOME...

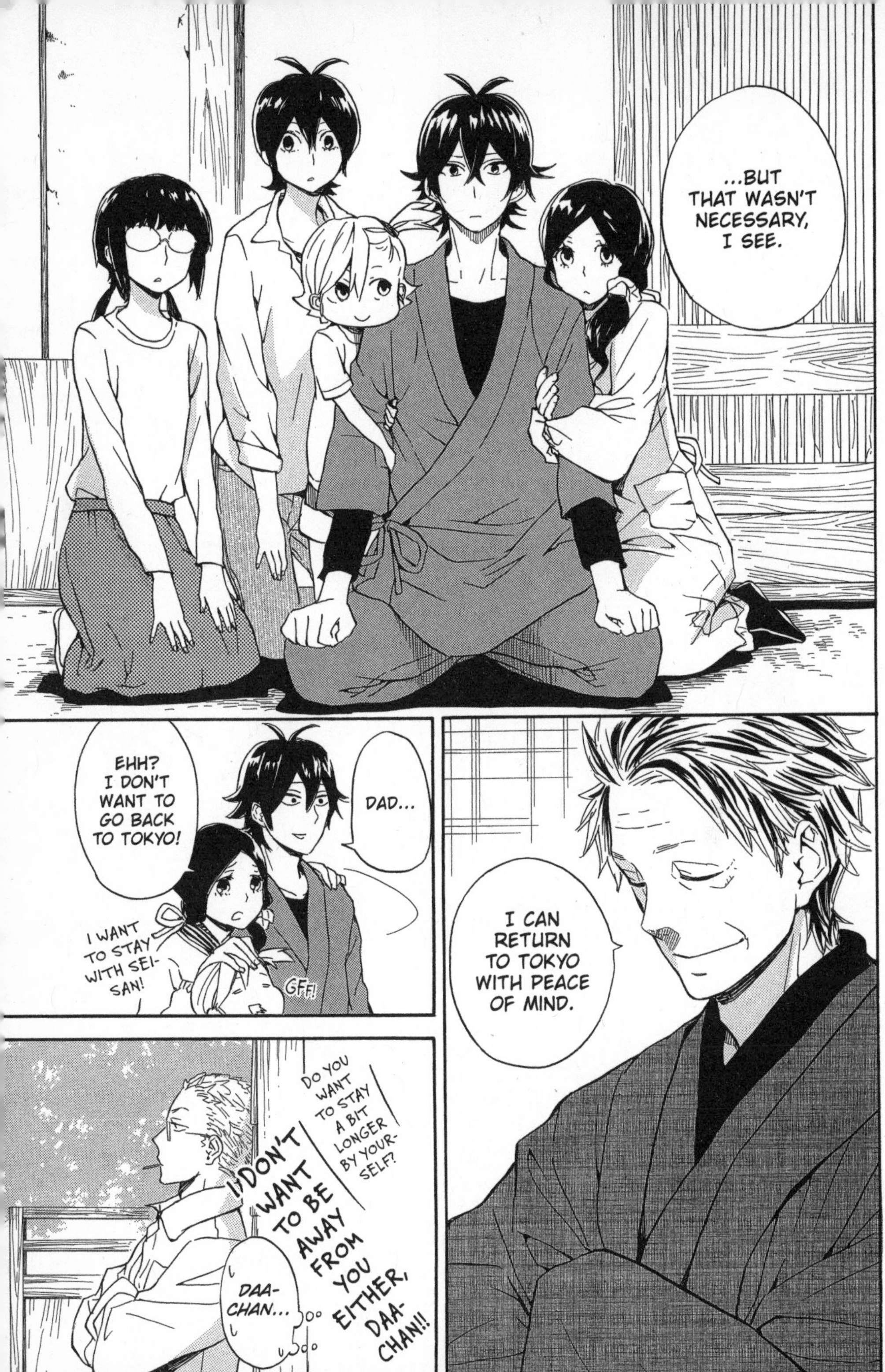
...BUT THAT WASN'T NECESSARY, I SEE.
I CAN RETURN TO TOKYO WITH PEACE OF MIND.
DAD...
EHH? I DON'T WANT TO GO BACK TO TOKYO!
I WANT TO STAY WITH SEI-SAN!
GFF!
DO YOU WANT TO STAY A BIT LONGER BY YOURSELF?
I DON'T WANT TO BE AWAY FROM YOU EITHER, DAA-CHAN!!
DAA-CHAN...

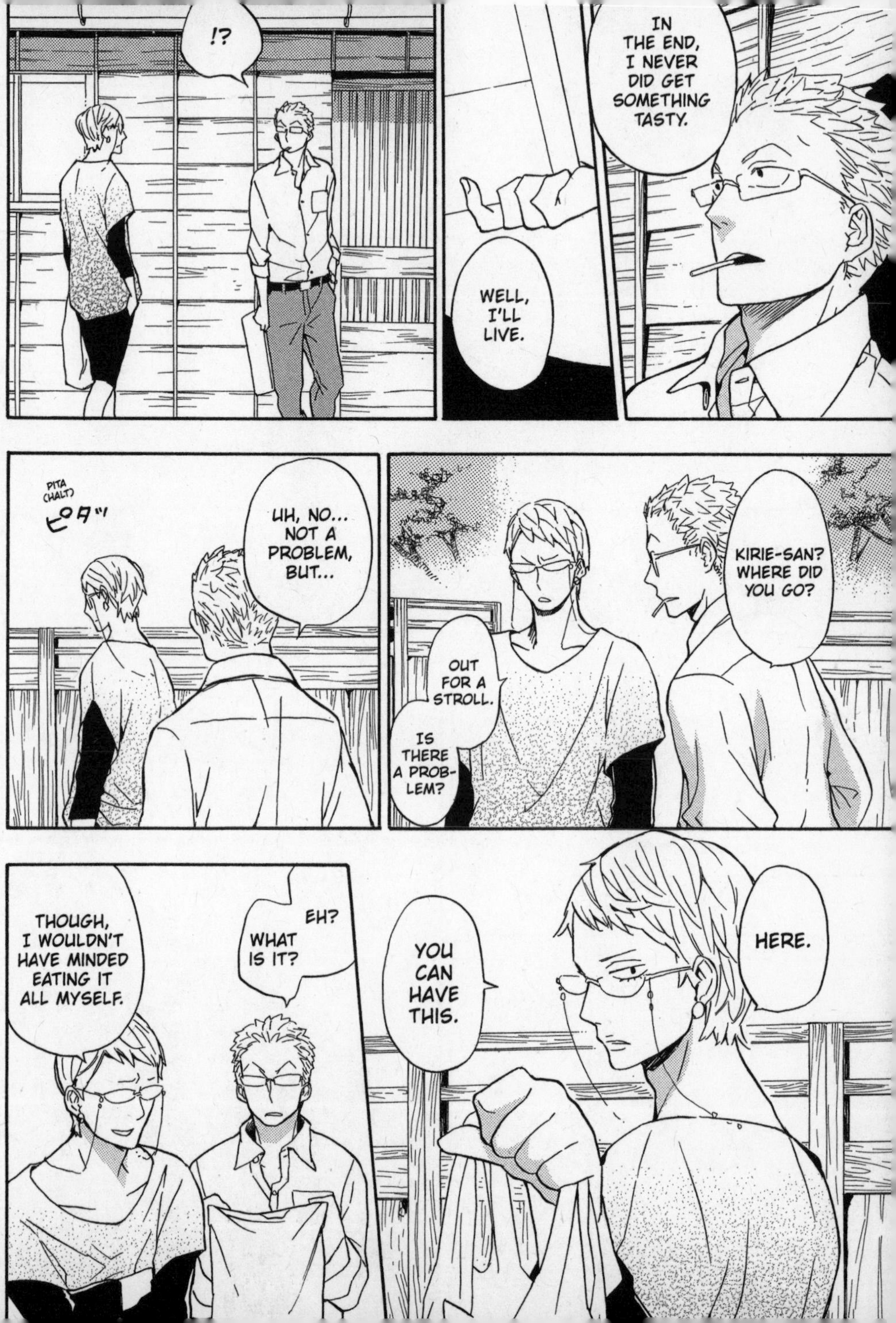
IN THE END, I NEVER DID GET SOMETHING TASTY.
WELL, I'LL LIVE.
!?
KIRIE-SAN? WHERE DID YOU GO?
OUT FOR A STROLL.
IS THERE A PROB-LEM?
UH, NO... NOT A PROBLEM, BUT...
PITA (HALT)
ピタッ
HERE.
YOU CAN HAVE THIS.
EH? WHAT IS IT?
THOUGH, I WOULDN'T HAVE MINDED EATING IT ALL MYSELF.

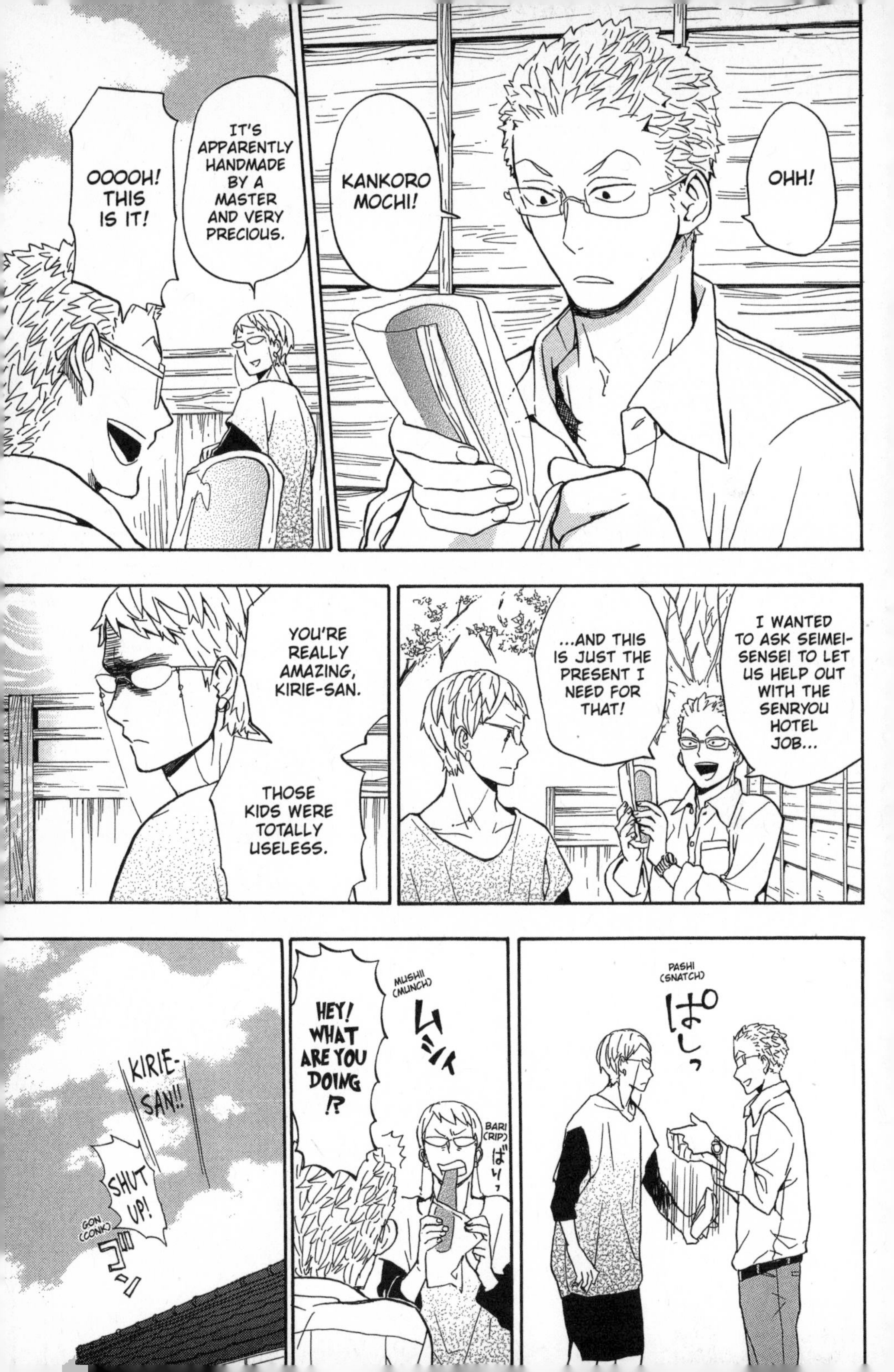
OHH!
KANKORO MOCHI!
IT'S APPARENTLY HANDMADE BY A MASTER AND VERY PRECIOUS.
OOOOH! THIS IS IT!
I WANTED TO ASK SEIMEI-SENSEI TO LET US HELP OUT WITH THE SENRYOU HOTEL JOB...
...AND THIS IS JUST THE PRESENT I NEED FOR THAT!
YOU'RE REALLY AMAZING, KIRIE-SAN.
THOSE KIDS WERE TOTALLY USELESS.
PASHI (SNATCH)
ぱしっ
BARI (RIP)
ばりっ
MUSHII (MUNCH)
ムシィ
HEY! WHAT ARE YOU DOING!?
KIRIE-SAN!!
SHUT UP!
GON (CONK)
ゴンッ

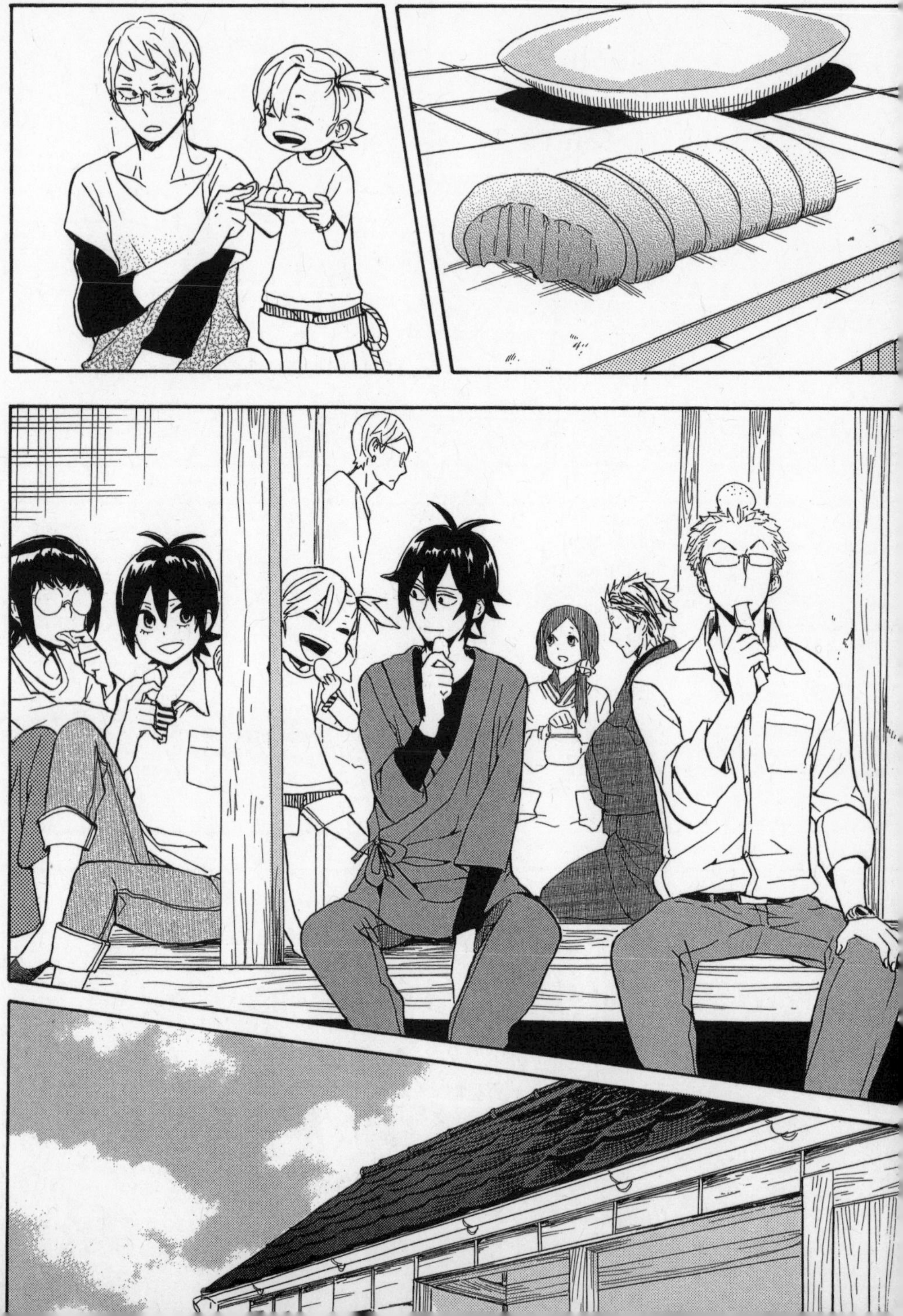

Act.82
NUKKA
(Translation: Warm)

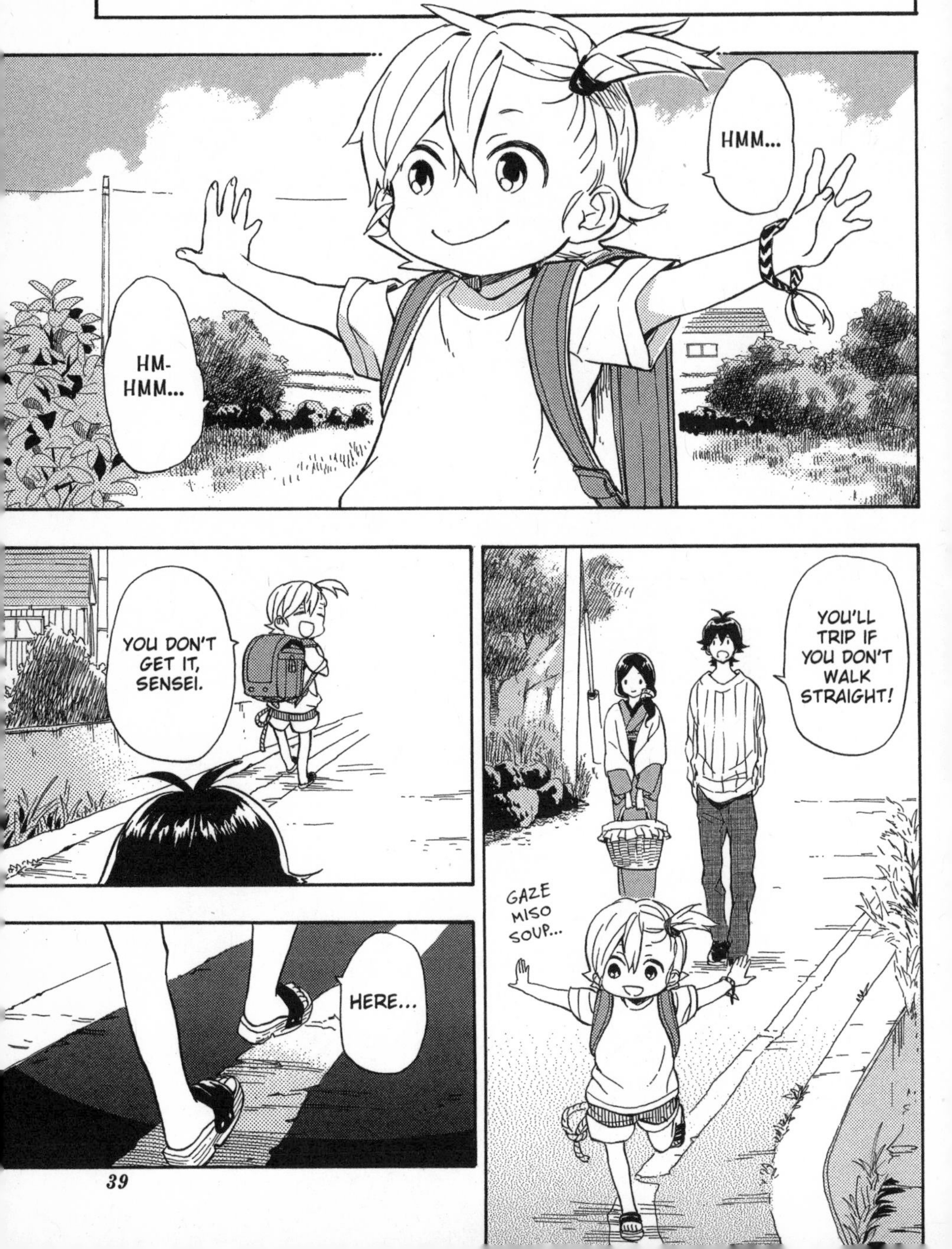
HMM...
HM-HMM...
YOU'LL TRIP IF YOU DON'T WALK STRAIGHT!
GAZE MISO SOUP...
YOU DON'T GET IT, SENSEI.
HERE...

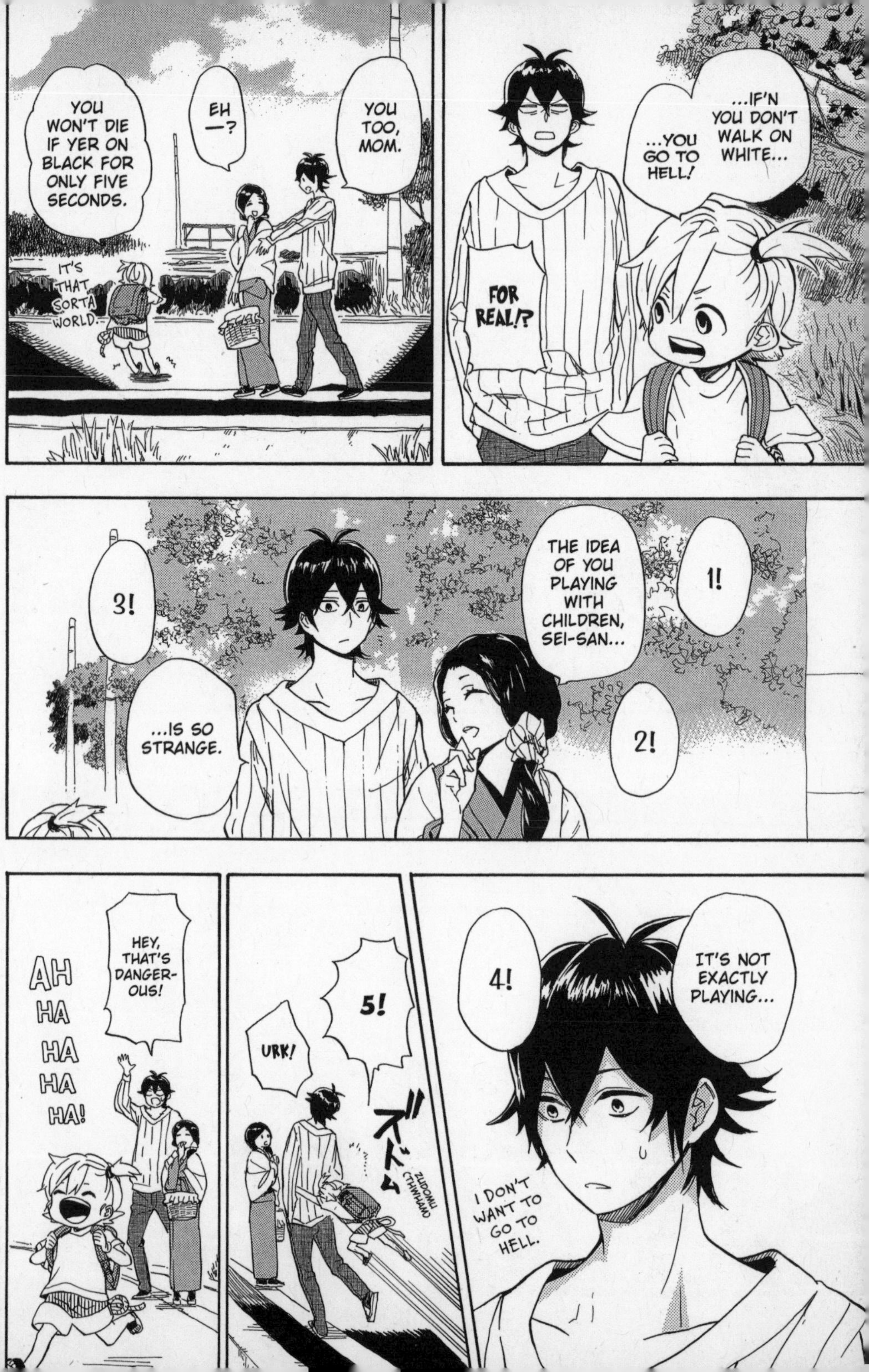
...IF'N YOU DON'T WALK ON WHITE...
...YOU GO TO HELL!
FOR REAL!?
YOU TOO, MOM.
EH—?
YOU WON'T DIE IF YER ON BLACK FOR ONLY FIVE SECONDS.
IT'S THAT SORTA WORLD...
1!
THE IDEA OF YOU PLAYING WITH CHILDREN, SEI-SAN...
2!
3!
...IS SO STRANGE.
IT'S NOT EXACTLY PLAYING...
4!
I DON'T WANT TO GO TO HELL.
5!
URK!
ズドム
ZUDOOM (THWHAM)
HEY, THAT'S DANGER-OUS!
AH HA HA HA HA!

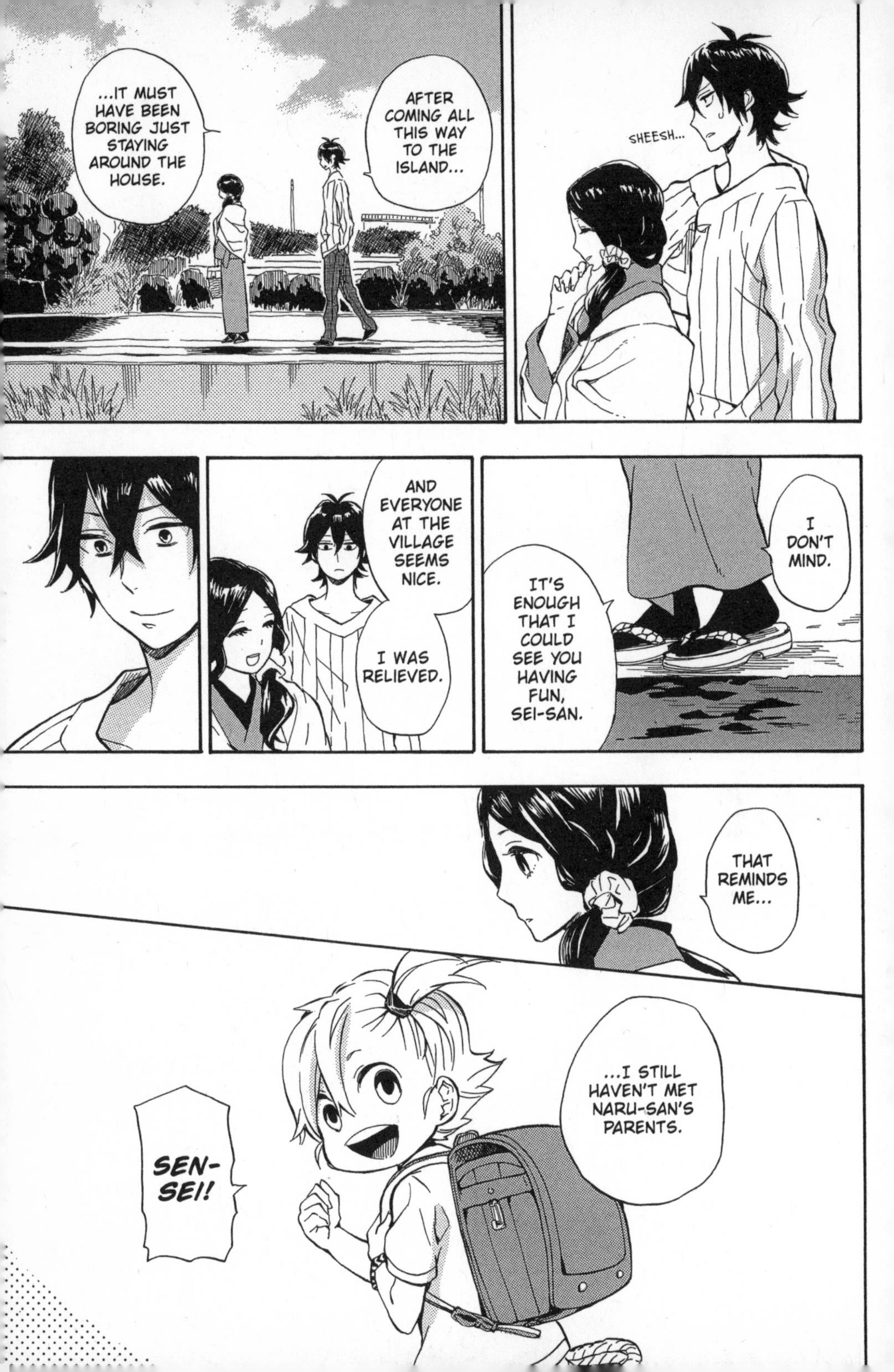
SHEESH...
AFTER COMING ALL THIS WAY TO THE ISLAND...
...IT MUST HAVE BEEN BORING JUST STAYING AROUND THE HOUSE.
I DON'T MIND.
IT'S ENOUGH THAT I COULD SEE YOU HAVING FUN, SEI-SAN.
AND EVERYONE AT THE VILLAGE SEEMS NICE.
I WAS RELIEVED.
THAT REMINDS ME...
...I STILL HAVEN'T MET NARU-SAN'S PARENTS.
SEN-SEI!

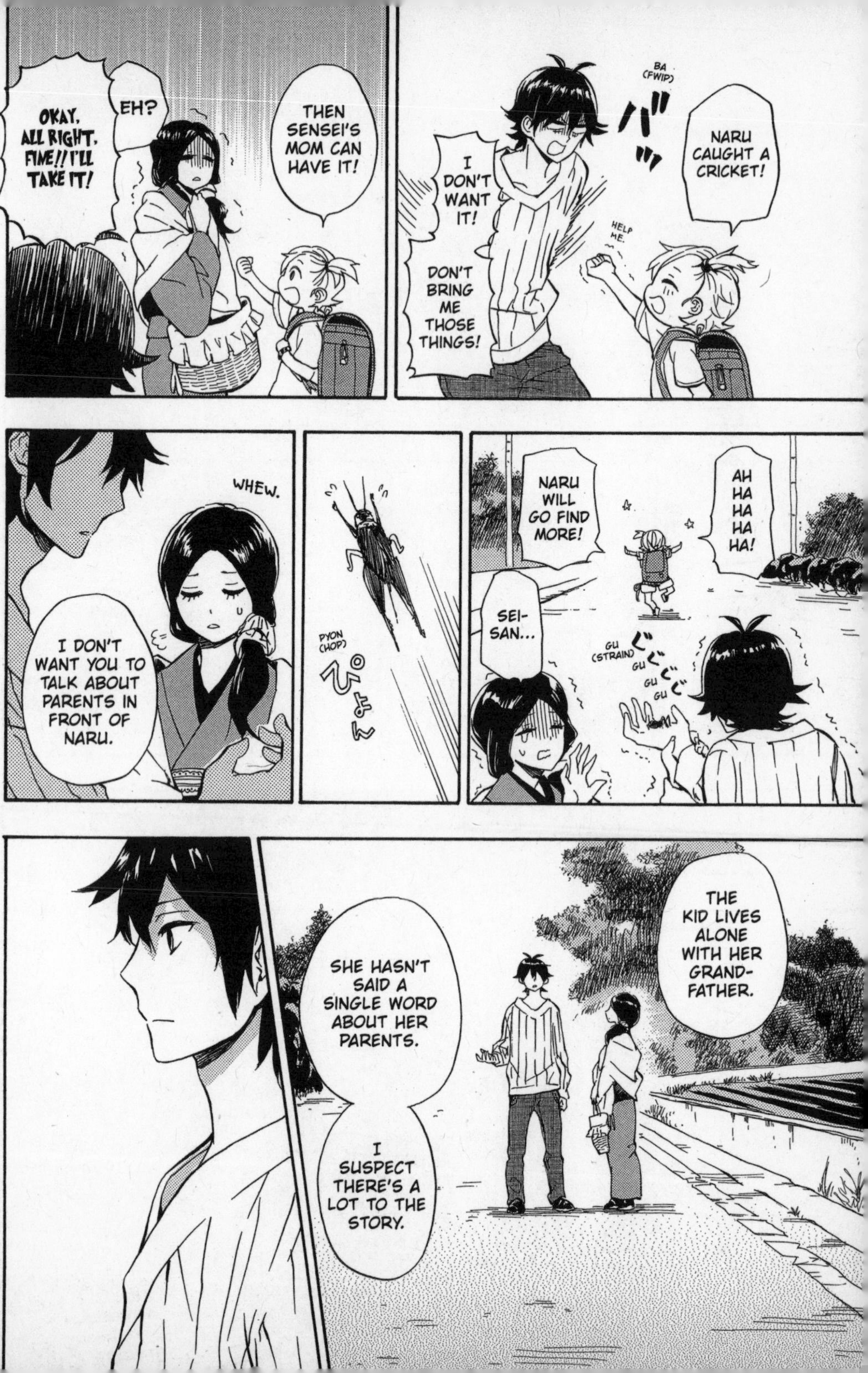
BA (FWIP)
NARU CAUGHT A CRICKET!
HELP ME.
I DON'T WANT IT!
DON'T BRING ME THOSE THINGS!
THEN SENSEI'S MOM CAN HAVE IT!
EH?
OKAY. ALL RIGHT. FINE!! I'LL TAKE IT!
AH HA HA HA HA!
NARU WILL GO FIND MORE!
SEI-SAN...
GU (STRAIN) GU GU GU
PYON (HOP)
WHEW.
I DON'T WANT YOU TO TALK ABOUT PARENTS IN FRONT OF NARU.
THE KID LIVES ALONE WITH HER GRAND-FATHER.
SHE HASN'T SAID A SINGLE WORD ABOUT HER PARENTS.
I SUSPECT THERE'S A LOT TO THE STORY.

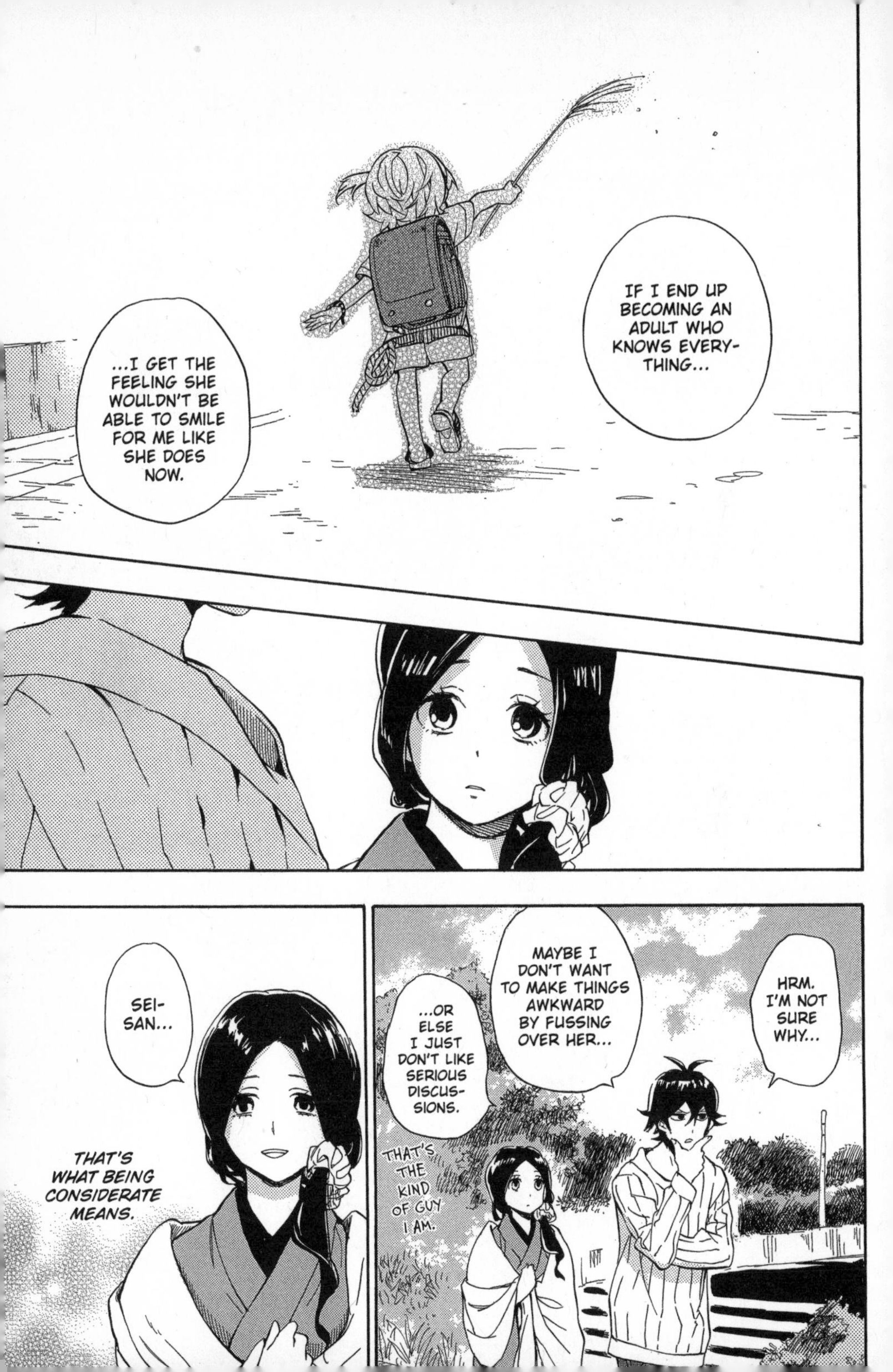
IF I END UP BECOMING AN ADULT WHO KNOWS EVERY-THING...
...I GET THE FEELING SHE WOULDN'T BE ABLE TO SMILE FOR ME LIKE SHE DOES NOW.
HRM. I'M NOT SURE WHY...
MAYBE I DON'T WANT TO MAKE THINGS AWKWARD BY FUSSING OVER HER...
...OR ELSE I JUST DON'T LIKE SERIOUS DISCUS-SIONS.
THAT'S THE KIND OF GUY I AM.
SEI-SAN...
THAT'S WHAT BEING CONSIDERATE MEANS.

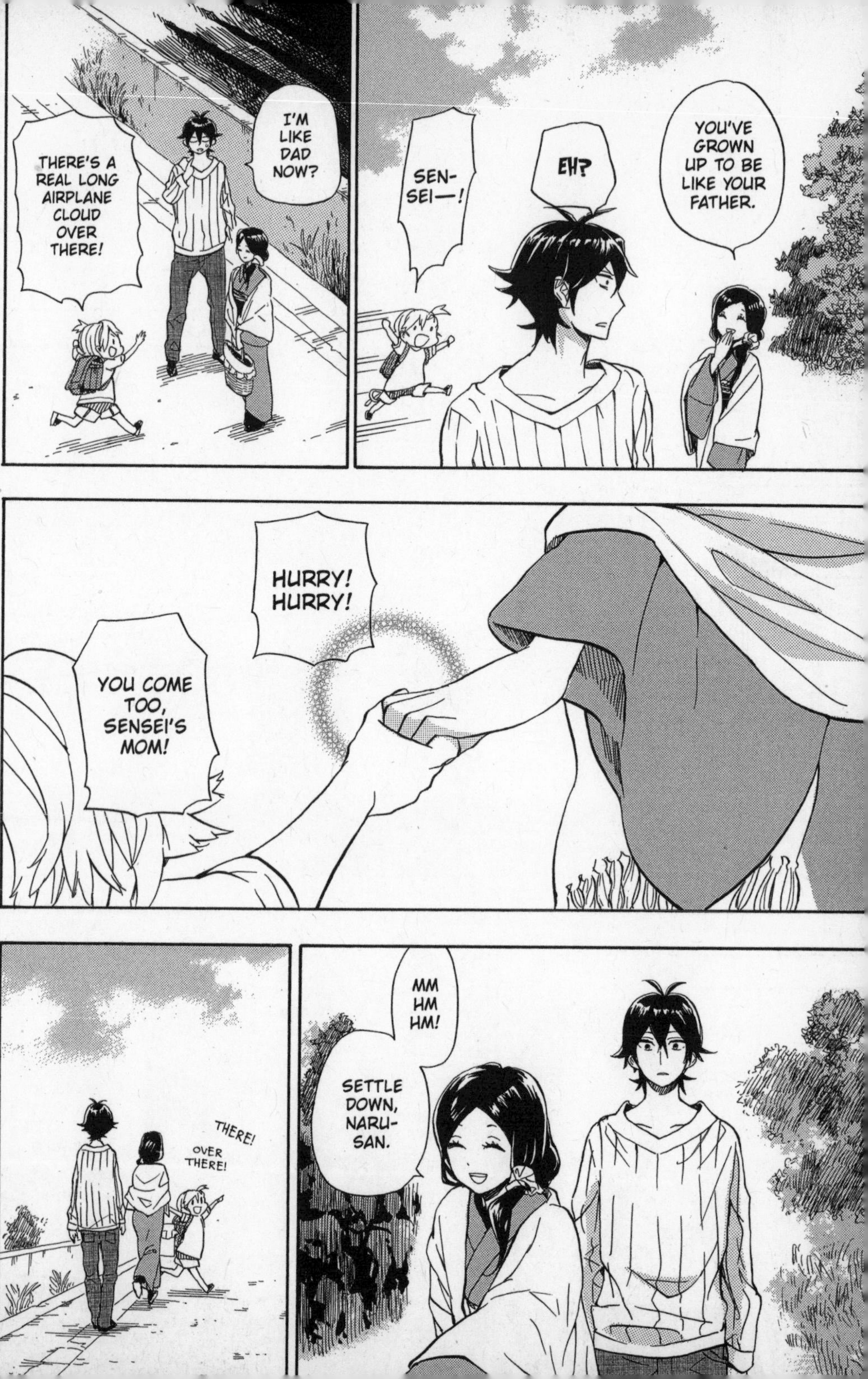
YOU'VE GROWN UP TO BE LIKE YOUR FATHER.
EH?
SEN-SEI—!
I'M LIKE DAD NOW?
THERE'S A REAL LONG AIRPLANE CLOUD OVER THERE!
HURRY! HURRY!
YOU COME TOO, SENSEI'S MOM!
MM HM HM!
SETTLE DOWN, NARU-SAN.
THERE!
OVER THERE!

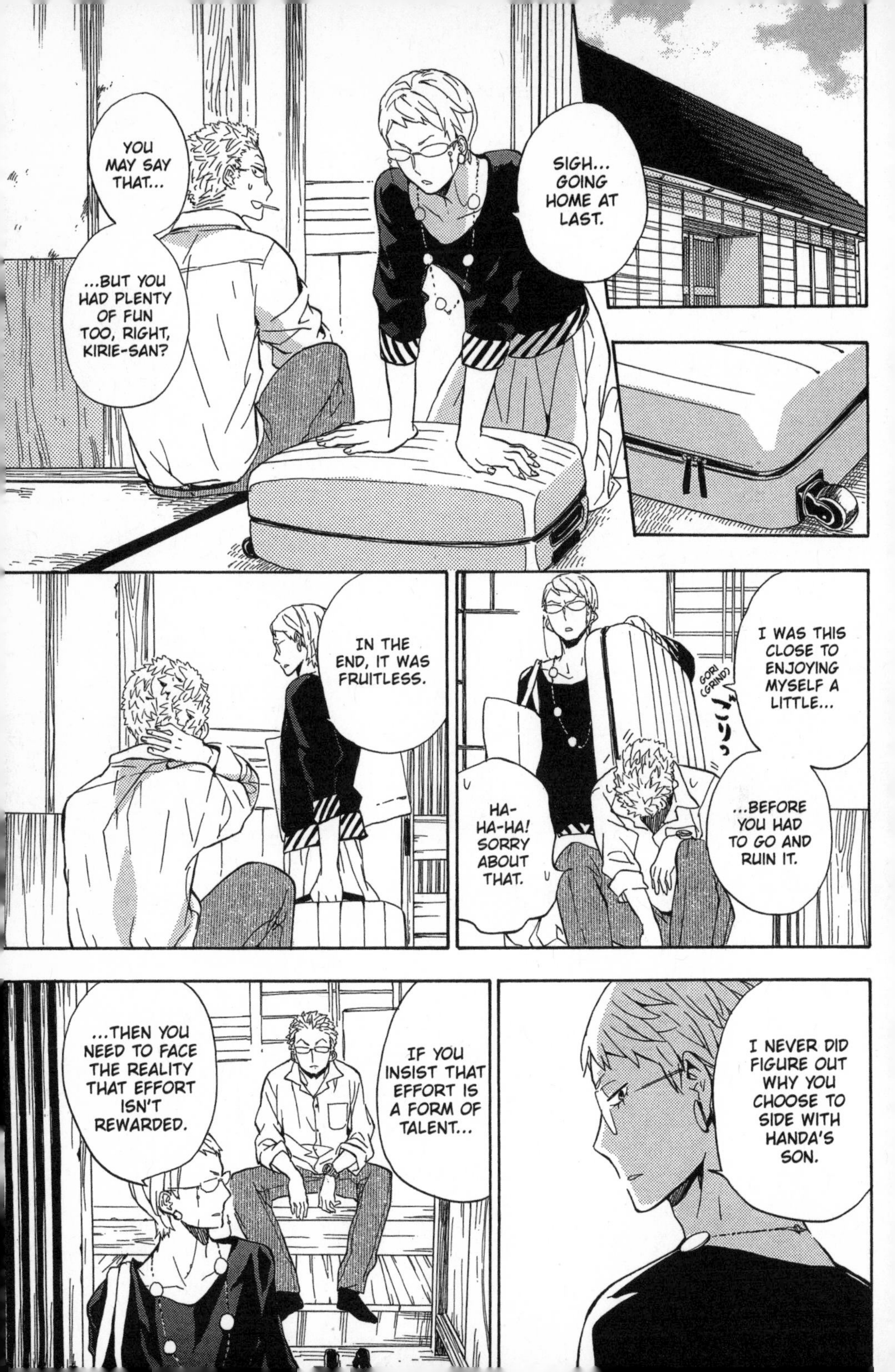
SIGH... GOING HOME AT LAST.
YOU MAY SAY THAT...
...BUT YOU HAD PLENTY OF FUN TOO, RIGHT, KIRIE-SAN?
I WAS THIS CLOSE TO ENJOYING MYSELF A LITTLE...
GORI (GRIND)
...BEFORE YOU HAD TO GO AND RUIN IT.
HA-HA-HA! SORRY ABOUT THAT.
IN THE END, IT WAS FRUITLESS.
I NEVER DID FIGURE OUT WHY YOU CHOOSE TO SIDE WITH HANDA'S SON.
IF YOU INSIST THAT EFFORT IS A FORM OF TALENT...
...THEN YOU NEED TO FACE THE REALITY THAT EFFORT ISN'T REWARDED.

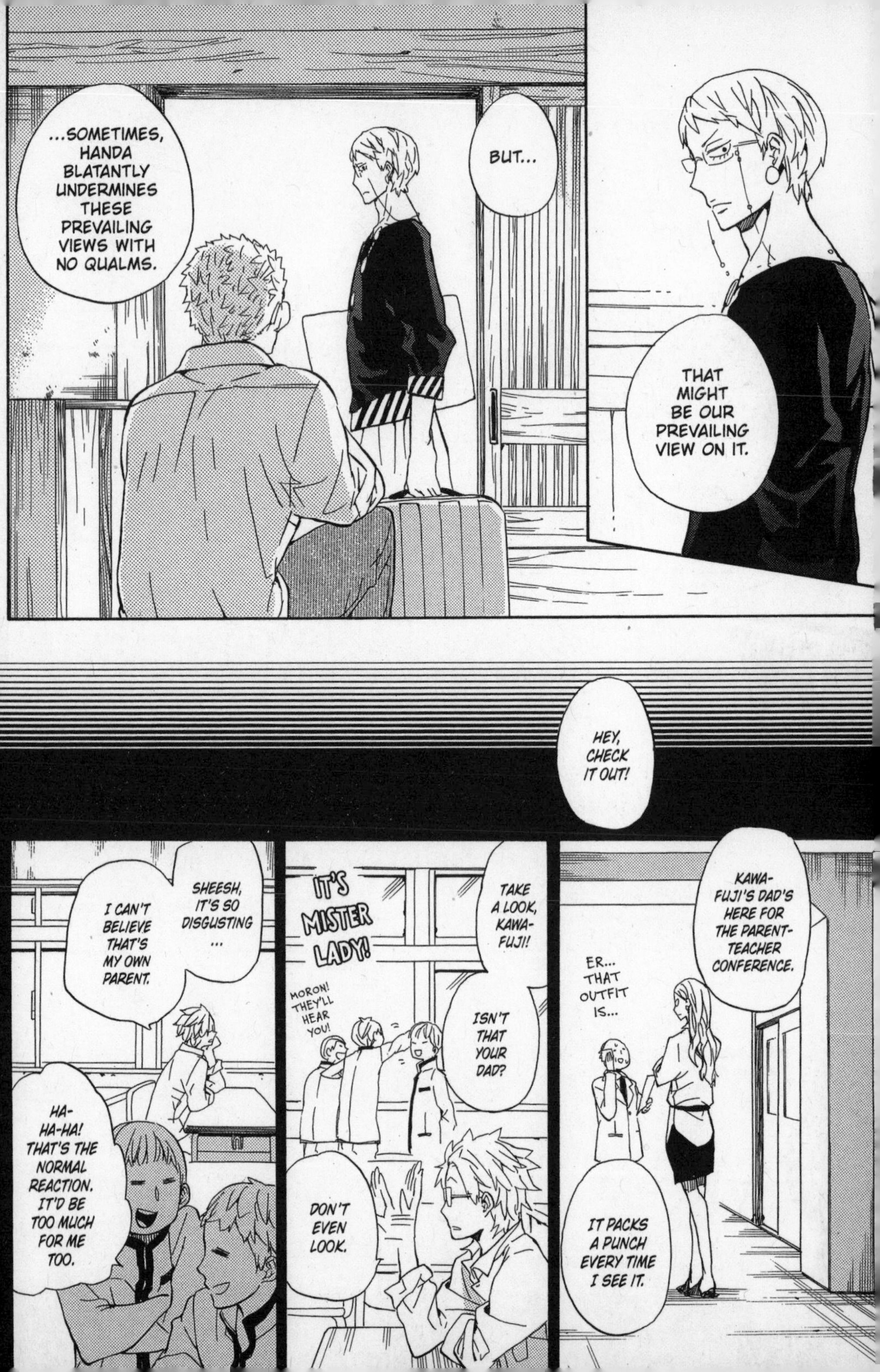
THAT MIGHT BE OUR PREVAILING VIEW ON IT.
BUT...
...SOMETIMES, HANDA BLATANTLY UNDERMINES THESE PREVAILING VIEWS WITH NO QUALMS.
HEY, CHECK IT OUT!
KAWA-FUJI'S DAD'S HERE FOR THE PARENT-TEACHER CONFERENCE.
ER... THAT OUTFIT IS...
IT PACKS A PUNCH EVERY TIME I SEE IT.
TAKE A LOOK, KAWA-FUJI!
IT'S MISTER LADY!
ISN'T THAT YOUR DAD?
MORON! THEY'LL HEAR YOU!
DON'T EVEN LOOK.
SHEESH, IT'S SO DISGUSTING...
I CAN'T BELIEVE THAT'S MY OWN PARENT.
HA-HA-HA! THAT'S THE NORMAL REACTION. IT'D BE TOO MUCH FOR ME TOO.

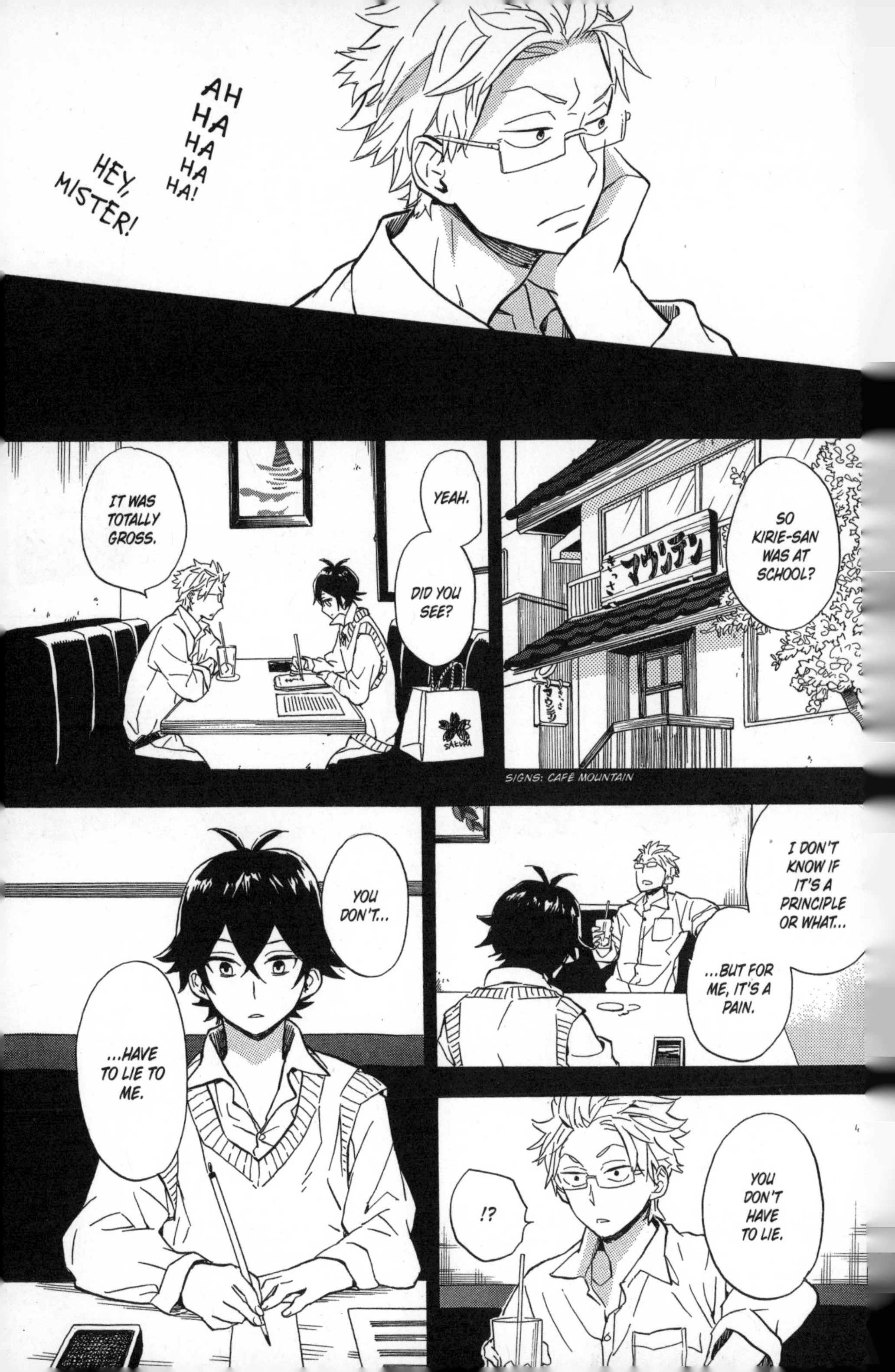
AH HA HA HA HA!
HEY, MISTER!
SO KIRIE-SAN WAS AT SCHOOL?
SIGNS: CAFÉ MOUNTAIN
YEAH.
DID YOU SEE?
IT WAS TOTALLY GROSS.
I DON'T KNOW IF IT'S A PRINCIPLE OR WHAT...
...BUT FOR ME, IT'S A PAIN.
YOU DON'T HAVE TO LIE.
!?
YOU DON'T...
...HAVE TO LIE TO ME.

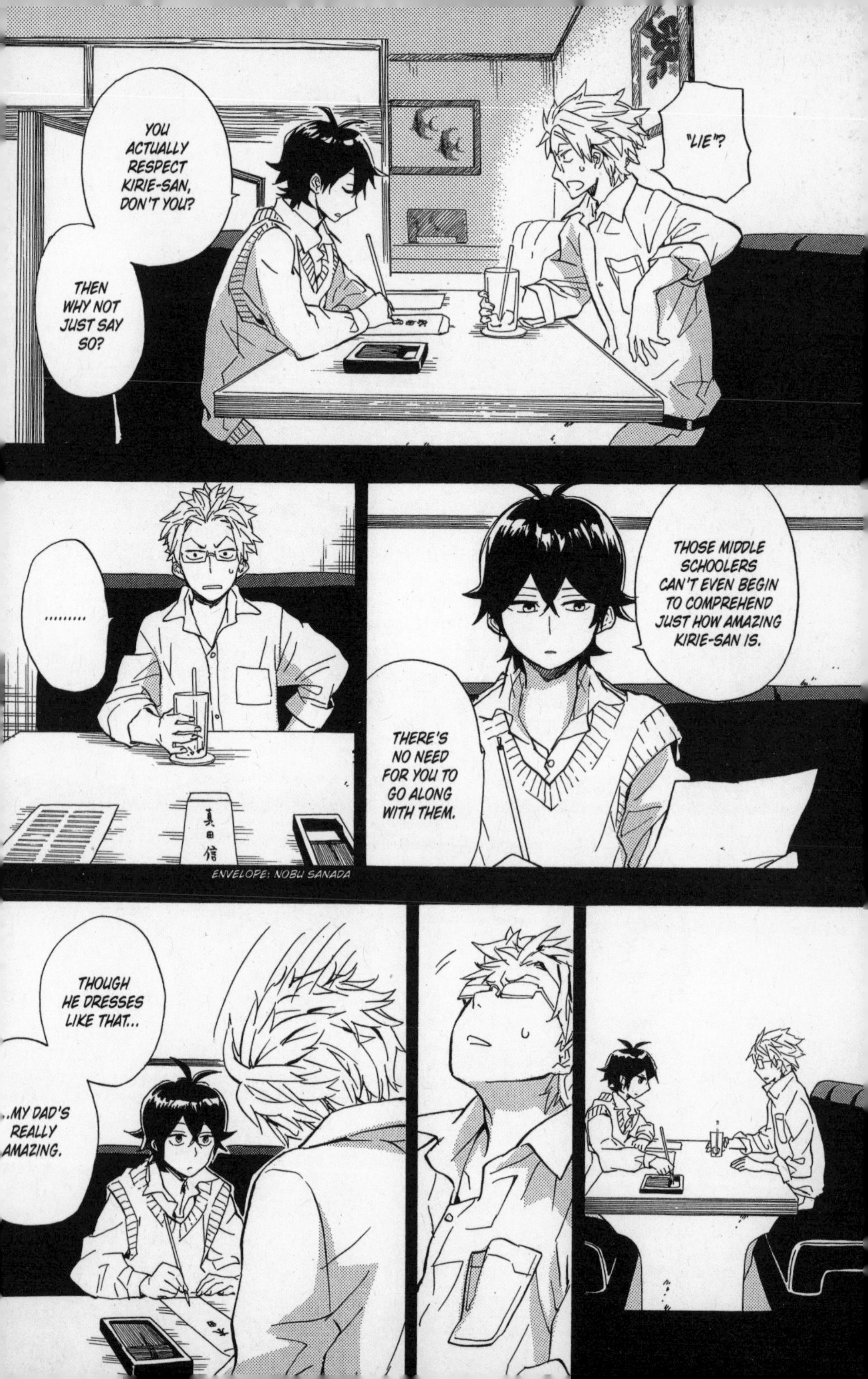
"LIE"?
YOU ACTUALLY RESPECT KIRIE-SAN, DON'T YOU?
THEN WHY NOT JUST SAY SO?
THOSE MIDDLE SCHOOLERS CAN'T EVEN BEGIN TO COMPREHEND JUST HOW AMAZING KIRIE-SAN IS.
THERE'S NO NEED FOR YOU TO GO ALONG WITH THEM.
....
真田信
ENVELOPE: NOBU SANADA
THOUGH HE DRESSES LIKE THAT...
..MY DAD'S REALLY AMAZING.

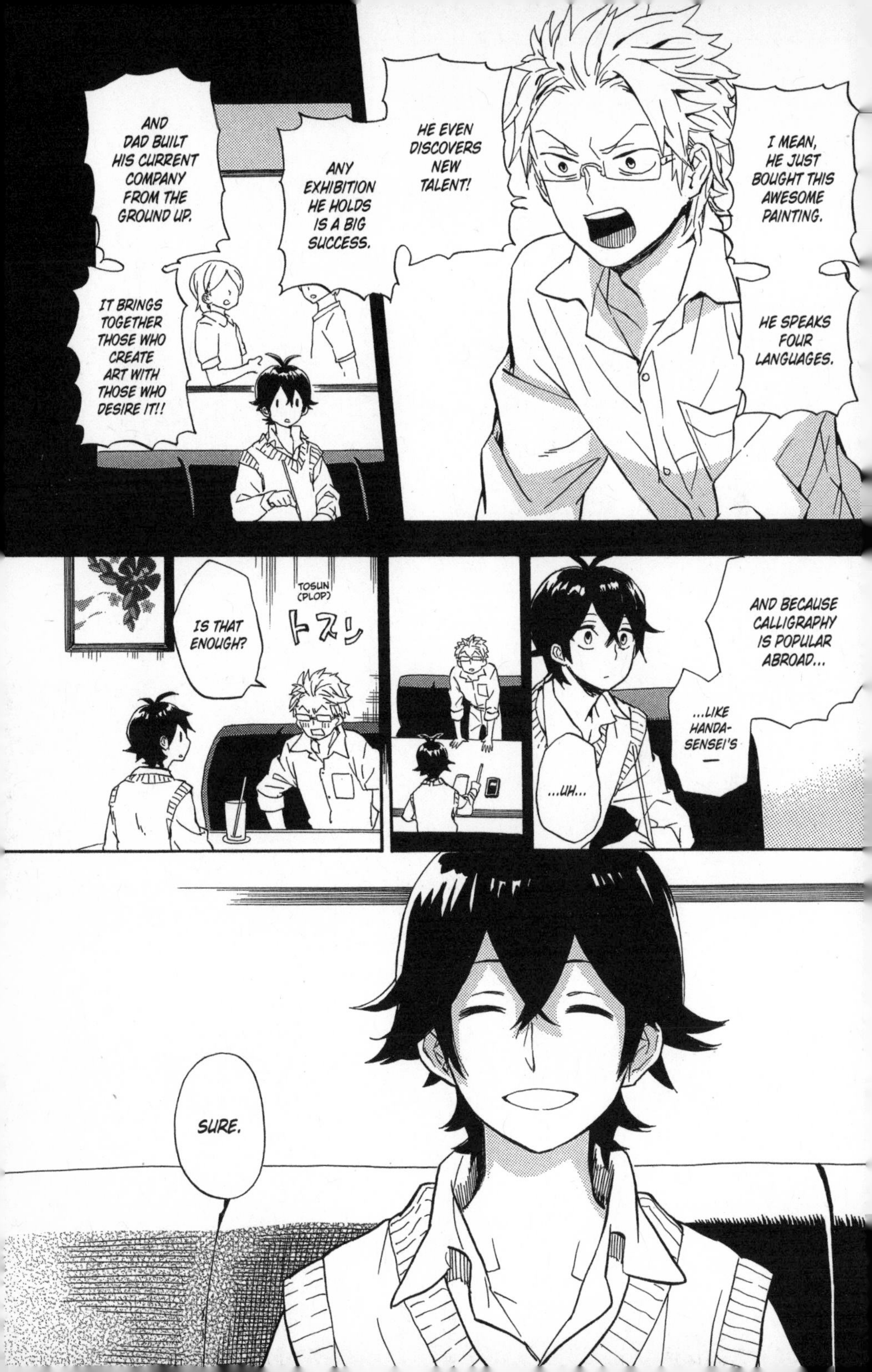
I MEAN, HE JUST BOUGHT THIS AWESOME PAINTING.
HE EVEN DISCOVERS NEW TALENT!
HE SPEAKS FOUR LANGUAGES.
ANY EXHIBITION HE HOLDS IS A BIG SUCCESS.
AND DAD BUILT HIS CURRENT COMPANY FROM THE GROUND UP.
IT BRINGS TOGETHER THOSE WHO CREATE ART WITH THOSE WHO DESIRE IT!!
AND BECAUSE CALLIGRAPHY IS POPULAR ABROAD...
...LIKE HANDA-SENSEI'S —
...UH...
TOSUN (PLOP)
トスン
IS THAT ENOUGH?
SURE.

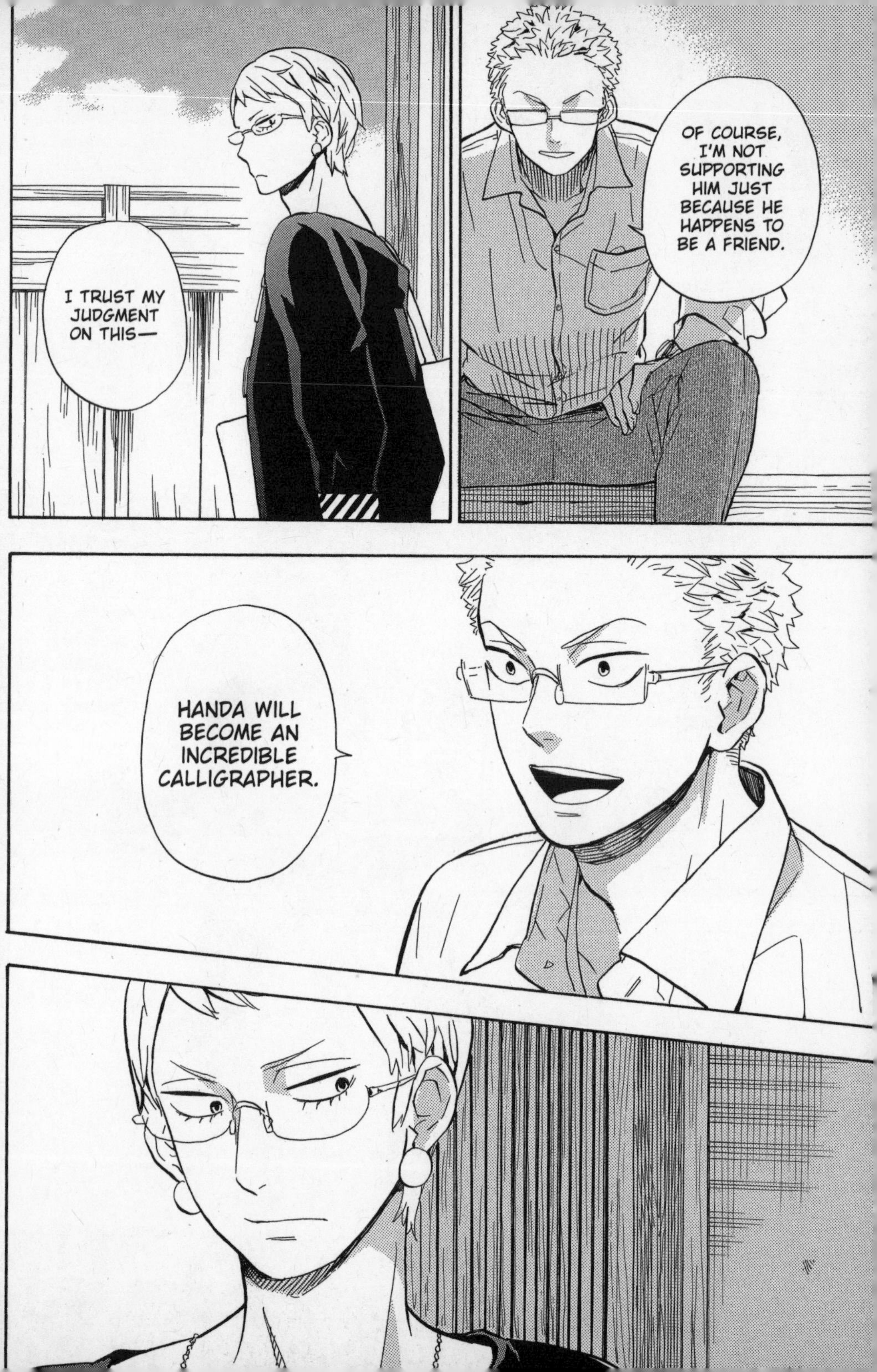
OF COURSE, I'M NOT SUPPORTING HIM JUST BECAUSE HE HAPPENS TO BE A FRIEND.
I TRUST MY JUDGMENT ON THIS—
HANDA WILL BECOME AN INCREDIBLE CALLIGRAPHER.

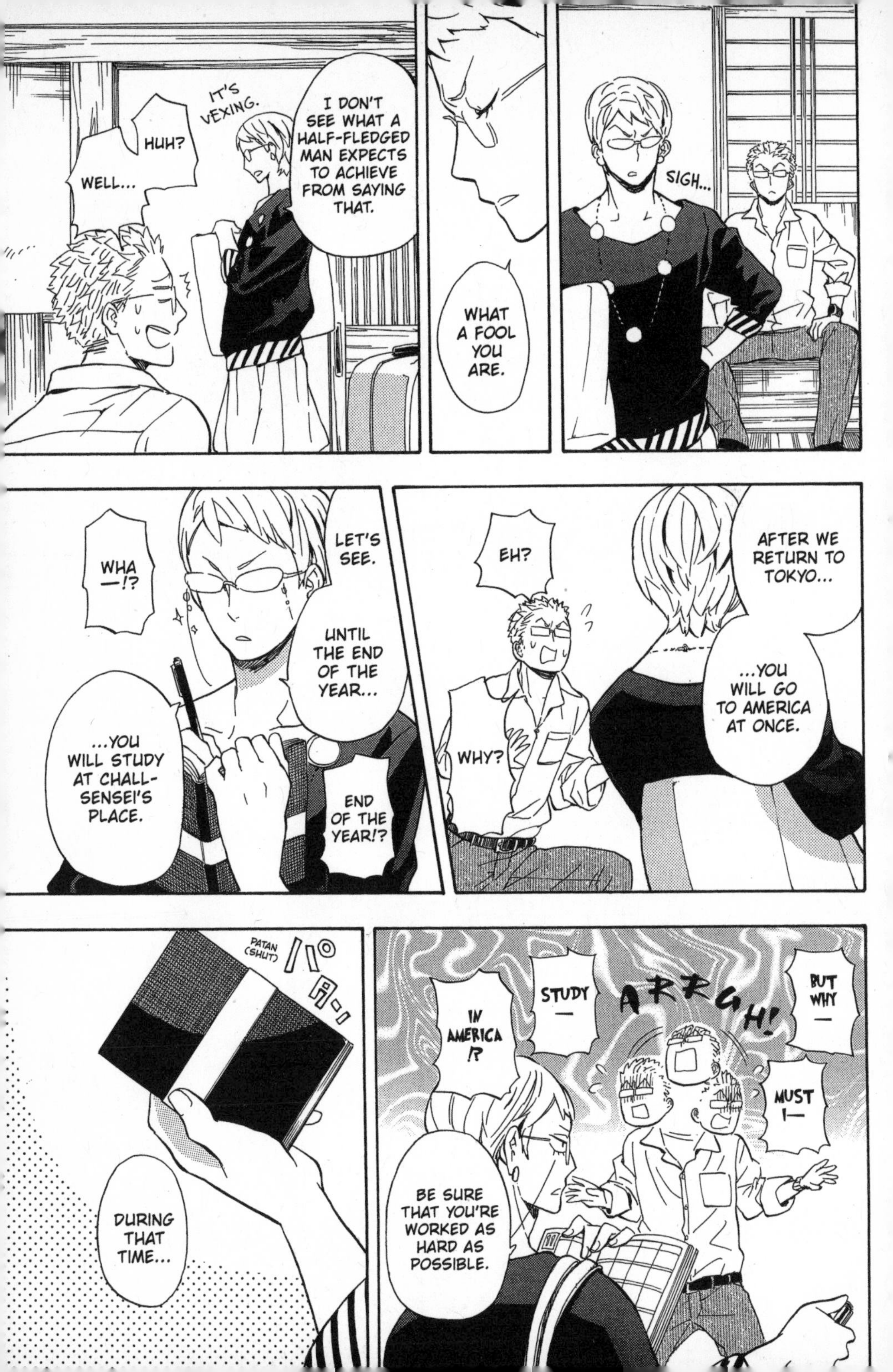
SIGH...
WHAT A FOOL YOU ARE.
I DON'T SEE WHAT A HALF-FLEDGED MAN EXPECTS TO ACHIEVE FROM SAYING THAT.
IT'S VEXING.
HUH?
WELL...
AFTER WE RETURN TO TOKYO...
EH?
...YOU WILL GO TO AMERICA AT ONCE.
WHY?
LET'S SEE.
WHA—!?
UNTIL THE END OF THE YEAR...
END OF THE YEAR!?
...YOU WILL STUDY AT CHALL-SENSEI'S PLACE.
BUT WHY —
ARRGH!
STUDY —
MUST I—
IN AMERICA!?
BE SURE THAT YOU'RE WORKED AS HARD AS POSSIBLE.
PATAN (SHUT)
DURING THAT TIME...

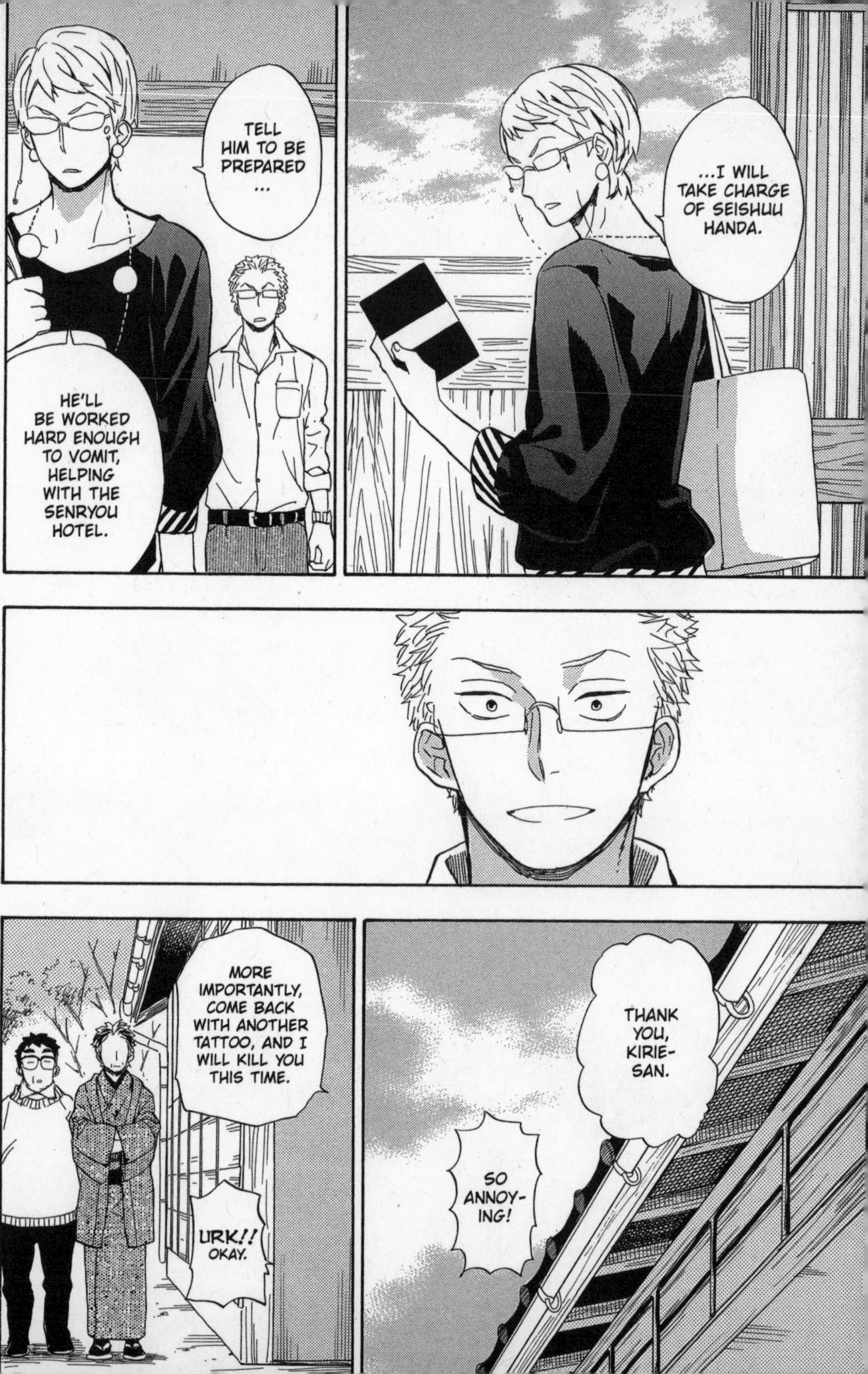
...I WILL TAKE CHARGE OF SEISHUU HANDA.
TELL HIM TO BE PREPARED ...
HE'LL BE WORKED HARD ENOUGH TO VOMIT, HELPING WITH THE SENRYOU HOTEL.
THANK YOU, KIRIE-SAN.
SO ANNOY-ING!
MORE IMPORTANTLY, COME BACK WITH ANOTHER TATTOO, AND I WILL KILL YOU THIS TIME.
URK!! OKAY.

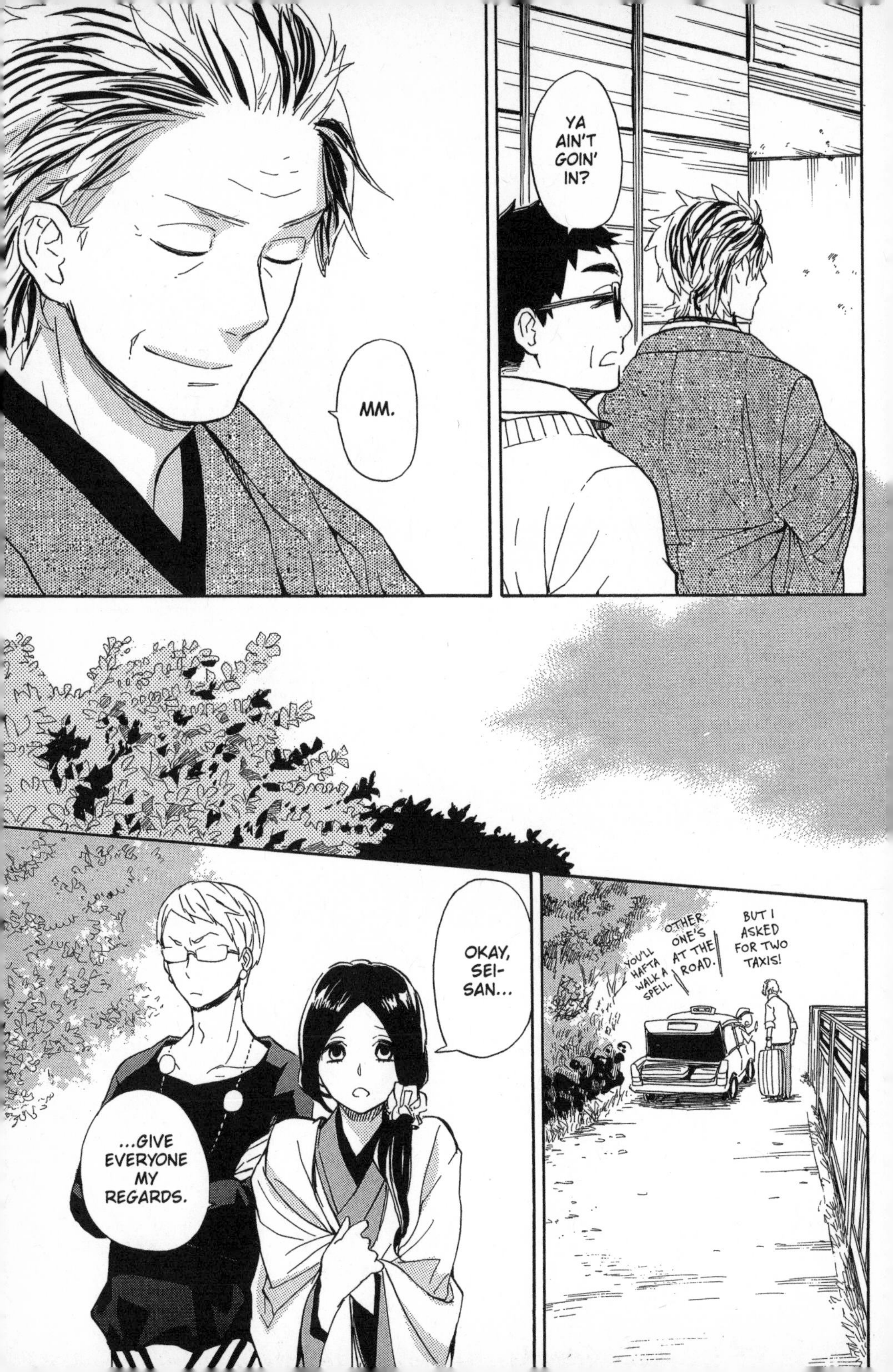
YA AIN'T GOIN' IN?
MM.
BUT I ASKED FOR TWO TAXIS!
OTHER ONE'S AT THE ROAD.
YOU'LL HAFTA WALK A SPELL.
OKAY, SEI-SAN...
...GIVE EVERYONE MY REGARDS.

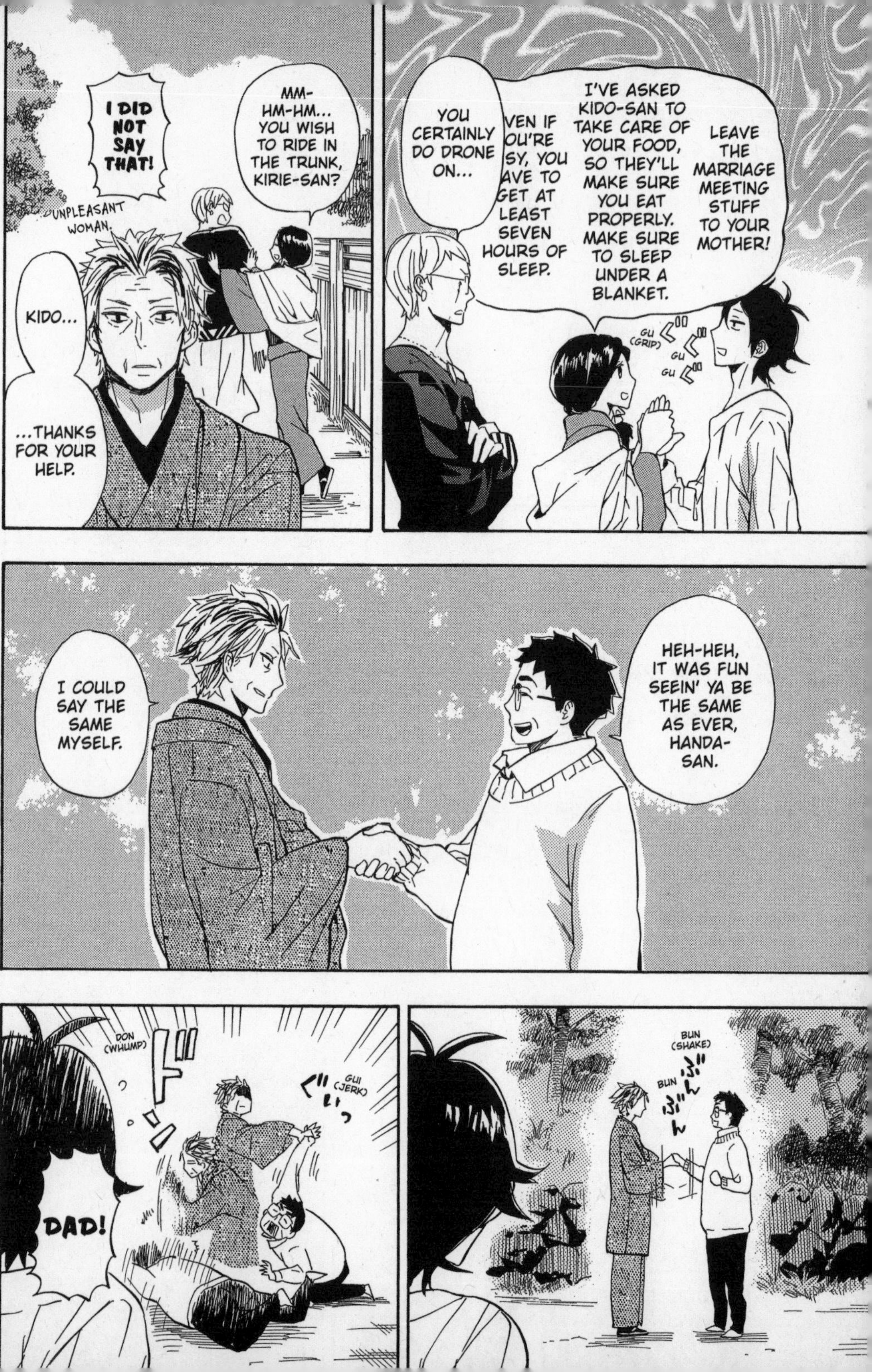
LEAVE THE MARRIAGE MEETING STUFF TO YOUR MOTHER!
I'VE ASKED KIDO-SAN TO TAKE CARE OF YOUR FOOD, SO THEY'LL MAKE SURE YOU EAT PROPERLY. MAKE SURE TO SLEEP UNDER A BLANKET.
VEN IF OU'RE SY, YOU AVE TO GET AT LEAST SEVEN HOURS OF SLEEP.
GU (GRIP)
GU
GU
YOU CERTAINLY DO DRONE ON...
MM-HM-HM... YOU WISH TO RIDE IN THE TRUNK, KIRIE-SAN?
I DID NOT SAY THAT!
UNPLEASANT WOMAN.
KIDO...
...THANKS FOR YOUR HELP.
HEH-HEH, IT WAS FUN SEEIN' YA BE THE SAME AS EVER, HANDA-SAN.
I COULD SAY THE SAME MYSELF.
BUN (SHAKE)
BUN
GUI (JERK)
DON (WHUMP)
DAD!

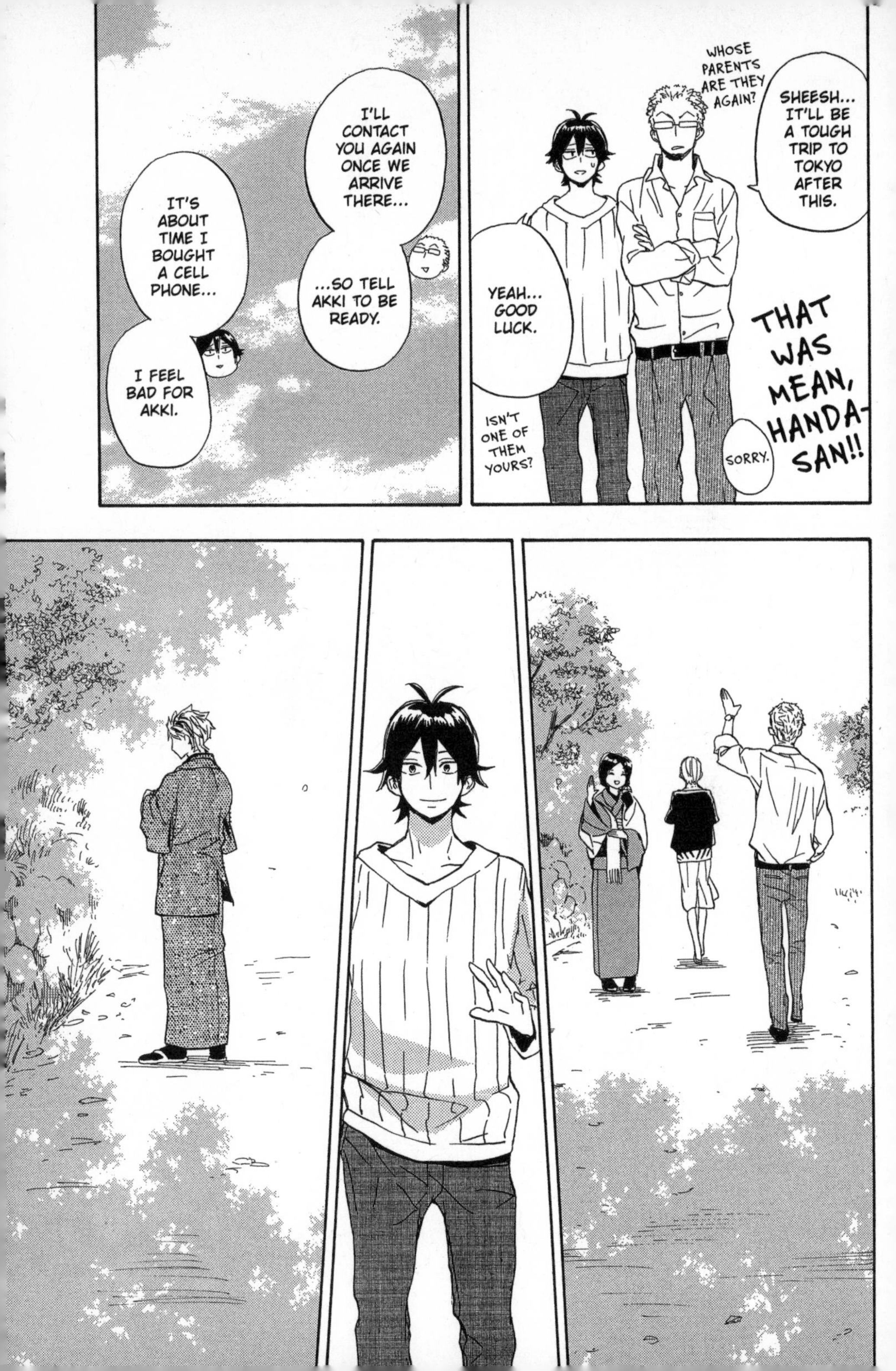
SHEESH... IT'LL BE A TOUGH TRIP TO TOKYO AFTER THIS.
WHOSE PARENTS ARE THEY AGAIN?
YEAH... GOOD LUCK.
THAT WAS MEAN, HANDA-SAN!!
SORRY.
ISN'T ONE OF THEM YOURS?
I'LL CONTACT YOU AGAIN ONCE WE ARRIVE THERE...
...SO TELL AKKI TO BE READY.
IT'S ABOUT TIME I BOUGHT A CELL PHONE...
I FEEL BAD FOR AKKI.

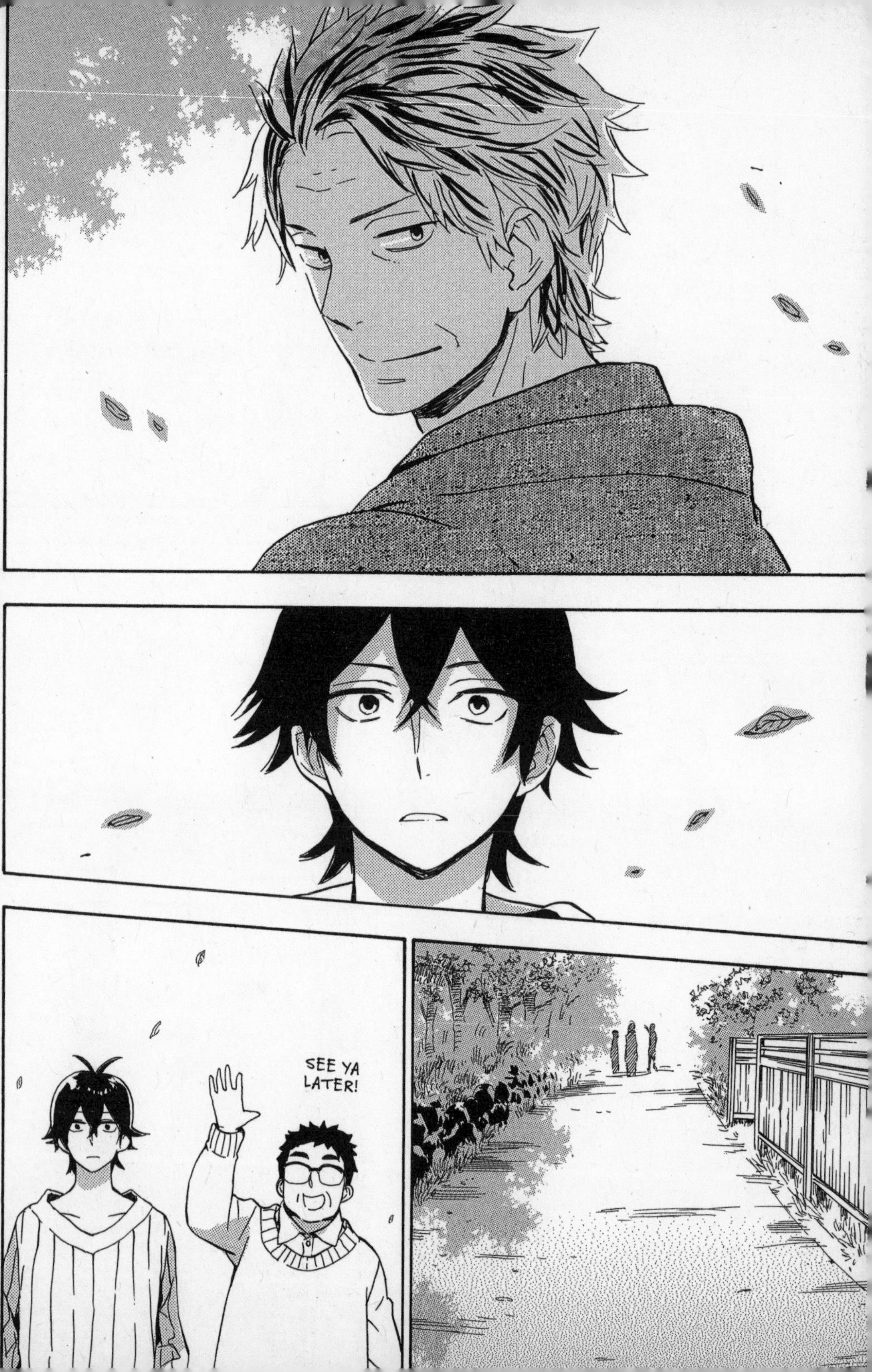
SEE YA LATER!

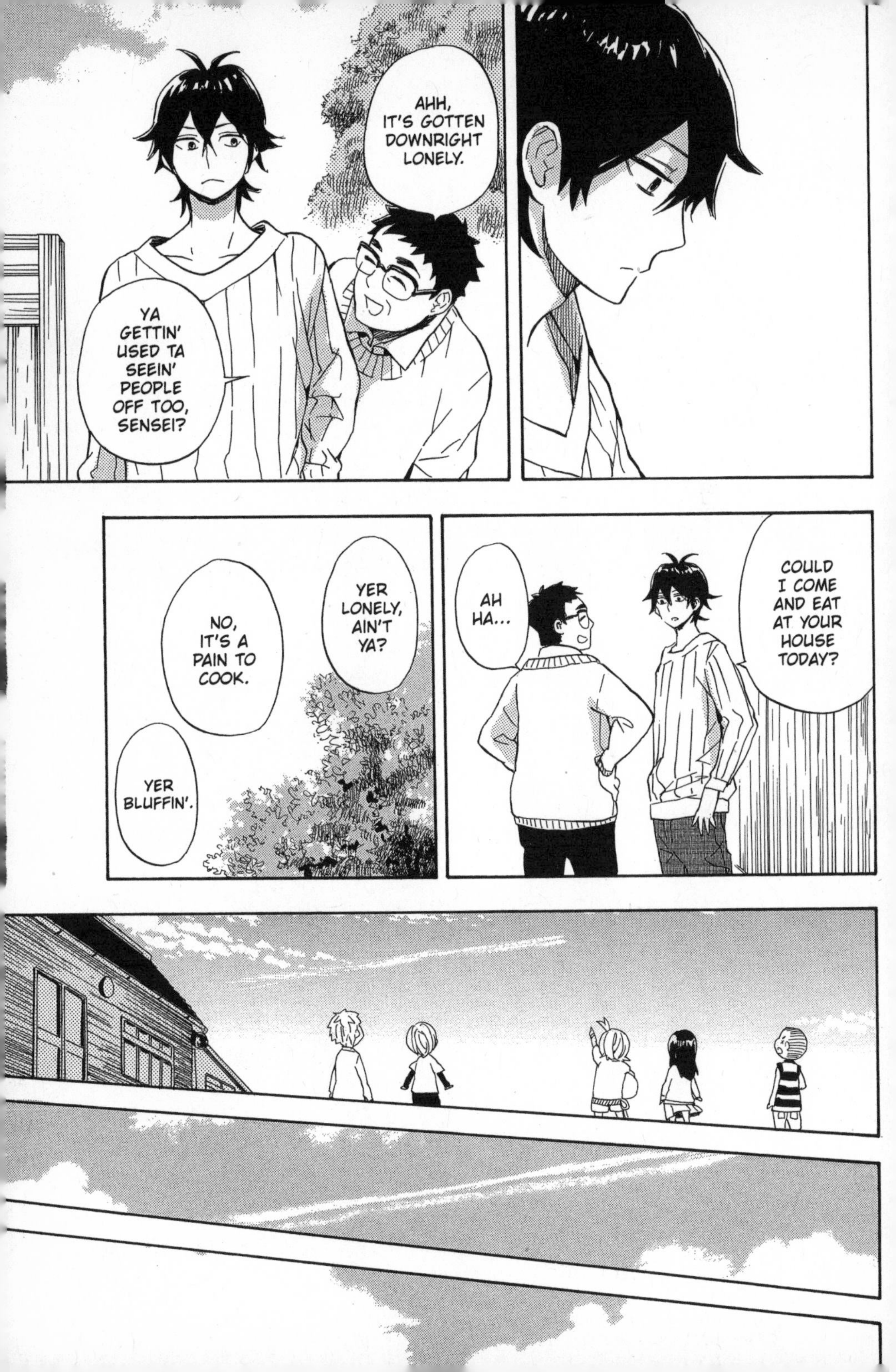
AHH, IT'S GOTTEN DOWNRIGHT LONELY.
YA GETTIN' USED TA SEEIN' PEOPLE OFF TOO, SENSEI?
COULD I COME AND EAT AT YOUR HOUSE TODAY?
AH HA...
YER LONELY, AIN'T YA?
NO, IT'S A PAIN TO COOK.
YER BLUFFIN'.

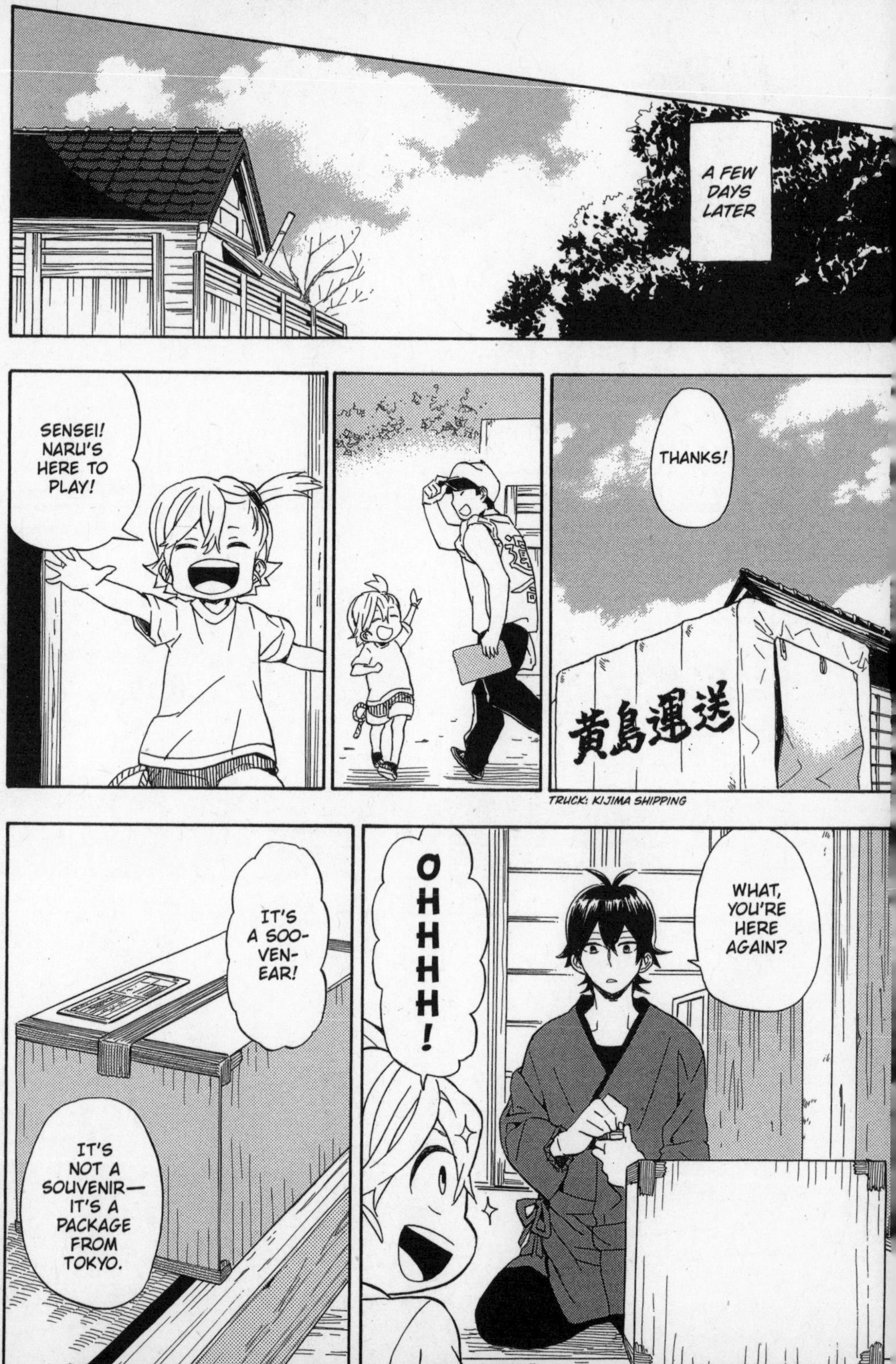
A FEW DAYS LATER
THANKS!
黄島運送
TRUCK: KIJIMA SHIPPING
SENSEI! NARU'S HERE TO PLAY!
WHAT, YOU'RE HERE AGAIN?
OHHHHH!
IT'S A SOO-VEN-EAR!
IT'S NOT A SOUVENIR—IT'S A PACKAGE FROM TOKYO.

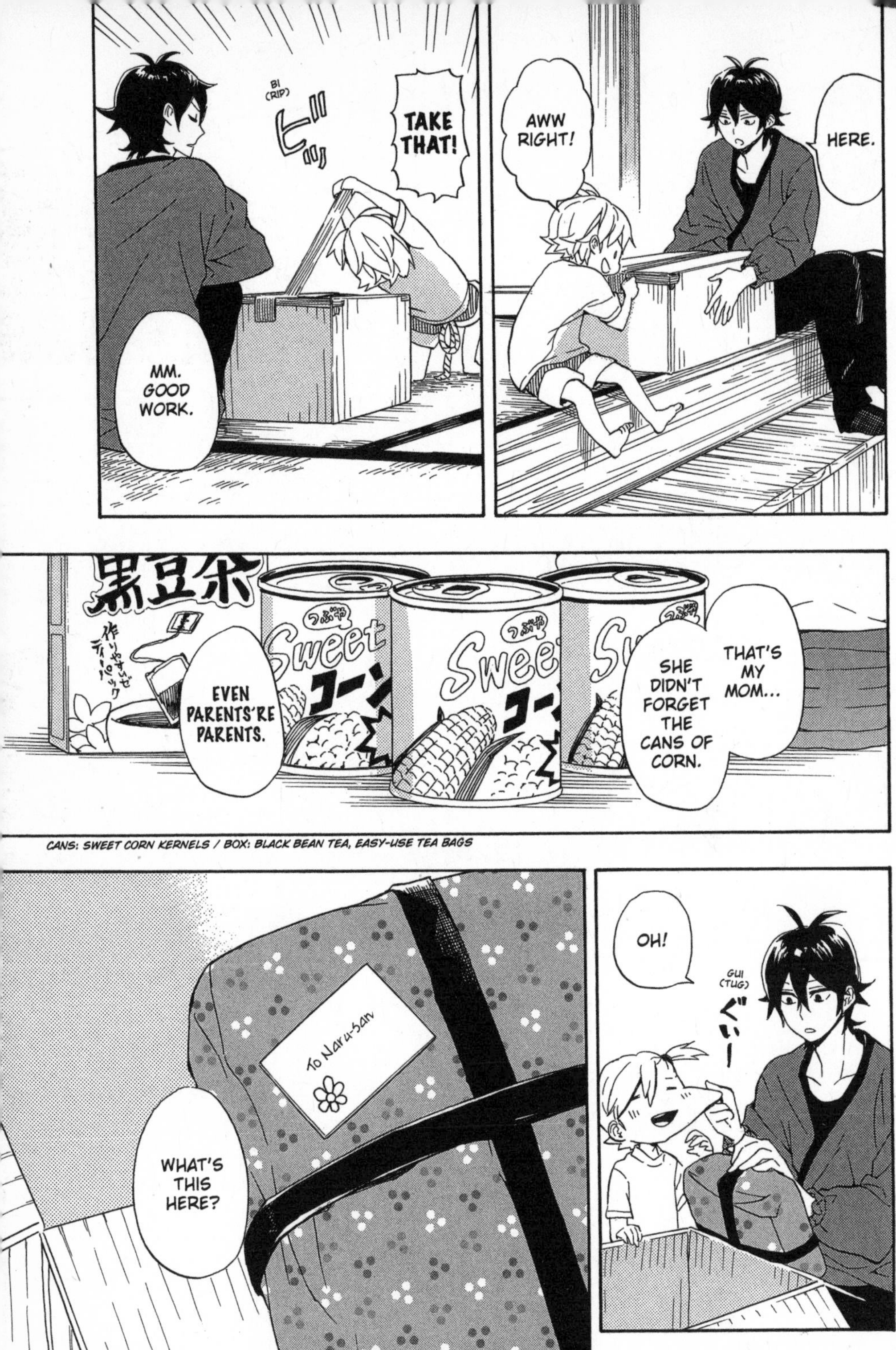
HERE.
AWW RIGHT!
TAKE THAT!
BI (RIP)
MM. GOOD WORK.
THAT'S MY MOM...
SHE DIDN'T FORGET THE CANS OF CORN.
EVEN PARENTS'RE PARENTS.
Sweet
OH!
GUI (TUG)
To Naru-san
WHAT'S THIS HERE?

CANS: SWEET CORN KERNELS / BOX: BLACK BEAN TEA, EASY-USE TEA BAGS

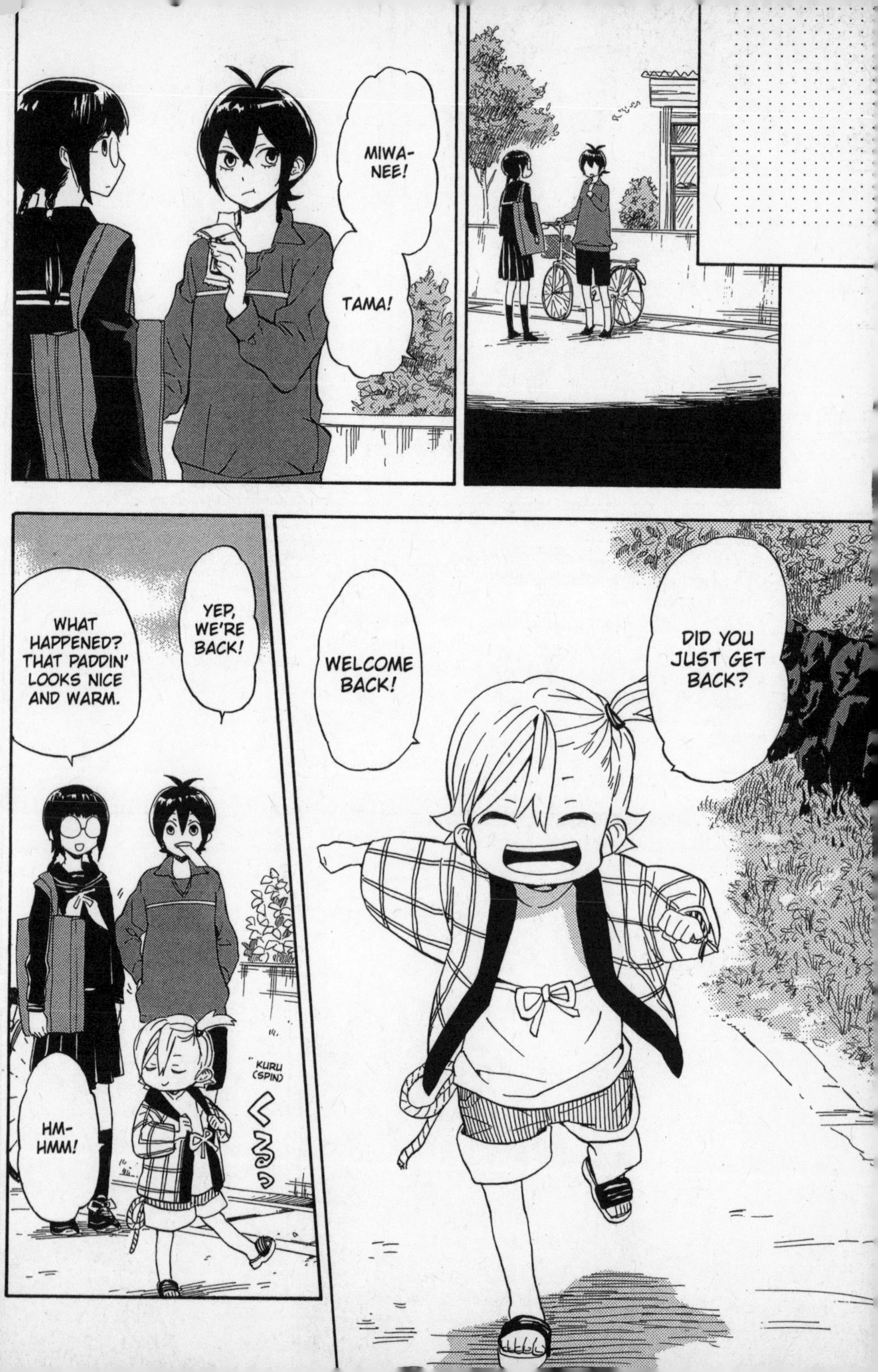
MIWA-NEE!
TAMA!
DID YOU JUST GET BACK?
WELCOME BACK!
YEP, WE'RE BACK!
WHAT HAPPENED? THAT PADDIN' LOOKS NICE AND WARM.
KURU (SPIN)
くるっ
HM-HMM!

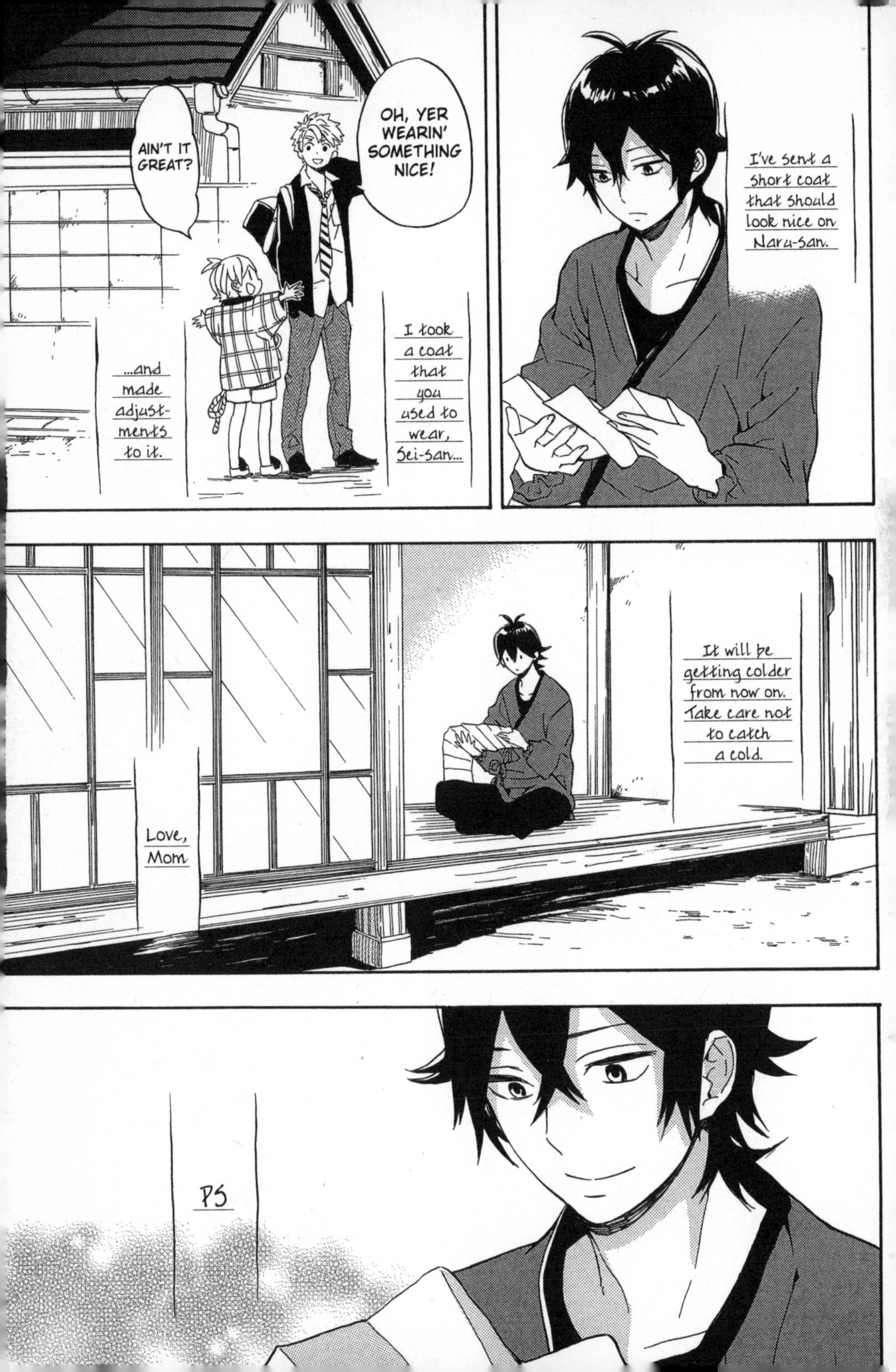
I've sent a short coat that should look nice on Naru-san.
OH, YER WEARIN' SOMETHING NICE!
AIN'T IT GREAT?
I took a coat that you used to wear, Sei-san...
...and made adjustments to it.
It will be getting colder from now on. Take care not to catch a cold.
Love, Mom
PS

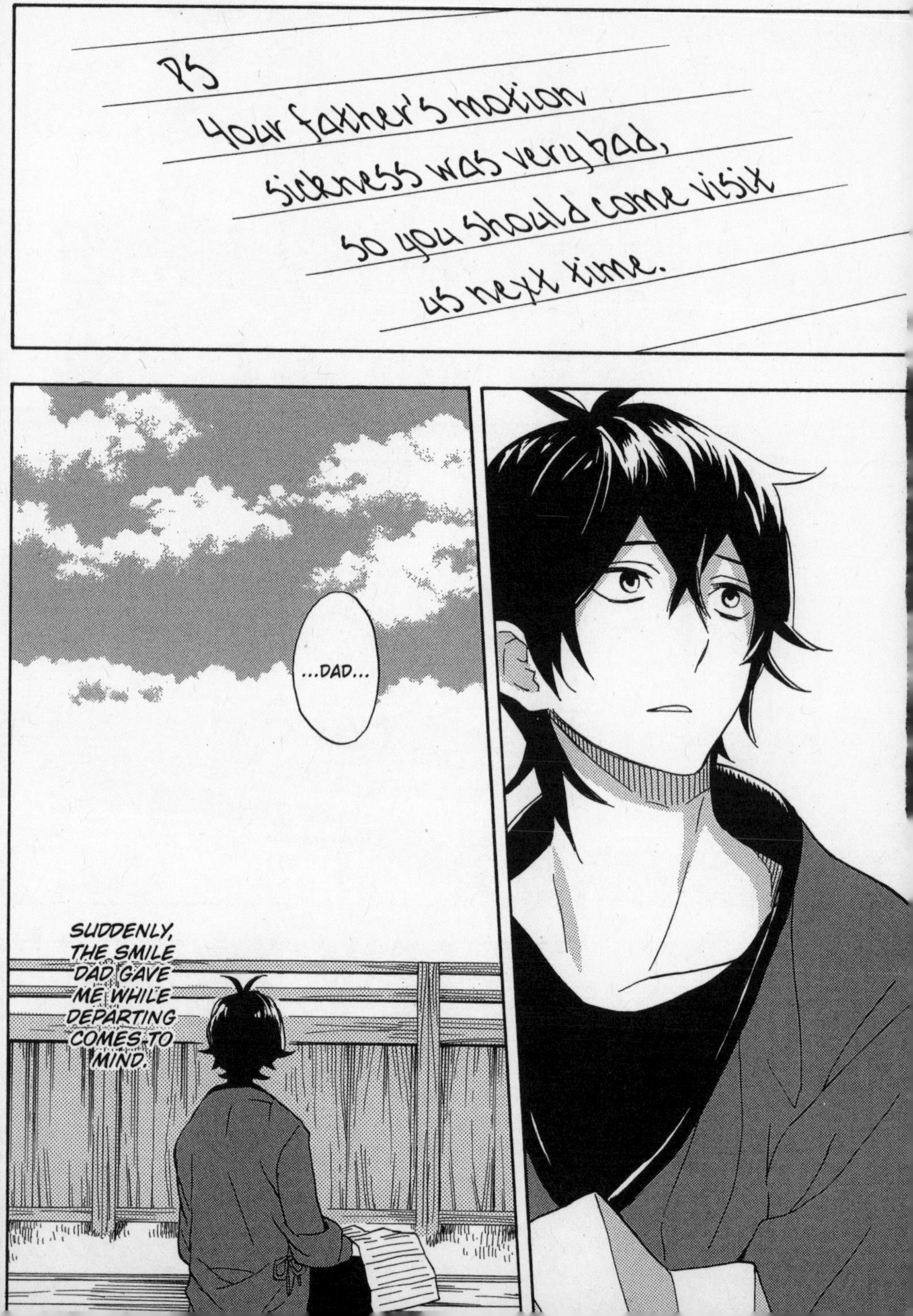
PS
Your father's motion sickness was very bad, so you should come visit us next time.
...DAD...
SUDDENLY, THE SMILE DAD GAVE ME WHILE DEPARTING COMES TO MIND.

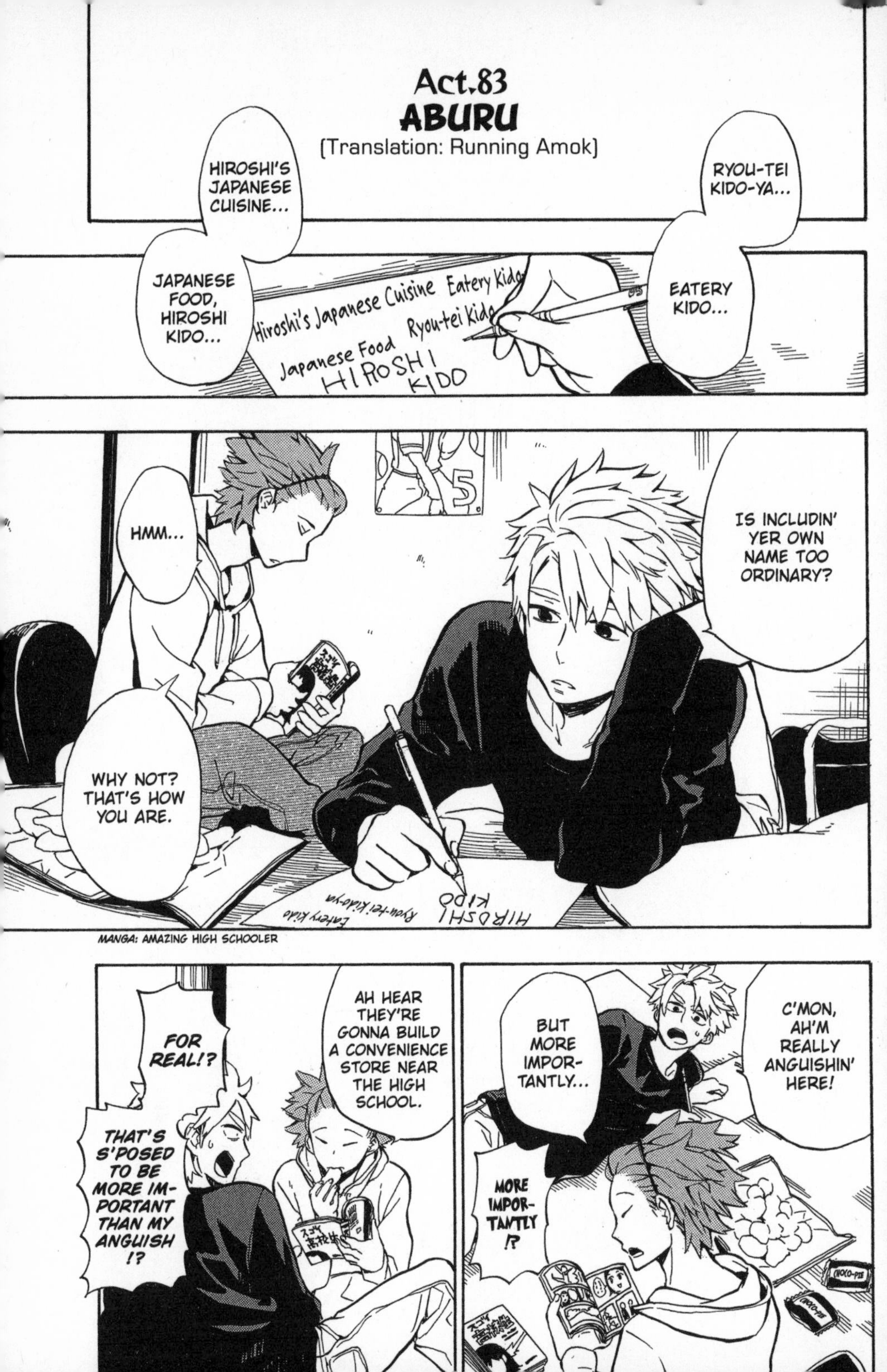
Act.83
ABURU
(Translation: Running Amok)
RYOU-TEI KIDO-YA...
HIROSHI'S JAPANESE CUISINE...
EATERY KIDO...
Hiroshi's Japanese Cuisine Eatery Kido
Ryou-tei Kido
Japanese Food HIROSHI KIDO
JAPANESE FOOD, HIROSHI KIDO...
IS INCLUDIN' YER OWN NAME TOO ORDINARY?
HMM...
WHY NOT? THAT'S HOW YOU ARE.
HIROSHI KIDO
Ryou-tei Kido-ya
Eatery Kido
MANGA: AMAZING HIGH SCHOOLER
C'MON, AH'M REALLY ANGUISHIN' HERE!
BUT MORE IMPOR-TANTLY...
MORE IMPOR-TANTLY !?
AH HEAR THEY'RE GONNA BUILD A CONVENIENCE STORE NEAR THE HIGH SCHOOL.
FOR REAL!?
THAT'S S'POSED TO BE MORE IM-PORTANT THAN MY ANGUISH !?

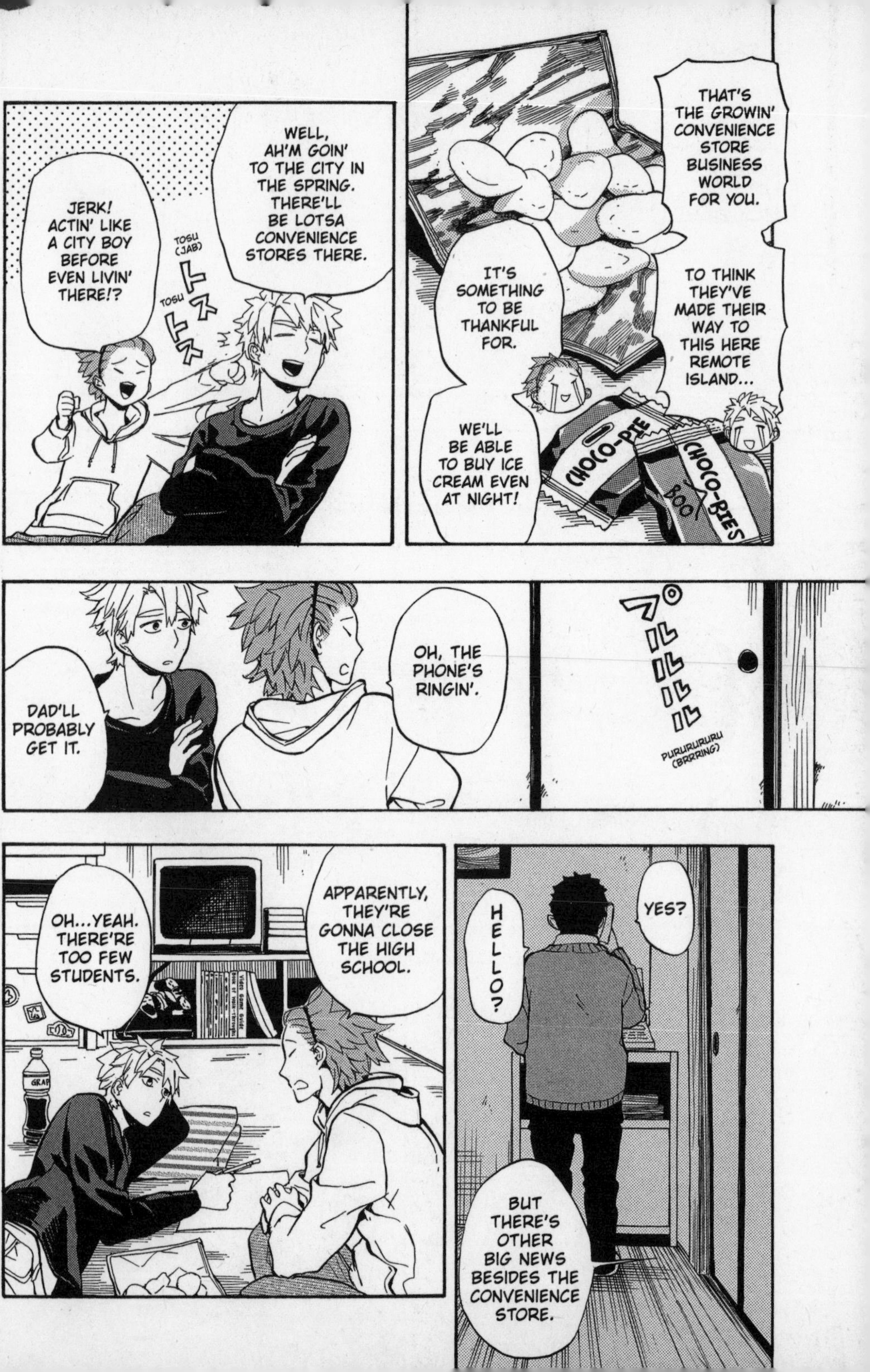
THAT'S THE GROWIN' CONVENIENCE STORE BUSINESS WORLD FOR YOU.
TO THINK THEY'VE MADE THEIR WAY TO THIS HERE REMOTE ISLAND...
IT'S SOMETHING TO BE THANKFUL FOR.
WE'LL BE ABLE TO BUY ICE CREAM EVEN AT NIGHT!
CHOCO-PIE
CHOCO-PIES
BOO
WELL, AH'M GOIN' TO THE CITY IN THE SPRING. THERE'LL BE LOTSA CONVENIENCE STORES THERE.
トス
TOSU (JAB)
トス
TOSU
JERK! ACTIN' LIKE A CITY BOY BEFORE EVEN LIVIN' THERE!?
プルルルル
PURURURURU (BRRRING)
OH, THE PHONE'S RINGIN'.
DAD'LL PROBABLY GET IT.
YES?
HELLO?
BUT THERE'S OTHER BIG NEWS BESIDES THE CONVENIENCE STORE.
APPARENTLY, THEY'RE GONNA CLOSE THE HIGH SCHOOL.
OH...YEAH. THERE'RE TOO FEW STUDENTS.

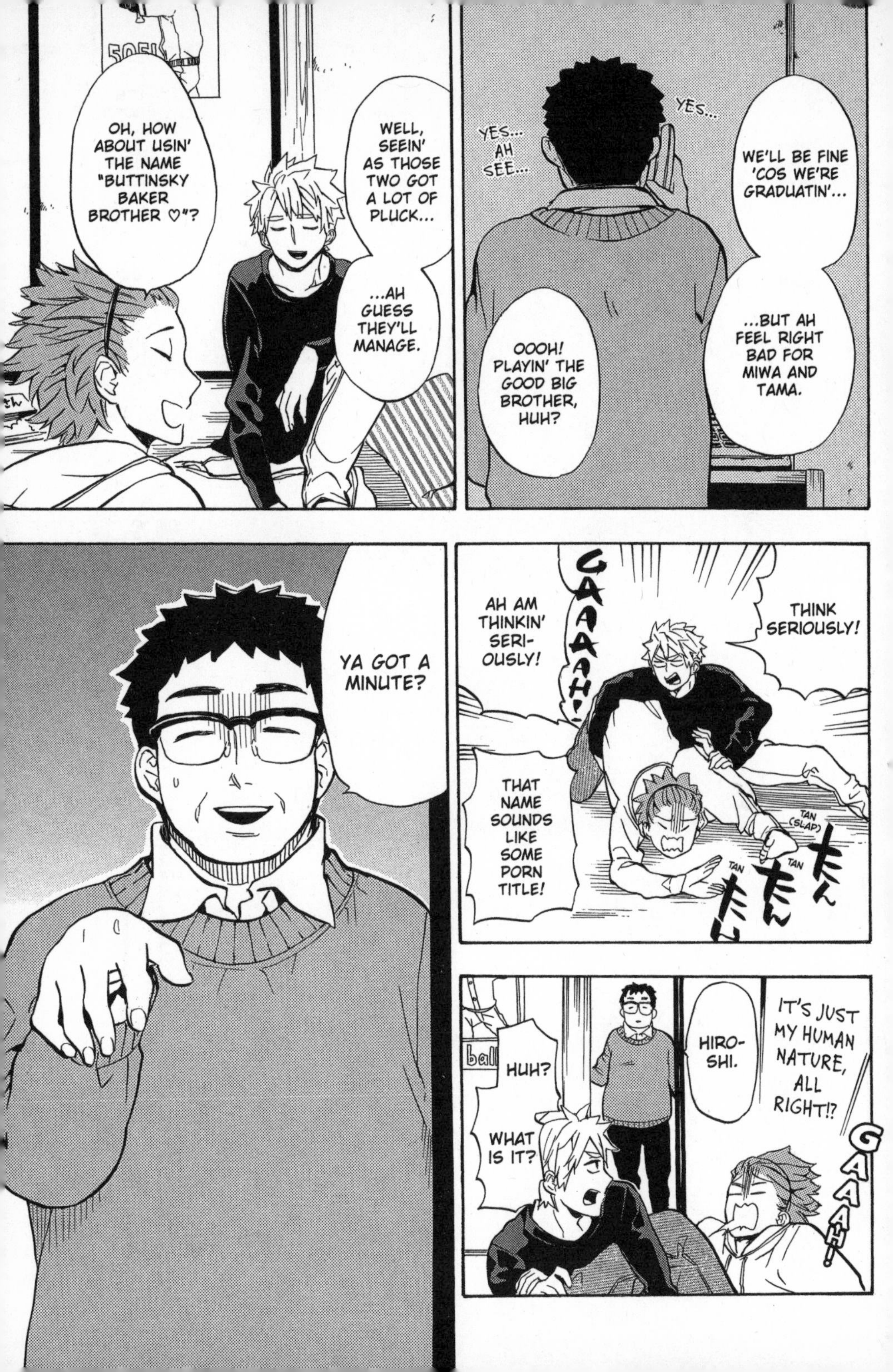
YES...
YES... AH SEE...
WE'LL BE FINE 'COS WE'RE GRADUATIN'...
...BUT AH FEEL RIGHT BAD FOR MIWA AND TAMA.
OOOH! PLAYIN' THE GOOD BIG BROTHER, HUH?
WELL, SEEIN' AS THOSE TWO GOT A LOT OF PLUCK...
...AH GUESS THEY'LL MANAGE.
OH, HOW ABOUT USIN' THE NAME "BUTTINSKY BAKER BROTHER ♡"?
THINK SERIOUSLY!
GAAAAH!
AH AM THINKIN' SERI-OUSLY!
THAT NAME SOUNDS LIKE SOME PORN TITLE!
TAN (SLAP)
TAN
TAN
IT'S JUST MY HUMAN NATURE, ALL RIGHT!?
GAAAAH!
HIRO-SHI.
HUH?
WHAT IS IT?
YA GOT A MINUTE?

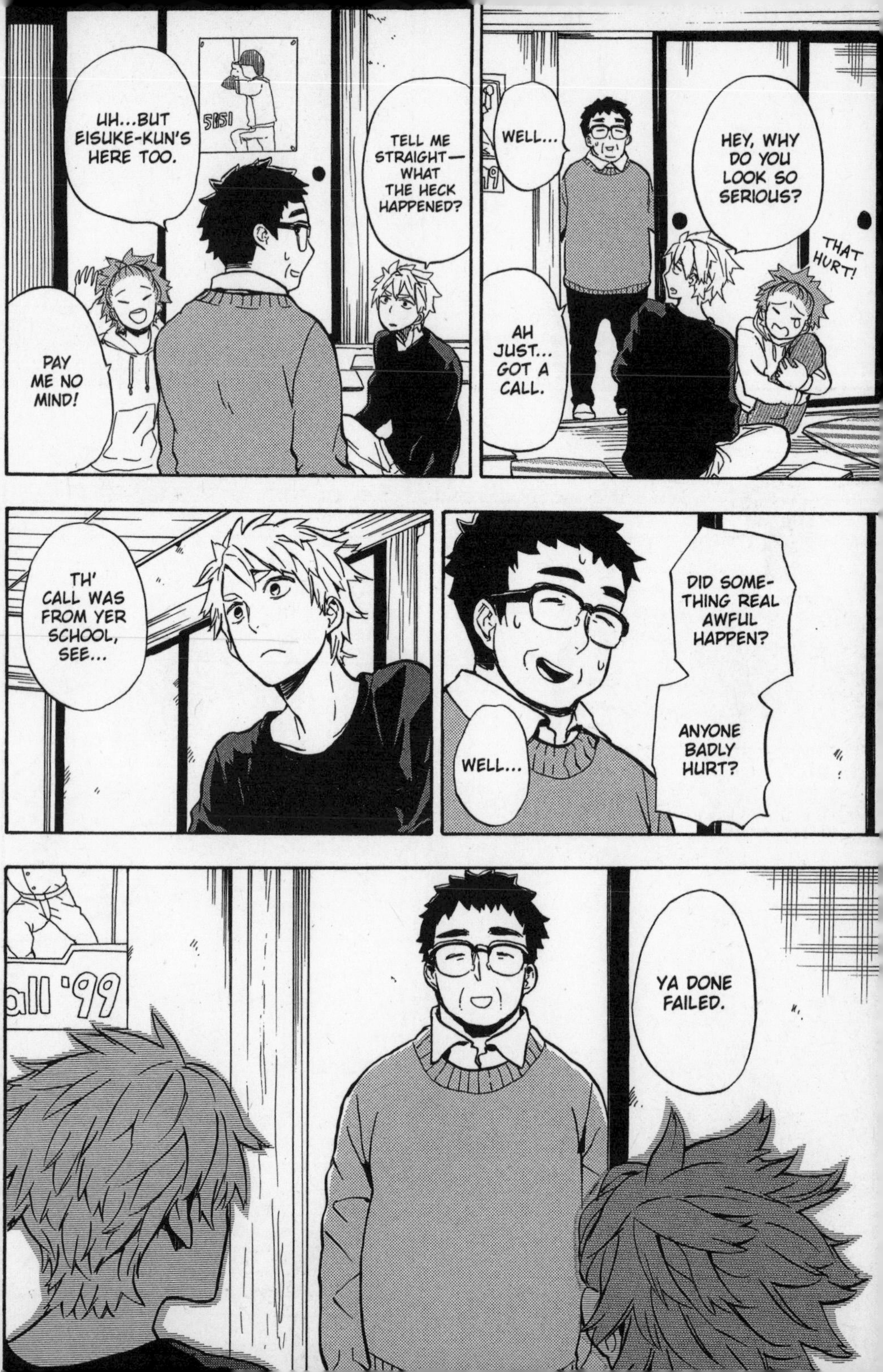
HEY, WHY DO YOU LOOK SO SERIOUS?
THAT HURT!
WELL...
AH JUST... GOT A CALL.
TELL ME STRAIGHT—WHAT THE HECK HAPPENED?
UH...BUT EISUKE-KUN'S HERE TOO.
PAY ME NO MIND!
DID SOME-THING REAL AWFUL HAPPEN?
ANYONE BADLY HURT?
WELL...
TH' CALL WAS FROM YER SCHOOL, SEE...
all '99
YA DONE FAILED.

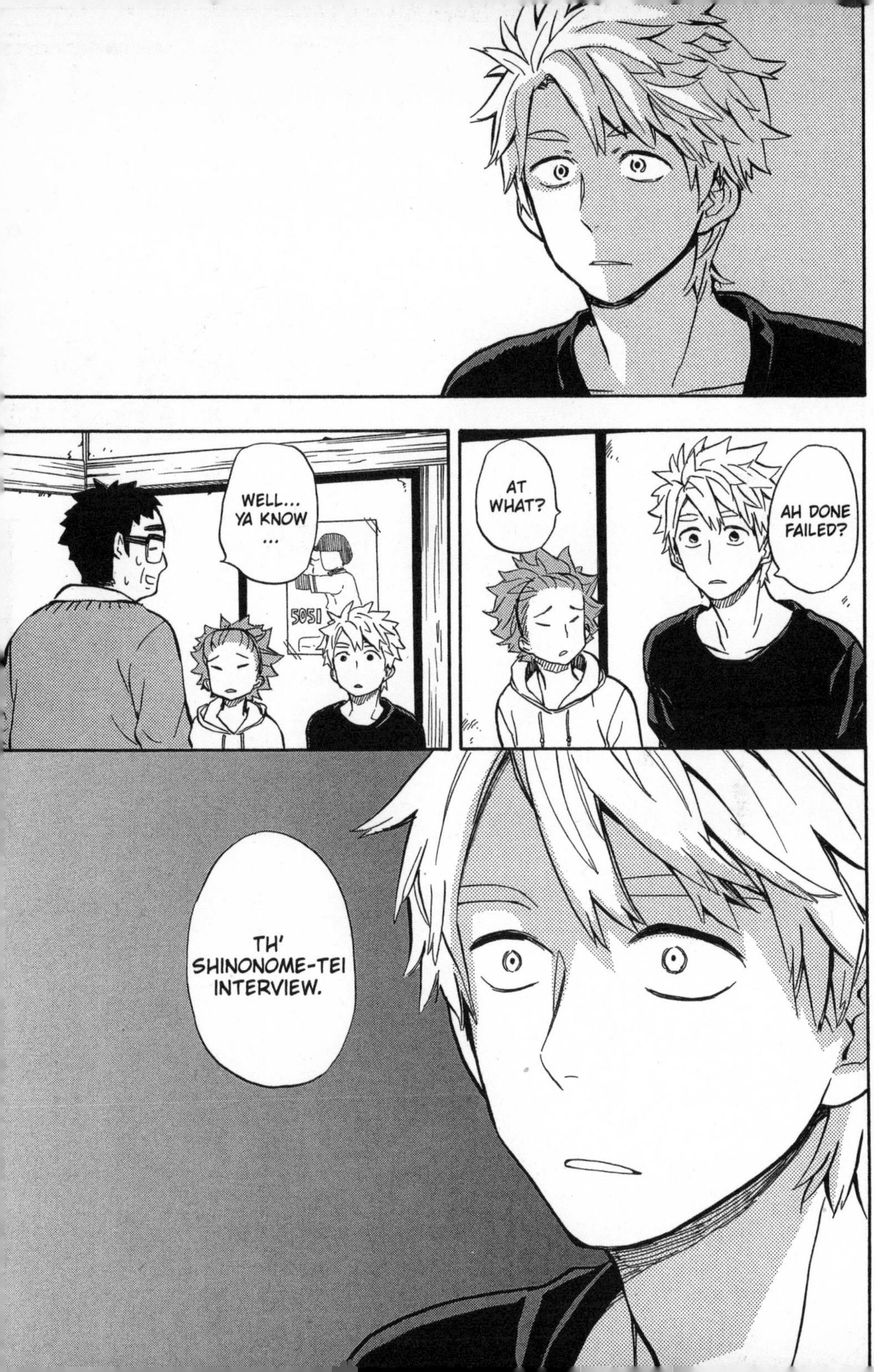
AH DONE FAILED?
AT WHAT?
WELL... YA KNOW ...
TH' SHINONOME-TEI INTERVIEW.

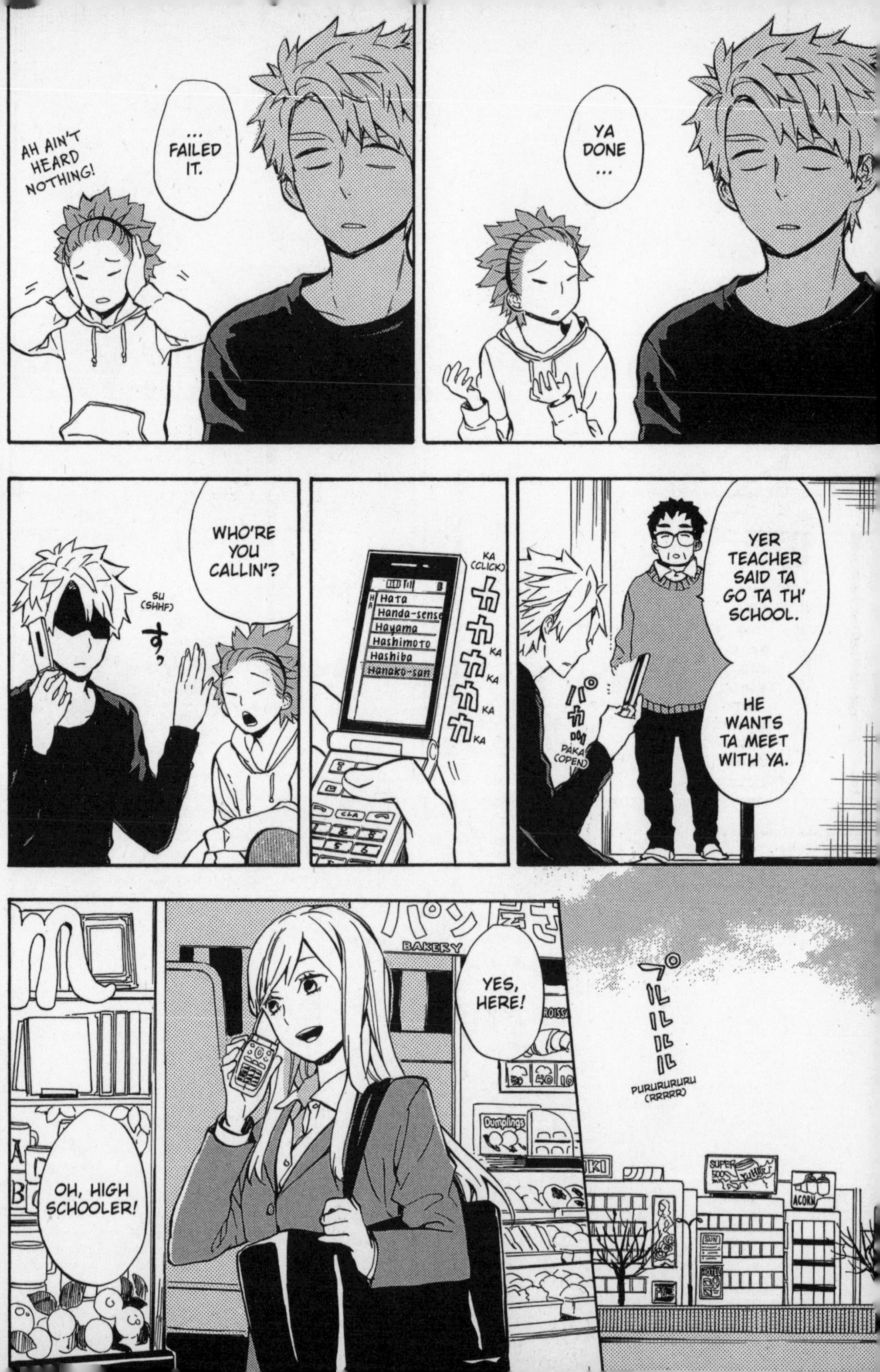

YA DONE ...
... FAILED IT.
AH AIN'T HEARD NOTHING!
YER TEACHER SAID TA GO TA TH' SCHOOL.
HE WANTS TA MEET WITH YA.
パカッ
PAKA (OPEN)
KA (CLICK)
カカカカカ
KA KA KA KA
Hata
Handa-sensei
Hayama
Hashimoto
Hashiba
Hanako-san
WHO'RE YOU CALLIN'?
SU (SHHF)
すっ
プルルルル
PURURURURU (RRRRR)
BAKERY
YES, HERE!
Dumplings
SUPER
ACORN
SUN
HOTEL
OH, HIGH SCHOOLER!

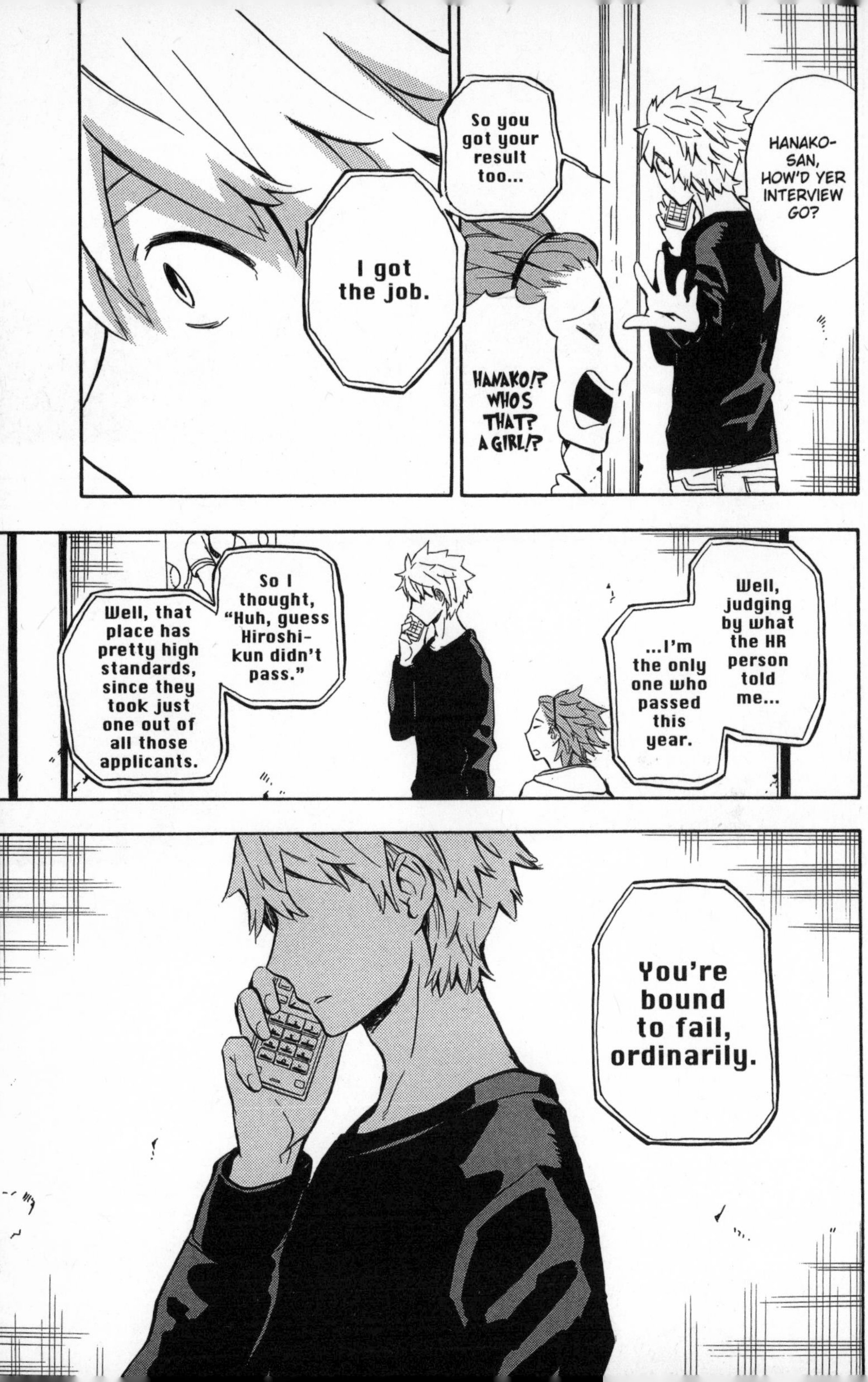
HANAKO-SAN, HOW'D YER INTERVIEW GO?
So you got your result too...
HANAKO!? WHOS THAT? A GIRL!?
I got the job.
Well, judging by what the HR person told me...
...I'm the only one who passed this year.
So I thought, "Huh, guess Hiroshi-kun didn't pass."
Well, that place has pretty high standards, since they took just one out of all those applicants.
You're bound to fail, ordinarily.

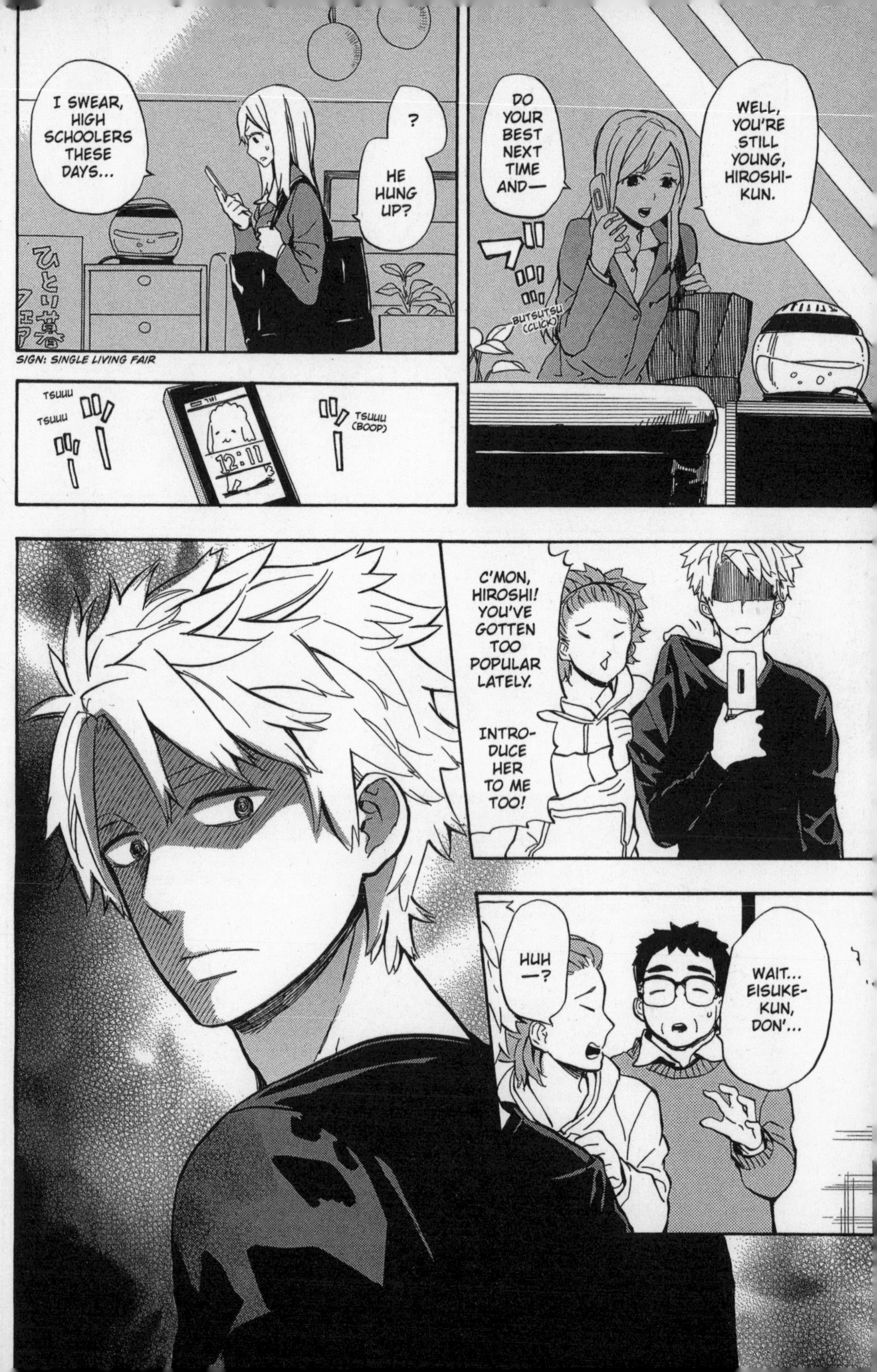
WELL, YOU'RE STILL YOUNG, HIROSHI-KUN.
DO YOUR BEST NEXT TIME AND—
BUTSUTSU (CLICK)
?
HE HUNG UP?
I SWEAR, HIGH SCHOOLERS THESE DAYS...
SIGN: SINGLE LIVING FAIR
TSUUU (BOOP)
12:11
TSUUU
TSUUU
C'MON, HIROSHI! YOU'VE GOTTEN TOO POPULAR LATELY.
INTRODUCE HER TO ME TOO!
WAIT... EISUKE-KUN, DON'...
HUH—?

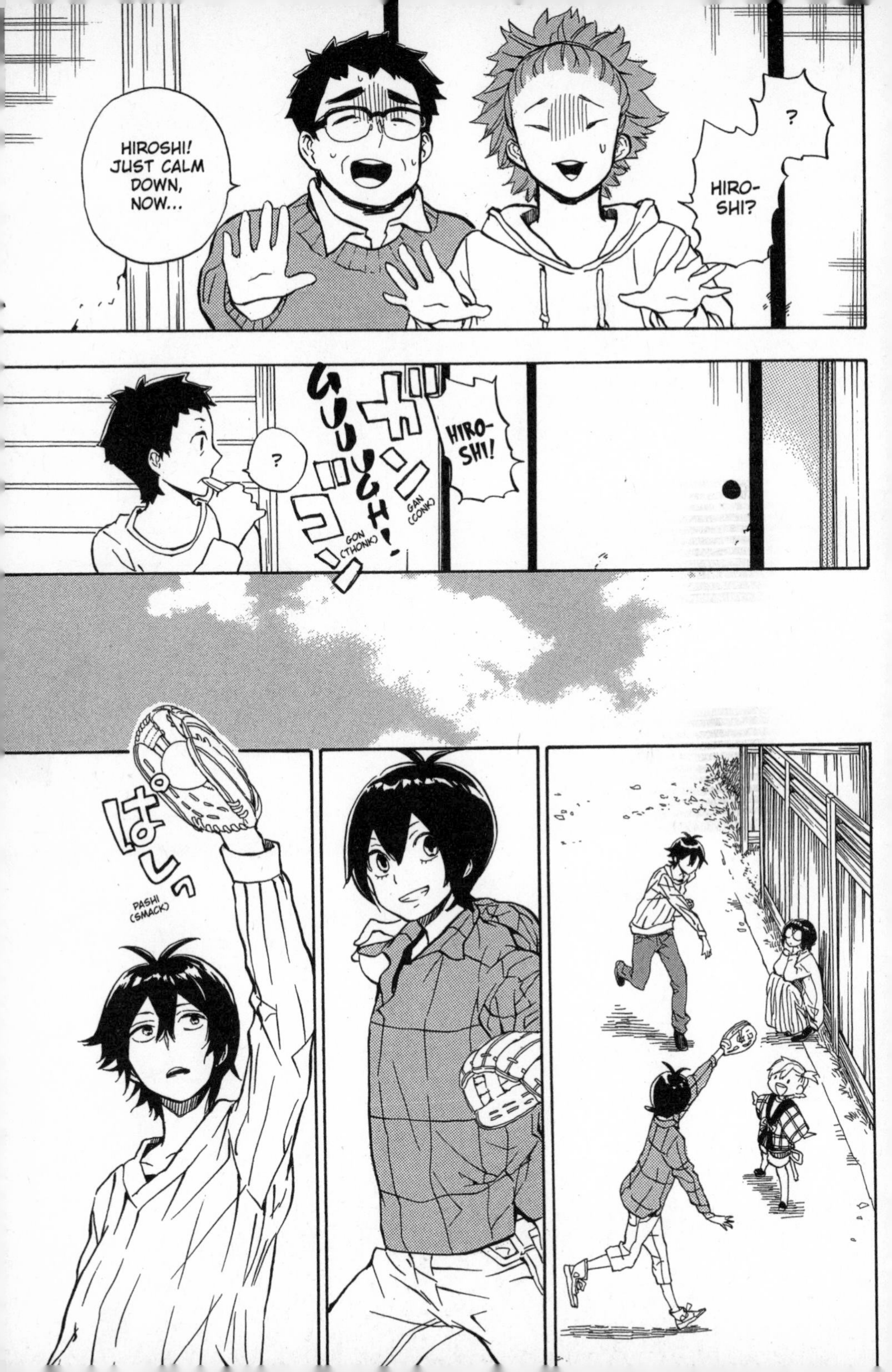
?
HIRO-SHI?
HIROSHI! JUST CALM DOWN, NOW...
HIRO-SHI!
ガン
GAN (CONK)
UUUGH!
ゴン
GON (THONK)
?
ぱしっ
PASHI (SMACK)

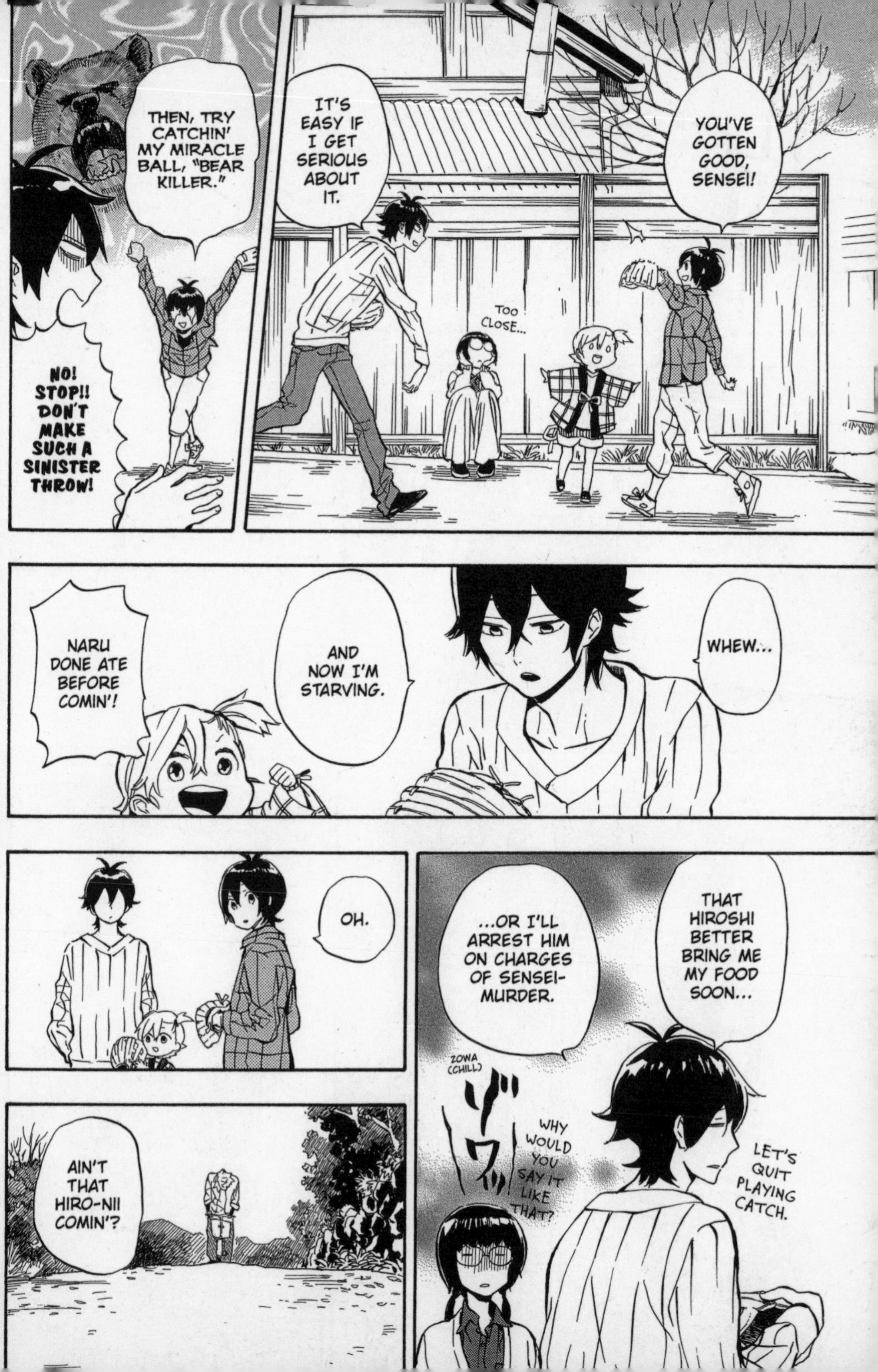
YOU'VE GOTTEN GOOD, SENSEI!
IT'S EASY IF I GET SERIOUS ABOUT IT.
TOO CLOSE...
THEN, TRY CATCHIN' MY MIRACLE BALL, "BEAR KILLER."
NO! STOP!! DON'T MAKE SUCH A SINISTER THROW!
WHEW...
AND NOW I'M STARVING.
NARU DONE ATE BEFORE COMIN'!
THAT HIROSHI BETTER BRING ME MY FOOD SOON...
...OR I'LL ARREST HIM ON CHARGES OF SENSEI-MURDER.
LET'S QUIT PLAYING CATCH.
WHY WOULD YOU SAY IT LIKE THAT?
ZOWA (CHILL)
OH.
AIN'T THAT HIRO-NII COMIN'?

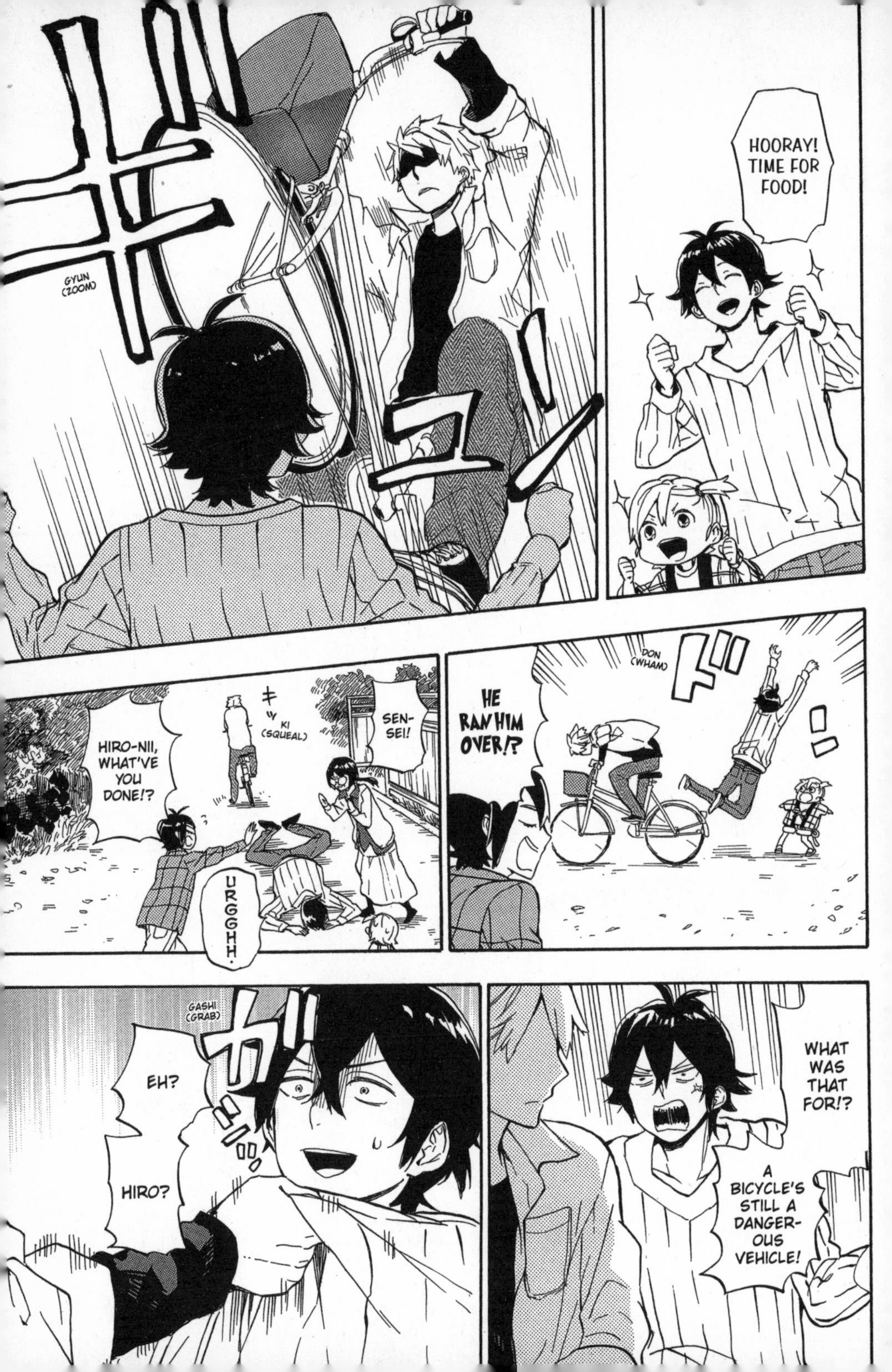
HOORAY! TIME FOR FOOD!
GYUN (ZOOM)
DON (WHAM)
HE RAN HIM OVER!?
SEN-SEI!
KI (SQUEAL)
HIRO-NII, WHAT'VE YOU DONE!?
URGGHH.
WHAT WAS THAT FOR!?
A BICYCLE'S STILL A DANGER-OUS VEHICLE!
GASHI (GRAB)
EH?
HIRO?

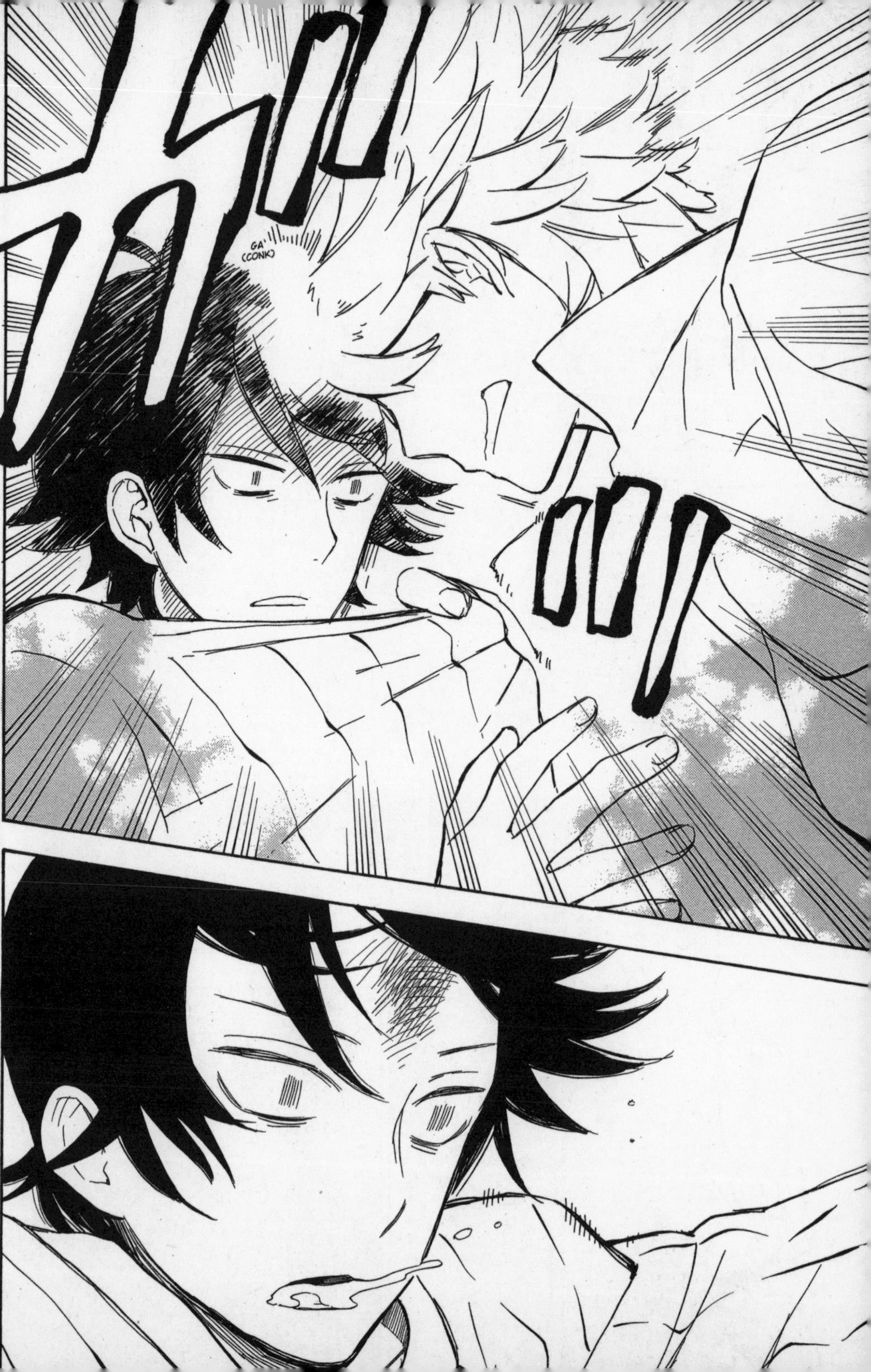
GA'
(CONK)

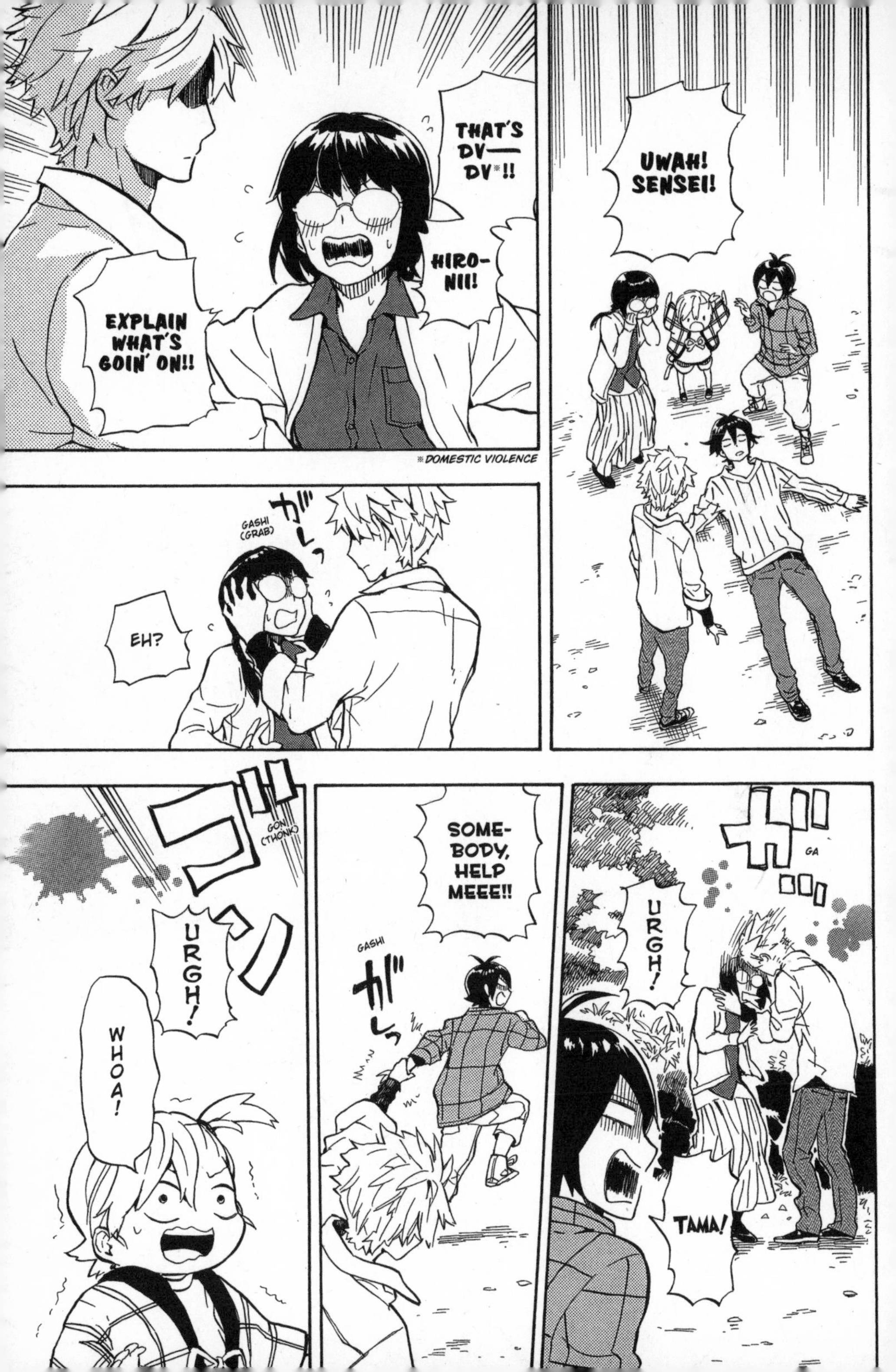
UWAH! SENSEI!
THAT'S DV— DV※!!
HIRO-NII!
EXPLAIN WHAT'S GOIN' ON!!
※DOMESTIC VIOLENCE
GASHI (GRAB)
EH?
GA
URGH!
TAMA!
SOME-BODY, HELP MEEE!!
GASHI
GON (THONK)
URGH!
WHOA!

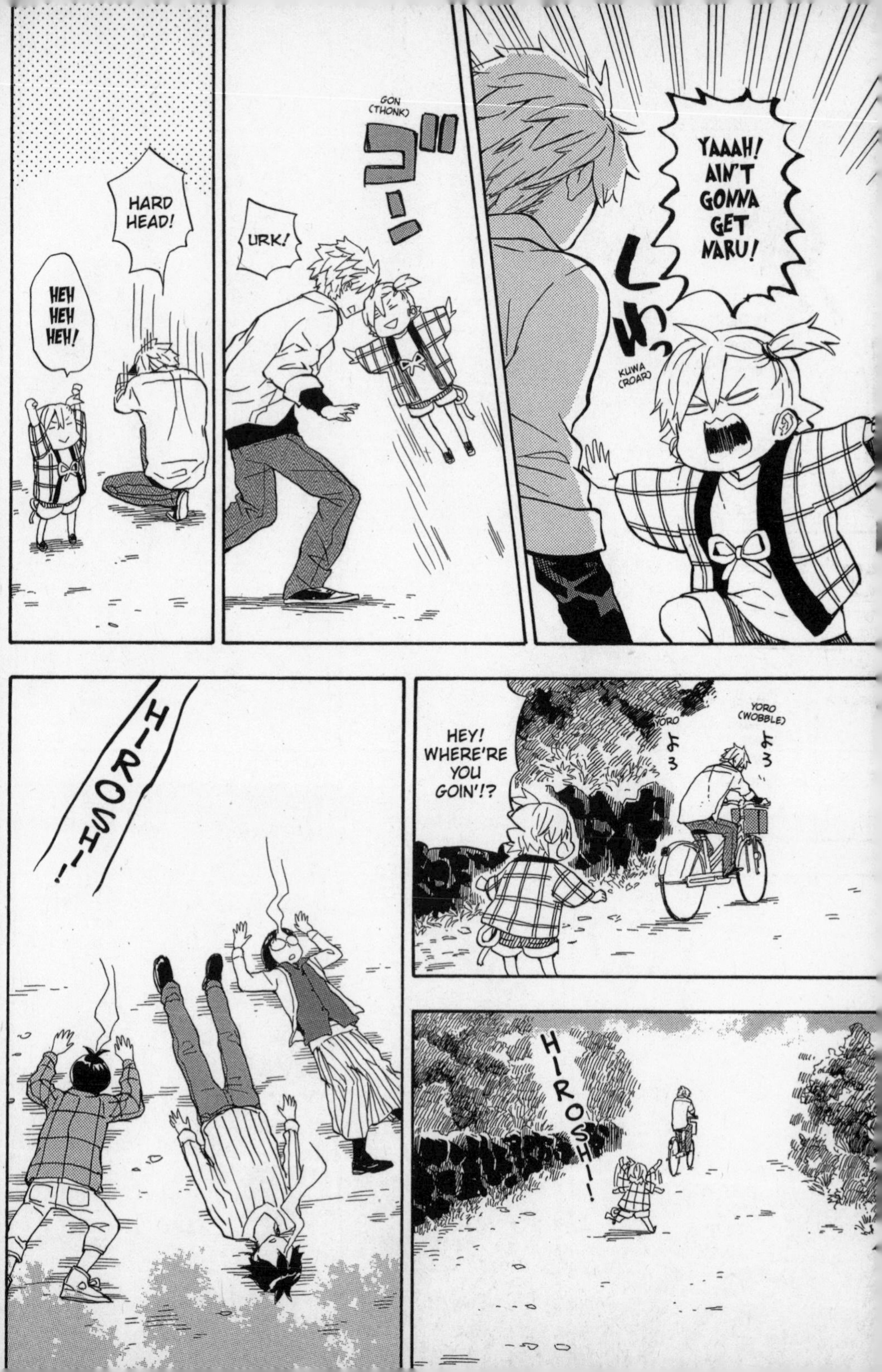
YAAAH! AIN'T GONNA GET NARU!
KUWA (ROAR)
GON (THONK)
URK!
HARD HEAD!
HEH HEH HEH!
YORO (WOBBLE)
YORO
HEY! WHERE'RE YOU GOIN'!?
HIROSHI!
HIROSHI-!

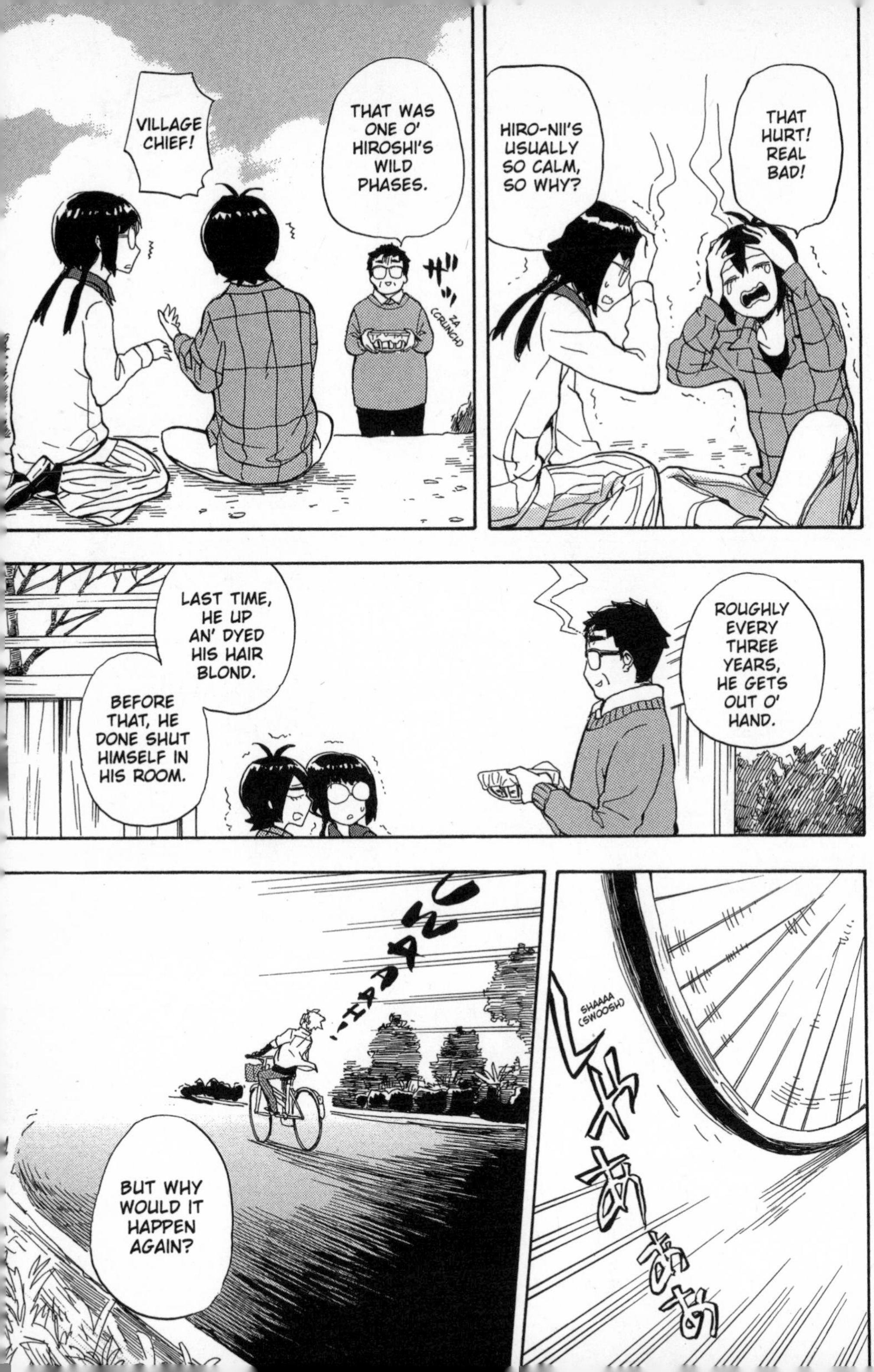
THAT HURT! REAL BAD!
HIRO-NII'S USUALLY SO CALM, SO WHY?
THAT WAS ONE O' HIROSHI'S WILD PHASES.
ZA (CRUNCH)
VILLAGE CHIEF!
ROUGHLY EVERY THREE YEARS, HE GETS OUT O' HAND.
LAST TIME, HE UP AN' DYED HIS HAIR BLOND.
BEFORE THAT, HE DONE SHUT HIMSELF IN HIS ROOM.
SHAAAA (SWOOSH)
UWAAAH!
BUT WHY WOULD IT HAPPEN AGAIN?

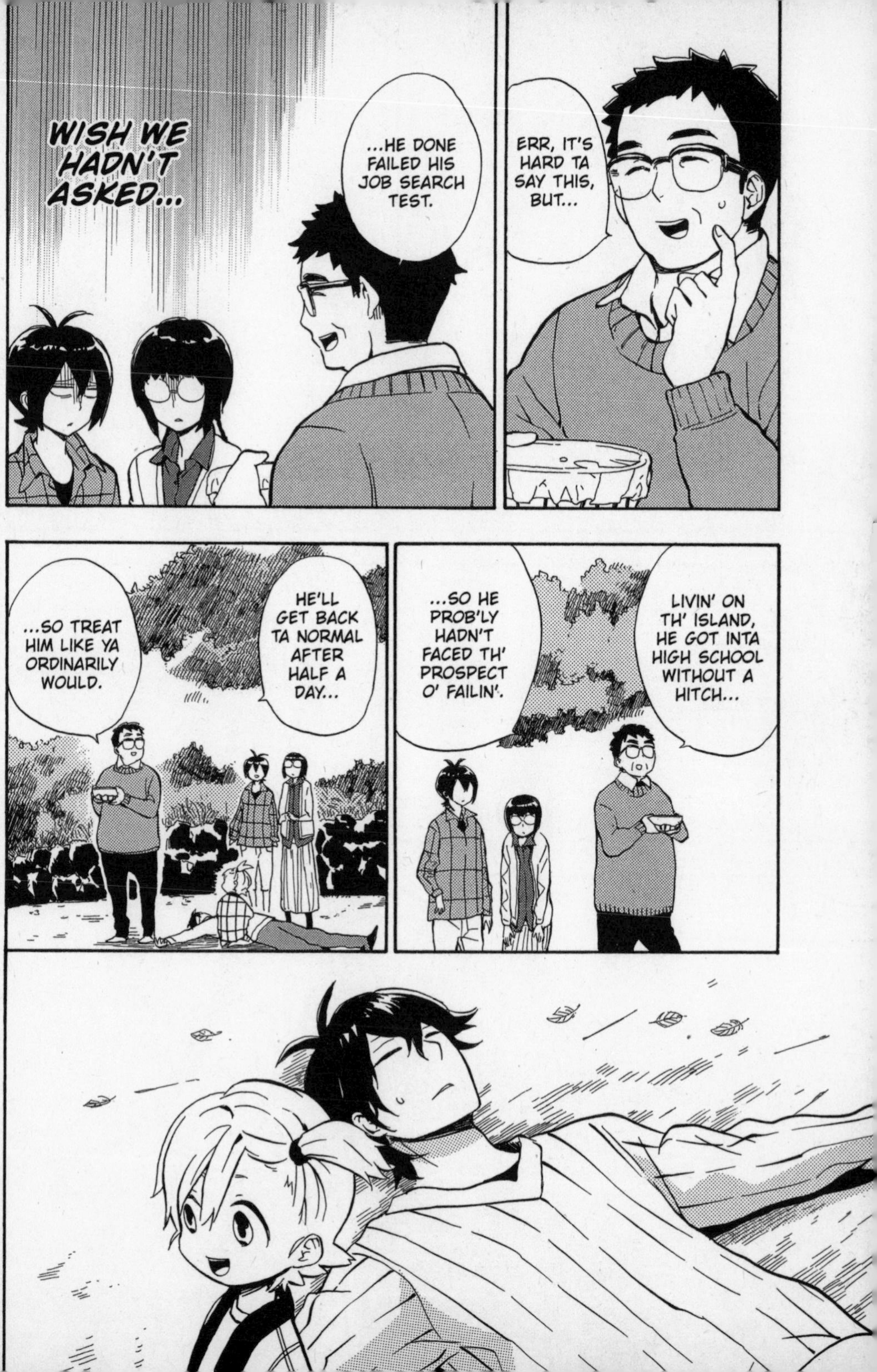
ERR, IT'S HARD TA SAY THIS, BUT...
...HE DONE FAILED HIS JOB SEARCH TEST.
WISH WE HADN'T ASKED...
LIVIN' ON TH' ISLAND, HE GOT INTA HIGH SCHOOL WITHOUT A HITCH...
...SO HE PROB'LY HADN'T FACED TH' PROSPECT O' FAILIN'.
HE'LL GET BACK TA NORMAL AFTER HALF A DAY...
...SO TREAT HIM LIKE YA ORDINARILY WOULD.

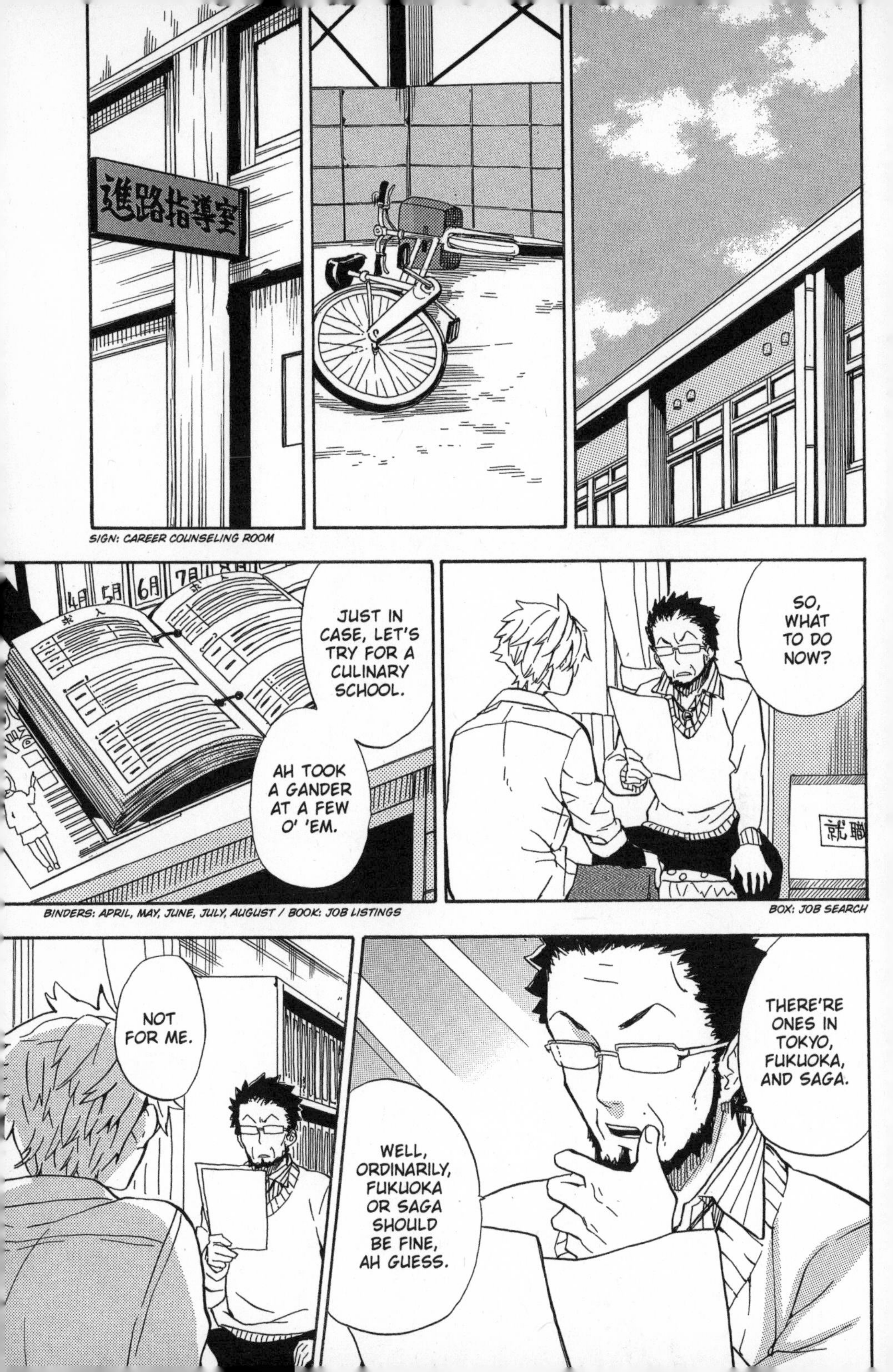
SIGN: CAREER COUNSELING ROOM
SO, WHAT TO DO NOW?
JUST IN CASE, LET'S TRY FOR A CULINARY SCHOOL.
AH TOOK A GANDER AT A FEW O' 'EM.
BINDERS: APRIL, MAY, JUNE, JULY, AUGUST / BOOK: JOB LISTINGS
BOX: JOB SEARCH
THERE'RE ONES IN TOKYO, FUKUOKA, AND SAGA.
WELL, ORDINARILY, FUKUOKA OR SAGA SHOULD BE FINE, AH GUESS.
NOT FOR ME.

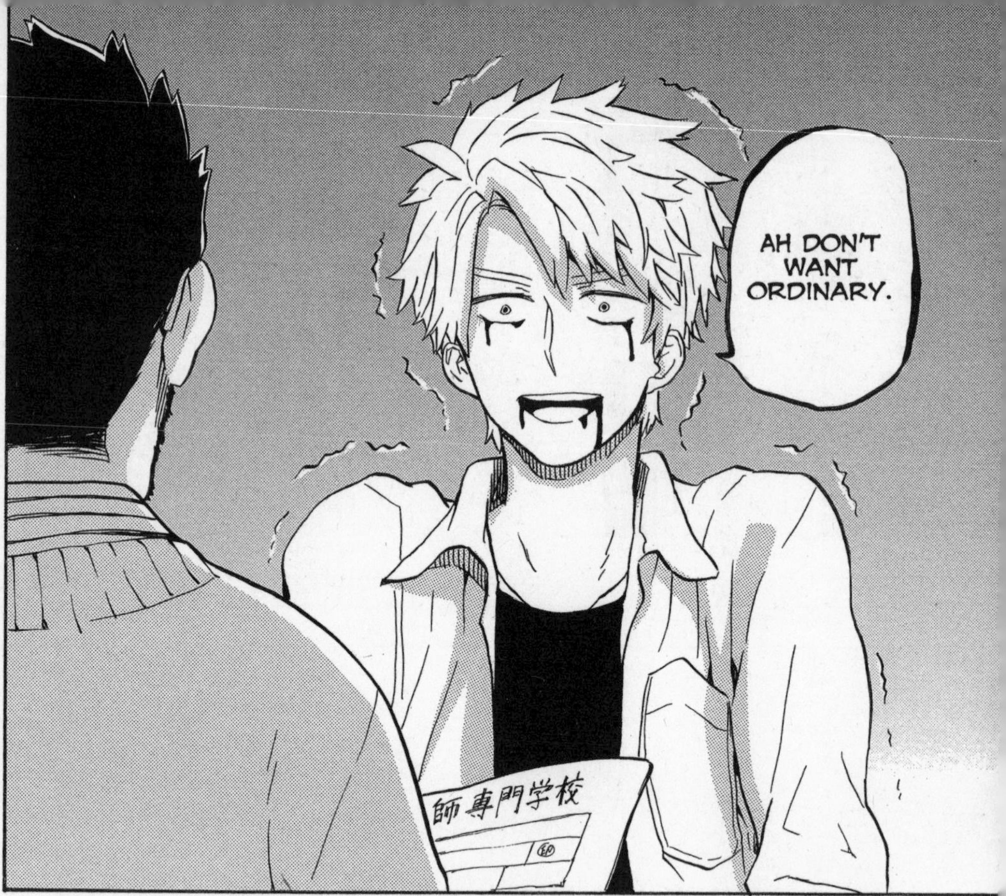
AH DON'T WANT ORDINARY.
師専門学校
PAPER: CULINARY SCHOOL

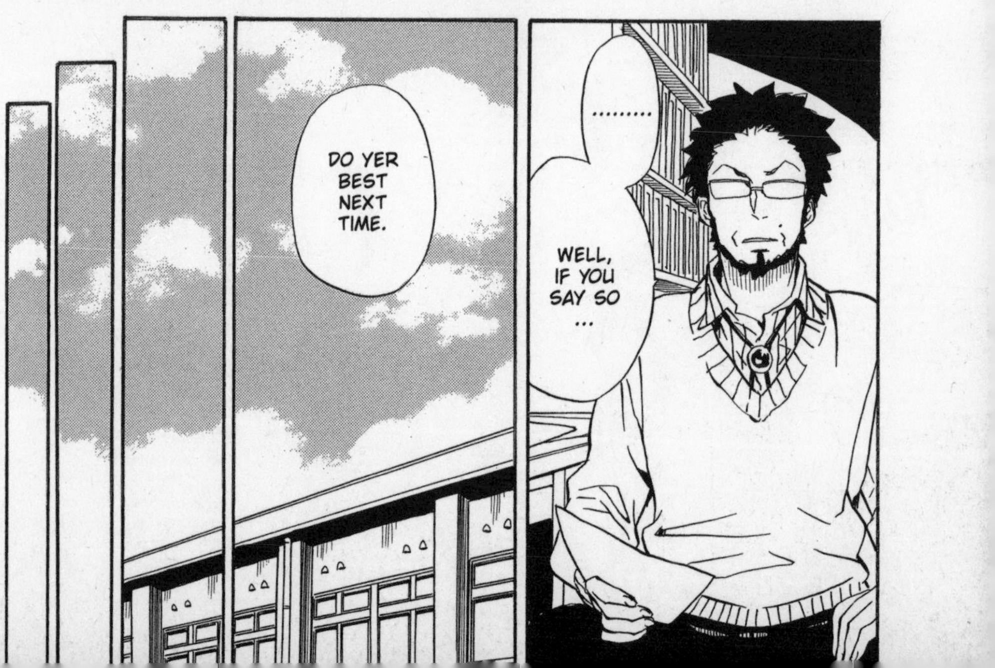
....
WELL, IF YOU SAY SO ...
DO YER BEST NEXT TIME.

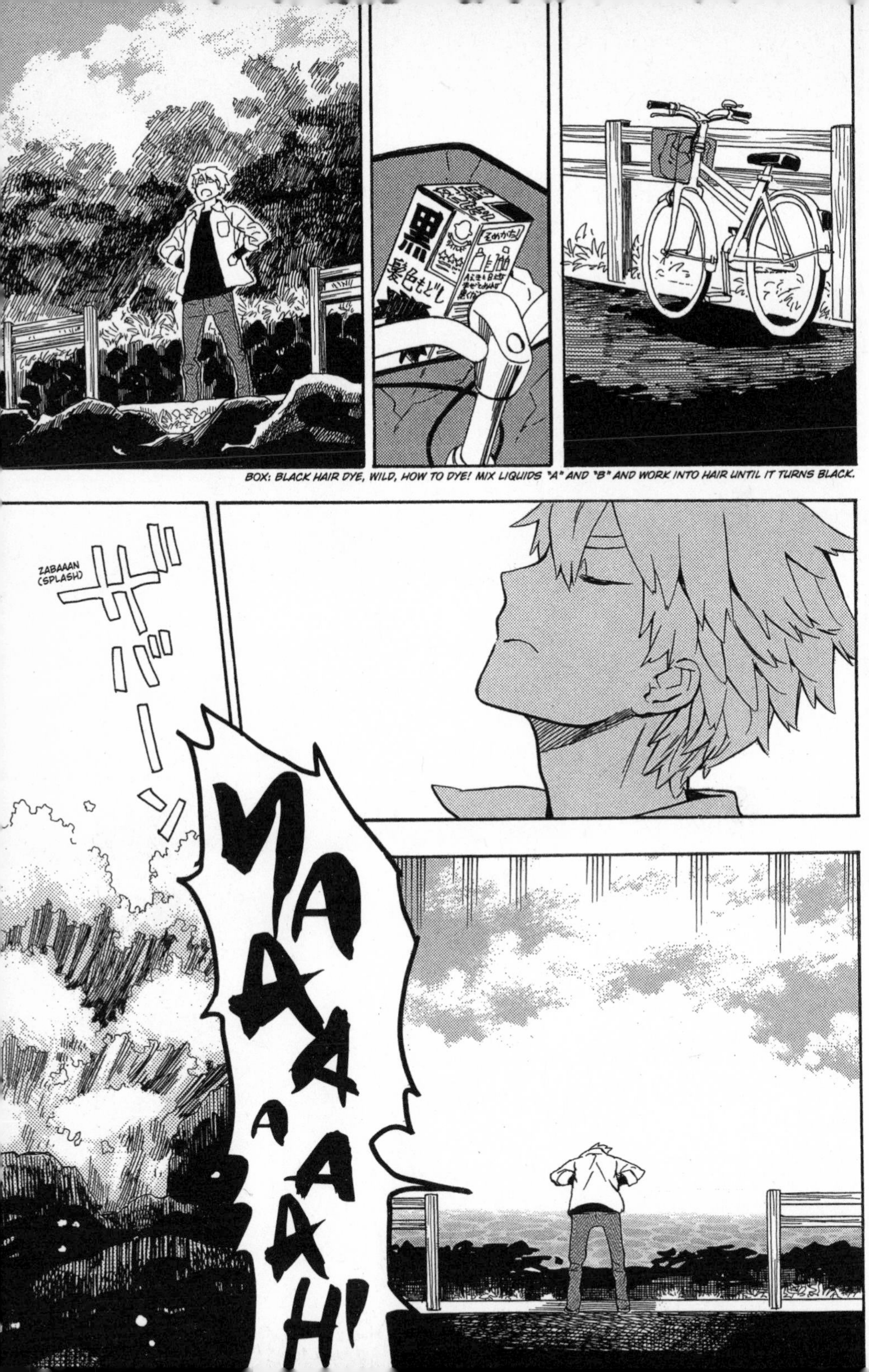
黒
髪色もどし
BOX: BLACK HAIR DYE, WILD, HOW TO DYE! MIX LIQUIDS "A" AND "B" AND WORK INTO HAIR UNTIL IT TURNS BLACK.
ザバーーン
ZABAAAN (SPLASH)
MAAAAAAH!

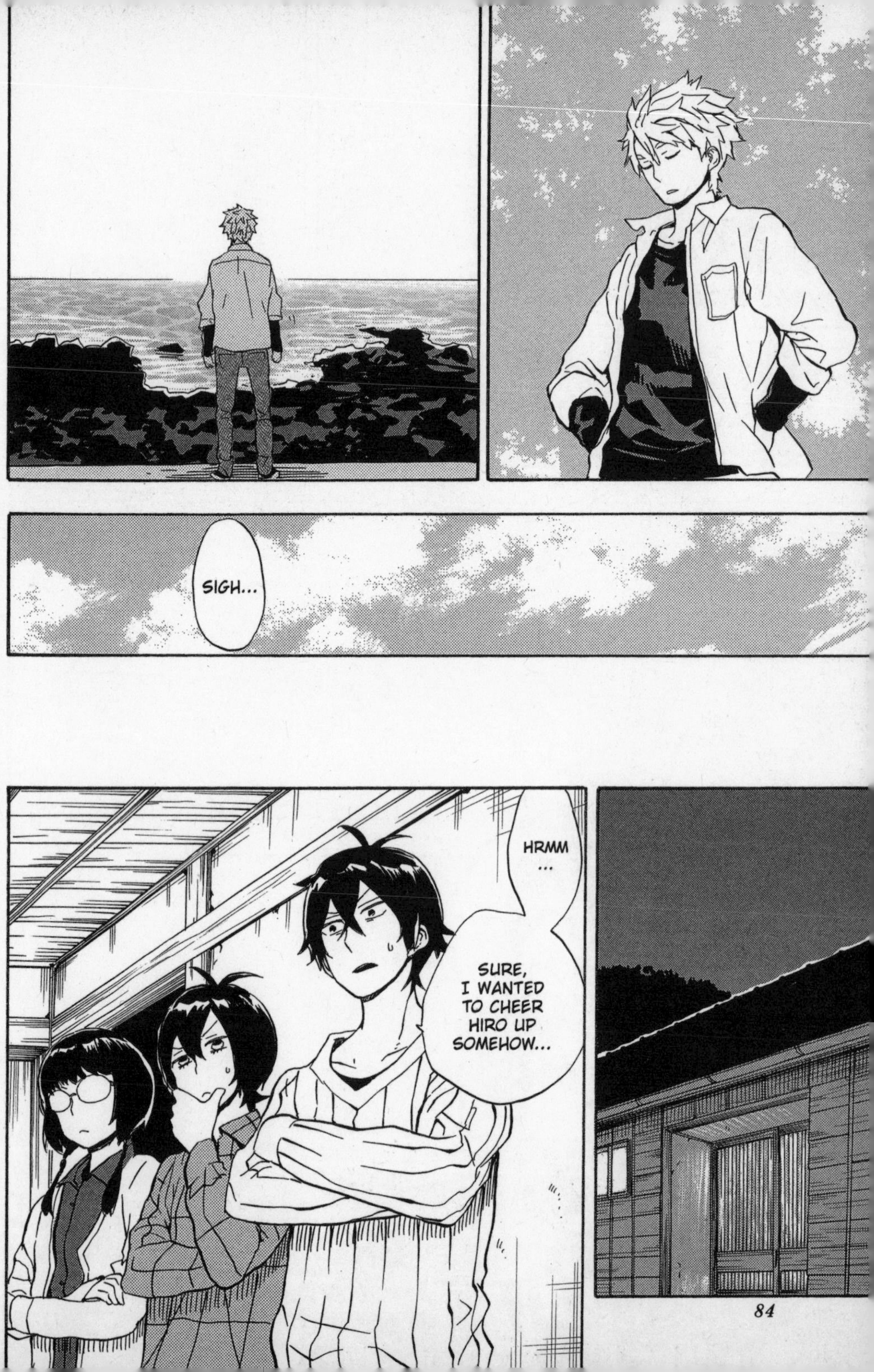
SIGH...
HRMM ...
SURE, I WANTED TO CHEER HIRO UP SOMEHOW...

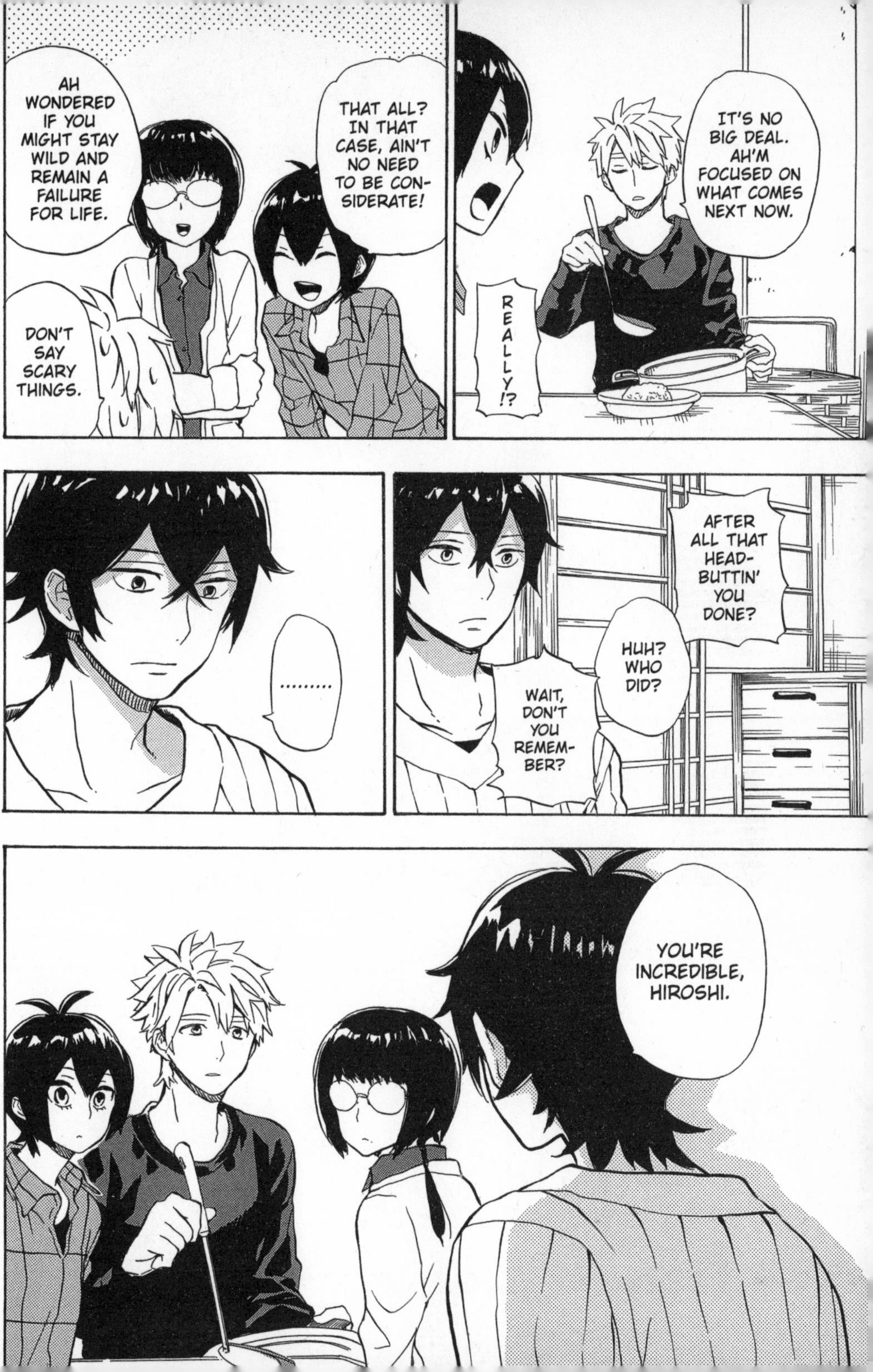
IT'S NO BIG DEAL. AH'M FOCUSED ON WHAT COMES NEXT NOW.
REALLY!?
THAT ALL? IN THAT CASE, AIN'T NO NEED TO BE CONSIDERATE!
AH WONDERED IF YOU MIGHT STAY WILD AND REMAIN A FAILURE FOR LIFE.
DON'T SAY SCARY THINGS.
AFTER ALL THAT HEADBUTTIN' YOU DONE?
HUH? WHO DID?
WAIT, DON'T YOU REMEMBER?
....
YOU'RE INCREDIBLE, HIROSHI.

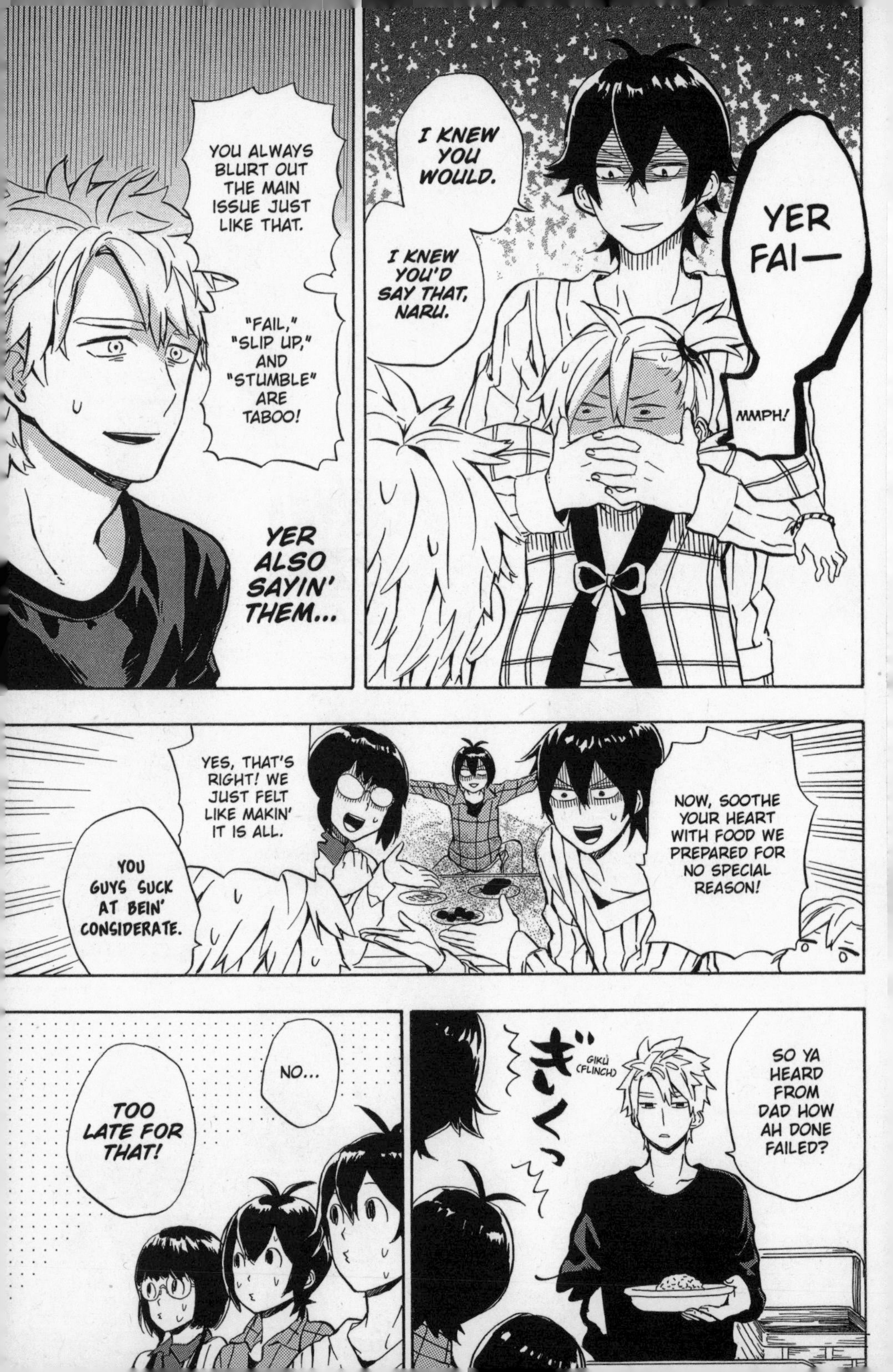
YER FAI—
MMPH!
I KNEW YOU WOULD.
I KNEW YOU'D SAY THAT, NARU.
YOU ALWAYS BLURT OUT THE MAIN ISSUE JUST LIKE THAT.
"FAIL," "SLIP UP," AND "STUMBLE" ARE TABOO!
YER ALSO SAYIN' THEM...
NOW, SOOTHE YOUR HEART WITH FOOD WE PREPARED FOR NO SPECIAL REASON!
YES, THAT'S RIGHT! WE JUST FELT LIKE MAKIN' IT IS ALL.
YOU GUYS SUCK AT BEIN' CONSIDERATE.
SO YA HEARD FROM DAD HOW AH DONE FAILED?
ぎくっ
GIKU (FLINCH)
NO...
TOO LATE FOR THAT!

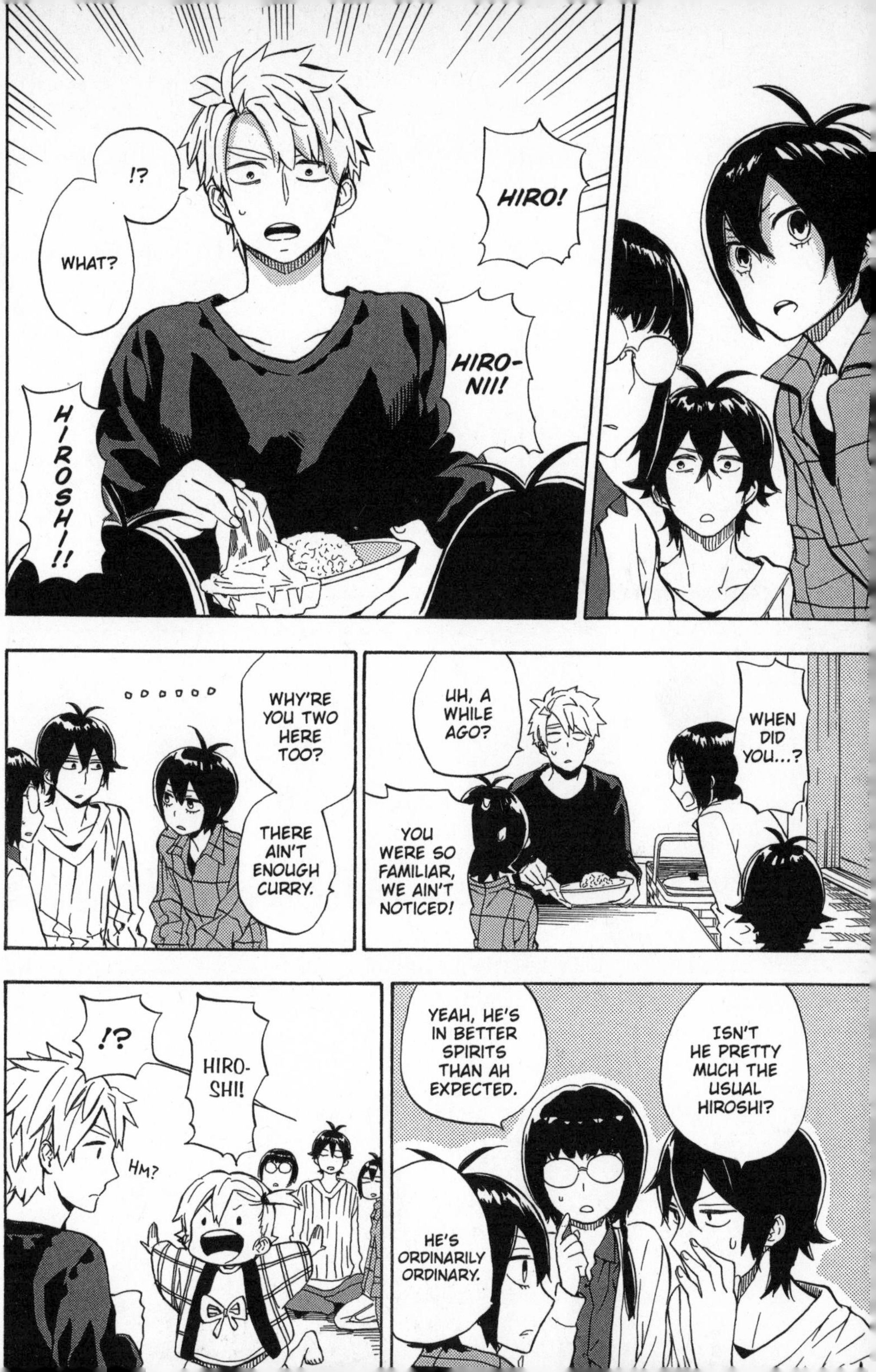
HIRO!
HIRO-NII!
!?
WHAT?
HIROSHI!!
WHEN DID YOU...?
UH, A WHILE AGO?
YOU WERE SO FAMILIAR, WE AIN'T NOTICED!
WHY'RE YOU TWO HERE TOO?
......
THERE AIN'T ENOUGH CURRY.
ISN'T HE PRETTY MUCH THE USUAL HIROSHI?
YEAH, HE'S IN BETTER SPIRITS THAN AH EXPECTED.
HE'S ORDINARILY ORDINARY.
HIRO-SHI!
!?
HM?

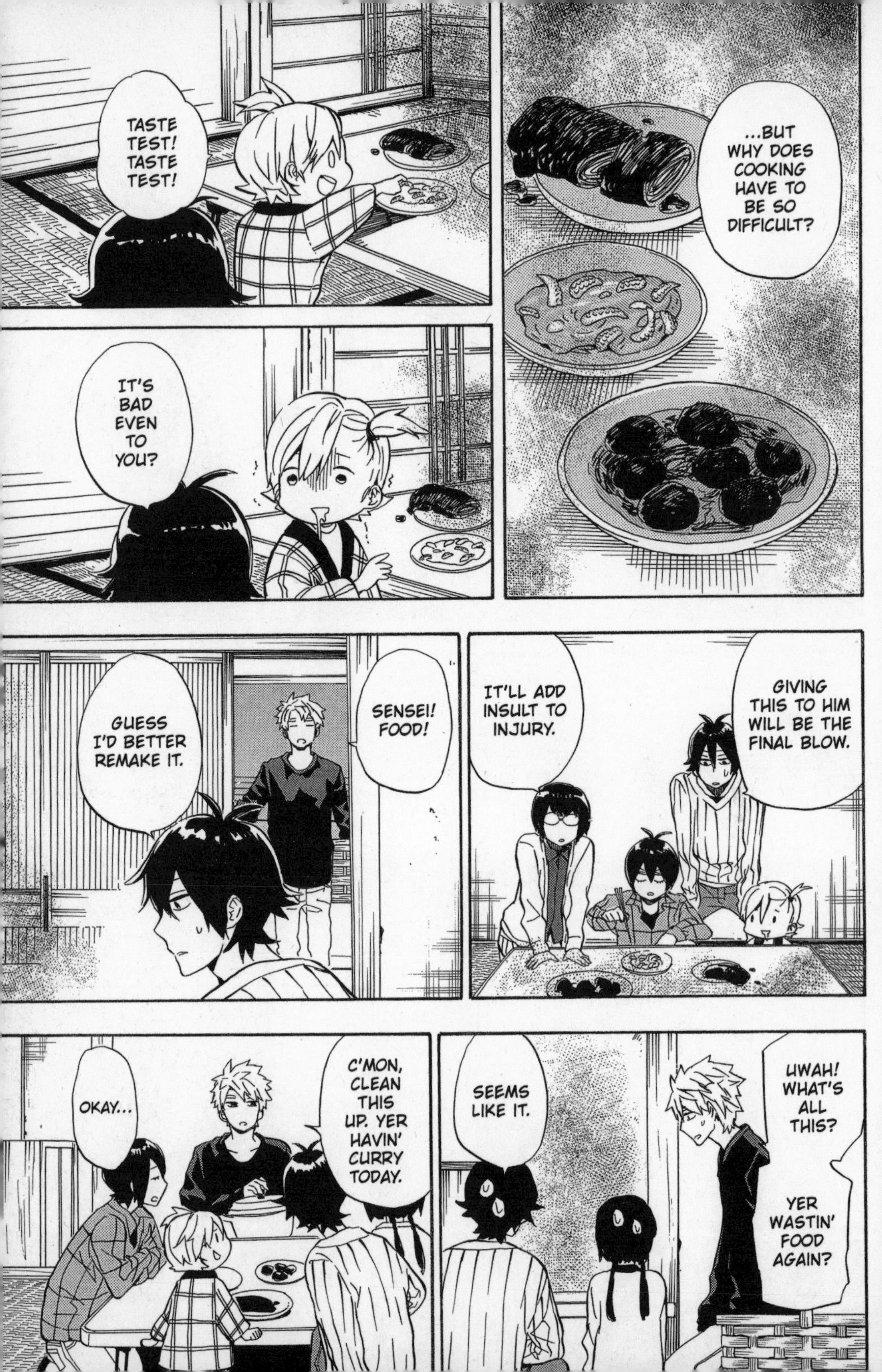
...BUT WHY DOES COOKING HAVE TO BE SO DIFFICULT?
TASTE TEST! TASTE TEST!
IT'S BAD EVEN TO YOU?
GIVING THIS TO HIM WILL BE THE FINAL BLOW.
IT'LL ADD INSULT TO INJURY.
SENSEI! FOOD!
GUESS I'D BETTER REMAKE IT.
UWAH! WHAT'S ALL THIS?
YER WASTIN' FOOD AGAIN?
SEEMS LIKE IT.
C'MON, CLEAN THIS UP. YER HAVIN' CURRY TODAY.
OKAY...

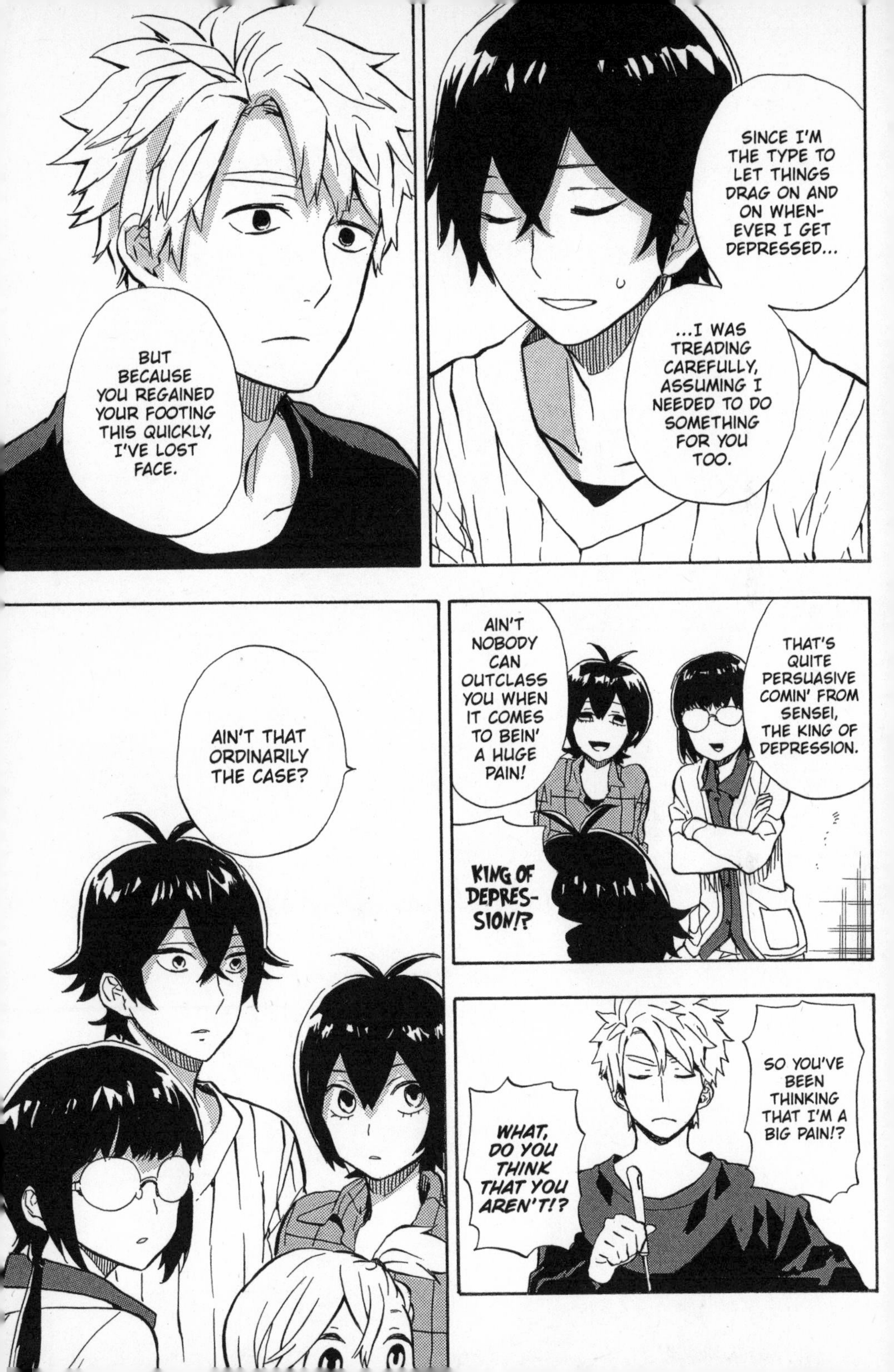
SINCE I'M THE TYPE TO LET THINGS DRAG ON AND ON WHEN-EVER I GET DEPRESSED...
...I WAS TREADING CAREFULLY, ASSUMING I NEEDED TO DO SOMETHING FOR YOU TOO.
BUT BECAUSE YOU REGAINED YOUR FOOTING THIS QUICKLY, I'VE LOST FACE.
THAT'S QUITE PERSUASIVE COMIN' FROM SENSEI, THE KING OF DEPRESSION.
AIN'T NOBODY CAN OUTCLASS YOU WHEN IT COMES TO BEIN' A HUGE PAIN!
KING OF DEPRES-SION!?
SO YOU'VE BEEN THINKING THAT I'M A BIG PAIN!?
WHAT, DO YOU THINK THAT YOU AREN'T!?
AIN'T THAT ORDINARILY THE CASE?

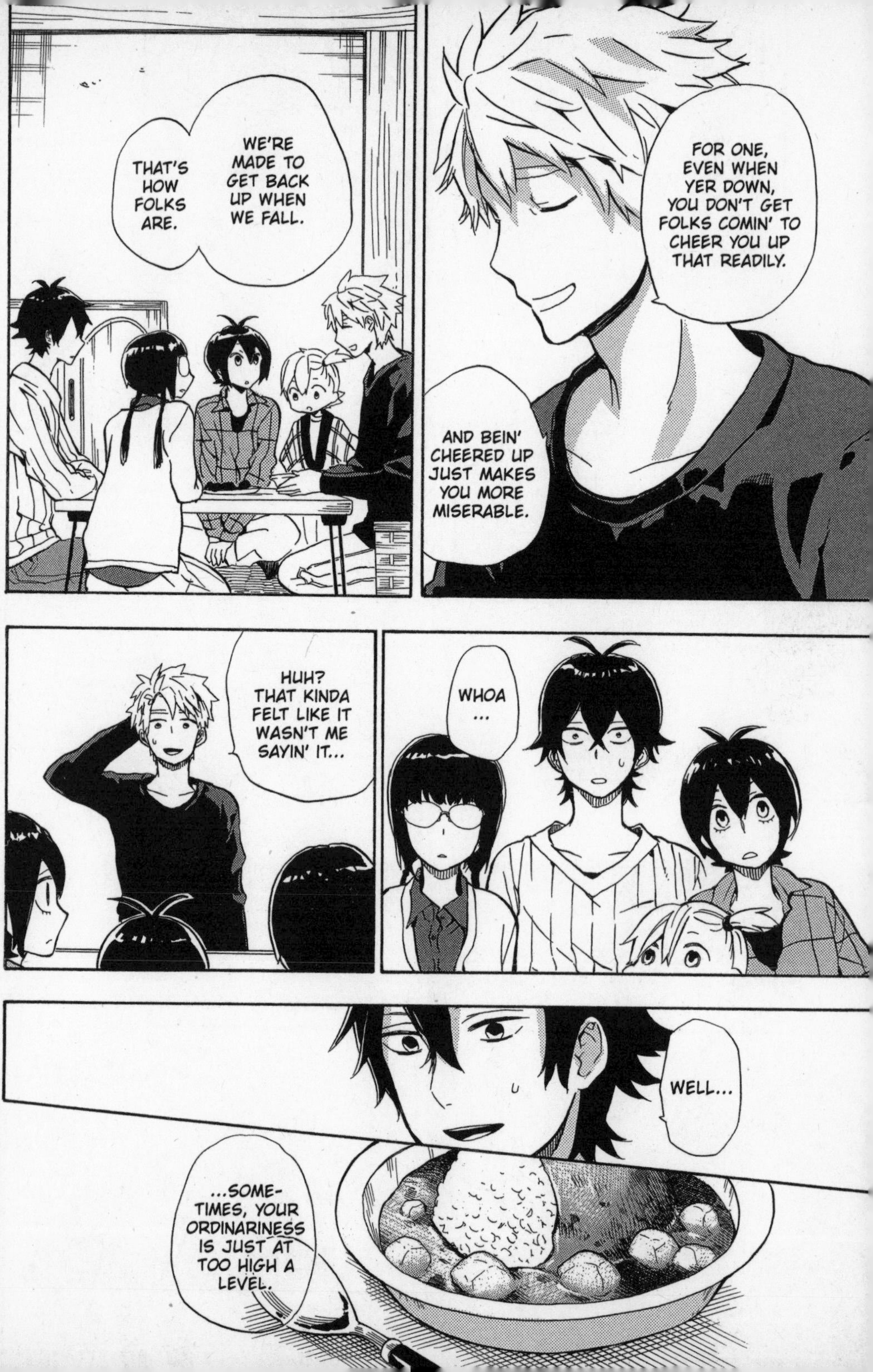
FOR ONE, EVEN WHEN YER DOWN, YOU DON'T GET FOLKS COMIN' TO CHEER YOU UP THAT READILY.
AND BEIN' CHEERED UP JUST MAKES YOU MORE MISERABLE.
WE'RE MADE TO GET BACK UP WHEN WE FALL.
THAT'S HOW FOLKS ARE.
WHOA ...
HUH? THAT KINDA FELT LIKE IT WASN'T ME SAYIN' IT...
WELL...
...SOME-TIMES, YOUR ORDINARINESS IS JUST AT TOO HIGH A LEVEL.

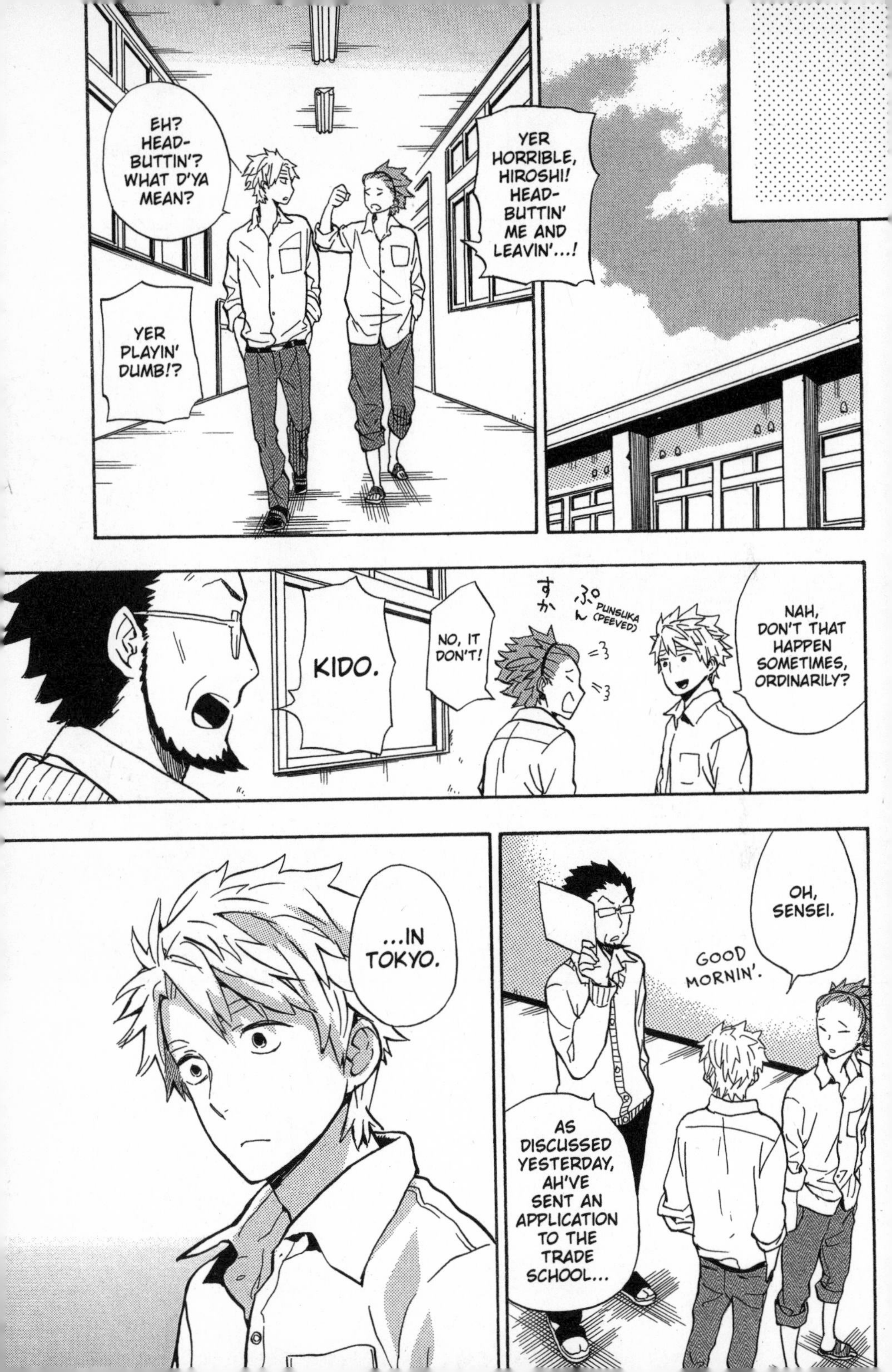
YER HORRIBLE, HIROSHI! HEAD-BUTTIN' ME AND LEAVIN'...!
EH? HEAD-BUTTIN'? WHAT D'YA MEAN?
YER PLAYIN' DUMB!?
NAH, DON'T THAT HAPPEN SOMETIMES, ORDINARILY?
ぷんすか
PUNSUKA (PEEVED)
NO, IT DON'T!
KIDO.
OH, SENSEI.
GOOD MORNIN'.
AS DISCUSSED YESTERDAY, AH'VE SENT AN APPLICATION TO THE TRADE SCHOOL...
...IN TOKYO.

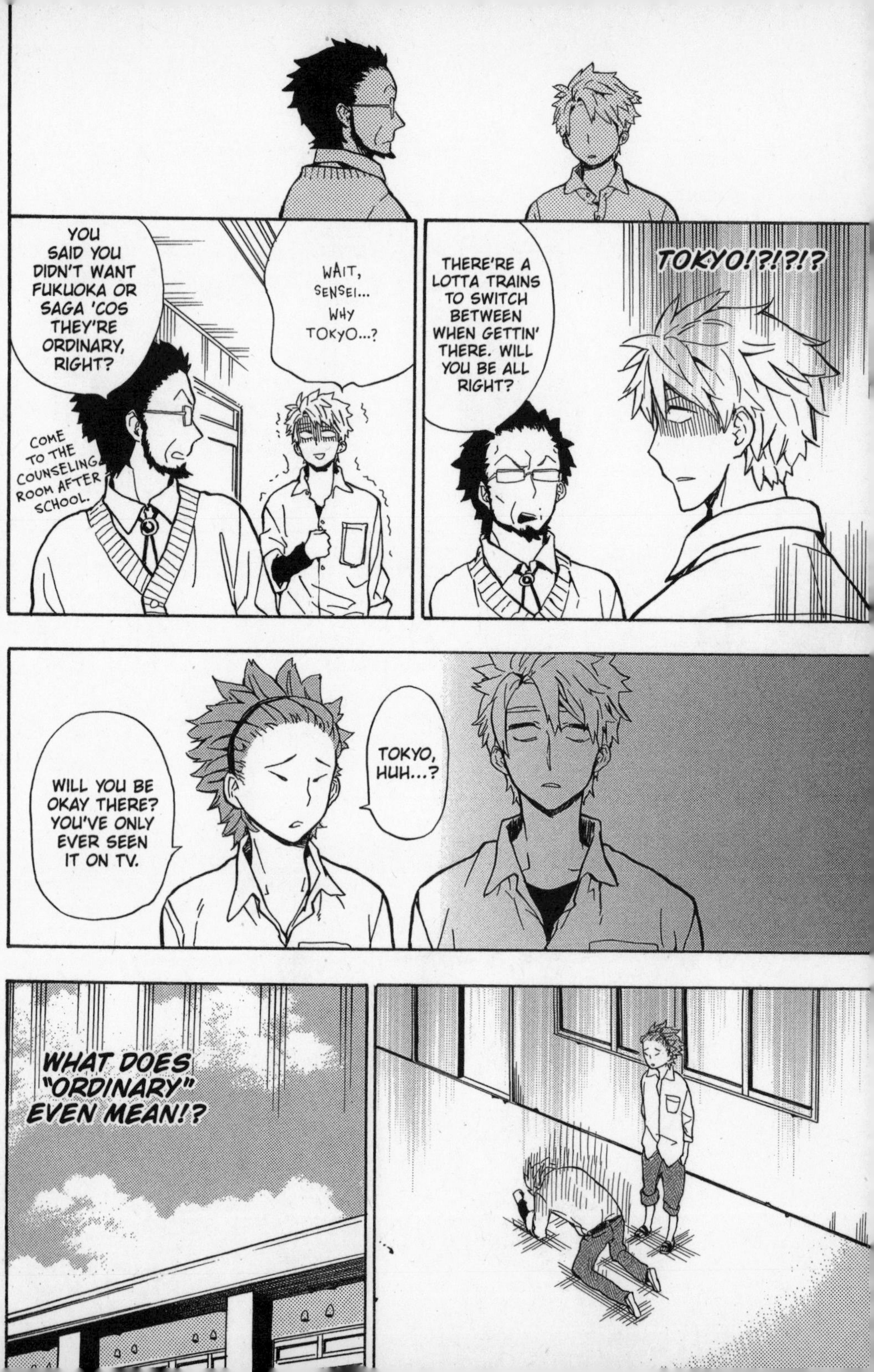
TOKYO!?!?!?
THERE'RE A LOTTA TRAINS TO SWITCH BETWEEN WHEN GETTIN' THERE. WILL YOU BE ALL RIGHT?
WAIT, SENSEI... WHY TOKYO...?
YOU SAID YOU DIDN'T WANT FUKUOKA OR SAGA 'COS THEY'RE ORDINARY, RIGHT?
COME TO THE COUNSELING ROOM AFTER SCHOOL.
TOKYO, HUH...?
WILL YOU BE OKAY THERE? YOU'VE ONLY EVER SEEN IT ON TV.
WHAT DOES "ORDINARY" EVEN MEAN!?

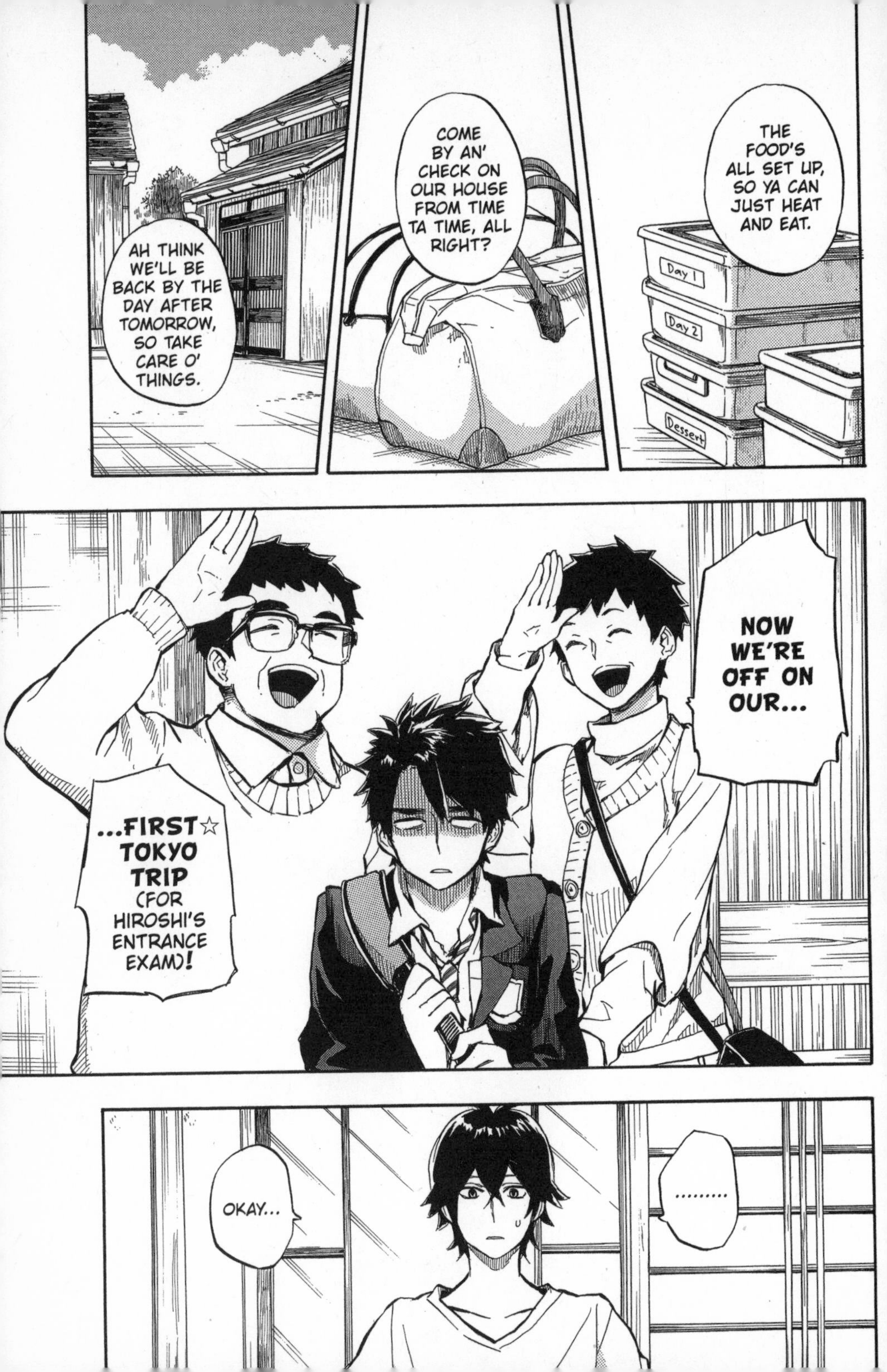
THE FOOD'S ALL SET UP, SO YA CAN JUST HEAT AND EAT.
Day 1
Day 2
Dessert
COME BY AN' CHECK ON OUR HOUSE FROM TIME TA TIME, ALL RIGHT?
AH THINK WE'LL BE BACK BY THE DAY AFTER TOMORROW, SO TAKE CARE O' THINGS.
NOW WE'RE OFF ON OUR...
...FIRST☆ TOKYO TRIP (FOR HIROSHI'S ENTRANCE EXAM)!
....
OKAY...

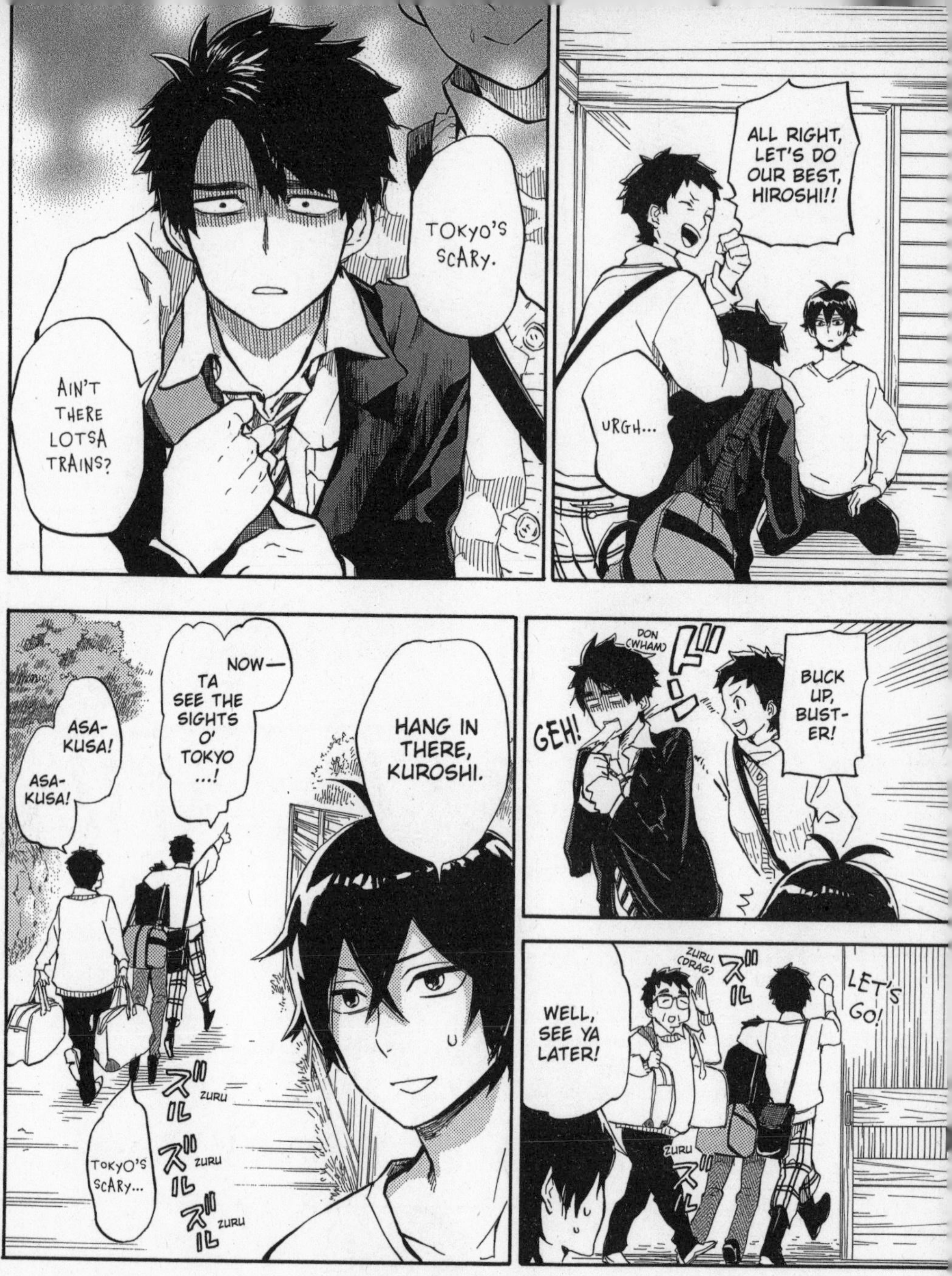
ALL RIGHT, LET'S DO OUR BEST, HIROSHI!!
URGH...
TOKYO'S SCARY.
AIN'T THERE LOTSA TRAINS?
BUCK UP, BUSTER!
DON (WHAM)
GEH!
LET'S GO!
ZURU (DRAG)
WELL, SEE YA LATER!
ZURU
HANG IN THERE, KUROSHI.
NOW— TA SEE THE SIGHTS O' TOKYO ...!
ASA-KUSA!
ASA-KUSA!
TOKYO'S SCARY...
ZURU
ZURU
ZURU

Act.84
YASHA TSUKURU
(Translation: Growing Vegetables)

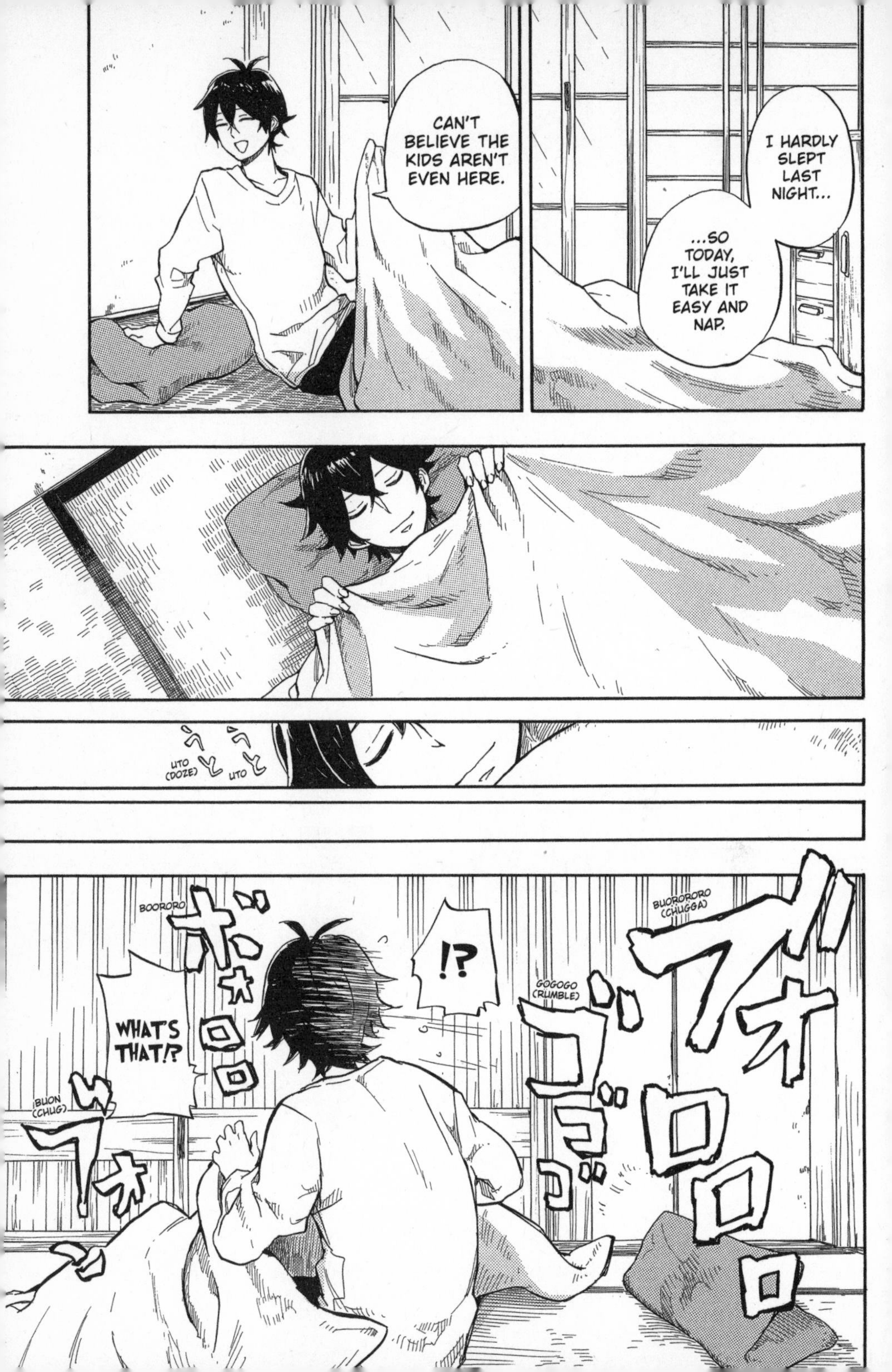
I HARDLY SLEPT LAST NIGHT...
...SO TODAY, I'LL JUST TAKE IT EASY AND NAP.
CAN'T BELIEVE THE KIDS AREN'T EVEN HERE.
UTO
UTO (DOZE)
BUORORORO (CHUGGA)
GOGOGO (RUMBLE)
!?
BOORORO
WHAT'S THAT!?
BUON (CHUG)

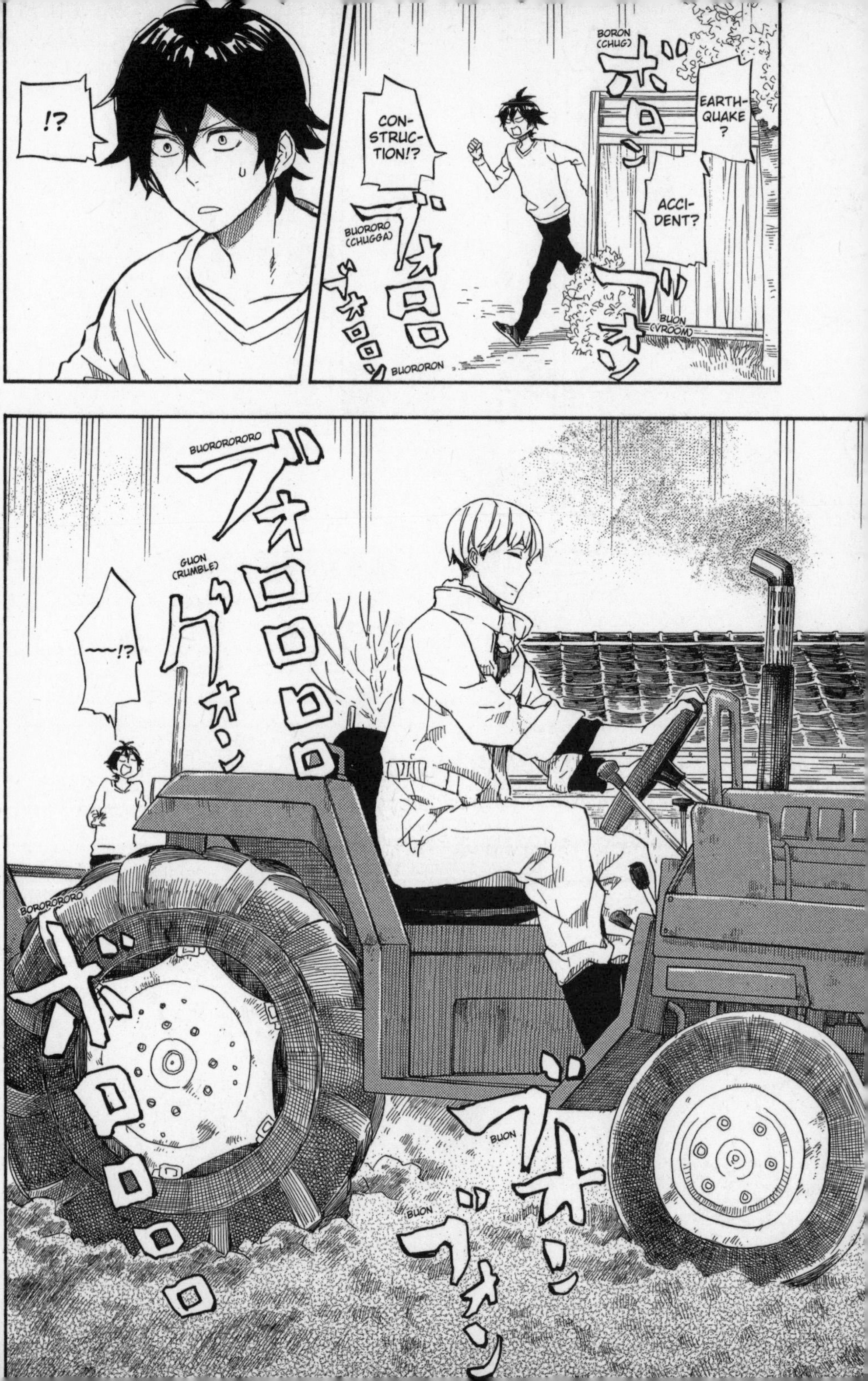
BORON (CHUG)
EARTH-QUAKE?
ACCI-DENT?
CON-STRUCTION!?
BUON (VROOM)
BUORORO (CHUGGA)
BUORORON
!?
BUORORORORO
GUON (RUMBLE)
——!?
BUON
BUON
BORORORORO

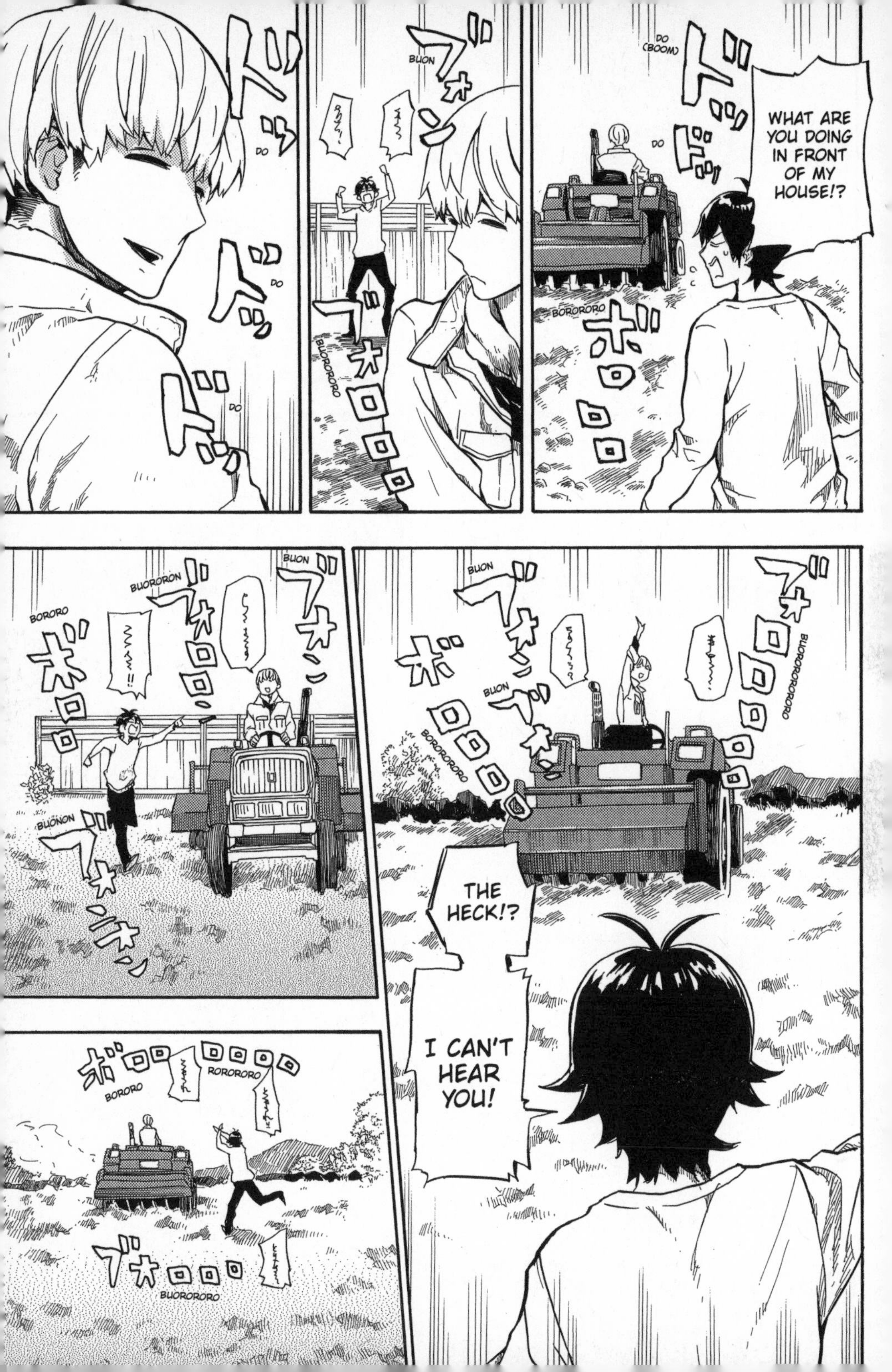

DO (BOOM)
DO
WHAT ARE YOU DOING IN FRONT OF MY HOUSE!?
BOROROROR
BUON
BUORORORO
DO
DO
DO
DO
BUORORORORO
BUON
BUON
BORORORORO
THE HECK!?
I CAN'T HEAR YOU!
BUON
BUORORON
BORORO
BUONON
RORORORO
BORORO
BUORORORO

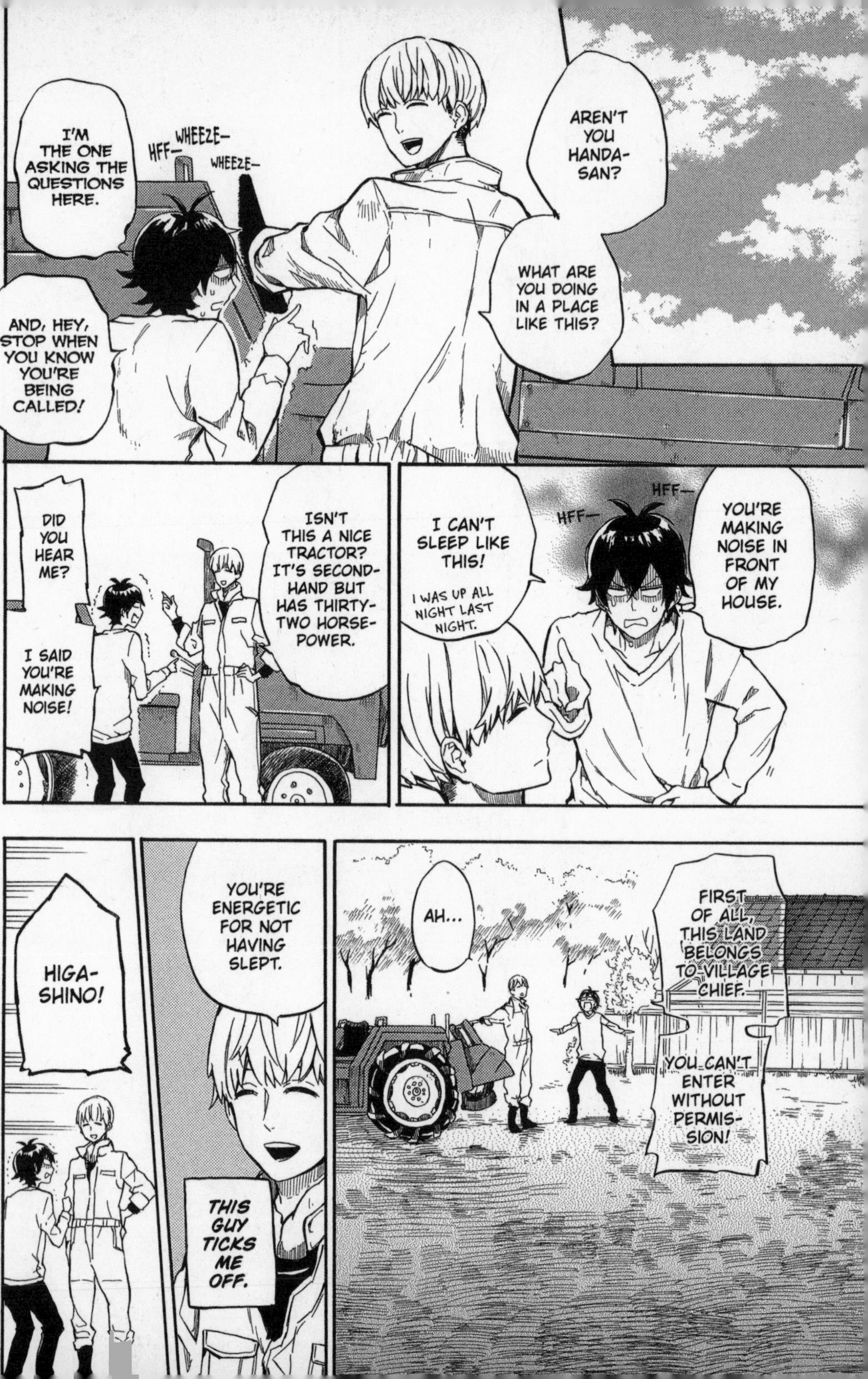
AREN'T YOU HANDA-SAN?
WHAT ARE YOU DOING IN A PLACE LIKE THIS?
I'M THE ONE ASKING THE QUESTIONS HERE.
HFF— WHEEZE— WHEEZE—
AND, HEY, STOP WHEN YOU KNOW YOU'RE BEING CALLED!
HFF— HFF—
YOU'RE MAKING NOISE IN FRONT OF MY HOUSE.
I CAN'T SLEEP LIKE THIS!
I WAS UP ALL NIGHT LAST NIGHT.
ISN'T THIS A NICE TRACTOR? IT'S SECOND-HAND BUT HAS THIRTY-TWO HORSE-POWER.
DID YOU HEAR ME?
I SAID YOU'RE MAKING NOISE!
FIRST OF ALL, THIS LAND BELONGS TO VILLAGE CHIEF.
AH...
YOU CAN'T ENTER WITHOUT PERMISSION!
YOU'RE ENERGETIC FOR NOT HAVING SLEPT.
THIS GUY TICKS ME OFF.
HIGA-SHINO!

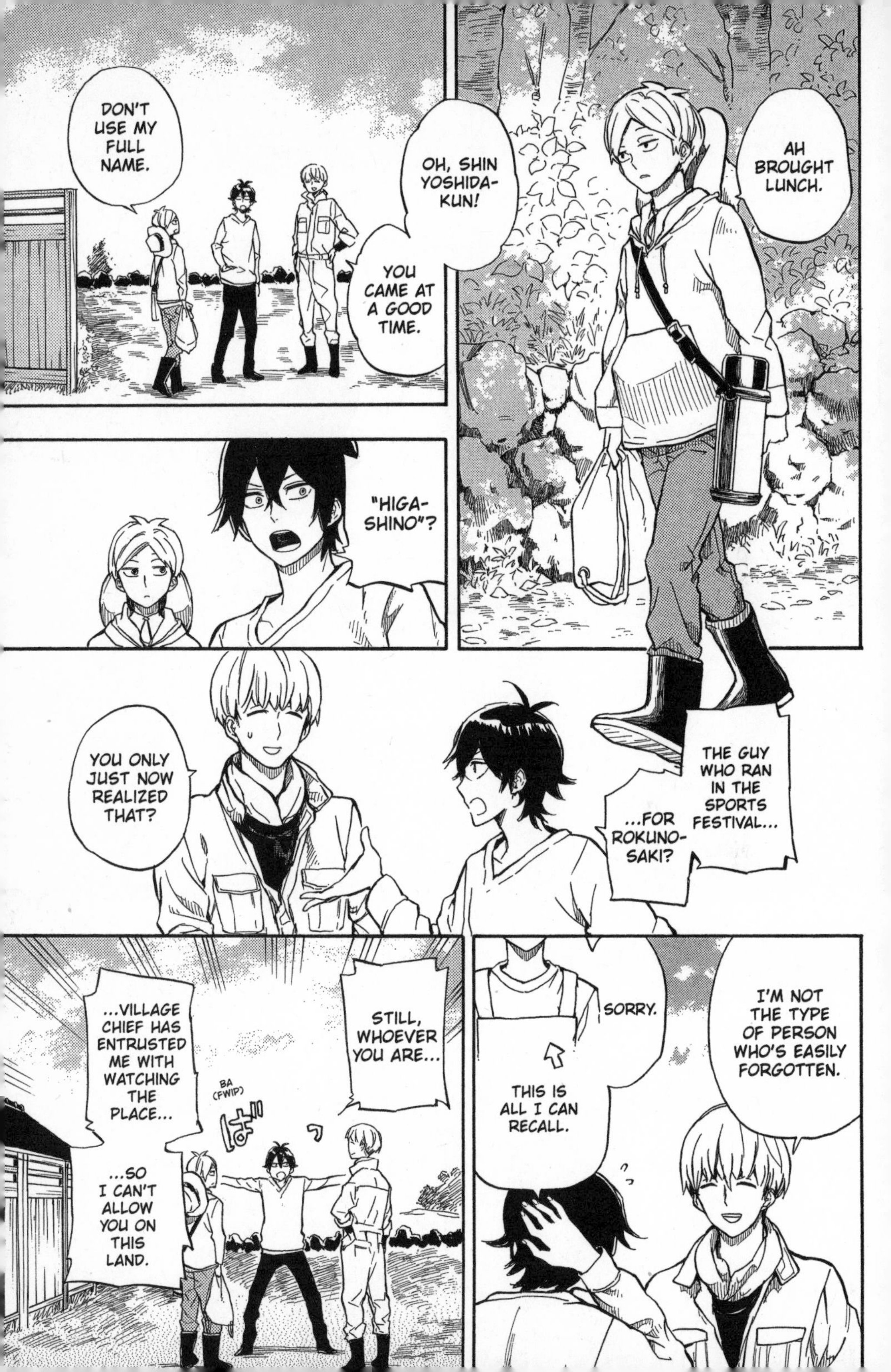
AH BROUGHT LUNCH.
OH, SHIN YOSHIDA-KUN!
YOU CAME AT A GOOD TIME.
DON'T USE MY FULL NAME.
"HIGA-SHINO"?
THE GUY WHO RAN IN THE SPORTS FESTIVAL...
...FOR ROKUNOSAKI?
YOU ONLY JUST NOW REALIZED THAT?
I'M NOT THE TYPE OF PERSON WHO'S EASILY FORGOTTEN.
SORRY.
THIS IS ALL I CAN RECALL.
STILL, WHOEVER YOU ARE...
...VILLAGE CHIEF HAS ENTRUSTED ME WITH WATCHING THE PLACE...
BA (FWIP)
ばっ
...SO I CAN'T ALLOW YOU ON THIS LAND.

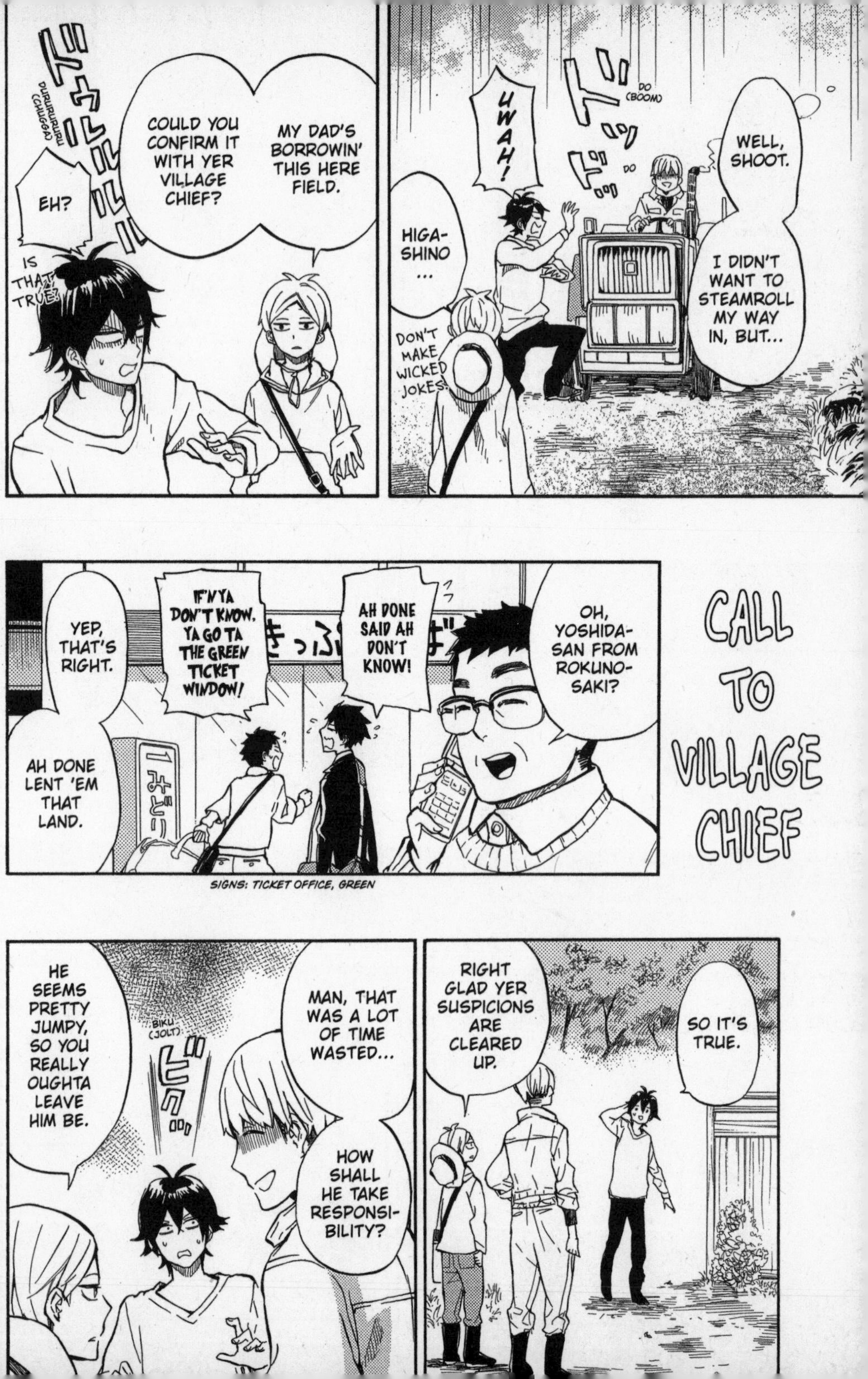
WELL, SHOOT.
I DIDN'T WANT TO STEAMROLL MY WAY IN, BUT...
DO (BOOM)
DO
UWAH!
HIGA-SHINO...
DON'T MAKE WICKED JOKES!
MY DAD'S BORROWIN' THIS HERE FIELD.
COULD YOU CONFIRM IT WITH YER VILLAGE CHIEF?
DURURURURU (CHUGGA)
EH?
IS THAT TRUE?
CALL TO VILLAGE CHIEF
OH, YOSHIDA-SAN FROM ROKUNO-SAKI?
AH DONE SAID AH DON'T KNOW!
IF'N YA DON'T KNOW, YA GO TA THE GREEN TICKET WINDOW!
YEP, THAT'S RIGHT.
AH DONE LENT 'EM THAT LAND.
SIGNS: TICKET OFFICE, GREEN
SO IT'S TRUE.
RIGHT GLAD YER SUSPICIONS ARE CLEARED UP.
MAN, THAT WAS A LOT OF TIME WASTED...
HOW SHALL HE TAKE RESPONSI-BILITY?
BIKU (JOLT)
HE SEEMS PRETTY JUMPY, SO YOU REALLY OUGHTA LEAVE HIM BE.

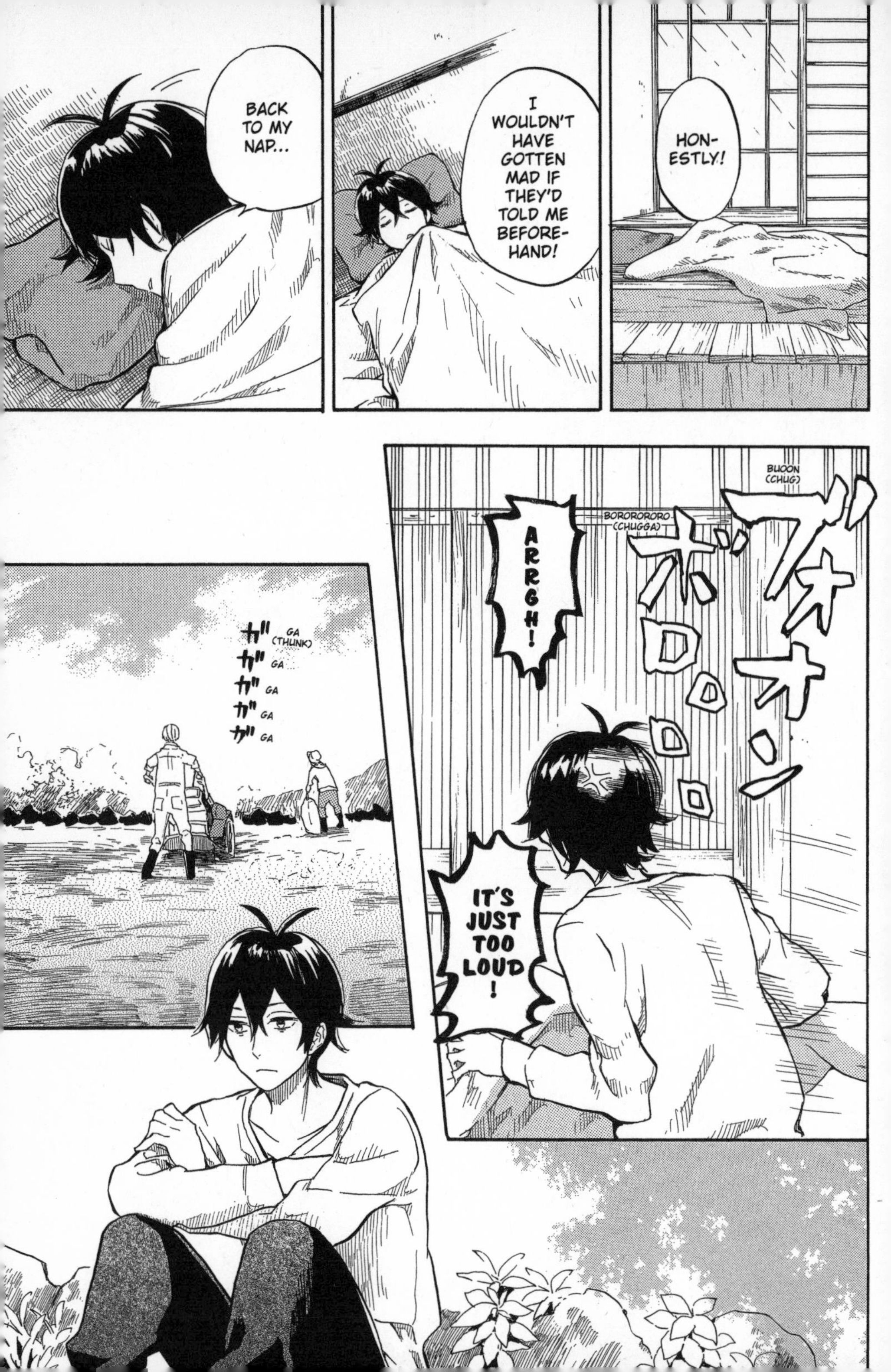
HON-
ESTLY!
I WOULDN'T HAVE GOTTEN MAD IF THEY'D TOLD ME BEFORE-
HAND!
BACK TO MY NAP...
BUOON (CHUG)
BORORORORO (CHUGGA)
ARRGH!
IT'S JUST TOO LOUD!
GA (THUNK)
GA
GA
GA
GA

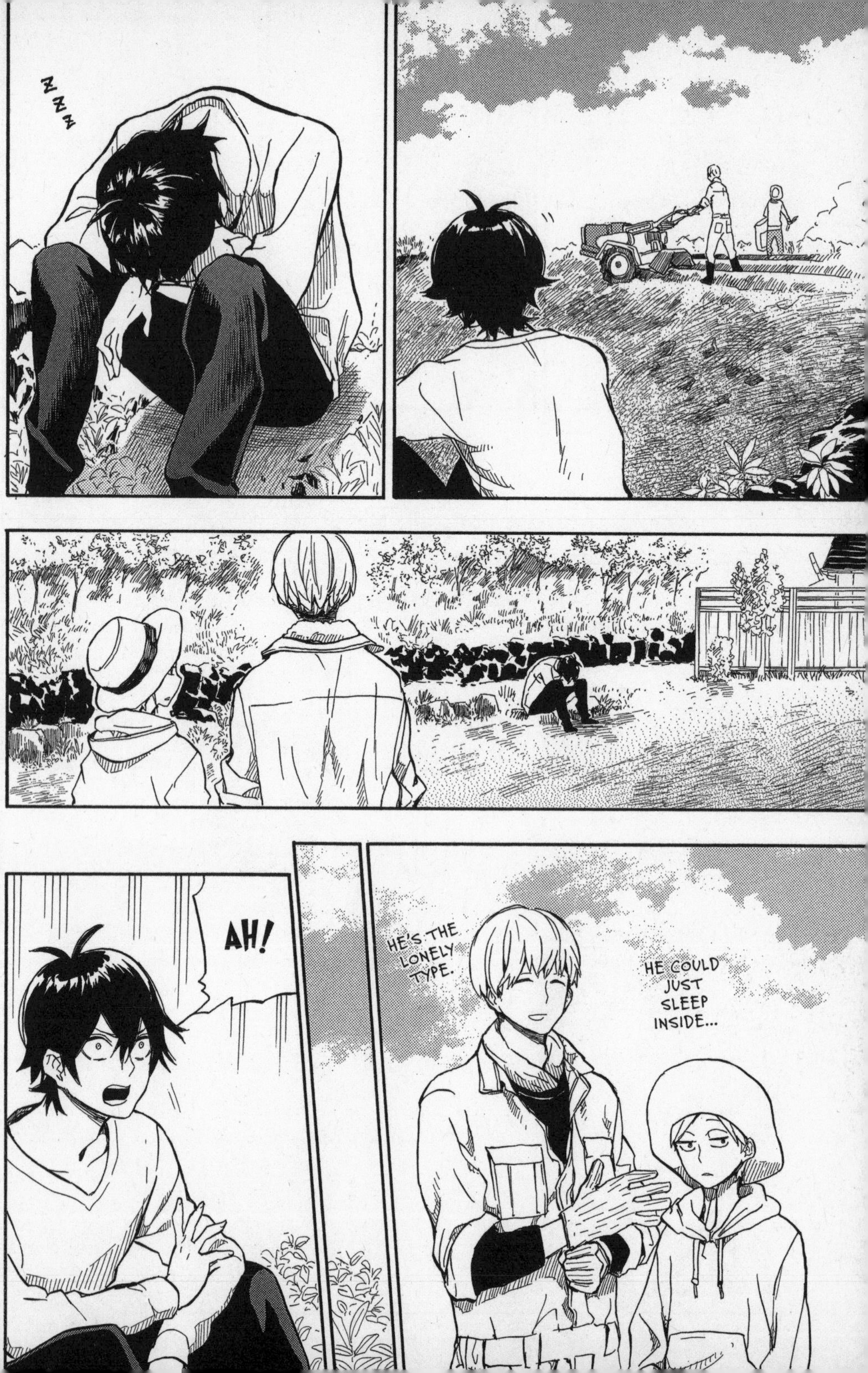
ZZZ
HE COULD JUST SLEEP INSIDE...
HE'S THE LONELY TYPE.
AH!

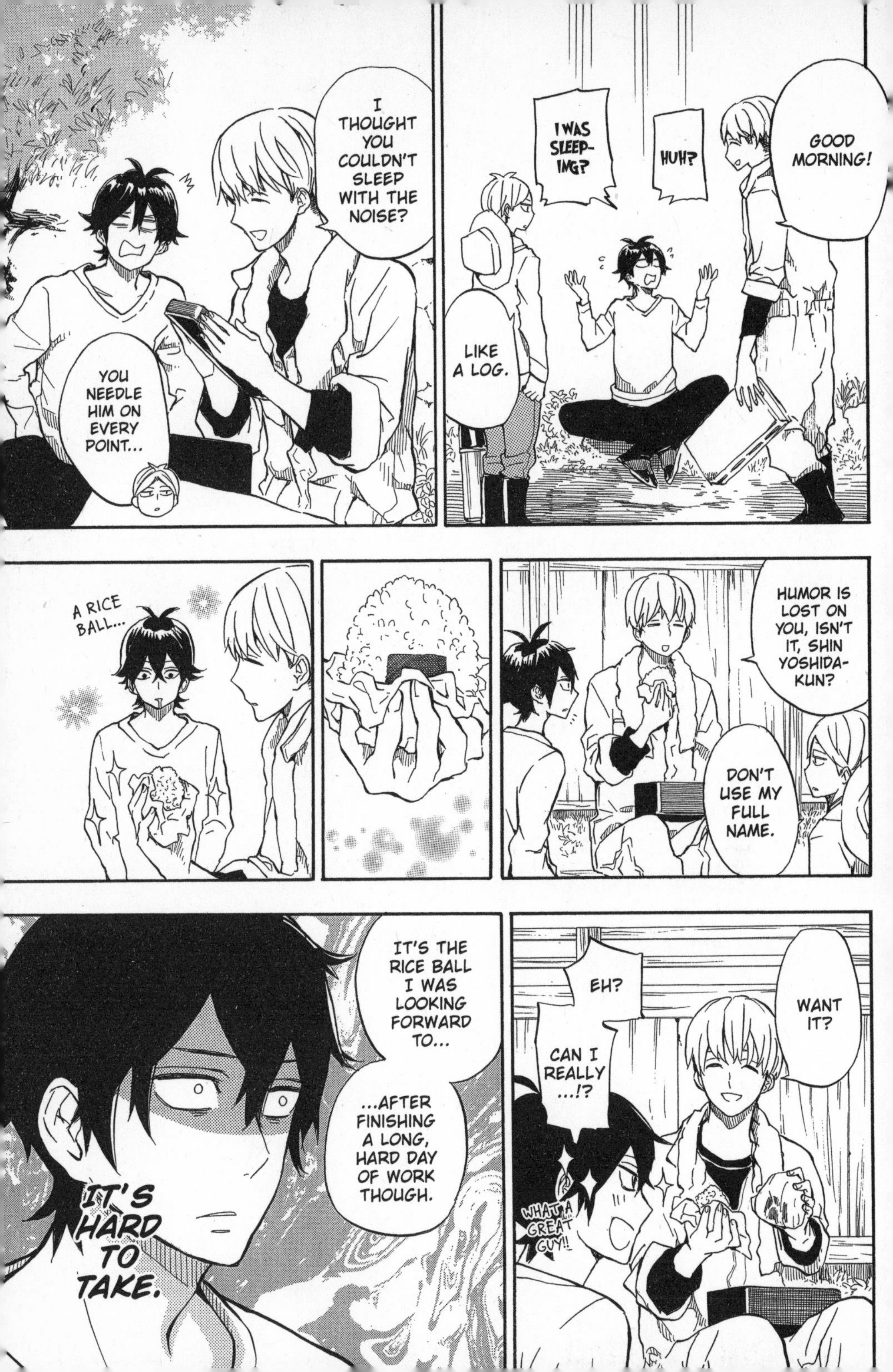
GOOD MORNING!
HUH?
I WAS SLEEP-ING?
LIKE A LOG.
I THOUGHT YOU COULDN'T SLEEP WITH THE NOISE?
YOU NEEDLE HIM ON EVERY POINT...
HUMOR IS LOST ON YOU, ISN'T IT, SHIN YOSHIDA-KUN?
DON'T USE MY FULL NAME.
A RICE BALL...
WANT IT?
EH?
CAN I REALLY ...!?
WHAT A GREAT GUY!!
IT'S THE RICE BALL I WAS LOOKING FORWARD TO...
...AFTER FINISHING A LONG, HARD DAY OF WORK THOUGH.
IT'S HARD TO TAKE.

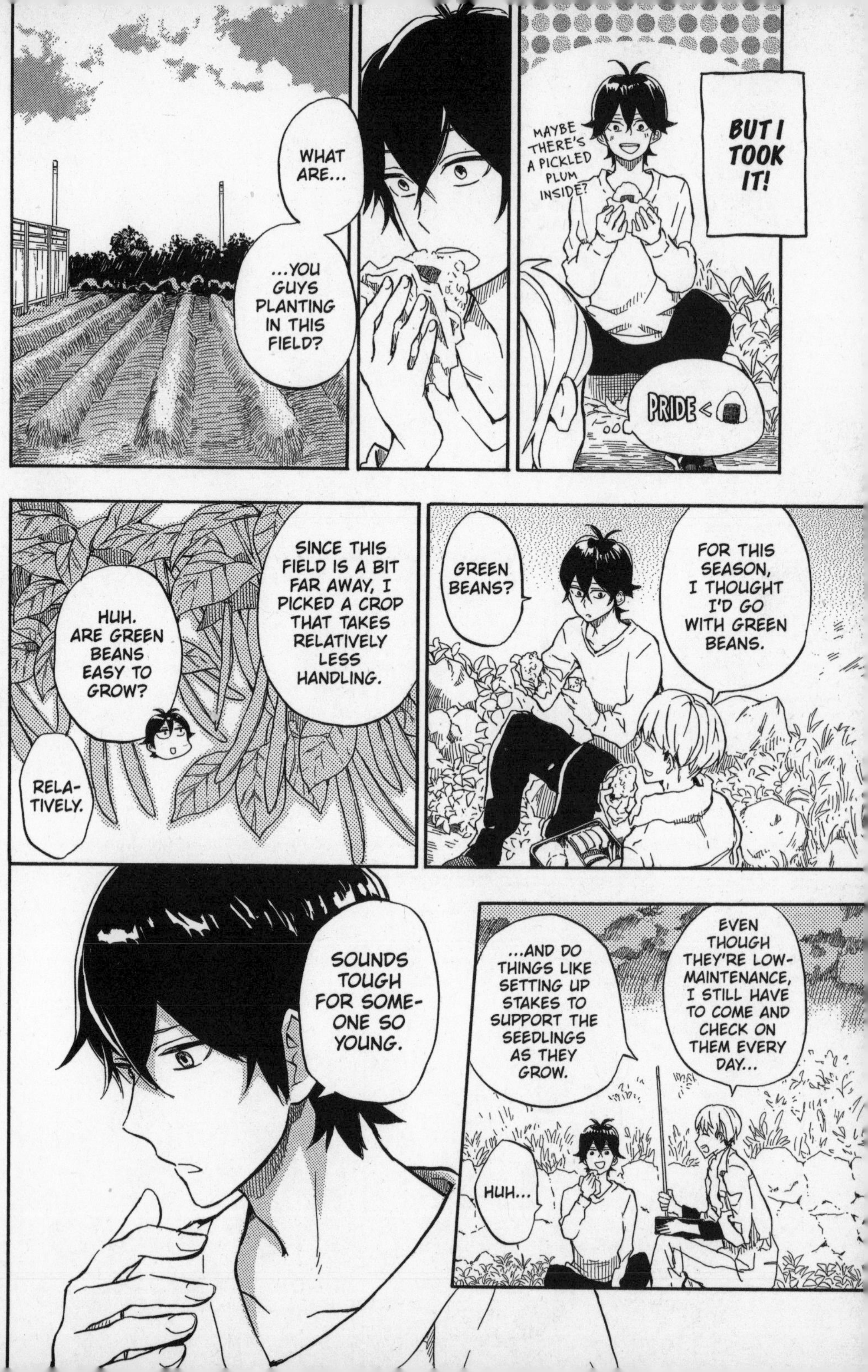
BUT I TOOK IT!
MAYBE THERE'S A PICKLED PLUM INSIDE?
PRIDE <
WHAT ARE...
...YOU GUYS PLANTING IN THIS FIELD?
FOR THIS SEASON, I THOUGHT I'D GO WITH GREEN BEANS.
GREEN BEANS?
SINCE THIS FIELD IS A BIT FAR AWAY, I PICKED A CROP THAT TAKES RELATIVELY LESS HANDLING.
HUH. ARE GREEN BEANS EASY TO GROW?
RELA-TIVELY.
EVEN THOUGH THEY'RE LOW-MAINTENANCE, I STILL HAVE TO COME AND CHECK ON THEM EVERY DAY...
...AND DO THINGS LIKE SETTING UP STAKES TO SUPPORT THE SEEDLINGS AS THEY GROW.
HUH...
SOUNDS TOUGH FOR SOME-ONE SO YOUNG.

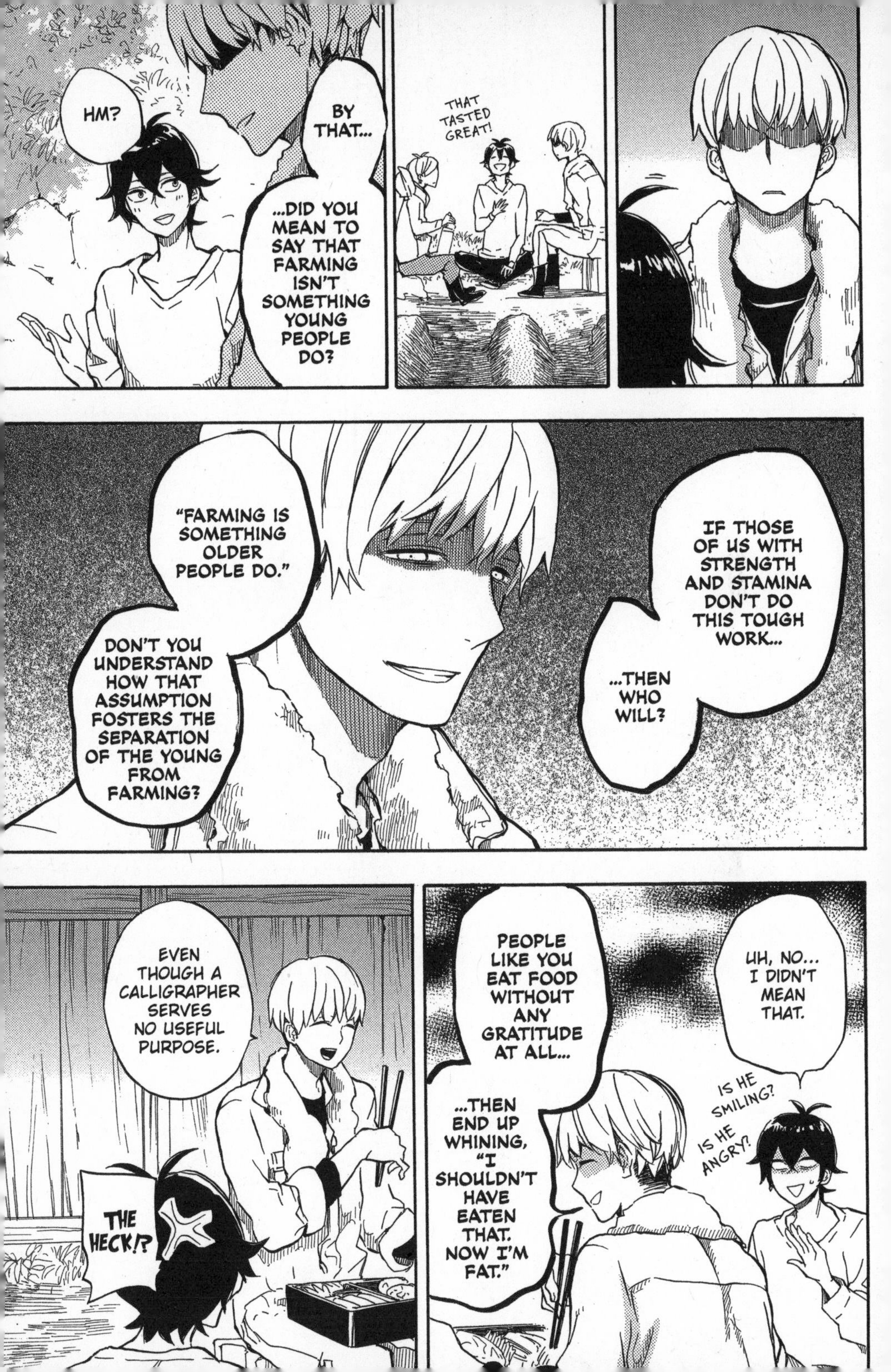
THAT TASTED GREAT!
BY THAT...
...DID YOU MEAN TO SAY THAT FARMING ISN'T SOMETHING YOUNG PEOPLE DO?
HM?
IF THOSE OF US WITH STRENGTH AND STAMINA DON'T DO THIS TOUGH WORK...
...THEN WHO WILL?
"FARMING IS SOMETHING OLDER PEOPLE DO."
DON'T YOU UNDERSTAND HOW THAT ASSUMPTION FOSTERS THE SEPARATION OF THE YOUNG FROM FARMING?
UH, NO... I DIDN'T MEAN THAT.
PEOPLE LIKE YOU EAT FOOD WITHOUT ANY GRATITUDE AT ALL...
IS HE SMILING?
IS HE ANGRY?
...THEN END UP WHINING, "I SHOULDN'T HAVE EATEN THAT. NOW I'M FAT."
EVEN THOUGH A CALLIGRAPHER SERVES NO USEFUL PURPOSE.
THE HECK!?

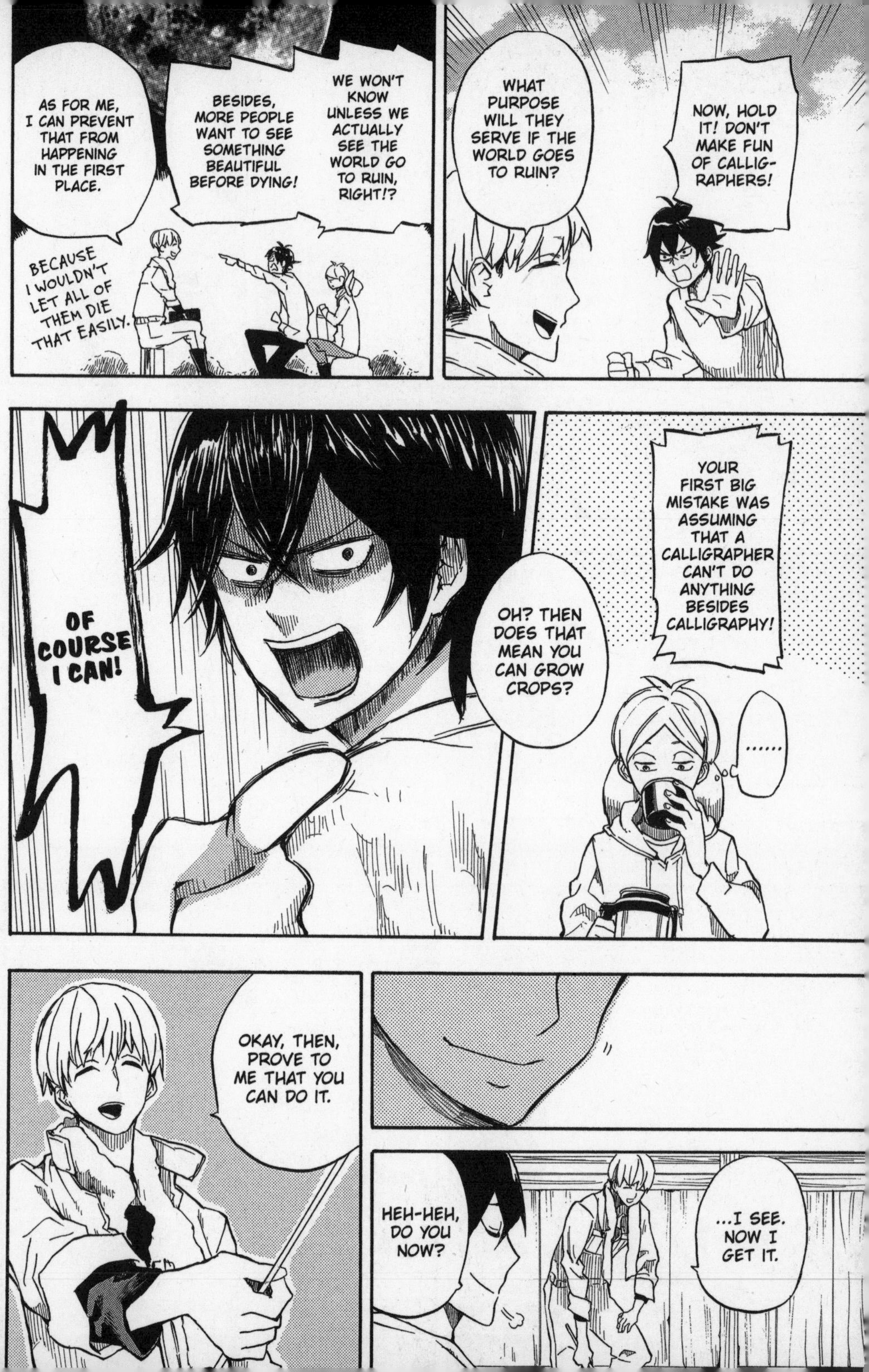
NOW, HOLD IT! DON'T MAKE FUN OF CALLIGRAPHERS!
WHAT PURPOSE WILL THEY SERVE IF THE WORLD GOES TO RUIN?
WE WON'T KNOW UNLESS WE ACTUALLY SEE THE WORLD GO TO RUIN, RIGHT!?
BESIDES, MORE PEOPLE WANT TO SEE SOMETHING BEAUTIFUL BEFORE DYING!
AS FOR ME, I CAN PREVENT THAT FROM HAPPENING IN THE FIRST PLACE.
BECAUSE I WOULDN'T LET ALL OF THEM DIE THAT EASILY.
YOUR FIRST BIG MISTAKE WAS ASSUMING THAT A CALLIGRAPHER CAN'T DO ANYTHING BESIDES CALLIGRAPHY!
......
OH? THEN DOES THAT MEAN YOU CAN GROW CROPS?
OF COURSE I CAN!
...I SEE. NOW I GET IT.
HEH-HEH, DO YOU NOW?
OKAY, THEN, PROVE TO ME THAT YOU CAN DO IT.

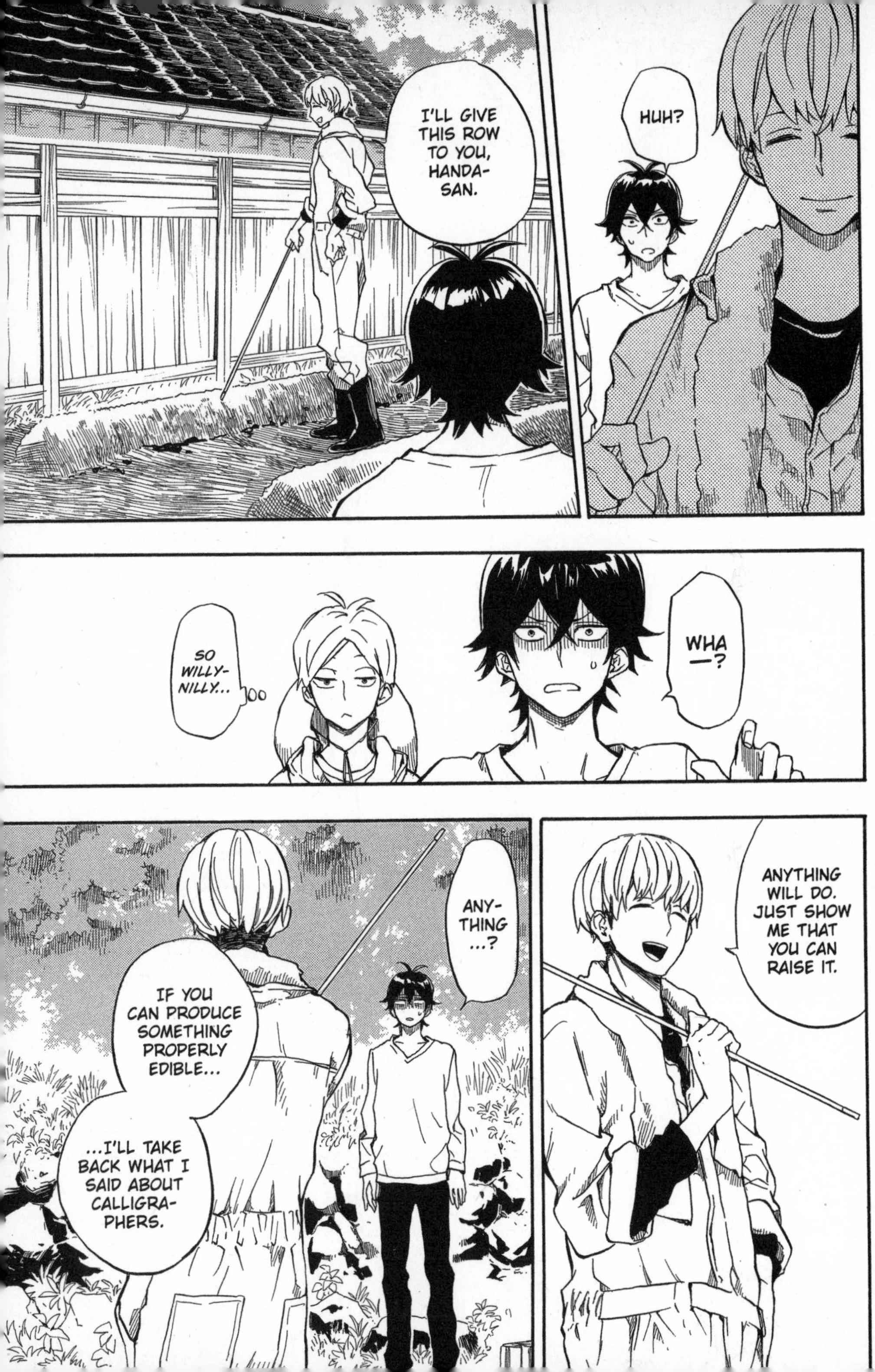
HUH?
I'LL GIVE THIS ROW TO YOU, HANDA-SAN.
WHA—?
SO WILLY-NILLY...
ANYTHING WILL DO. JUST SHOW ME THAT YOU CAN RAISE IT.
ANY-THING ...?
IF YOU CAN PRODUCE SOMETHING PROPERLY EDIBLE...
...I'LL TAKE BACK WHAT I SAID ABOUT CALLIGRA-PHERS.

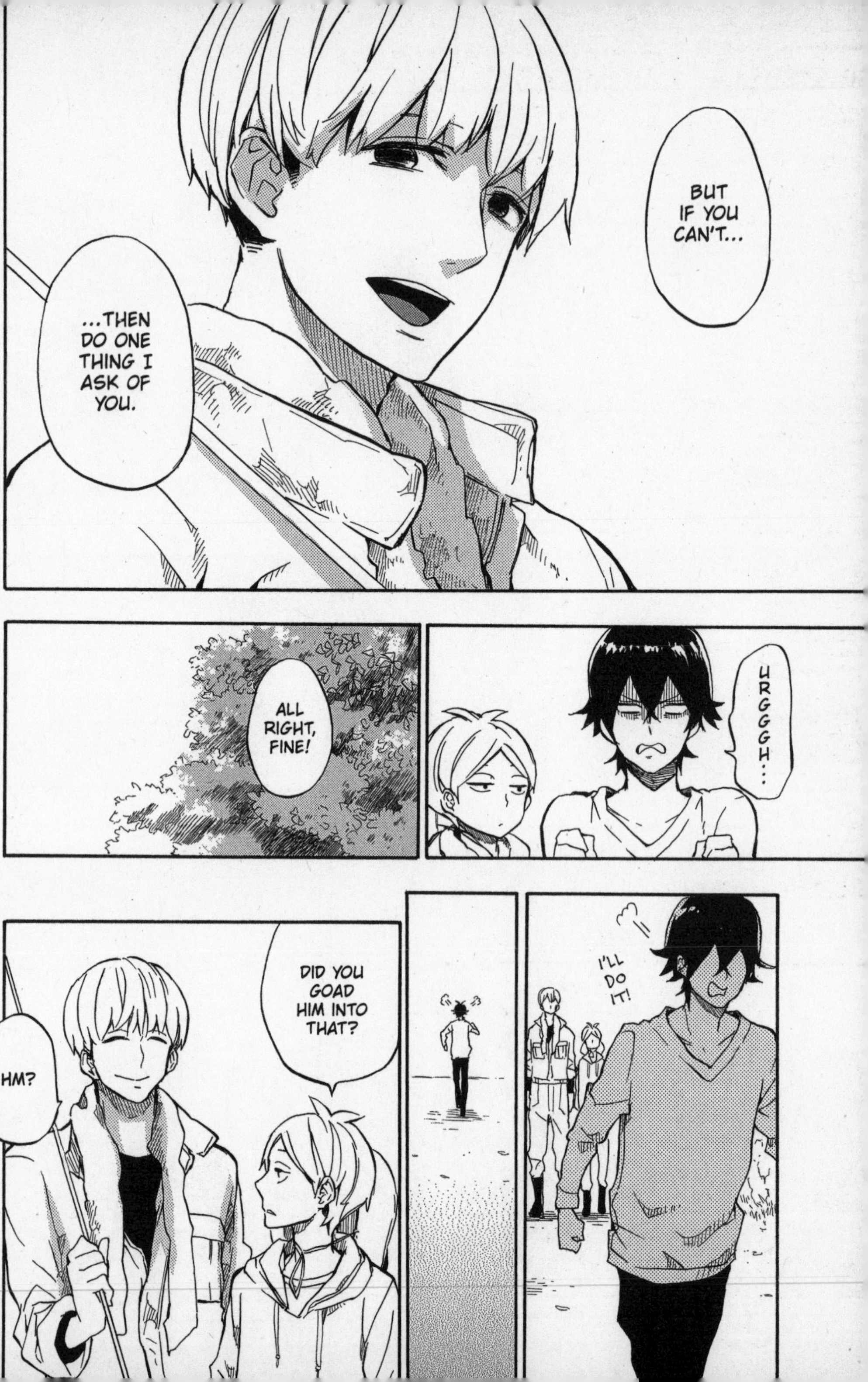
BUT IF YOU CAN'T...
...THEN DO ONE THING I ASK OF YOU.
URGGGH...
ALL RIGHT, FINE!
I'LL DO IT!
DID YOU GOAD HIM INTO THAT?
HM?

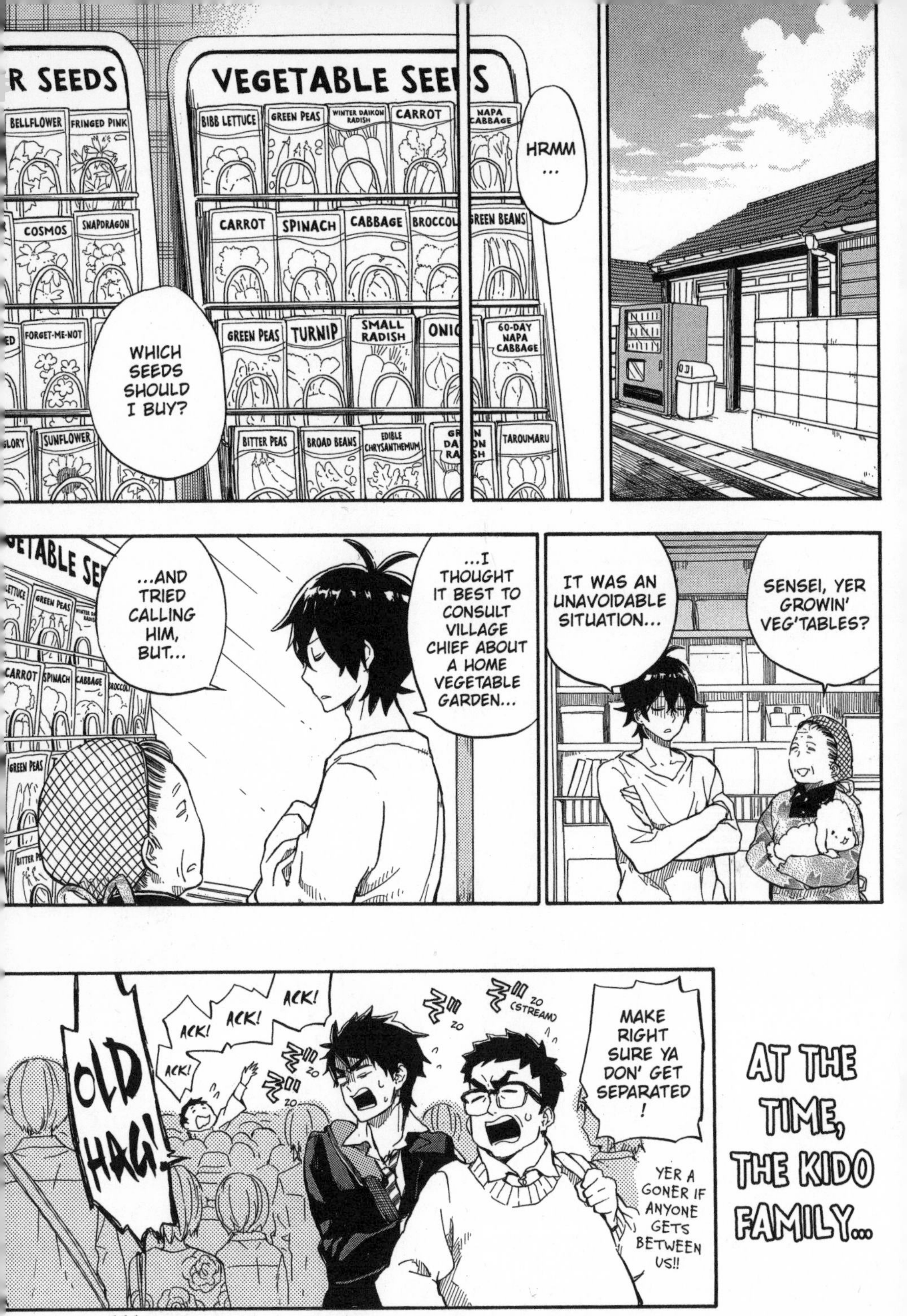
HRMM ...
VEGETABLE SEEDS
BIBB LETTUCE
GREEN PEAS
WINTER DAIKON RADISH
CARROT
NAPA CABBAGE
CARROT
SPINACH
CABBAGE
GREEN PEAS
TURNIP
SMALL RADISH
60-DAY NAPA CABBAGE
BITTER PEAS
BROAD BEANS
EDIBLE CHRYSANTHEMUM
TAROUMARU
R SEEDS
BELLFLOWER
FRINGED PINK
COSMOS
SNAPDRAGON
FORGET-ME-NOT
SUNFLOWER
WHICH SEEDS SHOULD I BUY?
SENSEI, YER GROWIN' VEG'TABLES?
IT WAS AN UNAVOIDABLE SITUATION...
...I THOUGHT IT BEST TO CONSULT VILLAGE CHIEF ABOUT A HOME VEGETABLE GARDEN...
...AND TRIED CALLING HIM, BUT...
AT THE TIME, THE KIDO FAMILY...
MAKE RIGHT SURE YA DON' GET SEPARATED!
YER A GONER IF ANYONE GETS BETWEEN US!!
ZO (STREAM)
ZO
ZO
ZO
ACK!
ACK!
ACK!
ACK!
OLD HAG!

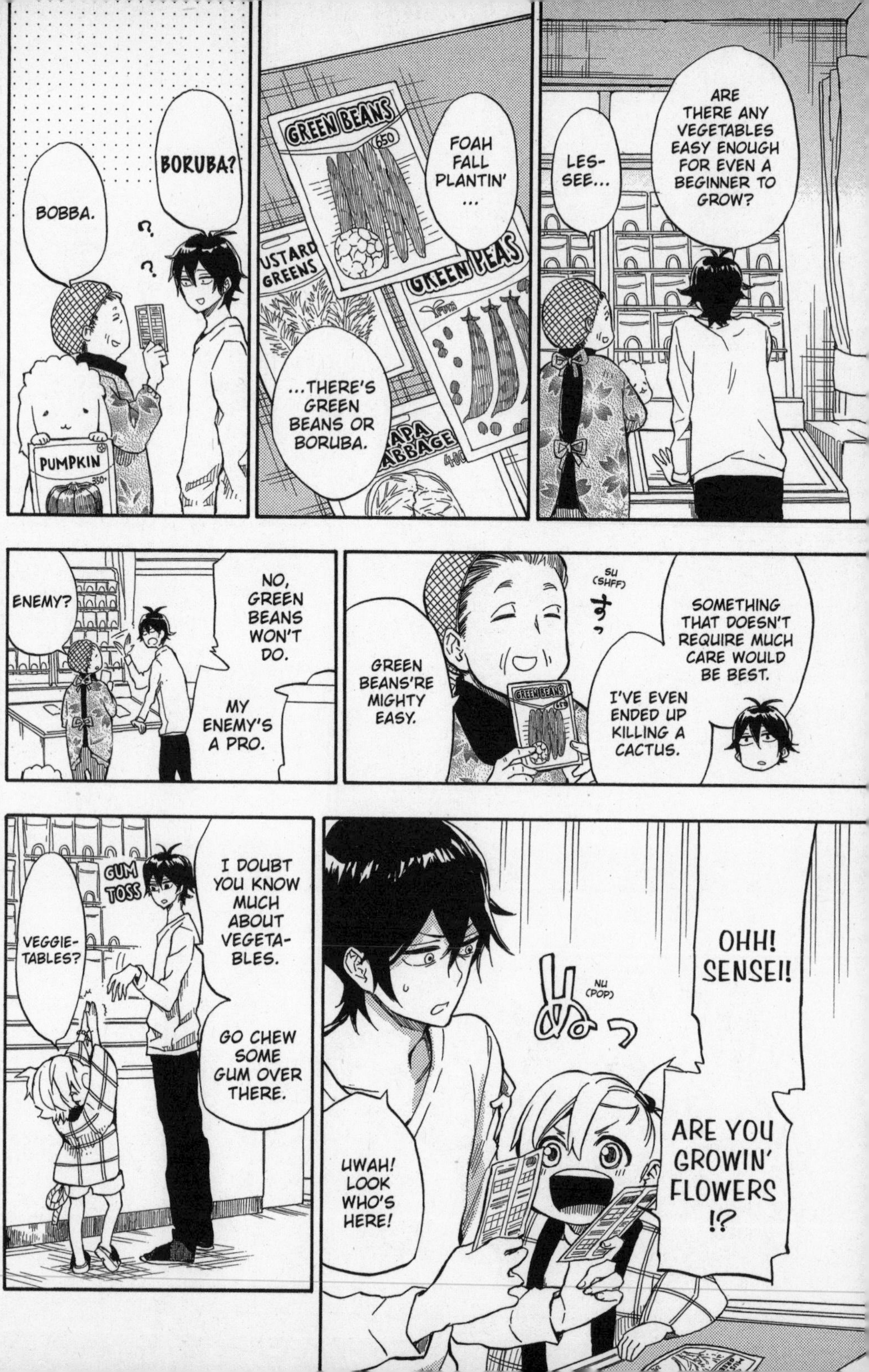

ARE THERE ANY VEGETABLES EASY ENOUGH FOR EVEN A BEGINNER TO GROW?
LES-SEE...
FOAH FALL PLANTIN' ...
GREEN BEANS
GREEN PEAS
...THERE'S GREEN BEANS OR BORUBA.
BORUBA?
BOBBA.
PUMPKIN
SOMETHING THAT DOESN'T REQUIRE MUCH CARE WOULD BE BEST.
I'VE EVEN ENDED UP KILLING A CACTUS.
SU (SHFF)
すっ
GREEN BEANS'RE MIGHTY EASY.
NO, GREEN BEANS WON'T DO.
MY ENEMY'S A PRO.
ENEMY?
OHH! SENSEI!
NU (POP)
ぬっ
ARE YOU GROWIN' FLOWERS !?
UWAH! LOOK WHO'S HERE!
I DOUBT YOU KNOW MUCH ABOUT VEGETA-BLES.
GO CHEW SOME GUM OVER THERE.
GUM TOSS
VEGGIE-TABLES?

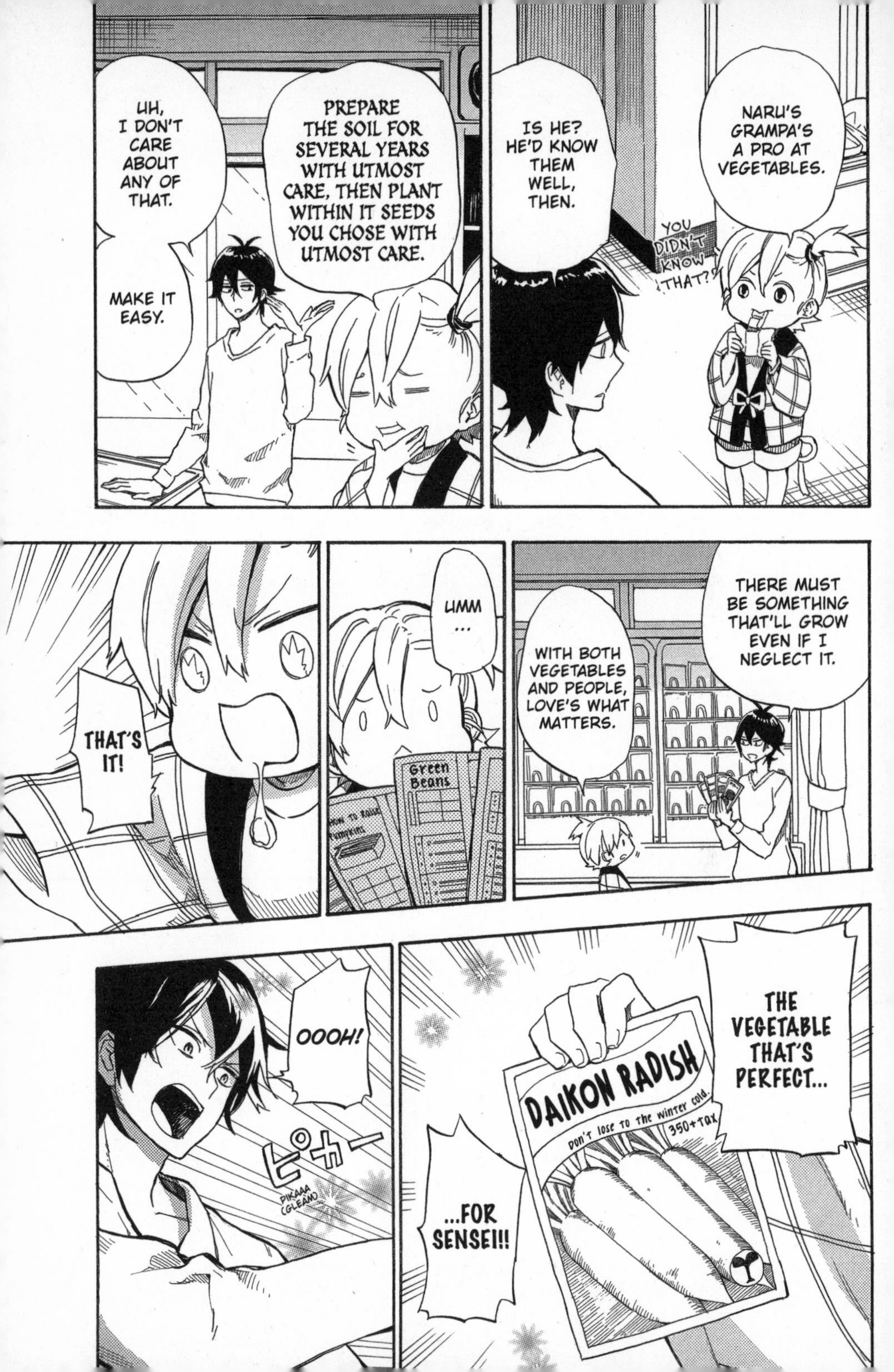
NARU'S GRAMPA'S A PRO AT VEGETABLES.
YOU DIDN'T KNOW THAT?
IS HE? HE'D KNOW THEM WELL, THEN.
PREPARE THE SOIL FOR SEVERAL YEARS WITH UTMOST CARE, THEN PLANT WITHIN IT SEEDS YOU CHOSE WITH UTMOST CARE.
UH, I DON'T CARE ABOUT ANY OF THAT.
MAKE IT EASY.
THERE MUST BE SOMETHING THAT'LL GROW EVEN IF I NEGLECT IT.
WITH BOTH VEGETABLES AND PEOPLE, LOVE'S WHAT MATTERS.
UMM ...
Green Beans
THAT'S IT!
THE VEGETABLE THAT'S PERFECT...
DAIKON RADISH
Don't lose to the winter cold.
350+tax
...FOR SENSEI!!!
OOOH!
ピカー
PIKAAA (GLEAM)

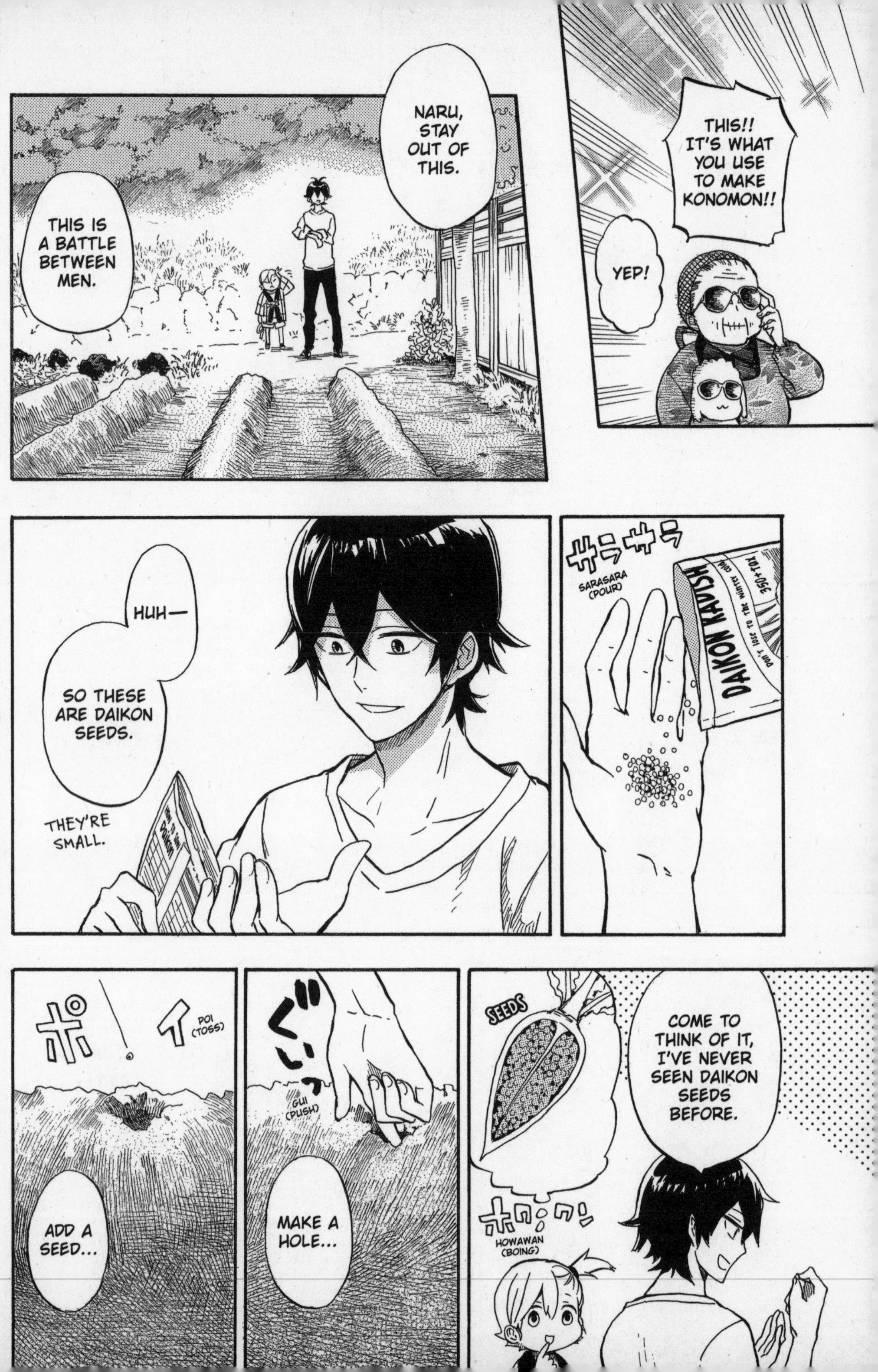
THIS!! IT'S WHAT YOU USE TO MAKE KONOMON!!
YEP!
NARU, STAY OUT OF THIS.
THIS IS A BATTLE BETWEEN MEN.
サラサラ
SARASARA (POUR)
DAIKON RADISH
HUH—
SO THESE ARE DAIKON SEEDS.
THEY'RE SMALL.
SEEDS
COME TO THINK OF IT, I'VE NEVER SEEN DAIKON SEEDS BEFORE.
ホワワン
HOWAWAN (BOING)
ぐいっ
GUI (PUSH)
MAKE A HOLE...
ポイ
POI (TOSS)
ADD A SEED...

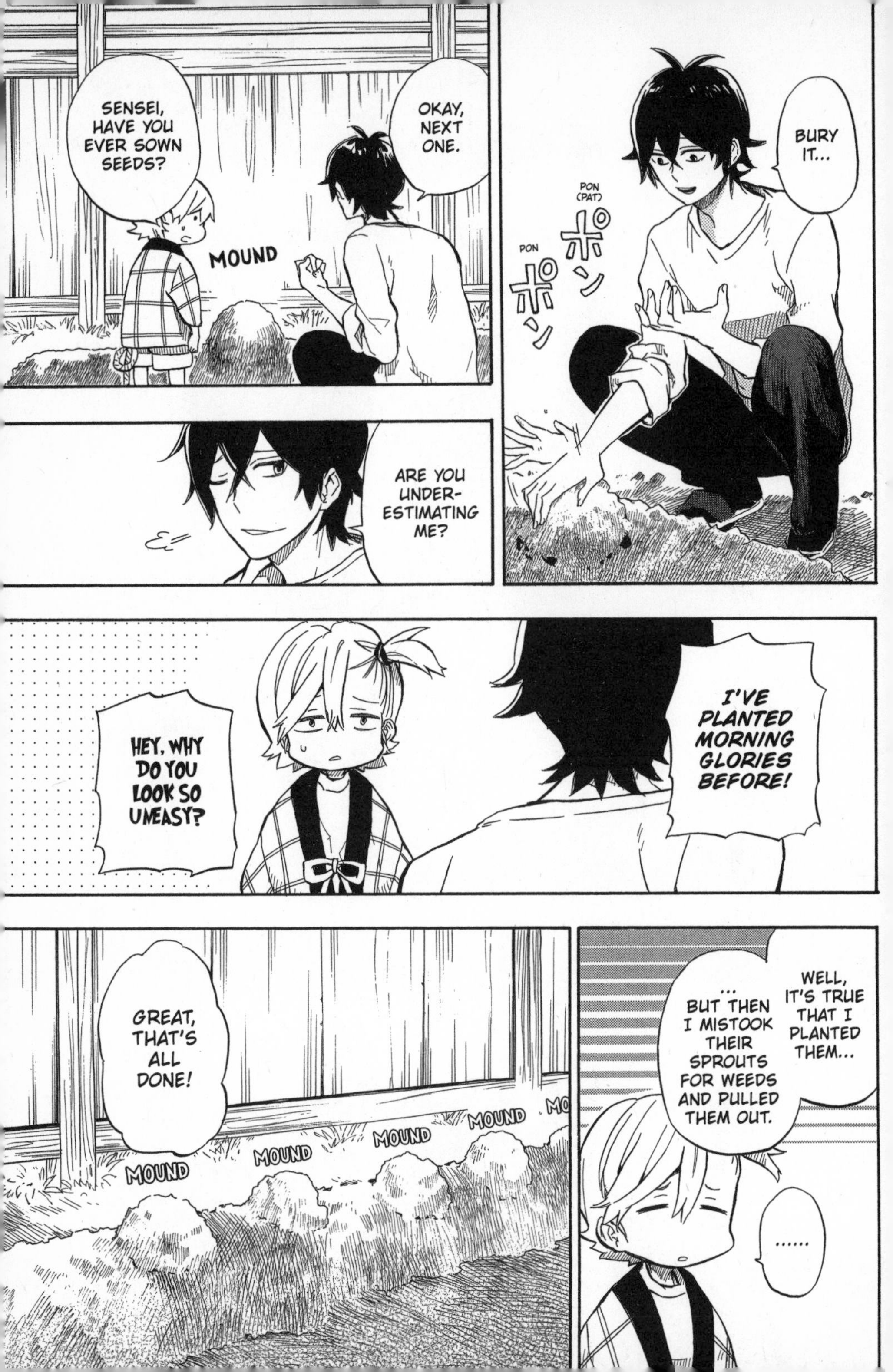
BURY IT...
PON (PAT)
ポン
PON
ポン
OKAY, NEXT ONE.
SENSEI, HAVE YOU EVER SOWN SEEDS?
MOUND
ARE YOU UNDER-ESTIMATING ME?
I'VE PLANTED MORNING GLORIES BEFORE!
HEY, WHY DO YOU LOOK SO UNEASY?
WELL, IT'S TRUE THAT I PLANTED THEM...
... BUT THEN I MISTOOK THEIR SPROUTS FOR WEEDS AND PULLED THEM OUT.
......
GREAT, THAT'S ALL DONE!
MOUND
MOUND
MOUND
MOUND

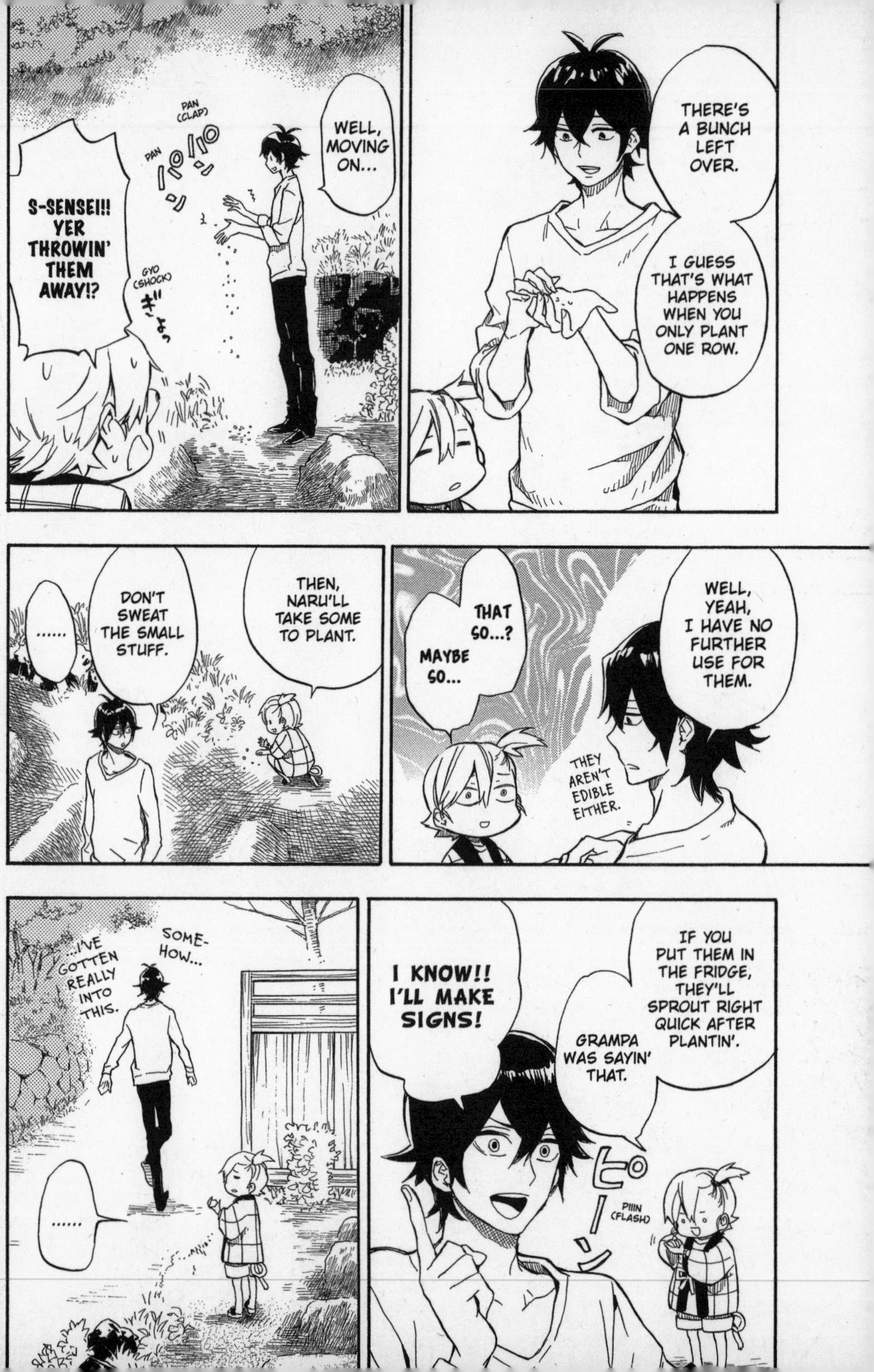
THERE'S A BUNCH LEFT OVER.
I GUESS THAT'S WHAT HAPPENS WHEN YOU ONLY PLANT ONE ROW.
WELL, MOVING ON...
PAN (CLAP)
PAN
S-SENSEI!! YER THROWIN' THEM AWAY!?
GYO (SHOCK)
WELL, YEAH, I HAVE NO FURTHER USE FOR THEM.
THAT SO...?
MAYBE SO...
THEY AREN'T EDIBLE EITHER.
THEN, NARU'LL TAKE SOME TO PLANT.
DON'T SWEAT THE SMALL STUFF.
......
IF YOU PUT THEM IN THE FRIDGE, THEY'LL SPROUT RIGHT QUICK AFTER PLANTIN'.
GRAMPA WAS SAYIN' THAT.
I KNOW!! I'LL MAKE SIGNS!
PIIIN (FLASH)
SOME-HOW...
...I'VE GOTTEN REALLY INTO THIS.
......

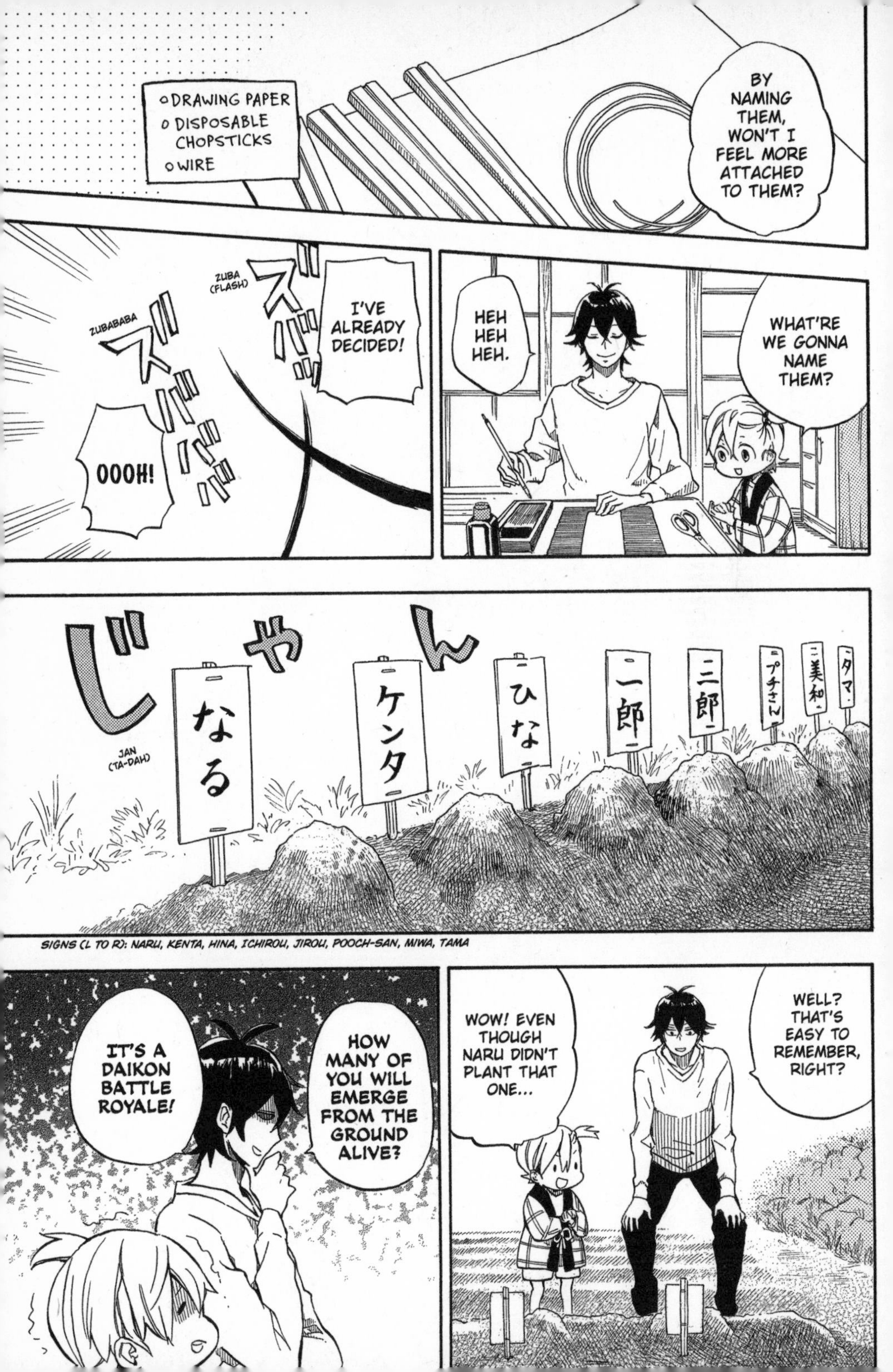
BY NAMING THEM, WON'T I FEEL MORE ATTACHED TO THEM?
○DRAWING PAPER
○DISPOSABLE CHOPSTICKS
○WIRE
WHAT'RE WE GONNA NAME THEM?
HEH HEH HEH.
I'VE ALREADY DECIDED!
ZUBA (FLASH)
ZUBABABA
OOOH!
じゃん
JAN (TA-DAH)
なる
ケンタ
ひな
一郎
二郎
プチさん
美和
タマ
SIGNS (L TO R): NARU, KENTA, HINA, ICHIROU, JIROU, POOCH-SAN, MIWA, TAMA
WELL? THAT'S EASY TO REMEMBER, RIGHT?
WOW! EVEN THOUGH NARU DIDN'T PLANT THAT ONE...
HOW MANY OF YOU WILL EMERGE FROM THE GROUND ALIVE?
IT'S A DAIKON BATTLE ROYALE!

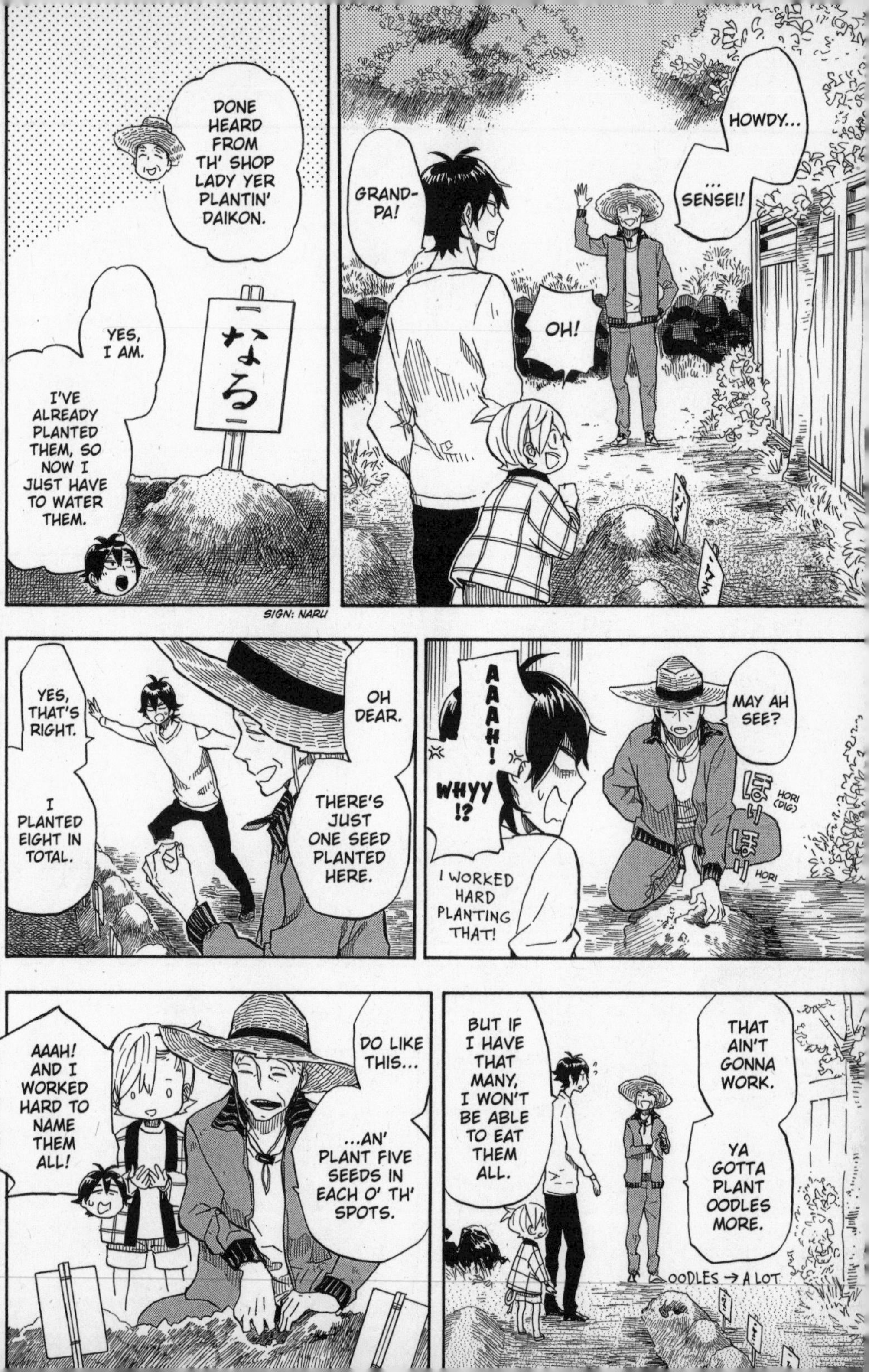
HOWDY...
...SENSEI!
GRAND-PA!
OH!
DONE HEARD FROM TH' SHOP LADY YER PLANTIN' DAIKON.
YES, I AM.
I'VE ALREADY PLANTED THEM, SO NOW I JUST HAVE TO WATER THEM.
なる
SIGN: NARU
MAY AH SEE?
HORI (DIG)
HORI
AAAH!
WHYY!?
I WORKED HARD PLANTING THAT!
OH DEAR.
YES, THAT'S RIGHT.
THERE'S JUST ONE SEED PLANTED HERE.
I PLANTED EIGHT IN TOTAL.
THAT AIN'T GONNA WORK.
YA GOTTA PLANT OODLES MORE.
BUT IF I HAVE THAT MANY, I WON'T BE ABLE TO EAT THEM ALL.
OODLES → A LOT
DO LIKE THIS...
...AN' PLANT FIVE SEEDS IN EACH O' TH' SPOTS.
AAAH! AND I WORKED HARD TO NAME THEM ALL!

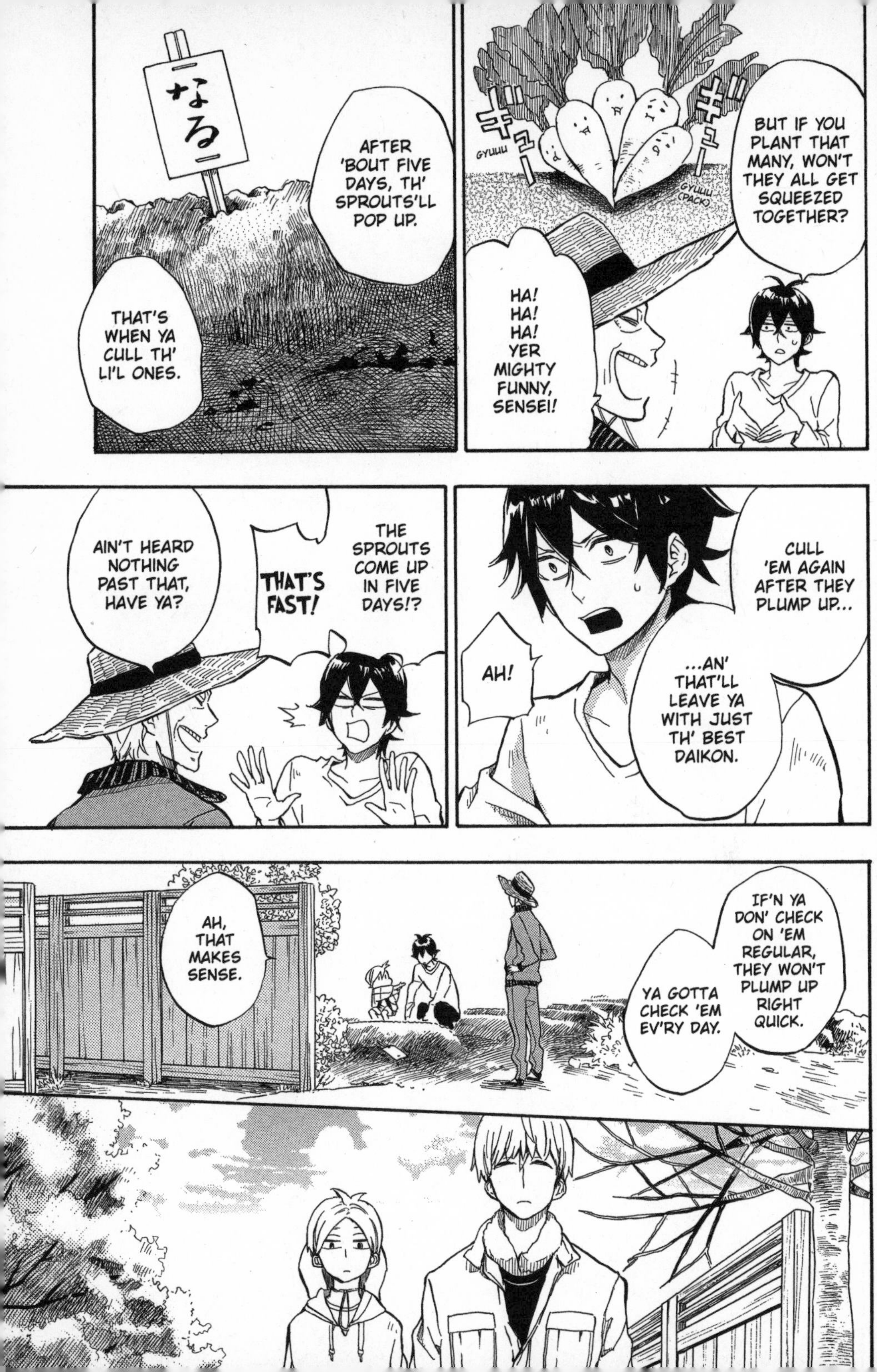
ギュー
GYUUU (PACK)
ギュー
GYUUU
BUT IF YOU PLANT THAT MANY, WON'T THEY ALL GET SQUEEZED TOGETHER?
HA! HA! HA! YER MIGHTY FUNNY, SENSEI!
なる
AFTER 'BOUT FIVE DAYS, TH' SPROUTS'LL POP UP.
THAT'S WHEN YA CULL TH' LI'L ONES.
CULL 'EM AGAIN AFTER THEY PLUMP UP...
AH!
...AN' THAT'LL LEAVE YA WITH JUST TH' BEST DAIKON.
THE SPROUTS COME UP IN FIVE DAYS!?
THAT'S FAST!
AIN'T HEARD NOTHING PAST THAT, HAVE YA?
IF'N YA DON' CHECK ON 'EM REGULAR, THEY WON'T PLUMP UP RIGHT QUICK.
YA GOTTA CHECK 'EM EV'RY DAY.
AH, THAT MAKES SENSE.

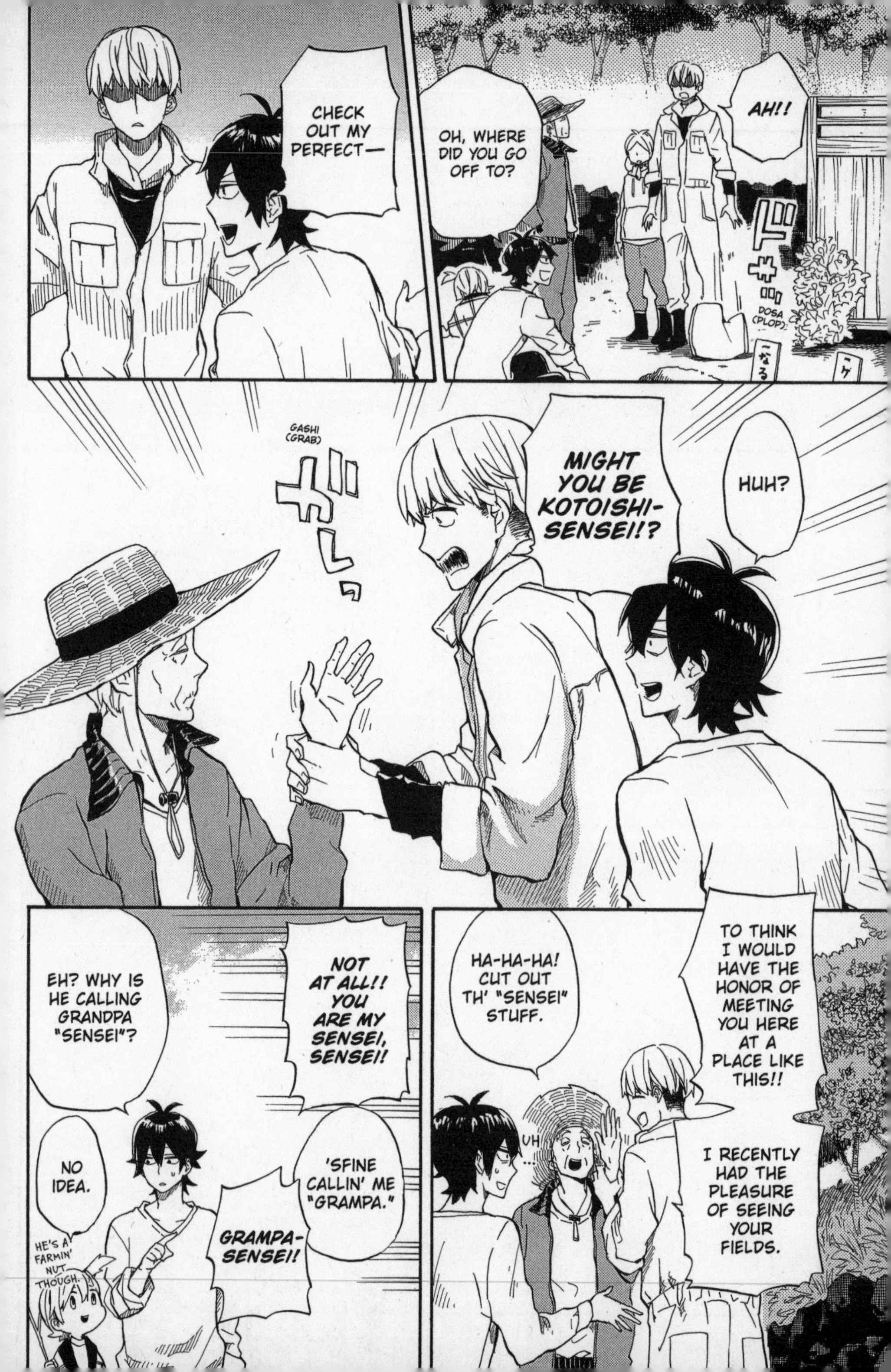
AH!!
OH, WHERE DID YOU GO OFF TO?
DOSA (PLOP)
CHECK OUT MY PERFECT—
HUH?
MIGHT YOU BE KOTOISHI-SENSEI!?
GASHI (GRAB)
TO THINK I WOULD HAVE THE HONOR OF MEETING YOU HERE AT A PLACE LIKE THIS!!
HA-HA-HA! CUT OUT TH' "SENSEI" STUFF.
UH ...
I RECENTLY HAD THE PLEASURE OF SEEING YOUR FIELDS.
NOT AT ALL!! YOU ARE MY SENSEI, SENSEI!
EH? WHY IS HE CALLING GRANDPA "SENSEI"?
'SFINE CALLIN' ME "GRAMPA."
GRAMPA-SENSEI!
NO IDEA.
HE'S A FARMIN' NUT THOUGH.

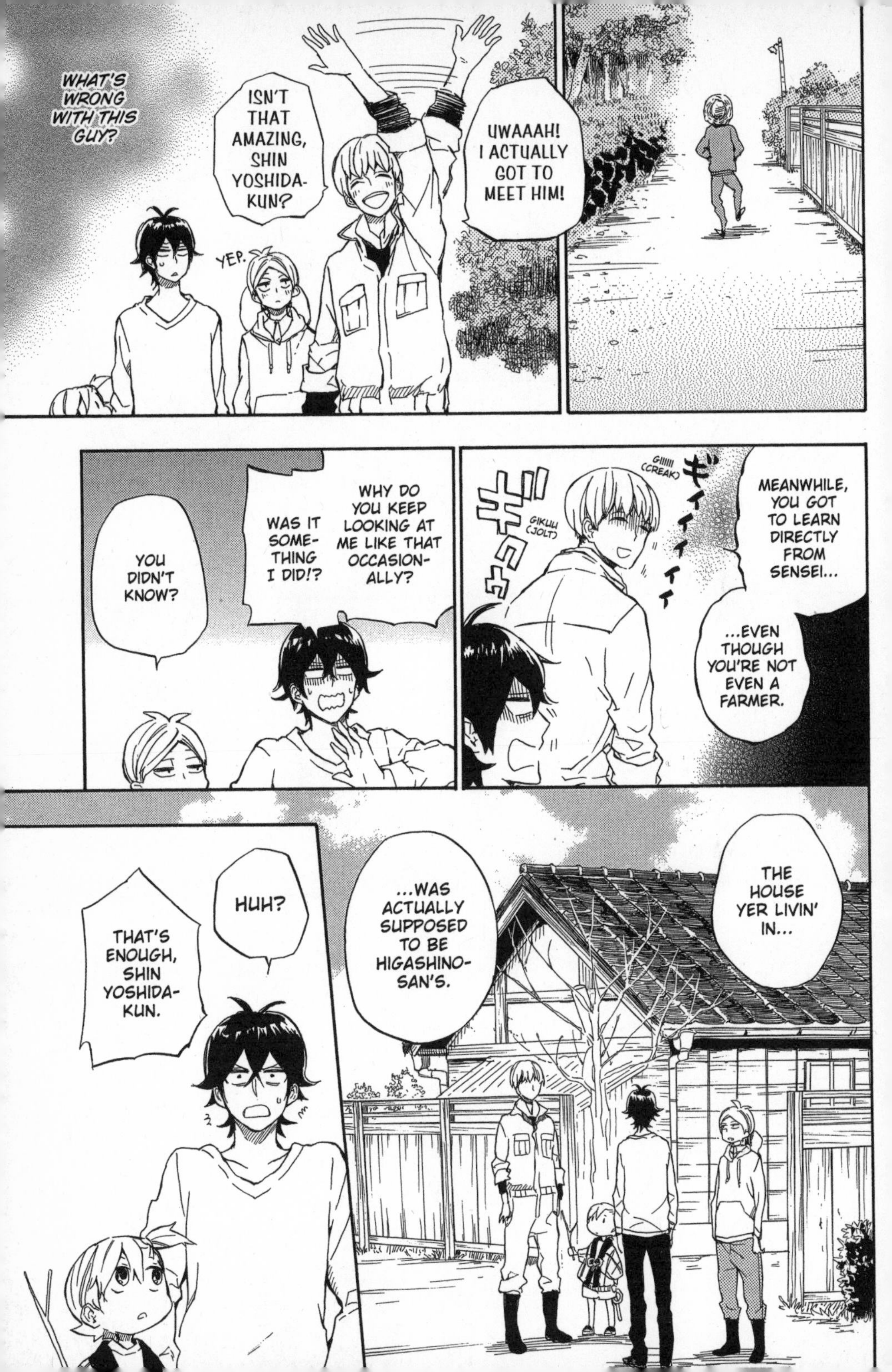
UWAAAH! I ACTUALLY GOT TO MEET HIM!
ISN'T THAT AMAZING, SHIN YOSHIDA-KUN?
YEP.
WHAT'S WRONG WITH THIS GUY?
MEANWHILE, YOU GOT TO LEARN DIRECTLY FROM SENSEI...
...EVEN THOUGH YOU'RE NOT EVEN A FARMER.
GIIIII (CREAK)
GIKUU (JOLT)
WHY DO YOU KEEP LOOKING AT ME LIKE THAT OCCASIONALLY?
WAS IT SOMETHING I DID!?
YOU DIDN'T KNOW?
THE HOUSE YER LIVIN' IN...
...WAS ACTUALLY SUPPOSED TO BE HIGASHINO-SAN'S.
HUH?
THAT'S ENOUGH, SHIN YOSHIDA-KUN.

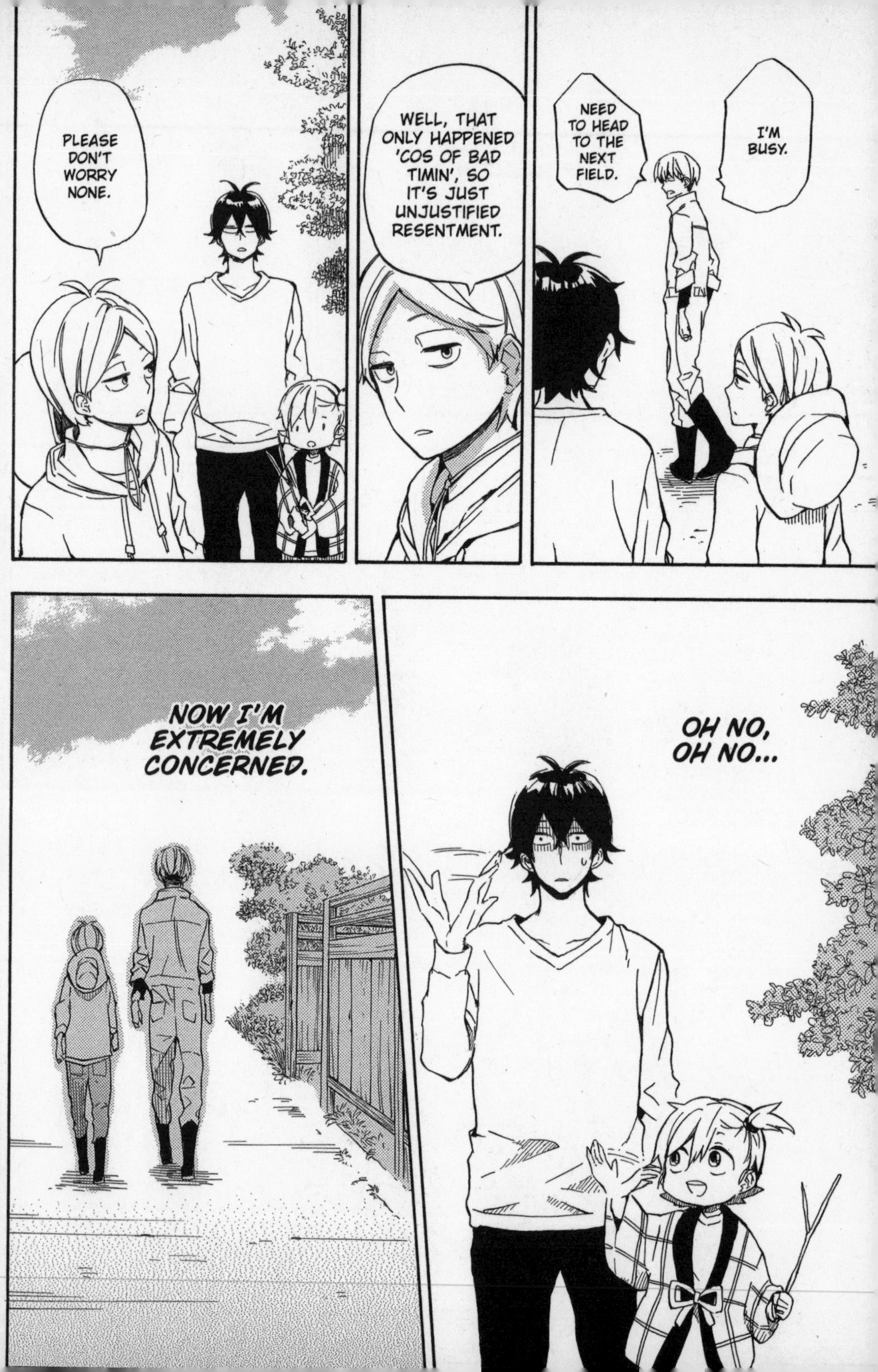
I'M BUSY.
NEED TO HEAD TO THE NEXT FIELD.
WELL, THAT ONLY HAPPENED 'COS OF BAD TIMIN', SO IT'S JUST UNJUSTIFIED RESENTMENT.
PLEASE DON'T WORRY NONE.
OH NO, OH NO...
NOW I'M EXTREMELY CONCERNED.

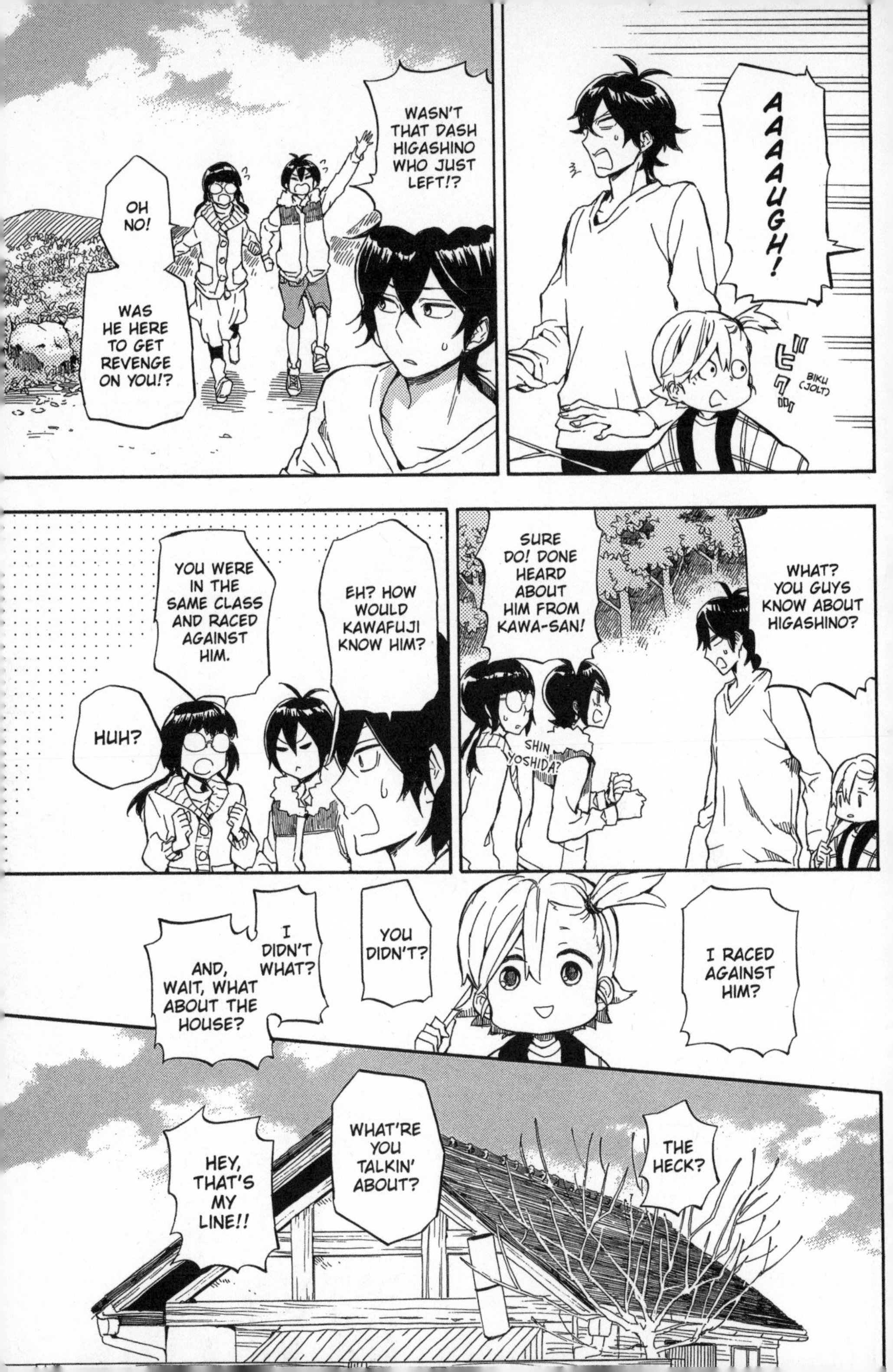
AAAAUGH!
BIKU (JOLT)
WASN'T THAT DASH HIGASHINO WHO JUST LEFT!?
OH NO!
WAS HE HERE TO GET REVENGE ON YOU!?
WHAT? YOU GUYS KNOW ABOUT HIGASHINO?
SURE DO! DONE HEARD ABOUT HIM FROM KAWA-SAN!
SHIN YOSHIDA?
EH? HOW WOULD KAWAFUJI KNOW HIM?
YOU WERE IN THE SAME CLASS AND RACED AGAINST HIM.
HUH?
I RACED AGAINST HIM?
YOU DIDN'T?
I DIDN'T WHAT?
AND, WAIT, WHAT ABOUT THE HOUSE?
THE HECK?
WHAT'RE YOU TALKIN' ABOUT?
HEY, THAT'S MY LINE!!

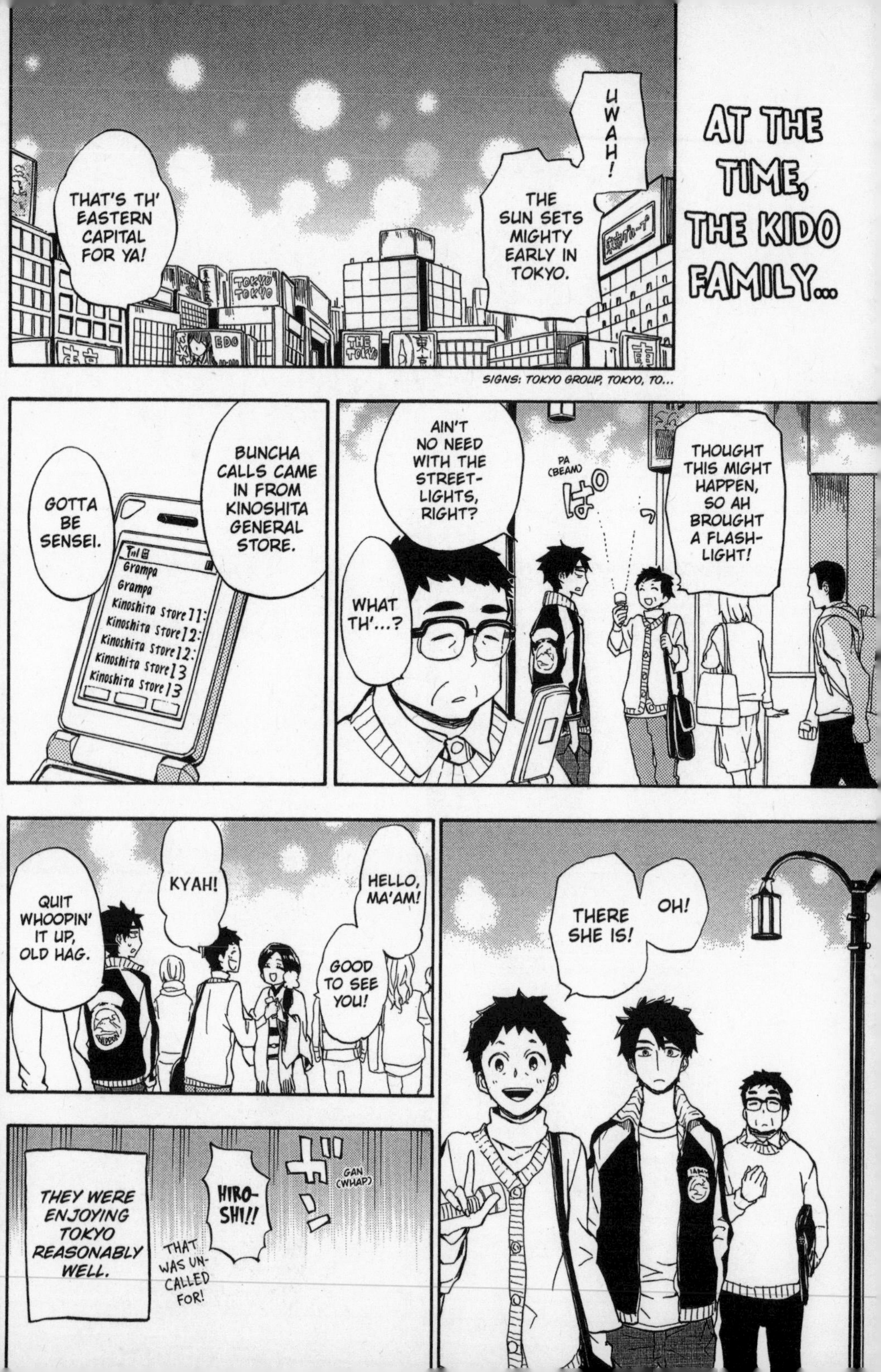
AT THE TIME, THE KIDO FAMILY...
UWAH!
THE SUN SETS MIGHTY EARLY IN TOKYO.
THAT'S TH' EASTERN CAPITAL FOR YA!
TOKYO TOKYO
EDO
THE TOKYO
SIGNS: TOKYO GROUP, TOKYO, TO...
THOUGHT THIS MIGHT HAPPEN, SO AH BROUGHT A FLASH-LIGHT!
PA (BEAM)
AIN'T NO NEED WITH THE STREET-LIGHTS, RIGHT?
WHAT TH'...?
BUNCHA CALLS CAME IN FROM KINOSHITA GENERAL STORE.
GOTTA BE SENSEI.
Grampa
Grampa
Kinoshita Store 11:
Kinoshita Store 12:
Kinoshita Store 12:
Kinoshita Store 13
Kinoshita Store 13
OH!
THERE SHE IS!
HELLO, MA'AM!
GOOD TO SEE YOU!
KYAH!
QUIT WHOOPIN' IT UP, OLD HAG.
GAN (WHAP)
HIRO-SHI!!
THAT WAS UN-CALLED FOR!
THEY WERE ENJOYING TOKYO REASONABLY WELL.

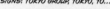

Act. 85
TAMAGO BA WATTARYA
(Translation: If You Break an Egg...)

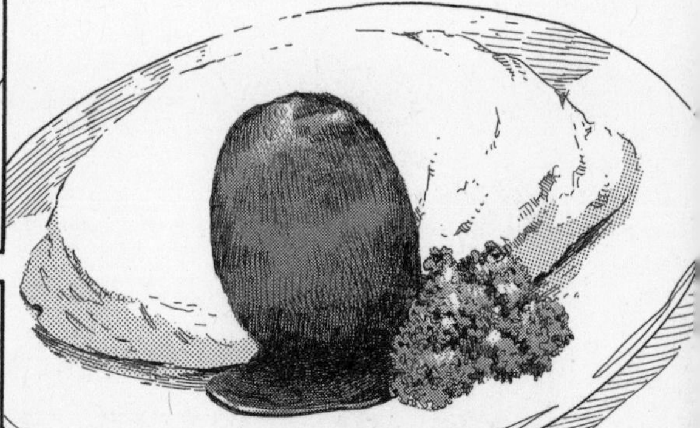
MODEL

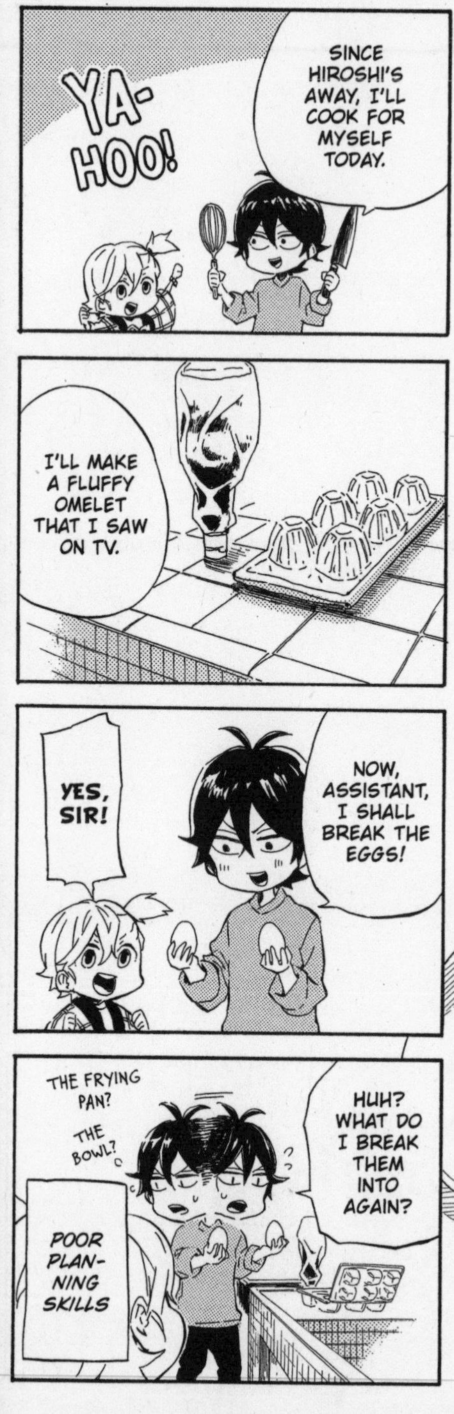
SINCE HIROSHI'S AWAY, I'LL COOK FOR MYSELF TODAY.
YA-HOO!
I'LL MAKE A FLUFFY OMELET THAT I SAW ON TV.
NOW, ASSISTANT, I SHALL BREAK THE EGGS!
YES, SIR!
HUH? WHAT DO I BREAK THEM INTO AGAIN?
THE FRYING PAN?
THE BOWL?
POOR PLAN-NING SKILLS

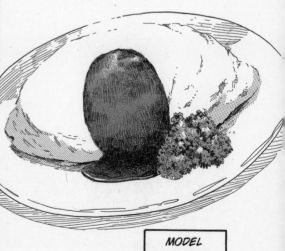

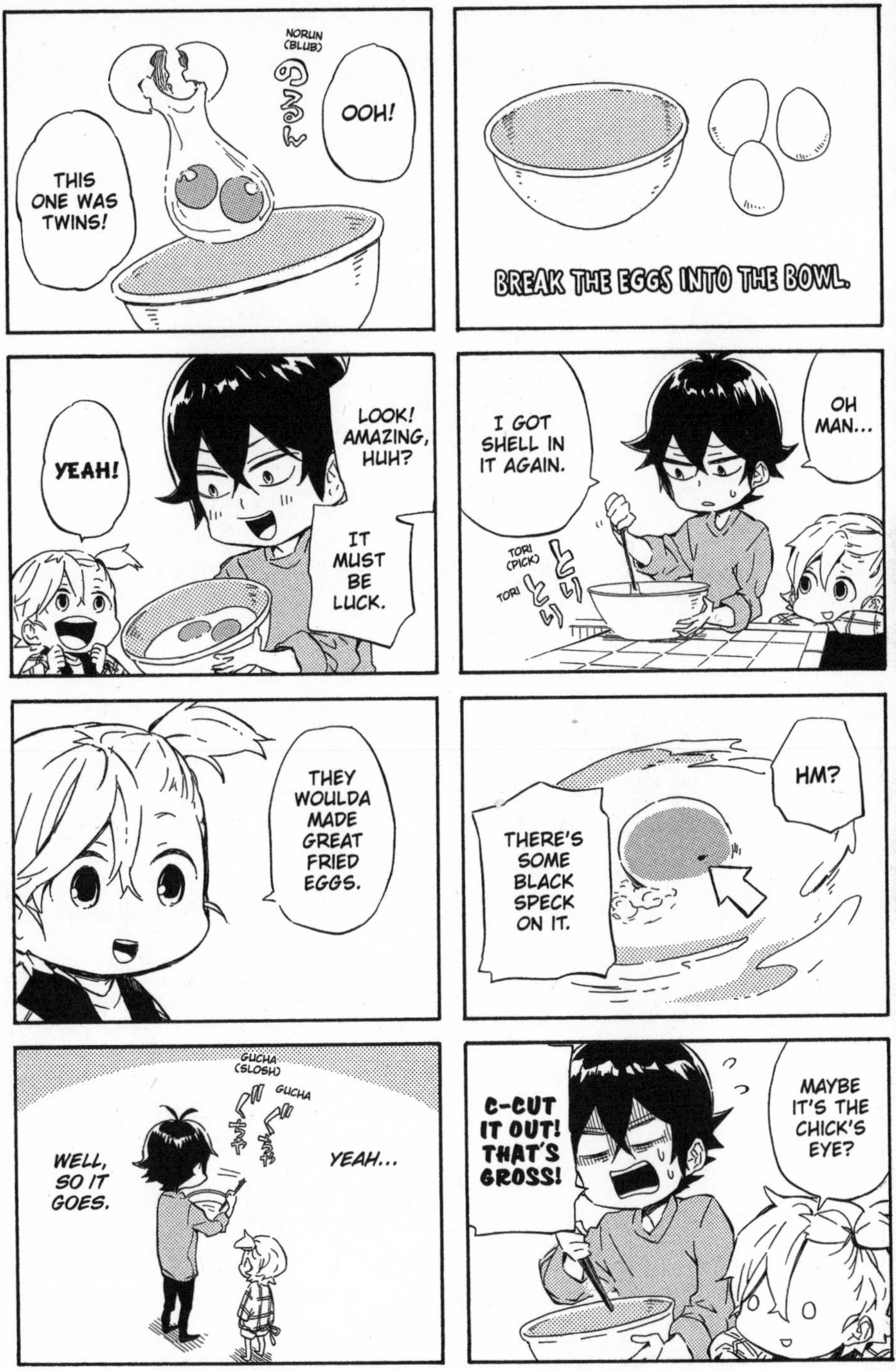
BREAK THE EGGS INTO THE BOWL.
NORUN (BLUB)
のるん
OOH!
THIS ONE WAS TWINS!
OH MAN...
I GOT SHELL IN IT AGAIN.
TORI (PICK)
とり
TORI
とり
LOOK! AMAZING, HUH?
IT MUST BE LUCK.
YEAH!
HM?
THERE'S SOME BLACK SPECK ON IT.
THEY WOULDA MADE GREAT FRIED EGGS.
MAYBE IT'S THE CHICK'S EYE?
C-CUT IT OUT! THAT'S GROSS!
GUCHA (SLOSH)
ぐちゃ
GUCHA
ぐちゃ
YEAH...
WELL, SO IT GOES.

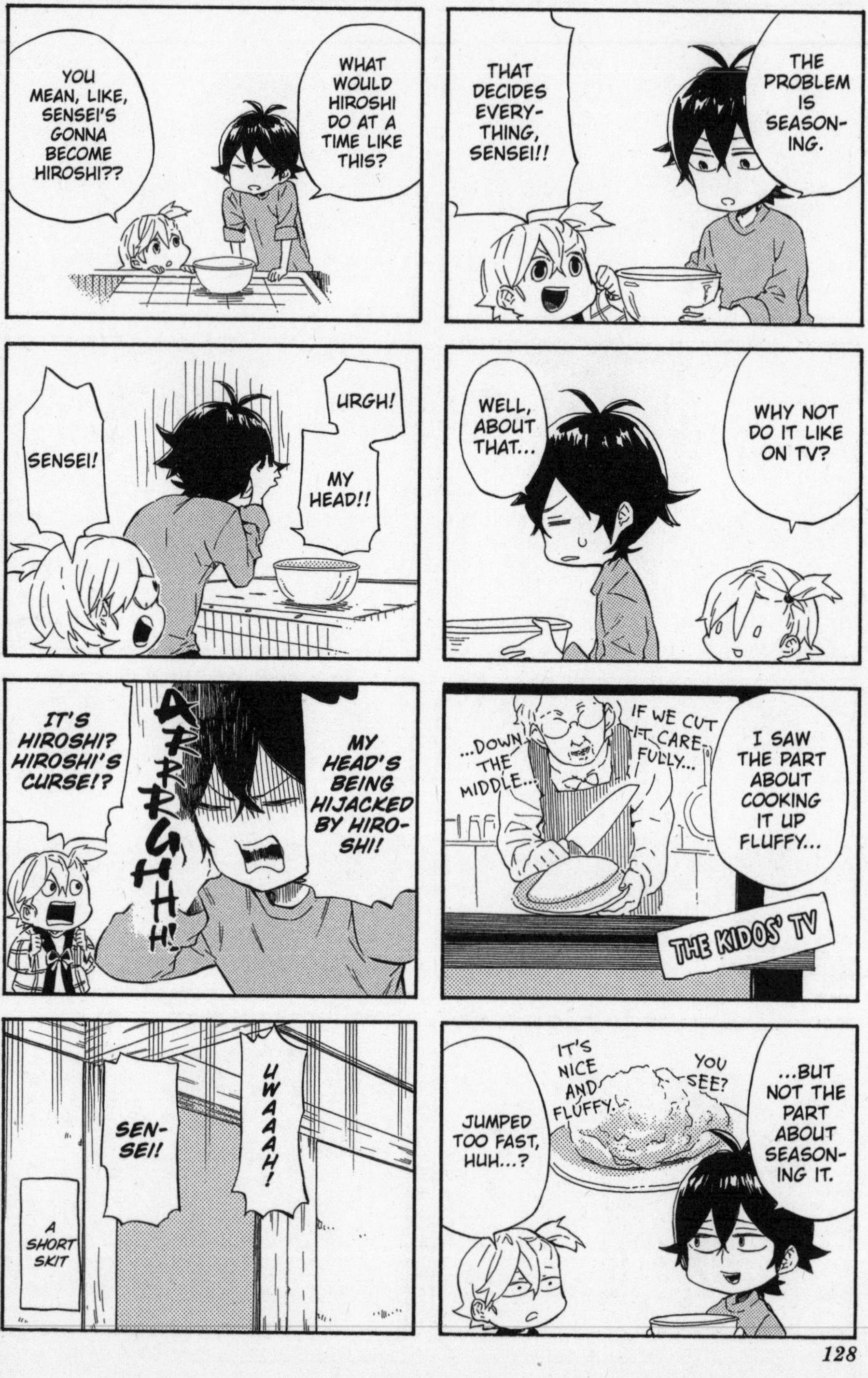
THE PROBLEM IS SEASON-ING.
THAT DECIDES EVERY-THING, SENSEI!!
WHAT WOULD HIROSHI DO AT A TIME LIKE THIS?
YOU MEAN, LIKE, SENSEI'S GONNA BECOME HIROSHI??
WHY NOT DO IT LIKE ON TV?
WELL, ABOUT THAT...
URGH!
MY HEAD!!
SENSEI!
I SAW THE PART ABOUT COOKING IT UP FLUFFY...
IF WE CUT IT CARE-FULLY...
...DOWN THE MIDDLE...
THE KIDOS' TV
MY HEAD'S BEING HIJACKED BY HIRO-SHI!
ARRRGHHH!
IT'S HIROSHI? HIROSHI'S CURSE!?
...BUT NOT THE PART ABOUT SEASON-ING IT.
YOU SEE?
IT'S NICE AND FLUFFY.
JUMPED TOO FAST, HUH...?
UWAAAH!
SEN-SEI!
A SHORT SKIT

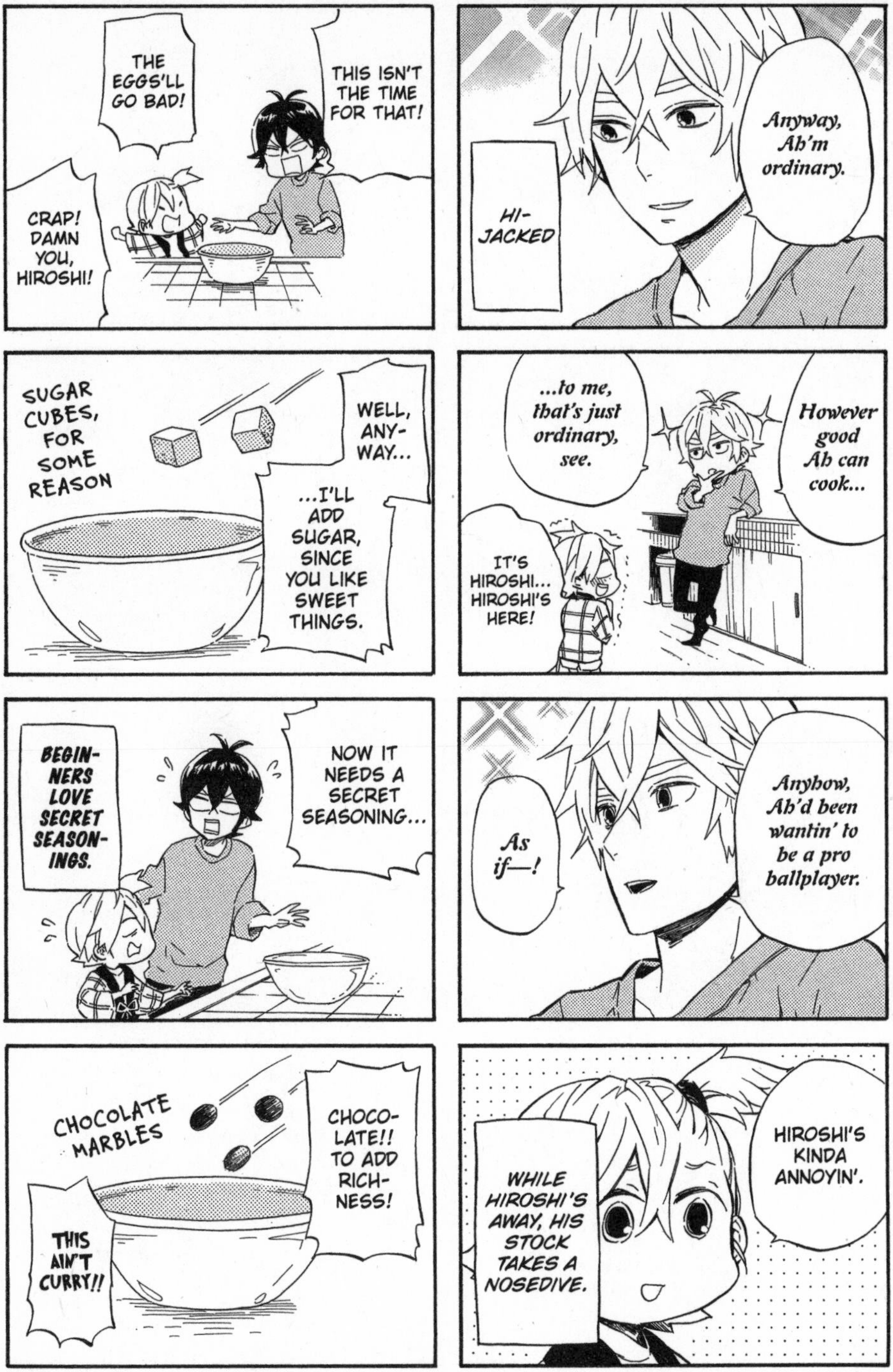
Anyway, Ah'm ordinary.
HI-JACKED
However good Ah can cook...
...to me, that's just ordinary, see.
IT'S HIROSHI... HIROSHI'S HERE!
Anyhow, Ah'd been wantin' to be a pro ballplayer.
As if—!
HIROSHI'S KINDA ANNOYIN'.
WHILE HIROSHI'S AWAY, HIS STOCK TAKES A NOSEDIVE.
THIS ISN'T THE TIME FOR THAT!
THE EGGS'LL GO BAD!
CRAP! DAMN YOU, HIROSHI!
WELL, ANY-WAY...
...I'LL ADD SUGAR, SINCE YOU LIKE SWEET THINGS.
SUGAR CUBES, FOR SOME REASON
NOW IT NEEDS A SECRET SEASONING...
BEGIN-NERS LOVE SECRET SEASON-INGS.
CHOCO-LATE!! TO ADD RICH-NESS!
CHOCOLATE MARBLES
THIS AIN'T CURRY!!

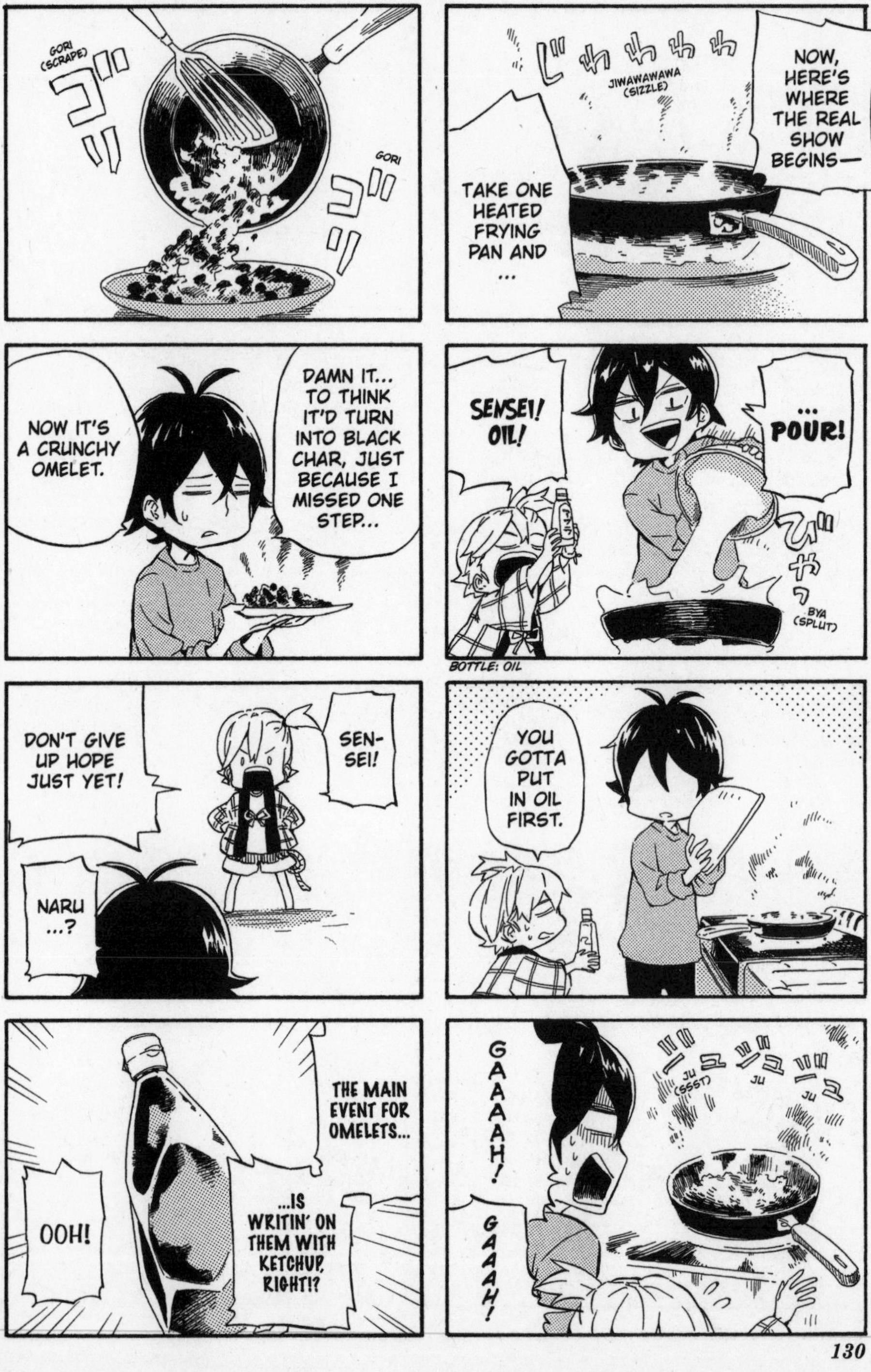

NOW, HERE'S WHERE THE REAL SHOW BEGINS—
TAKE ONE HEATED FRYING PAN AND ...
JIWAWAWAWA (SIZZLE)
SENSEI! OIL!
... POUR!
BYA (SPLUT)
BOTTLE: OIL
YOU GOTTA PUT IN OIL FIRST.
GAAAAH!
GAAAH!
JU (SSST)
JU
JU
GORI (SCRAPE)
GORI
DAMN IT... TO THINK IT'D TURN INTO BLACK CHAR, JUST BECAUSE I MISSED ONE STEP...
NOW IT'S A CRUNCHY OMELET.
SEN-SEI!
DON'T GIVE UP HOPE JUST YET!
NARU ...?
THE MAIN EVENT FOR OMELETS...
...IS WRITIN' ON THEM WITH KETCHUP, RIGHT!?
OOH!

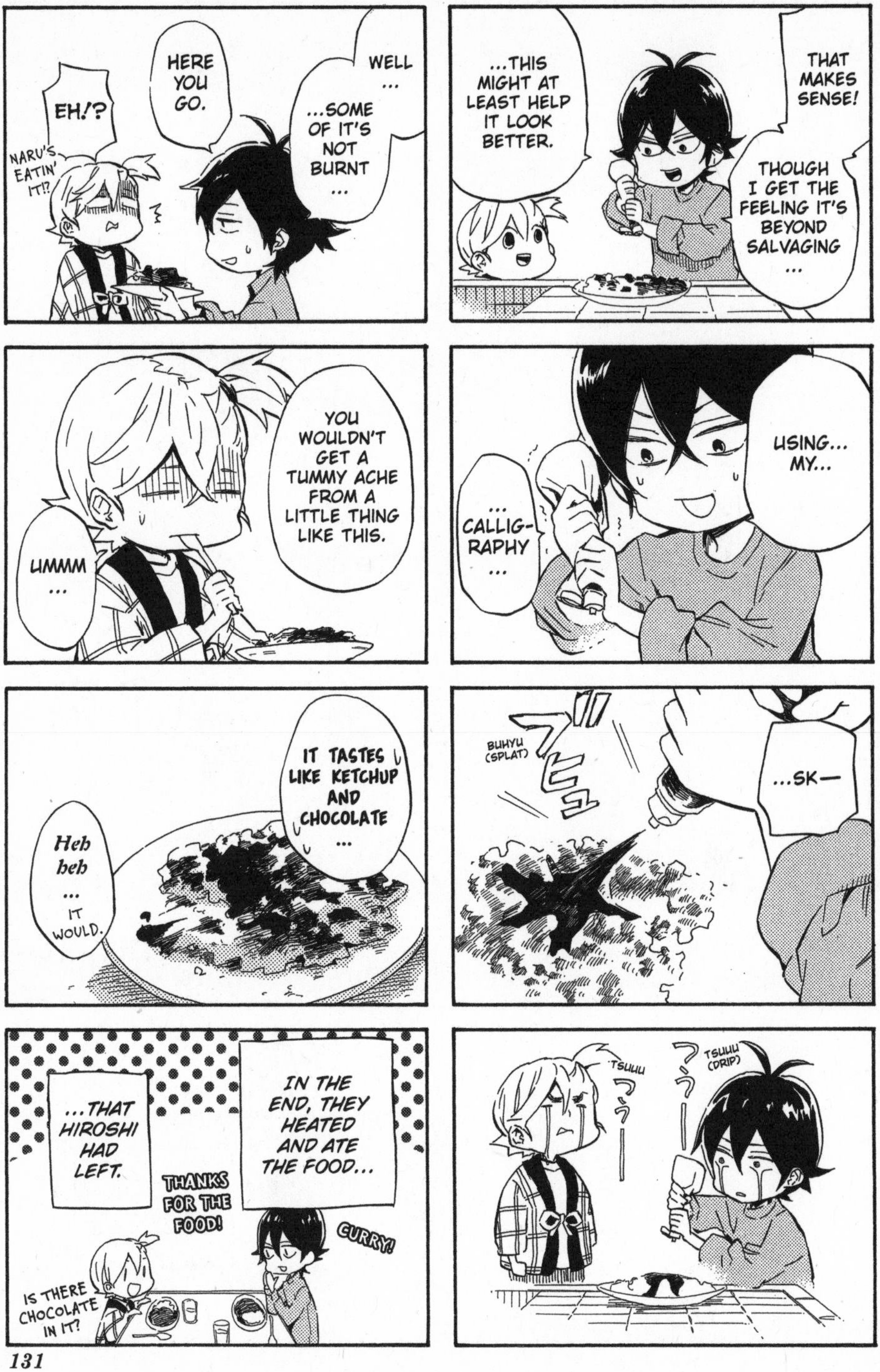
THAT MAKES SENSE!
THOUGH I GET THE FEELING IT'S BEYOND SALVAGING ...
...THIS MIGHT AT LEAST HELP IT LOOK BETTER.
WELL ...
...SOME OF IT'S NOT BURNT ...
HERE YOU GO.
EH!?
NARU'S EATIN' IT!?
USING... MY...
... CALLIG-RAPHY ...
YOU WOULDN'T GET A TUMMY ACHE FROM A LITTLE THING LIKE THIS.
UMMM ...
...SK—
BUHYU (SPLAT)
IT TASTES LIKE KETCHUP AND CHOCOLATE ...
Heh heh ... IT WOULD.
TSUUU (DRIP)
TSUUU
IN THE END, THEY HEATED AND ATE THE FOOD...
...THAT HIROSHI HAD LEFT.
CURRY!
THANKS FOR THE FOOD!
IS THERE CHOCOLATE IN IT?

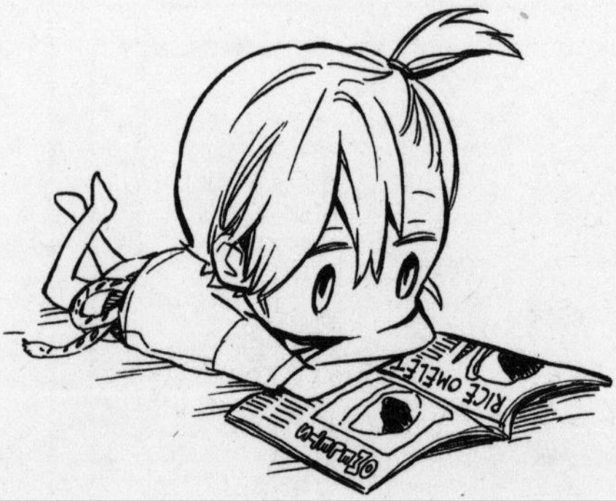
RICE OMELET

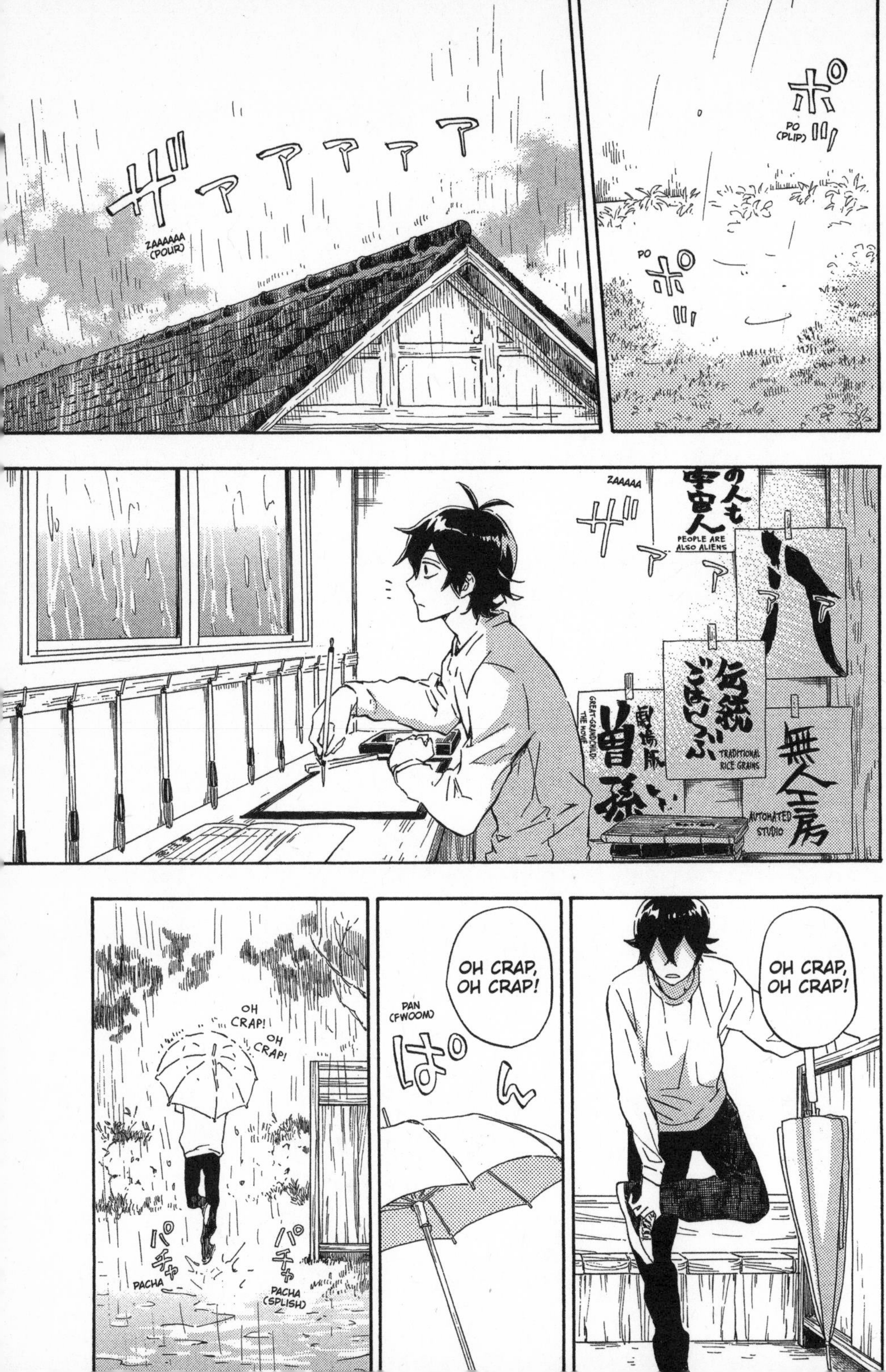
PO (PLIP)
PO
ZAAAAAA (POUR)
ZAAAAA
宇宙人の人も
PEOPLE ARE ALSO ALIENS
伝統ごはんぶ
TRADITIONAL RICE GRAINS
曽孫
GREAT-GRANDCHILD: THE MOVIE
無人工房
AUTOMATED STUDIO
OH CRAP, OH CRAP!
PAN (FWOOM)
OH CRAP, OH CRAP!
OH CRAP!
OH CRAP!
PACHA
PACHA (SPLISH)

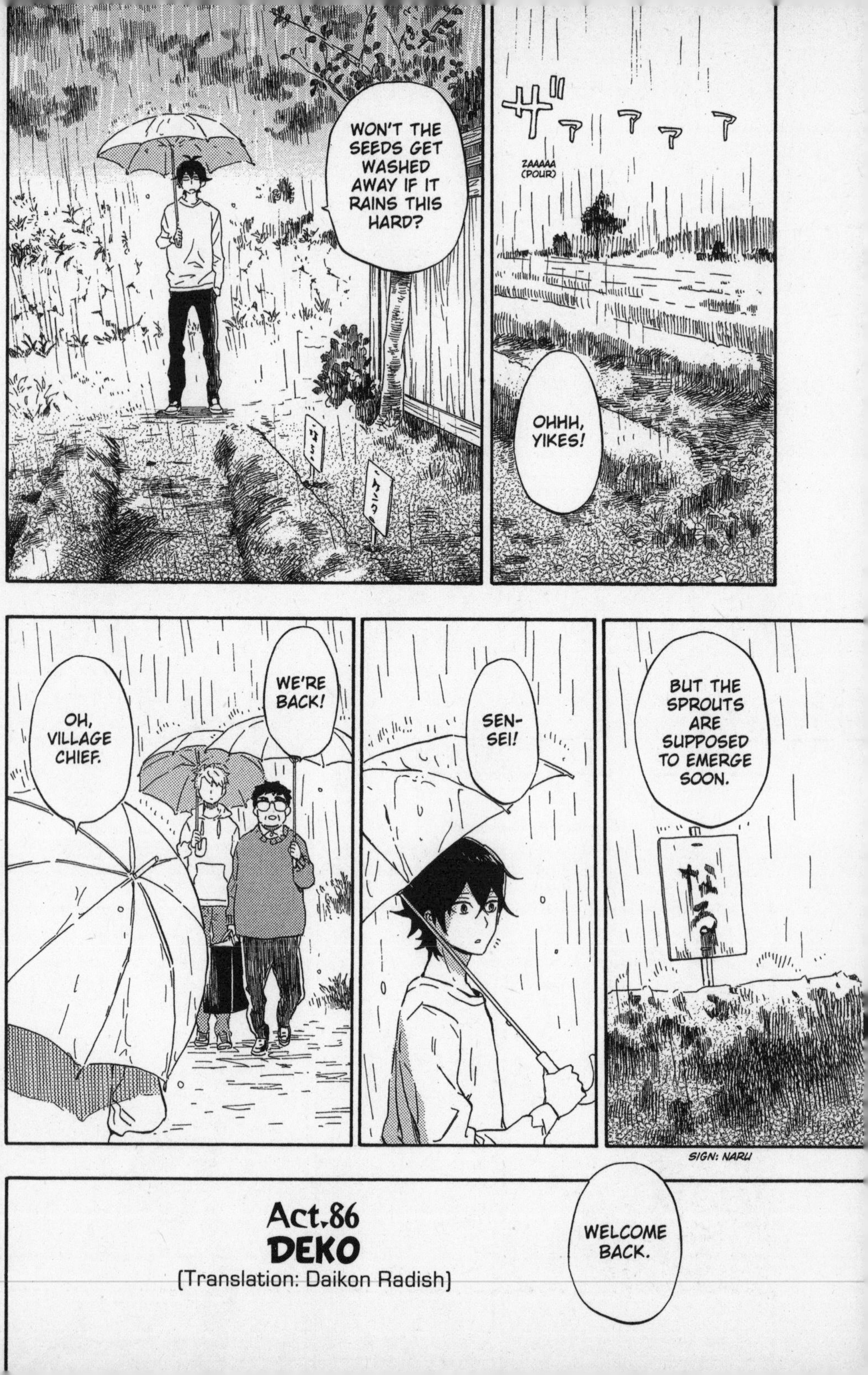
ザァァァァ
ZAAAAA (POUR)
OHHH, YIKES!
WON'T THE SEEDS GET WASHED AWAY IF IT RAINS THIS HARD?
BUT THE SPROUTS ARE SUPPOSED TO EMERGE SOON.
SIGN: NARU
SEN-SEI!
WE'RE BACK!
OH, VILLAGE CHIEF.
WELCOME BACK.
Act.86
DEKO
(Translation: Daikon Radish)

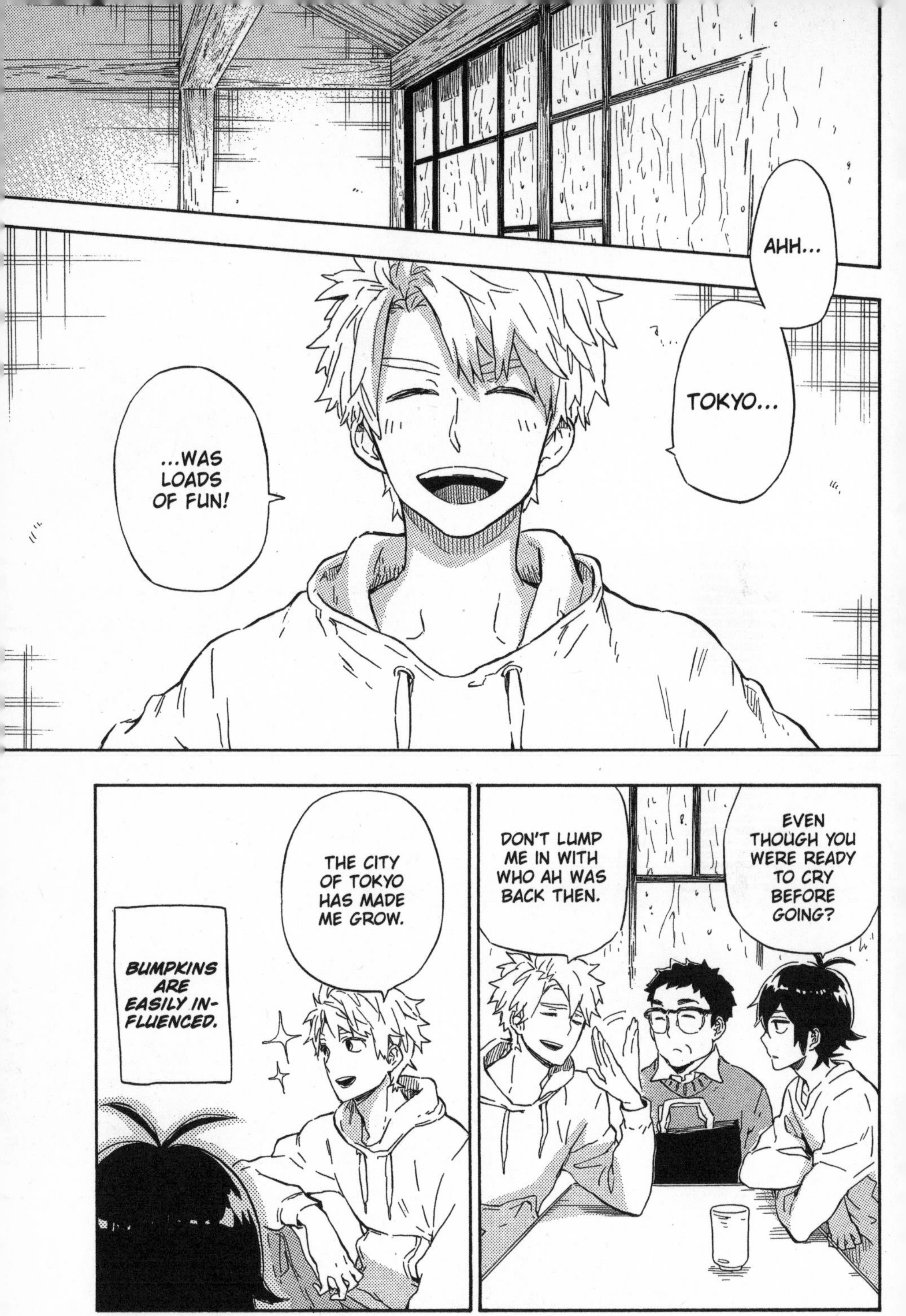
AHH...
TOKYO...
...WAS LOADS OF FUN!
EVEN THOUGH YOU WERE READY TO CRY BEFORE GOING?
DON'T LUMP ME IN WITH WHO AH WAS BACK THEN.
THE CITY OF TOKYO HAS MADE ME GROW.
BUMPKINS ARE EASILY IN-FLUENCED.

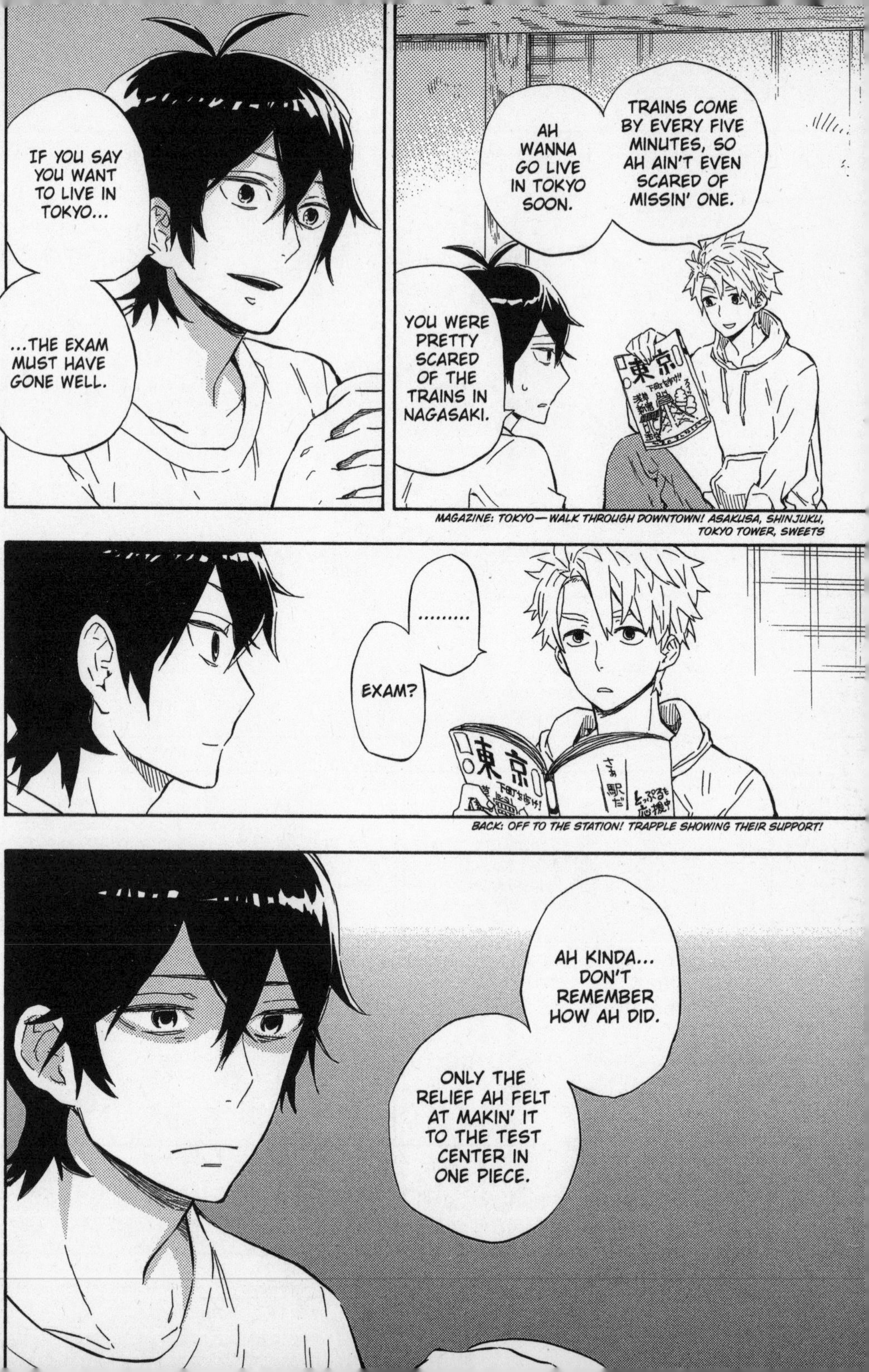
TRAINS COME BY EVERY FIVE MINUTES, SO AH AIN'T EVEN SCARED OF MISSIN' ONE.
AH WANNA GO LIVE IN TOKYO SOON.
YOU WERE PRETTY SCARED OF THE TRAINS IN NAGASAKI.
IF YOU SAY YOU WANT TO LIVE IN TOKYO...
...THE EXAM MUST HAVE GONE WELL.
MAGAZINE: TOKYO— WALK THROUGH DOWNTOWN! ASAKUSA, SHINJUKU, TOKYO TOWER, SWEETS
....
EXAM?
BACK: OFF TO THE STATION! TRAPPLE SHOWING THEIR SUPPORT!
AH KINDA... DON'T REMEMBER HOW AH DID.
ONLY THE RELIEF AH FELT AT MAKIN' IT TO THE TEST CENTER IN ONE PIECE.

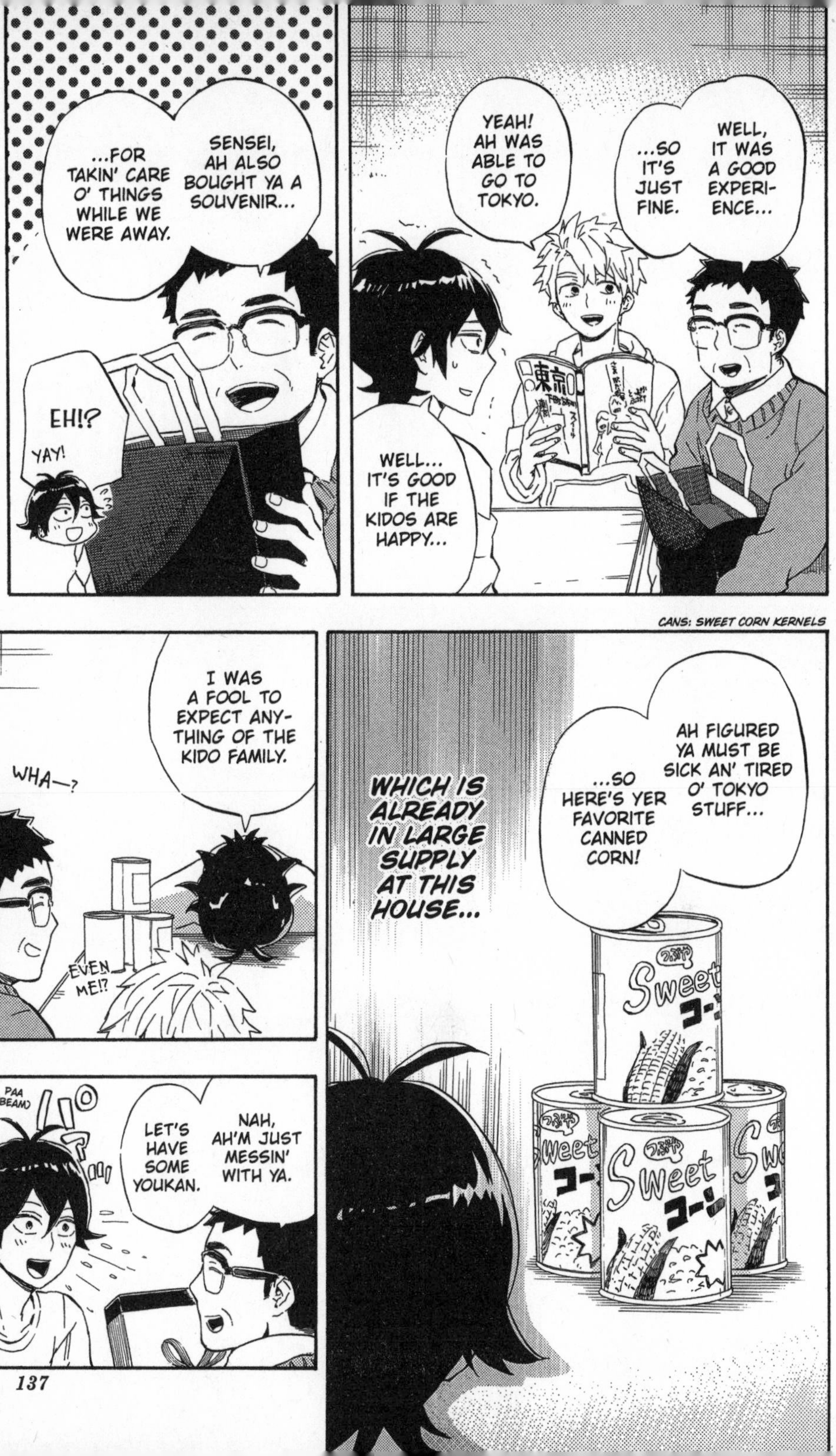
WELL, IT WAS A GOOD EXPERIENCE...
...SO IT'S JUST FINE.
YEAH! AH WAS ABLE TO GO TO TOKYO.
...
WELL... IT'S GOOD IF THE KIDOS ARE HAPPY...
SENSEI, AH ALSO BOUGHT YA A SOUVENIR...
...FOR TAKIN' CARE O' THINGS WHILE WE WERE AWAY.
EH!?
YAY!
CANS: SWEET CORN KERNELS
AH FIGURED YA MUST BE SICK AN' TIRED O' TOKYO STUFF...
...SO HERE'S YER FAVORITE CANNED CORN!
WHICH IS ALREADY IN LARGE SUPPLY AT THIS HOUSE...
Sweet
I WAS A FOOL TO EXPECT ANYTHING OF THE KIDO FAMILY.
WHA—?
EVEN ME!?
NAH, AH'M JUST MESSIN' WITH YA.
LET'S HAVE SOME YOUKAN.
PAA (BEAM)

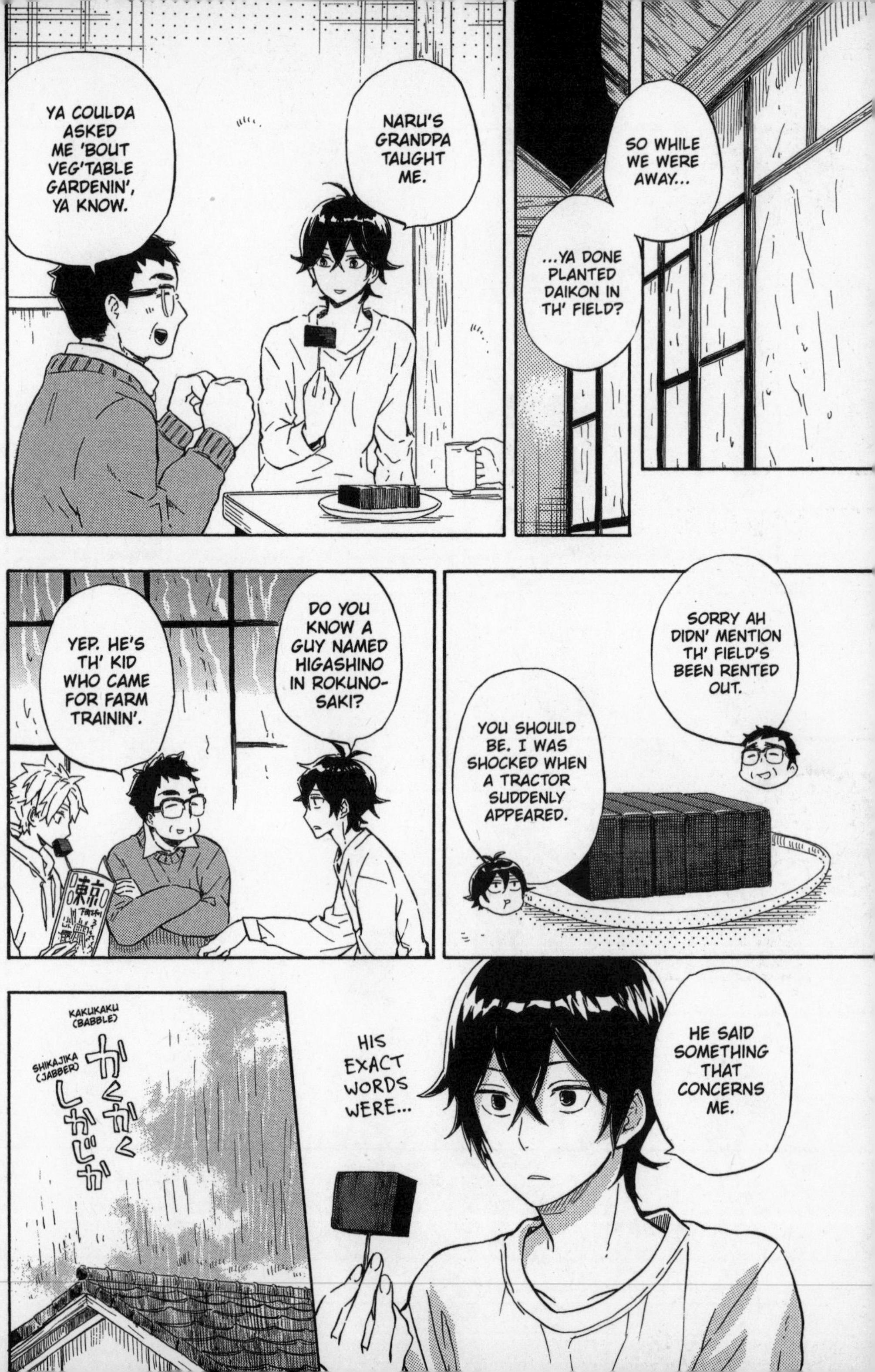
SO WHILE WE WERE AWAY...
...YA DONE PLANTED DAIKON IN TH' FIELD?
NARU'S GRANDPA TAUGHT ME.
YA COULDA ASKED ME 'BOUT VEG'TABLE GARDENIN', YA KNOW.
SORRY AH DIDN' MENTION TH' FIELD'S BEEN RENTED OUT.
YOU SHOULD BE. I WAS SHOCKED WHEN A TRACTOR SUDDENLY APPEARED.
DO YOU KNOW A GUY NAMED HIGASHINO IN ROKUNO-SAKI?
YEP. HE'S TH' KID WHO CAME FOR FARM TRAININ'.
東京
HE SAID SOMETHING THAT CONCERNS ME.
HIS EXACT WORDS WERE...
かくかく
KAKUKAKU (BABBLE)
しかじか
SHIKAJIKA (JABBER)

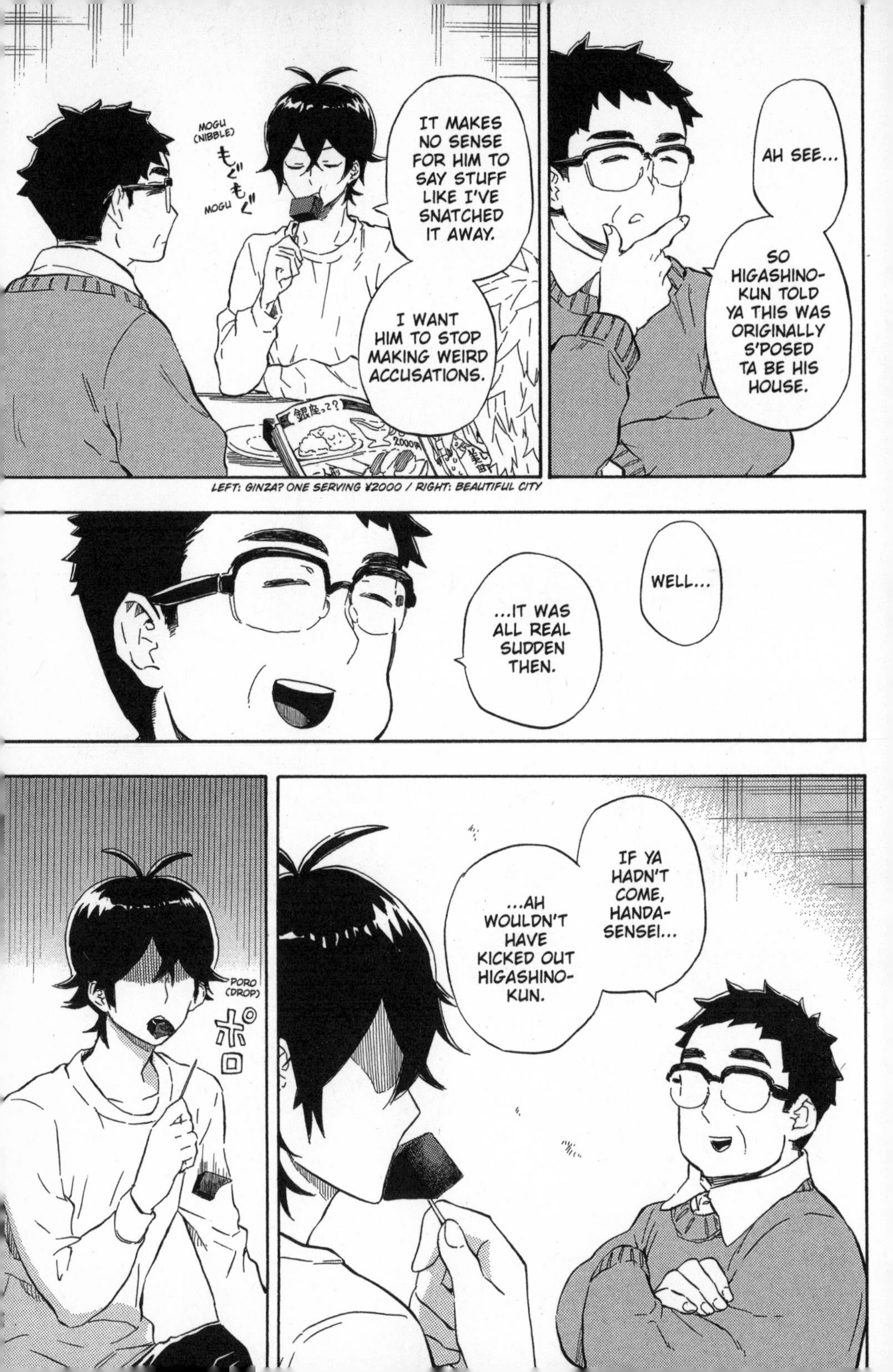
AH SEE...
SO HIGASHINO-KUN TOLD YA THIS WAS ORIGINALLY S'POSED TA BE HIS HOUSE.
IT MAKES NO SENSE FOR HIM TO SAY STUFF LIKE I'VE SNATCHED IT AWAY.
MOGU (NIBBLE) もぐもぐ MOGU
I WANT HIM TO STOP MAKING WEIRD ACCUSATIONS.
LEFT: GINZA? ONE SERVING ¥2000 / RIGHT: BEAUTIFUL CITY
WELL...
...IT WAS ALL REAL SUDDEN THEN.
IF YA HADN'T COME, HANDA-SENSEI...
...AH WOULDN'T HAVE KICKED OUT HIGASHINO-KUN.
PORO (DROP) ポロ

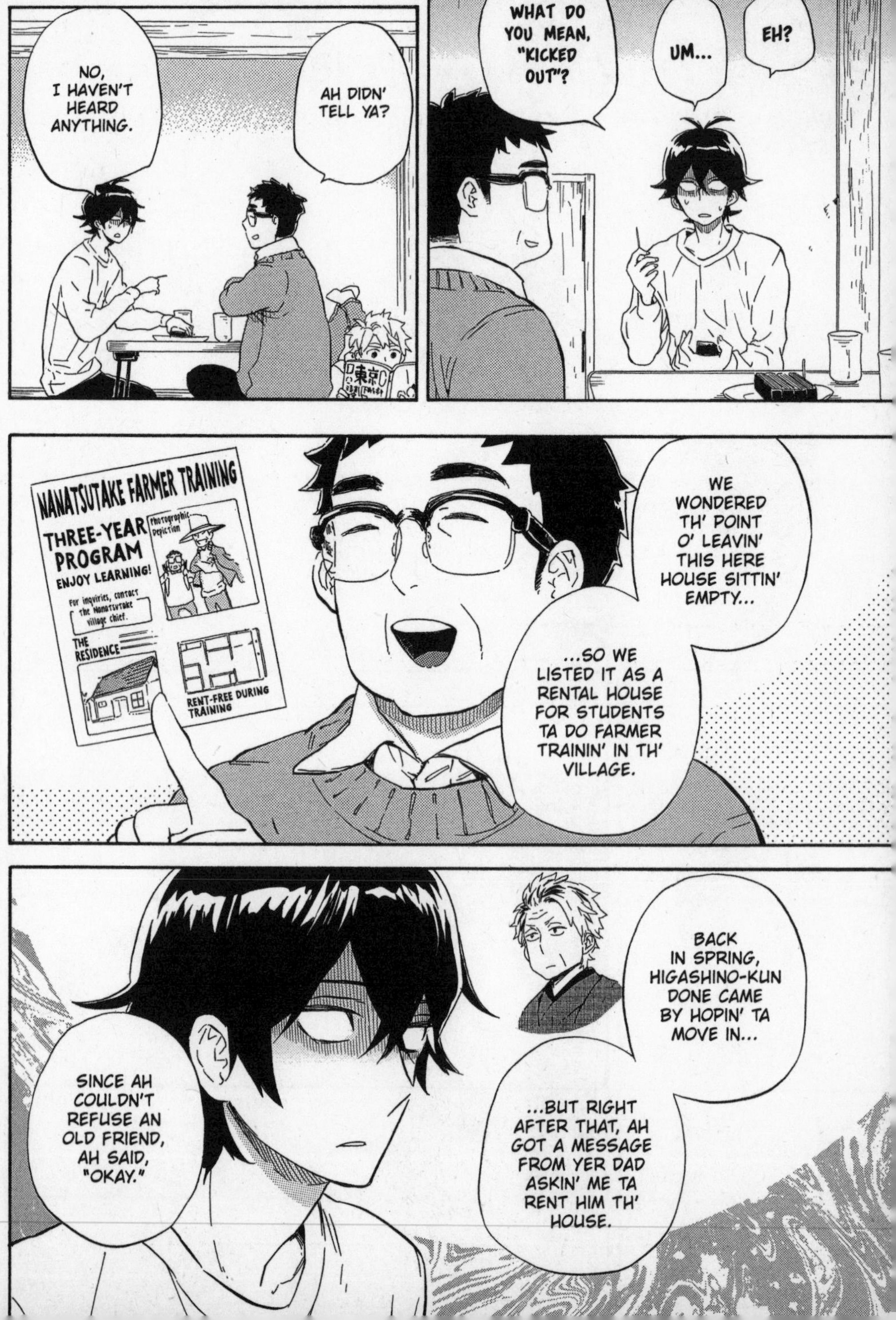
EH?
UM...
WHAT DO YOU MEAN, "KICKED OUT"?
AH DIDN' TELL YA?
NO, I HAVEN'T HEARD ANYTHING.
WE WONDERED TH' POINT O' LEAVIN' THIS HERE HOUSE SITTIN' EMPTY...
...SO WE LISTED IT AS A RENTAL HOUSE FOR STUDENTS TA DO FARMER TRAININ' IN TH' VILLAGE.
NANATSUTAKE FARMER TRAINING
THREE-YEAR PROGRAM
ENJOY LEARNING!
Photographic Depiction
For inquiries, contact the Nanatsutake village chief.
THE RESIDENCE
RENT-FREE DURING TRAINING
BACK IN SPRING, HIGASHINO-KUN DONE CAME BY HOPIN' TA MOVE IN...
...BUT RIGHT AFTER THAT, AH GOT A MESSAGE FROM YER DAD ASKIN' ME TA RENT HIM TH' HOUSE.
SINCE AH COULDN'T REFUSE AN OLD FRIEND, AH SAID, "OKAY."

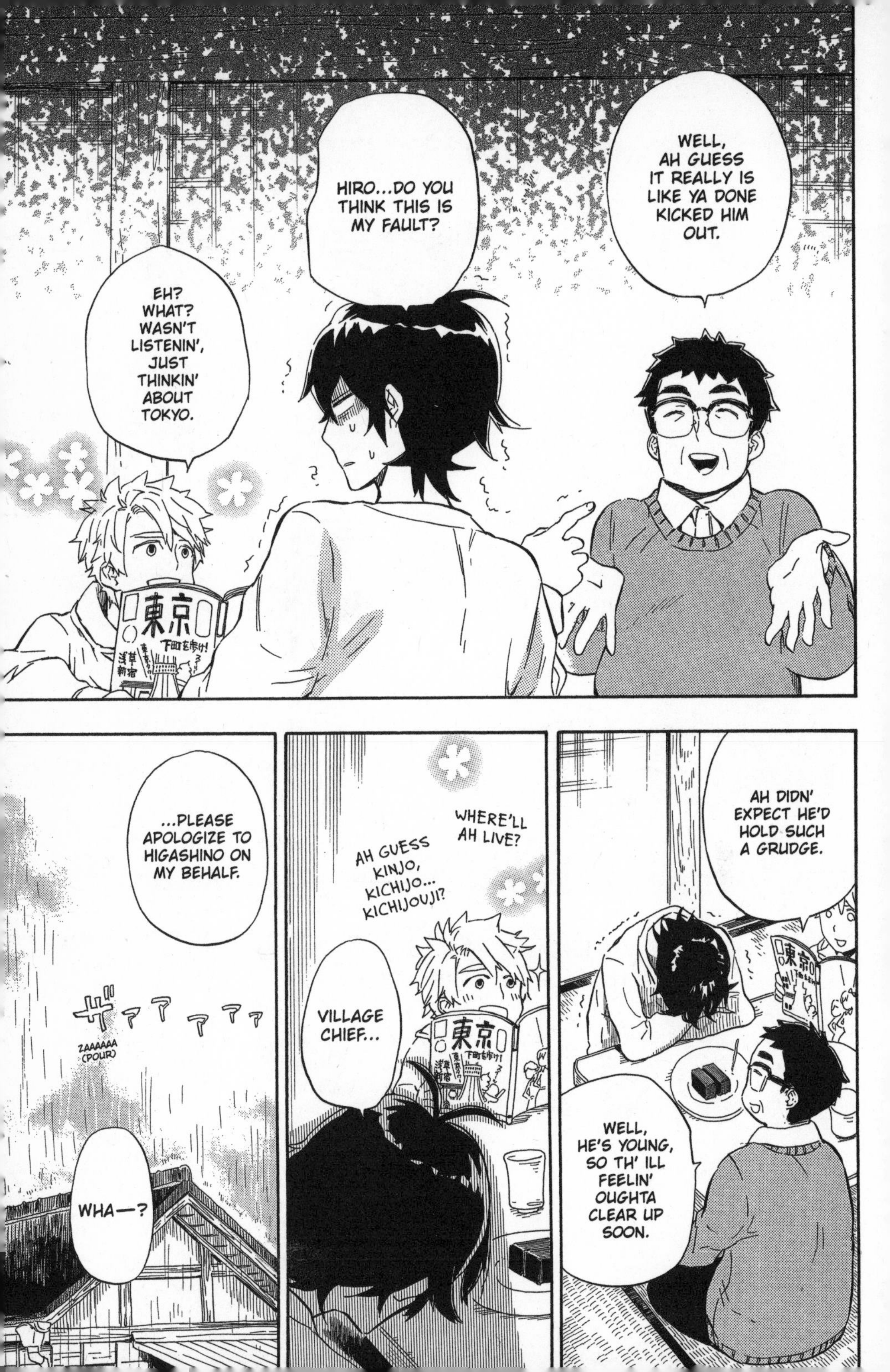
WELL, AH GUESS IT REALLY IS LIKE YA DONE KICKED HIM OUT.
HIRO...DO YOU THINK THIS IS MY FAULT?
EH? WHAT? WASN'T LISTENIN', JUST THINKIN' ABOUT TOKYO.
東京
AH DIDN' EXPECT HE'D HOLD SUCH A GRUDGE.
WELL, HE'S YOUNG, SO TH' ILL FEELIN' OUGHTA CLEAR UP SOON.
WHERE'LL AH LIVE?
AH GUESS KINJO, KICHIJO... KICHIJOUJI?
VILLAGE CHIEF...
東京
...PLEASE APOLOGIZE TO HIGASHINO ON MY BEHALF.
ザァアァアァ
ZAAAAAA (POUR)
WHA—?

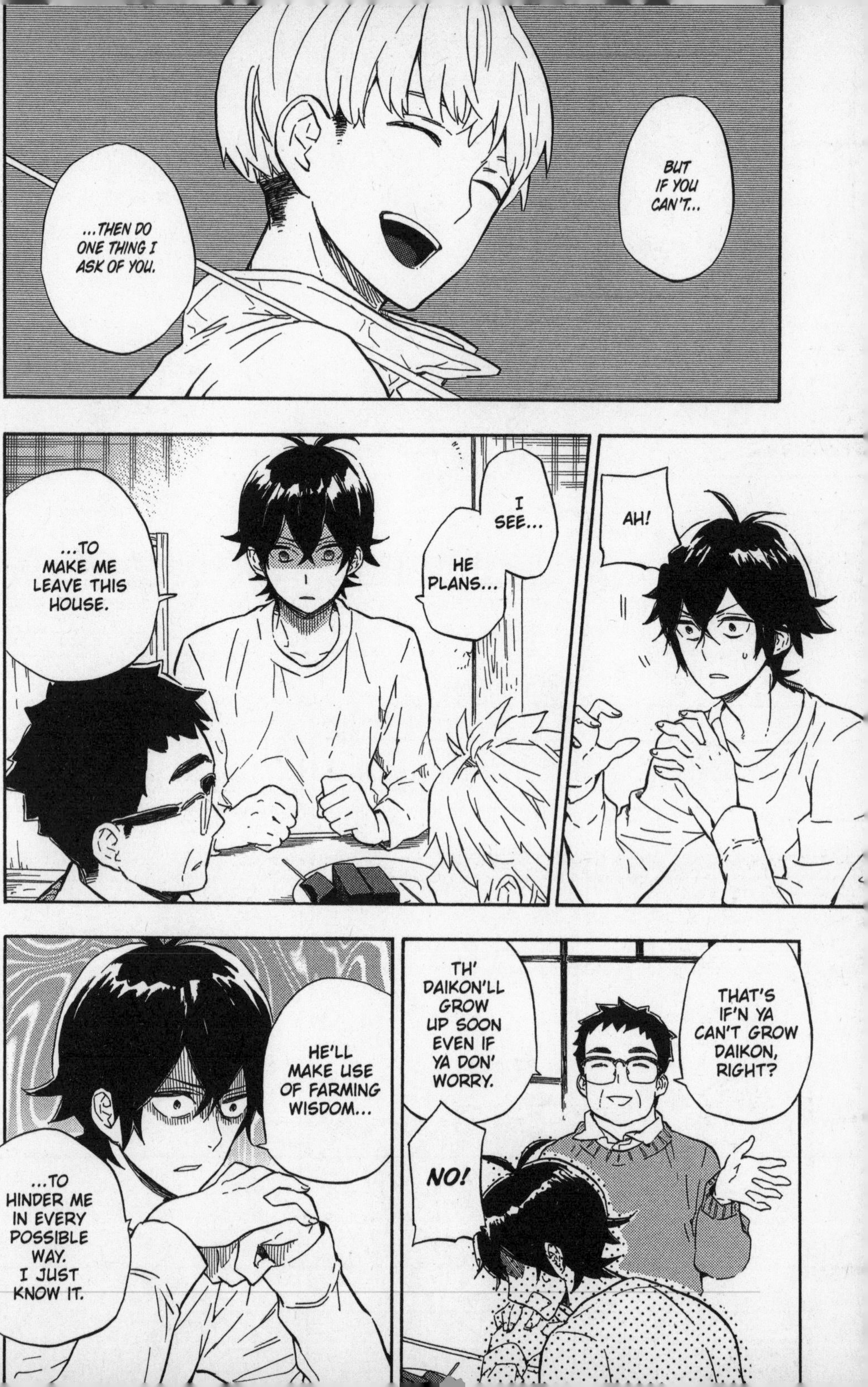
BUT IF YOU CAN'T...
...THEN DO ONE THING I ASK OF YOU.
AH!
I SEE...
HE PLANS...
...TO MAKE ME LEAVE THIS HOUSE.
THAT'S IF'N YA CAN'T GROW DAIKON, RIGHT?
TH' DAIKON'LL GROW UP SOON EVEN IF YA DON' WORRY.
NO!
HE'LL MAKE USE OF FARMING WISDOM...
...TO HINDER ME IN EVERY POSSIBLE WAY. I JUST KNOW IT.

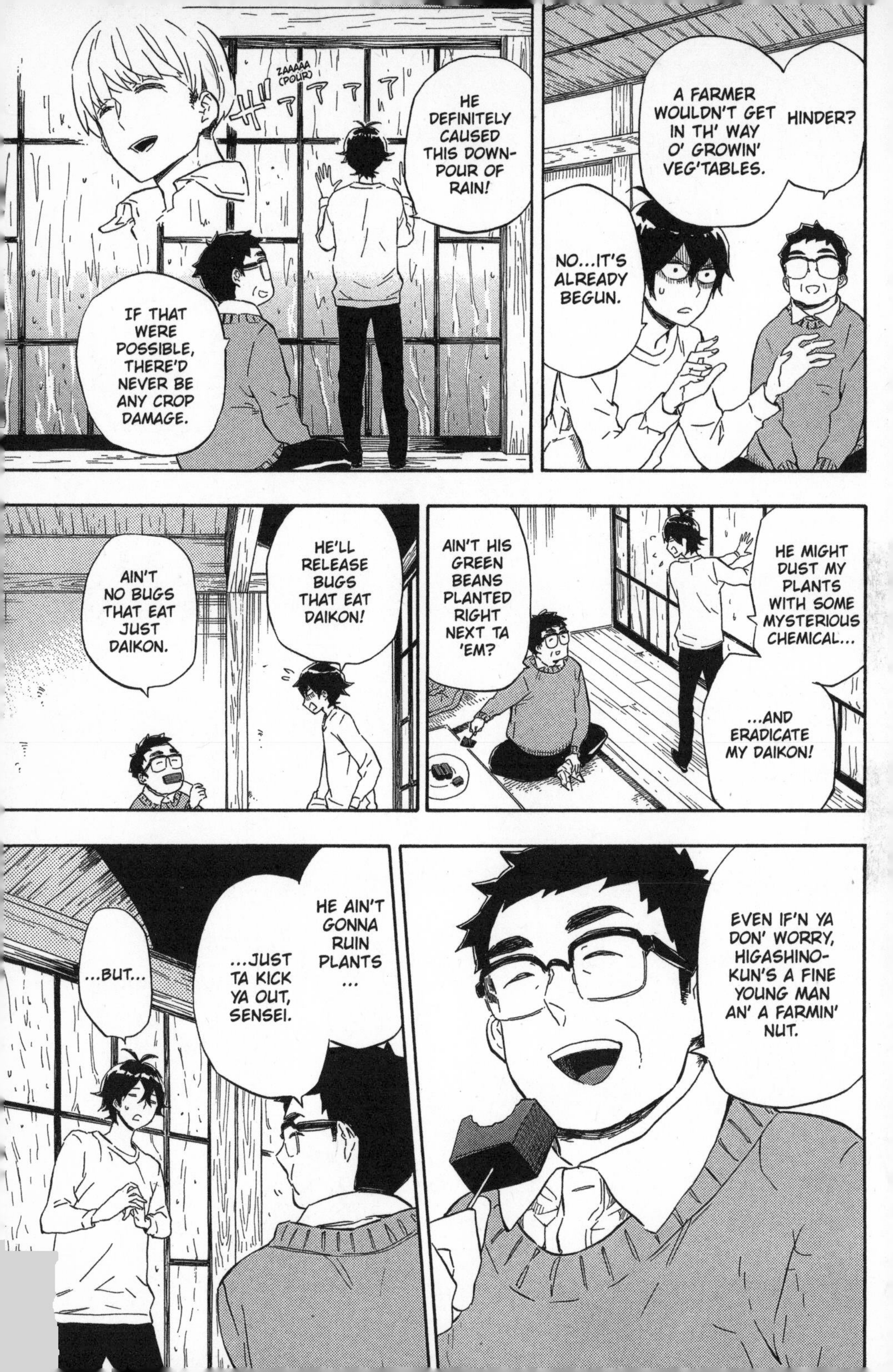
HINDER?
A FARMER WOULDN'T GET IN TH' WAY O' GROWIN' VEG'TABLES.
NO...IT'S ALREADY BEGUN.
ZAAAAA (POUR)
ザァァァァ
HE DEFINITELY CAUSED THIS DOWNPOUR OF RAIN!
IF THAT WERE POSSIBLE, THERE'D NEVER BE ANY CROP DAMAGE.
HE MIGHT DUST MY PLANTS WITH SOME MYSTERIOUS CHEMICAL...
...AND ERADICATE MY DAIKON!
AIN'T HIS GREEN BEANS PLANTED RIGHT NEXT TA 'EM?
HE'LL RELEASE BUGS THAT EAT DAIKON!
AIN'T NO BUGS THAT EAT JUST DAIKON.
EVEN IF'N YA DON' WORRY, HIGASHINO-KUN'S A FINE YOUNG MAN AN' A FARMIN' NUT.
HE AIN'T GONNA RUIN PLANTS...
...JUST TA KICK YA OUT, SENSEI.
...BUT...

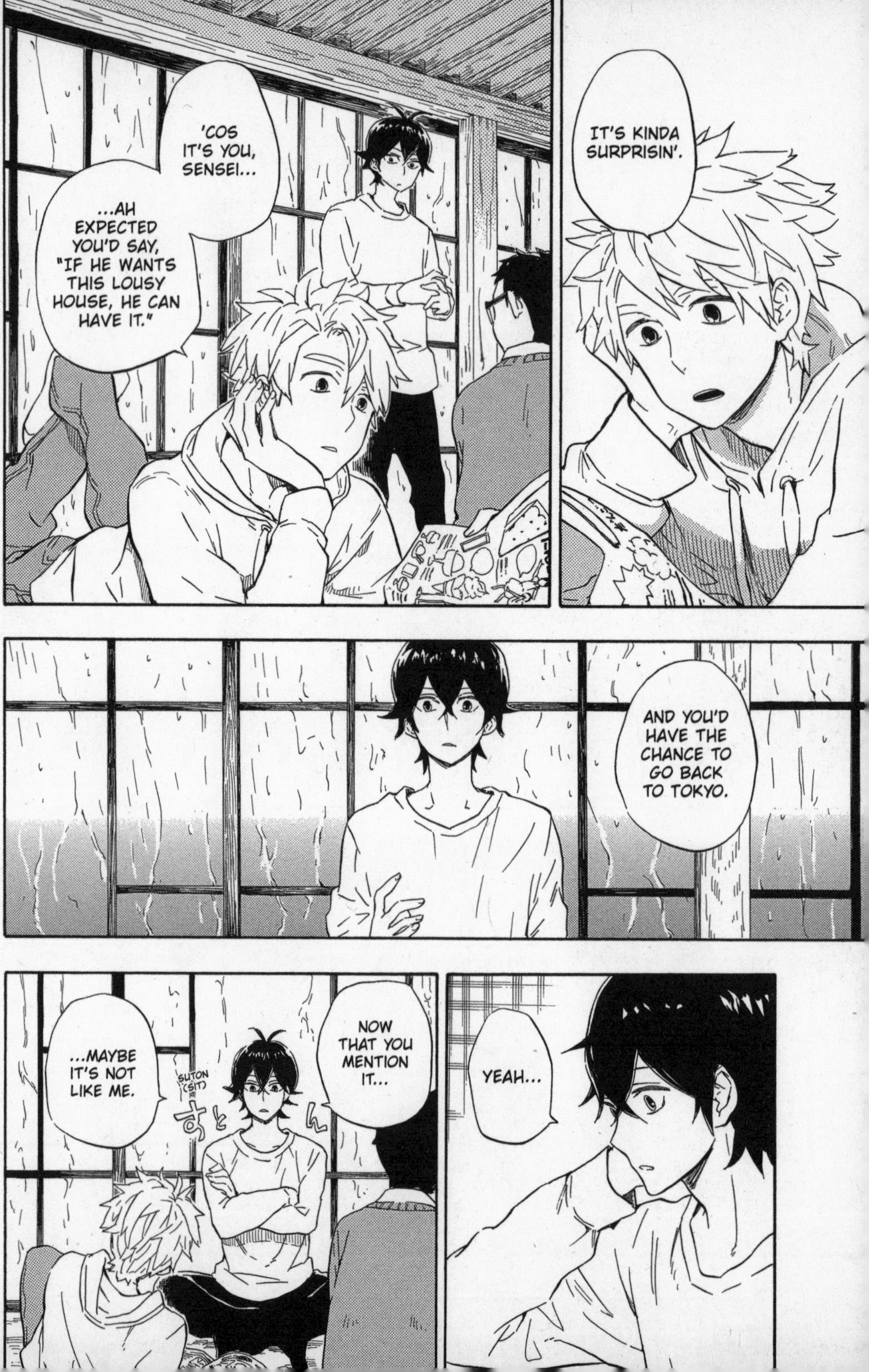
IT'S KINDA SURPRISIN'.
'COS IT'S YOU, SENSEI...
...AH EXPECTED YOU'D SAY, "IF HE WANTS THIS LOUSY HOUSE, HE CAN HAVE IT."
AND YOU'D HAVE THE CHANCE TO GO BACK TO TOKYO.
YEAH...
NOW THAT YOU MENTION IT...
SUTON (SIT)
すとん
...MAYBE IT'S NOT LIKE ME.

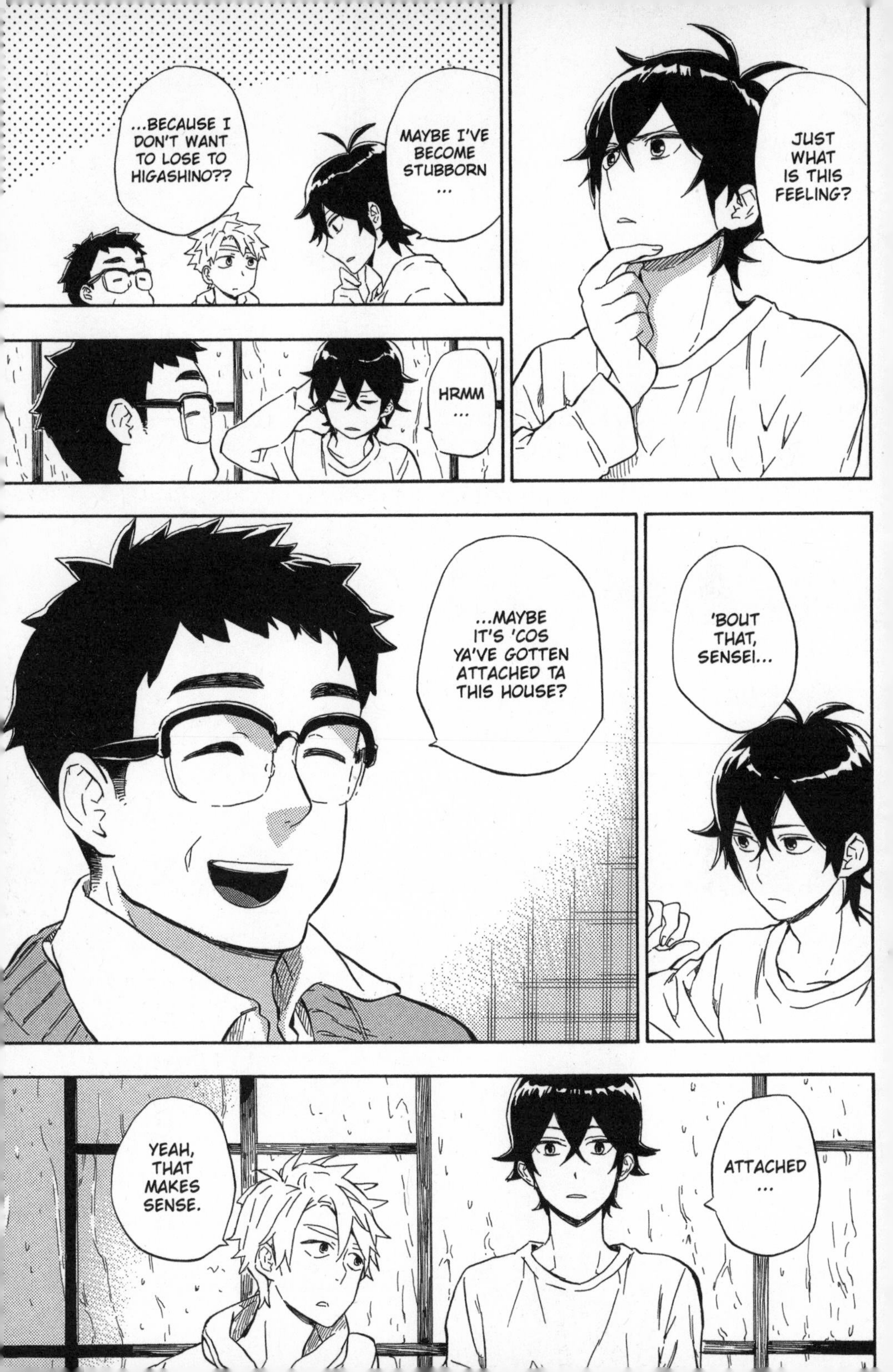
JUST WHAT IS THIS FEELING?
MAYBE I'VE BECOME STUBBORN ...
...BECAUSE I DON'T WANT TO LOSE TO HIGASHINO??
HRMM ...
'BOUT THAT, SENSEI...
...MAYBE IT'S 'COS YA'VE GOTTEN ATTACHED TA THIS HOUSE?
ATTACHED ...
YEAH, THAT MAKES SENSE.

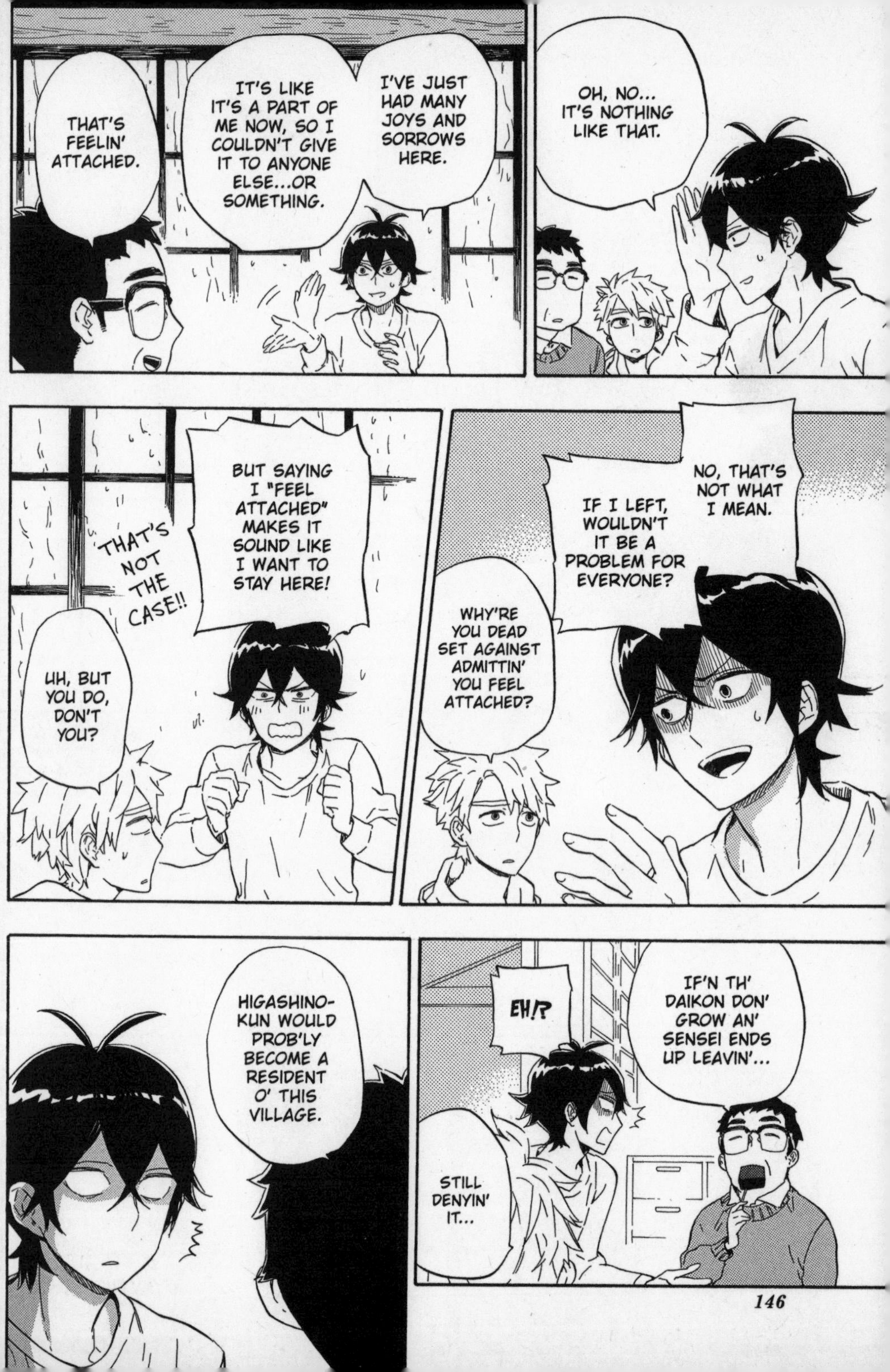
OH, NO... IT'S NOTHING LIKE THAT.
I'VE JUST HAD MANY JOYS AND SORROWS HERE.
IT'S LIKE IT'S A PART OF ME NOW, SO I COULDN'T GIVE IT TO ANYONE ELSE...OR SOMETHING.
THAT'S FEELIN' ATTACHED.
NO, THAT'S NOT WHAT I MEAN.
IF I LEFT, WOULDN'T IT BE A PROBLEM FOR EVERYONE?
WHY'RE YOU DEAD SET AGAINST ADMITTIN' YOU FEEL ATTACHED?
BUT SAYING I "FEEL ATTACHED" MAKES IT SOUND LIKE I WANT TO STAY HERE!
THAT'S NOT THE CASE!!
UH, BUT YOU DO, DON'T YOU?
IF'N TH' DAIKON DON' GROW AN' SENSEI ENDS UP LEAVIN'...
EH!?
STILL DENYIN' IT...
HIGASHINO-KUN WOULD PROB'LY BECOME A RESIDENT O' THIS VILLAGE.

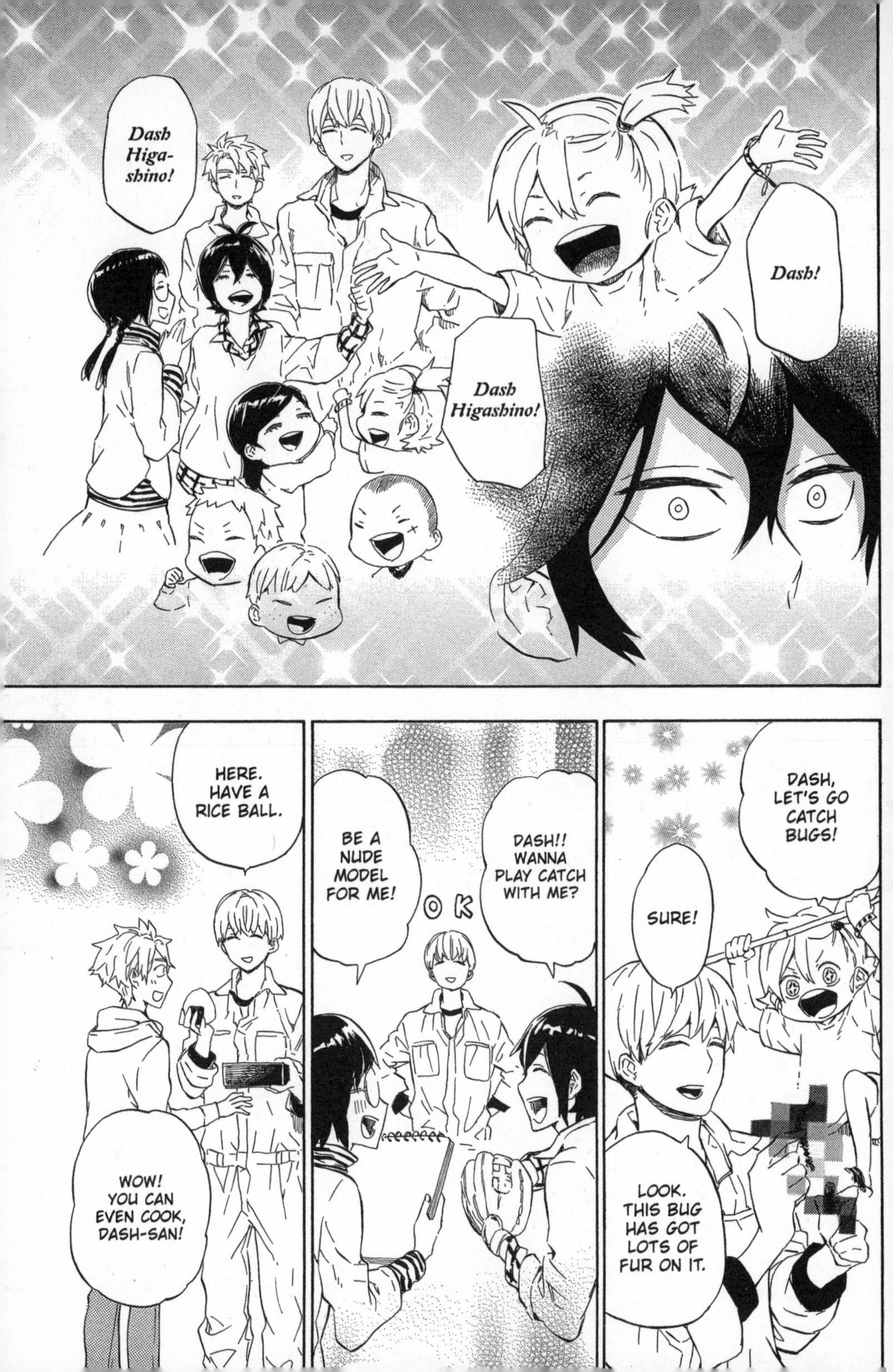
Dash!
Dash Higashino!
Dash Higa-shino!
DASH, LET'S GO CATCH BUGS!
SURE!
LOOK. THIS BUG HAS GOT LOTS OF FUR ON IT.
DASH!! WANNA PLAY CATCH WITH ME?
O K
BE A NUDE MODEL FOR ME!
HERE. HAVE A RICE BALL.
WOW! YOU CAN EVEN COOK, DASH-SAN!

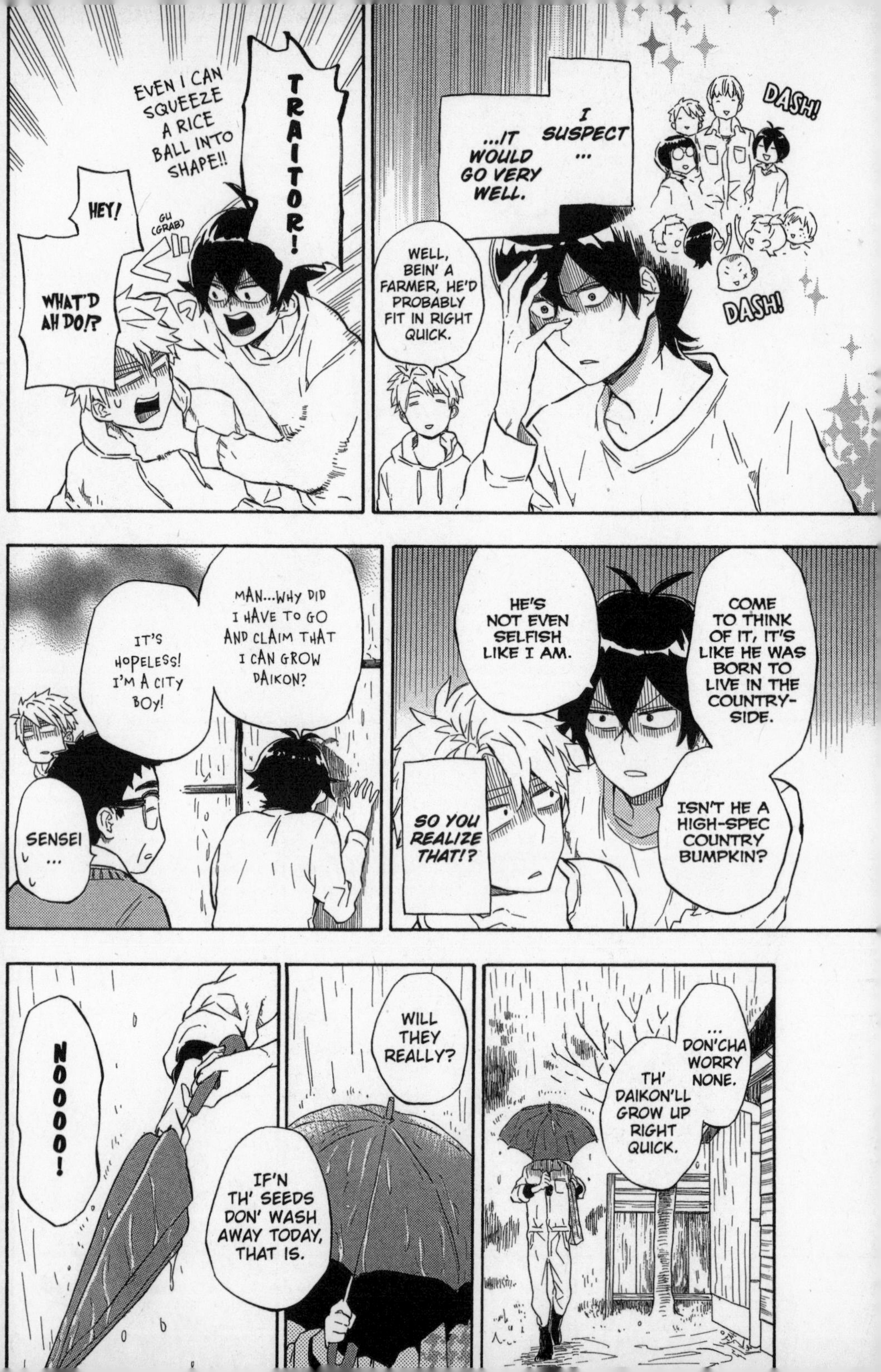
I SUSPECT...
...IT WOULD GO VERY WELL.
WELL, BEIN' A FARMER, HE'D PROBABLY FIT IN RIGHT QUICK.
DASH!
DASH!
TRAITOR!
EVEN I CAN SQUEEZE A RICE BALL INTO SHAPE!!
GU (GRAB)
HEY!
WHAT'D AH DO!?
COME TO THINK OF IT, IT'S LIKE HE WAS BORN TO LIVE IN THE COUNTRY-SIDE.
HE'S NOT EVEN SELFISH LIKE I AM.
ISN'T HE A HIGH-SPEC COUNTRY BUMPKIN?
SO YOU REALIZE THAT!?
MAN...WHY DID I HAVE TO GO AND CLAIM THAT I CAN GROW DAIKON?
IT'S HOPELESS! I'M A CITY BOY!
SENSEI...
...DON'CHA WORRY NONE.
TH' DAIKON'LL GROW UP RIGHT QUICK.
WILL THEY REALLY?
IF'N TH' SEEDS DON' WASH AWAY TODAY, THAT IS.
NOOOOO!

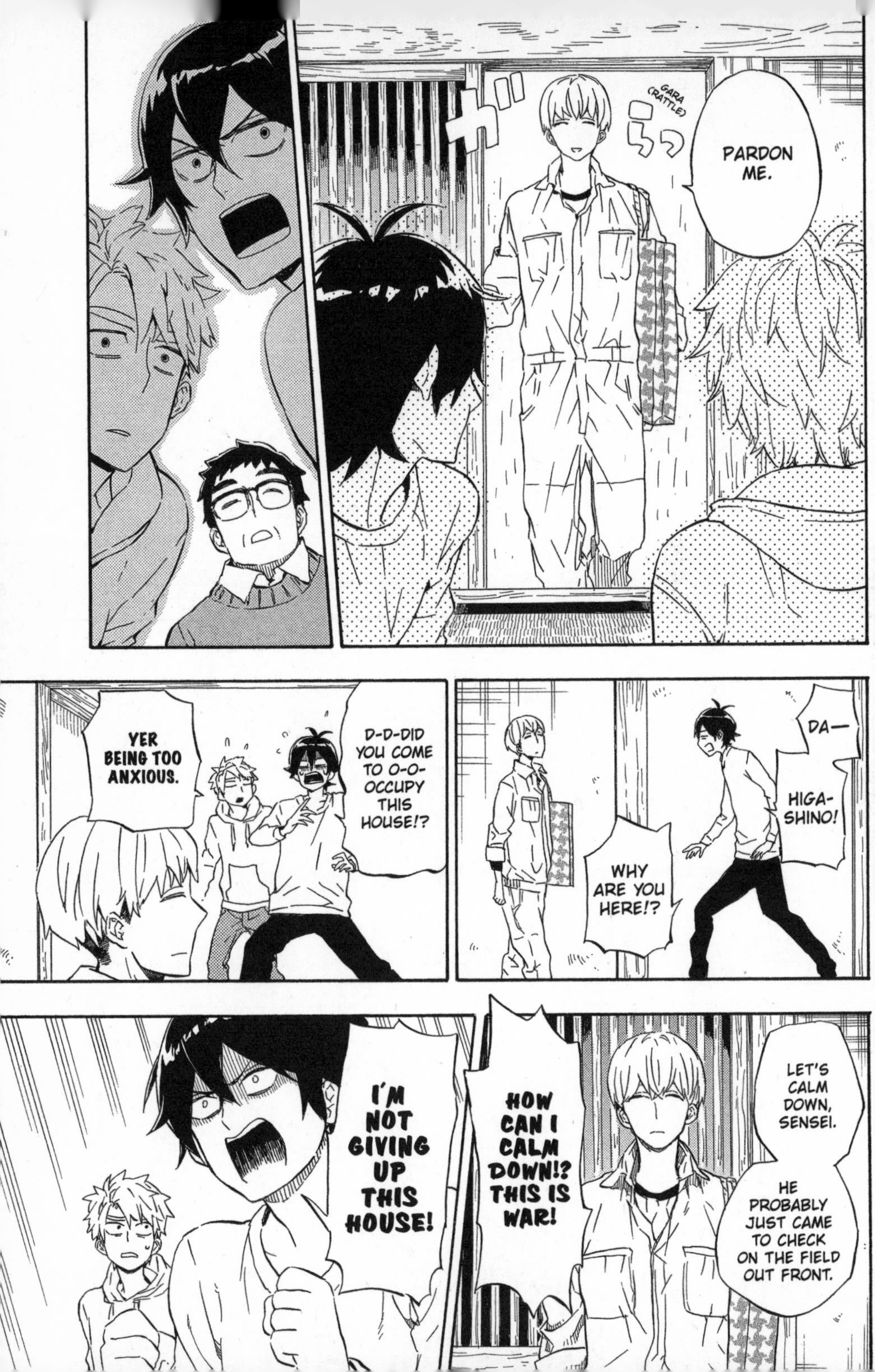
GARA (RATTLE)
PARDON ME.
DA—
HIGA-SHINO!
WHY ARE YOU HERE!?
D-D-DID YOU COME TO O-O-OCCUPY THIS HOUSE!?
YER BEING TOO ANXIOUS.
LET'S CALM DOWN, SENSEI.
HE PROBABLY JUST CAME TO CHECK ON THE FIELD OUT FRONT.
HOW CAN I CALM DOWN!? THIS IS WAR!
I'M NOT GIVING UP THIS HOUSE!

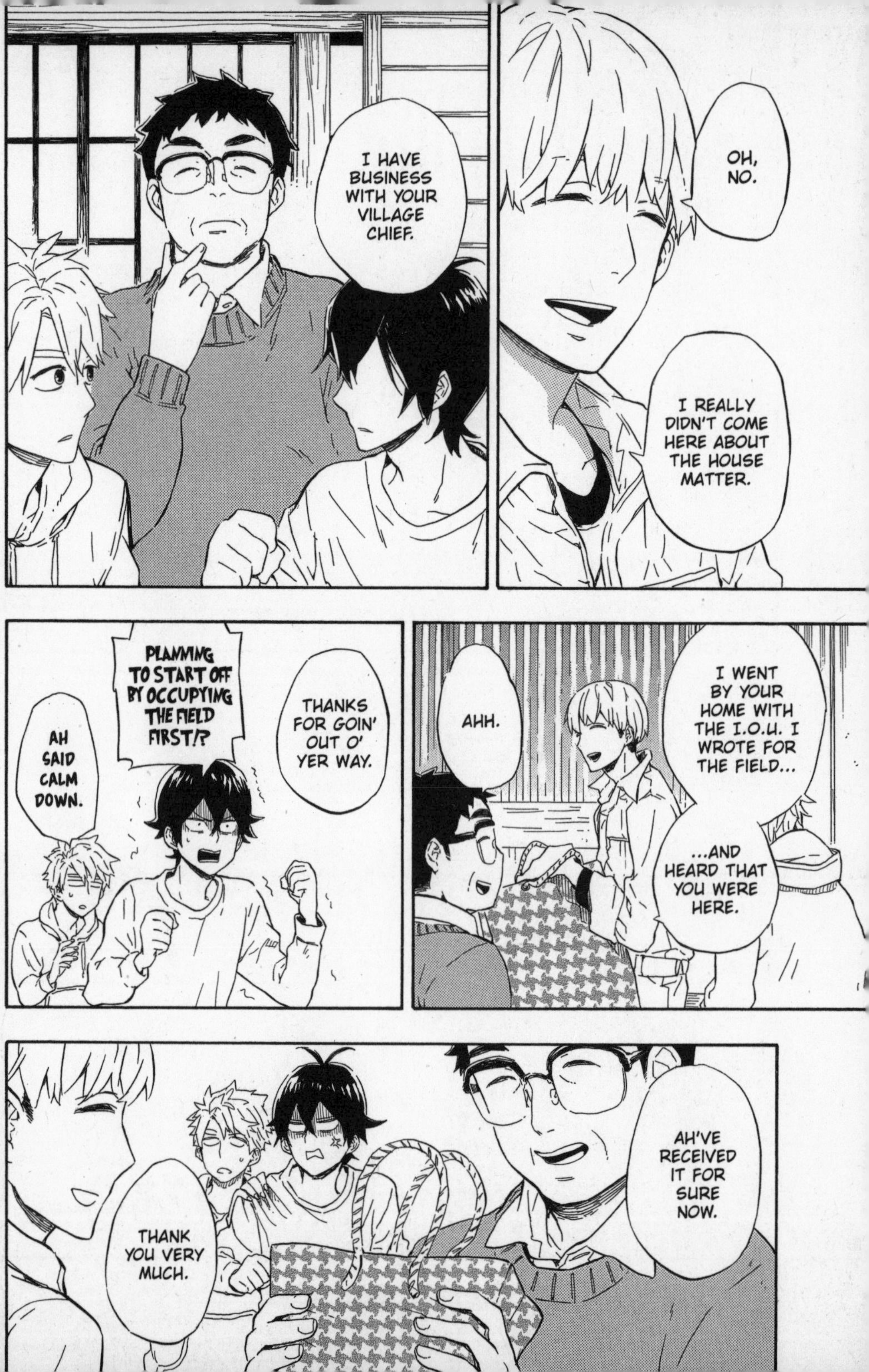
OH, NO.
I REALLY DIDN'T COME HERE ABOUT THE HOUSE MATTER.
I HAVE BUSINESS WITH YOUR VILLAGE CHIEF.
I WENT BY YOUR HOME WITH THE I.O.U. I WROTE FOR THE FIELD...
...AND HEARD THAT YOU WERE HERE.
AHH.
THANKS FOR GOIN' OUT O' YER WAY.
PLANNING TO START OFF BY OCCUPYING THE FIELD FIRST!?
AH SAID CALM DOWN.
AH'VE RECEIVED IT FOR SURE NOW.
THANK YOU VERY MUCH.

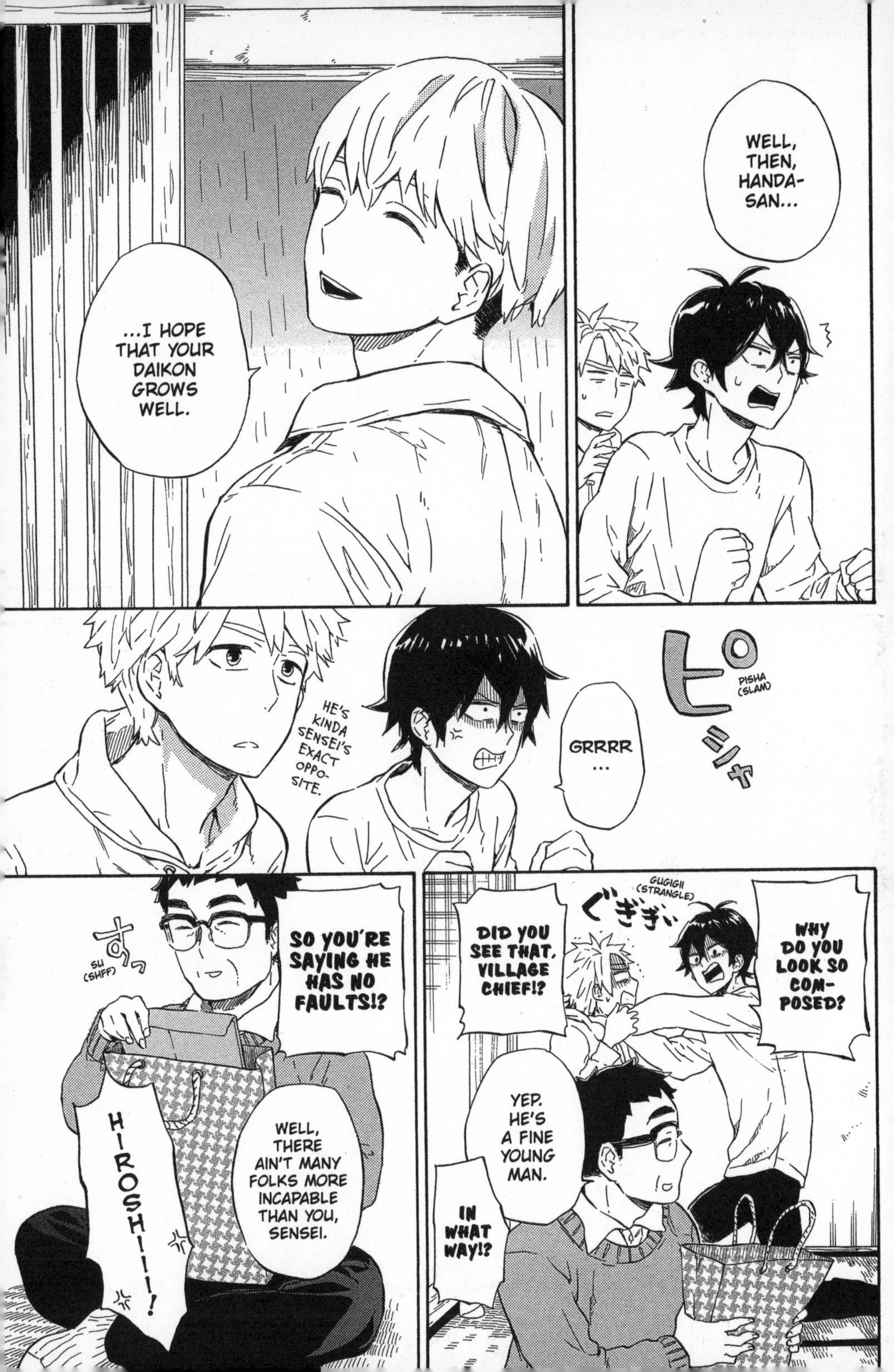

WELL, THEN, HANDA-SAN...
...I HOPE THAT YOUR DAIKON GROWS WELL.
ピシャ
PISHA (SLAM)
GRRRR...
HE'S KINDA SENSEI'S EXACT OPPO-SITE.
WHY DO YOU LOOK SO COM-POSED?
ぐぎぎぃ
GUGIGII (STRANGLE)
DID YOU SEE THAT, VILLAGE CHIEF!?
YEP. HE'S A FINE YOUNG MAN.
IN WHAT WAY!?
SO YOU'RE SAYING HE HAS NO FAULTS!?
すっ
SU (SHFF)
WELL, THERE AIN'T MANY FOLKS MORE INCAPABLE THAN YOU, SENSEI.
HIROSHI!!!!

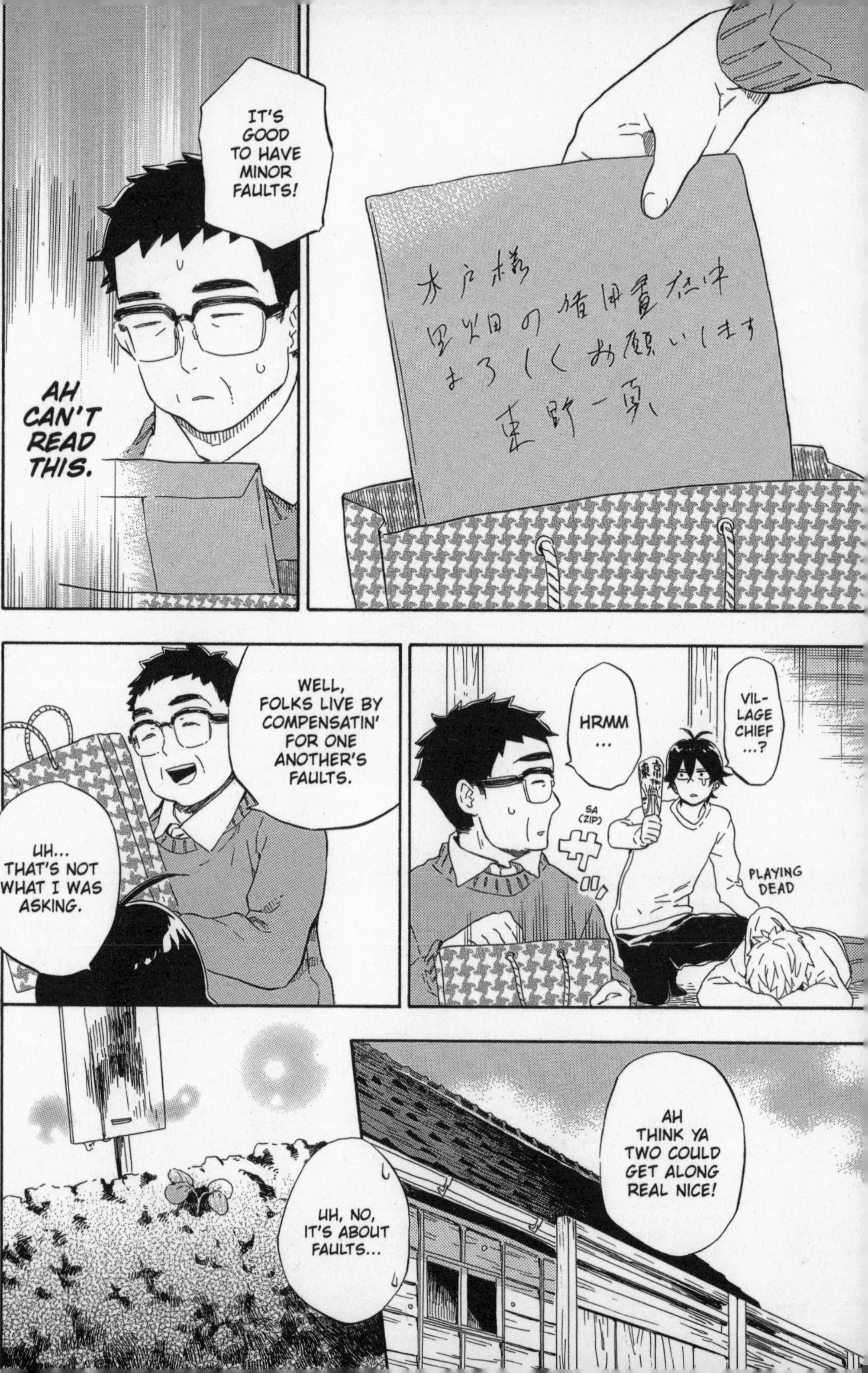
よろしくお願いします
IT'S GOOD TO HAVE MINOR FAULTS!
AH CAN'T READ THIS.
VIL-LAGE CHIEF ...?
HRMM ...
SA (ZIP)
PLAYING DEAD
WELL, FOLKS LIVE BY COMPENSATIN' FOR ONE ANOTHER'S FAULTS.
UH... THAT'S NOT WHAT I WAS ASKING.
AH THINK YA TWO COULD GET ALONG REAL NICE!
UH, NO, IT'S ABOUT FAULTS...

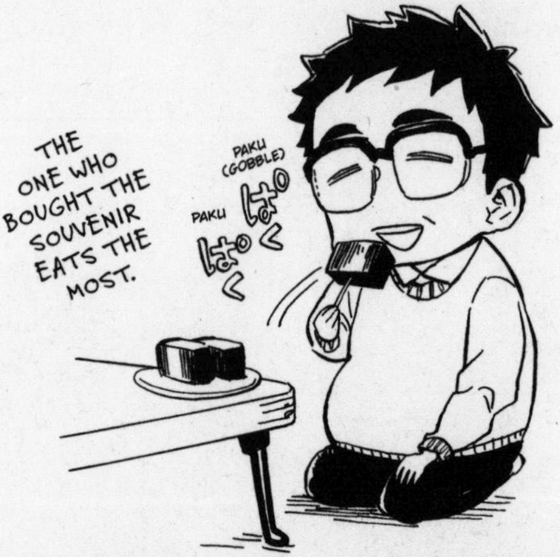
THE ONE WHO BOUGHT THE SOUVENIR EATS THE MOST.
PAKU (GOBBLE)
ぱく
PAKU
ぱく

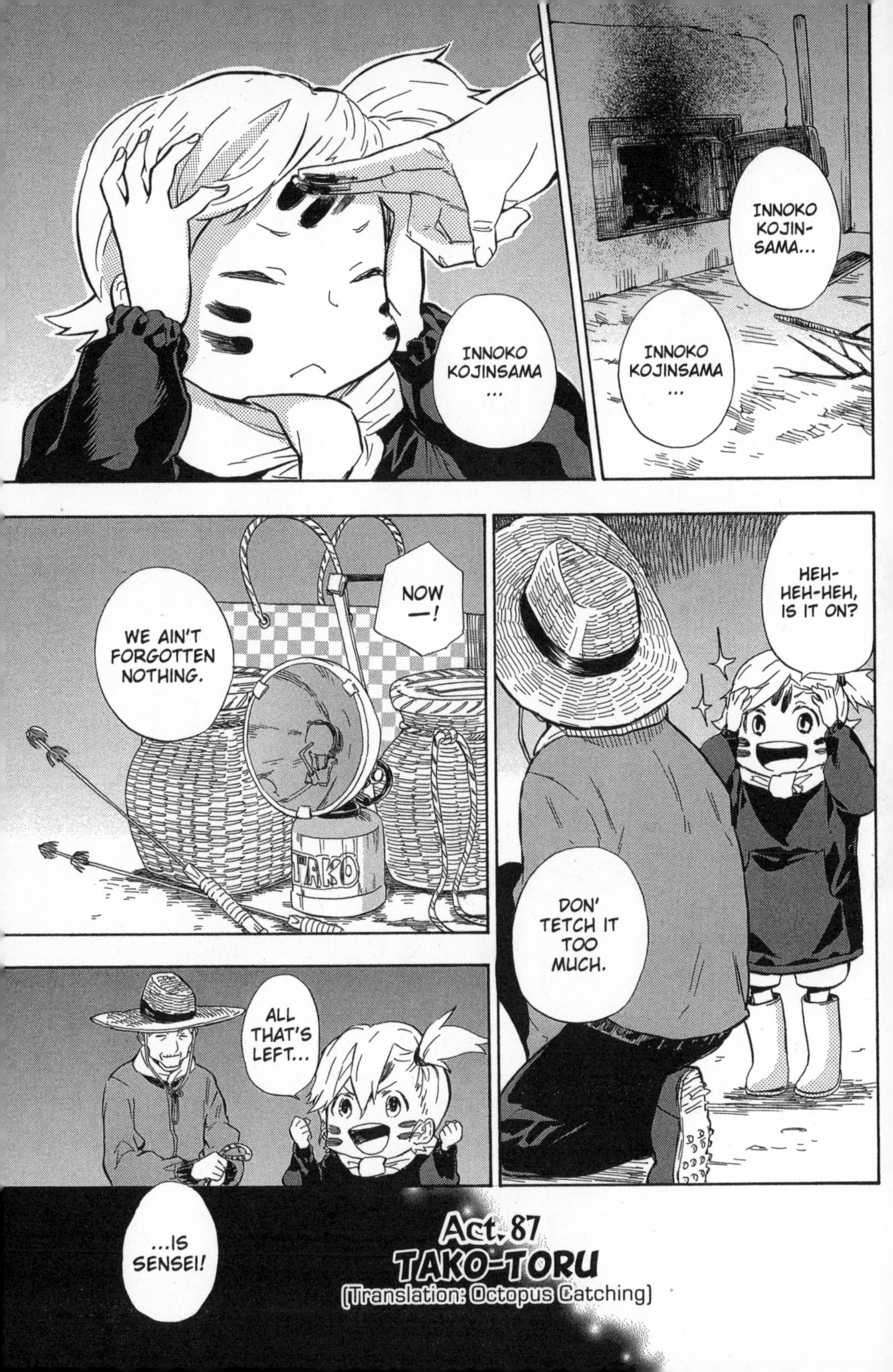
INNOKO KOJIN-SAMA...
INNOKO KOJINSAMA ...
INNOKO KOJINSAMA ...
HEH-HEH-HEH, IS IT ON?
DON' TETCH IT TOO MUCH.
NOW —!
WE AIN'T FORGOTTEN NOTHING.
ALL THAT'S LEFT...
...IS SENSEI!

Act. 87
TAKO-TORU
(Translation: Octopus Catching)

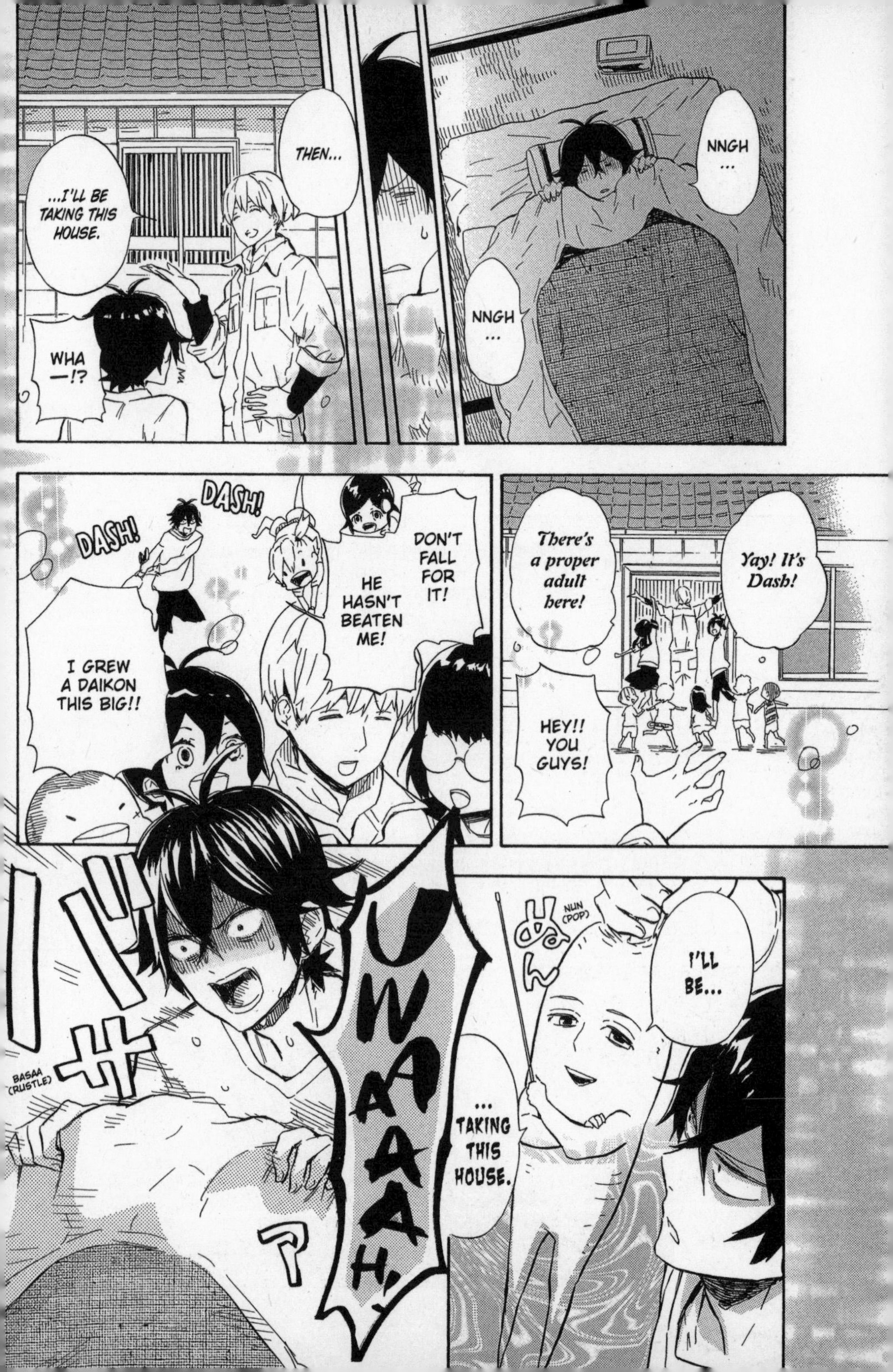
NNGH...
NNGH...
THEN...
...I'LL BE TAKING THIS HOUSE.
WHA—!?
Yay! It's Dash!
There's a proper adult here!
HEY!! YOU GUYS!
DON'T FALL FOR IT!
HE HASN'T BEATEN ME!
DASH!
DASH!
I GREW A DAIKON THIS BIG!!
ぬん
NUN (POP)
I'LL BE...
...TAKING THIS HOUSE.
UWAAAAH!
BASAA (RUSTLE)

BIKU (JOLT)
KON (KNOCK)
KON

SEN- SEI!

DO (DUN)
DO
DO

I FEEL SICK.

WHAT WAS WITH THAT DREAM??

BROKE OUT IN A SWEAT...

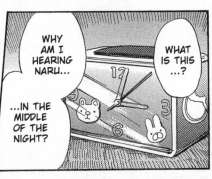

WHY AM I HEARING NARU...

...IN THE MIDDLE OF THE NIGHT?

WHAT IS THIS ...?

WE'RE GONNA CATCH OCTOPUS !!

BAAAN (TA-DAAAH)

HOW DID YOU GET IN HERE!?

BIKU

SHA (SWISH)

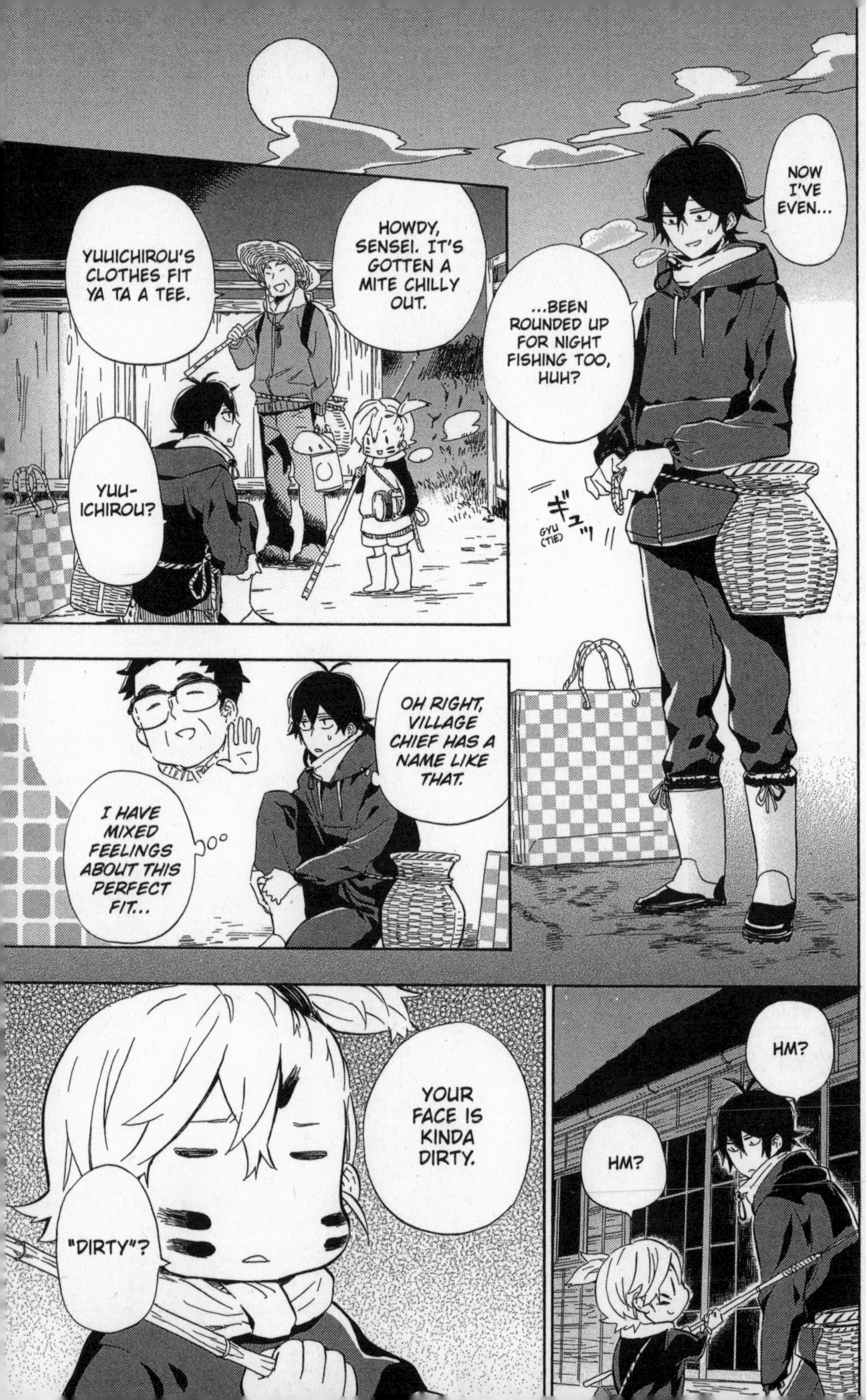
NOW I'VE EVEN...
...BEEN ROUNDED UP FOR NIGHT FISHING TOO, HUH?
ギュッ
GYU (TIE)
HOWDY, SENSEI. IT'S GOTTEN A MITE CHILLY OUT.
YUUICHIROU'S CLOTHES FIT YA TA A TEE.
YUU-ICHIROU?
OH RIGHT, VILLAGE CHIEF HAS A NAME LIKE THAT.
I HAVE MIXED FEELINGS ABOUT THIS PERFECT FIT...
HM?
HM?
YOUR FACE IS KINDA DIRTY.
"DIRTY"?

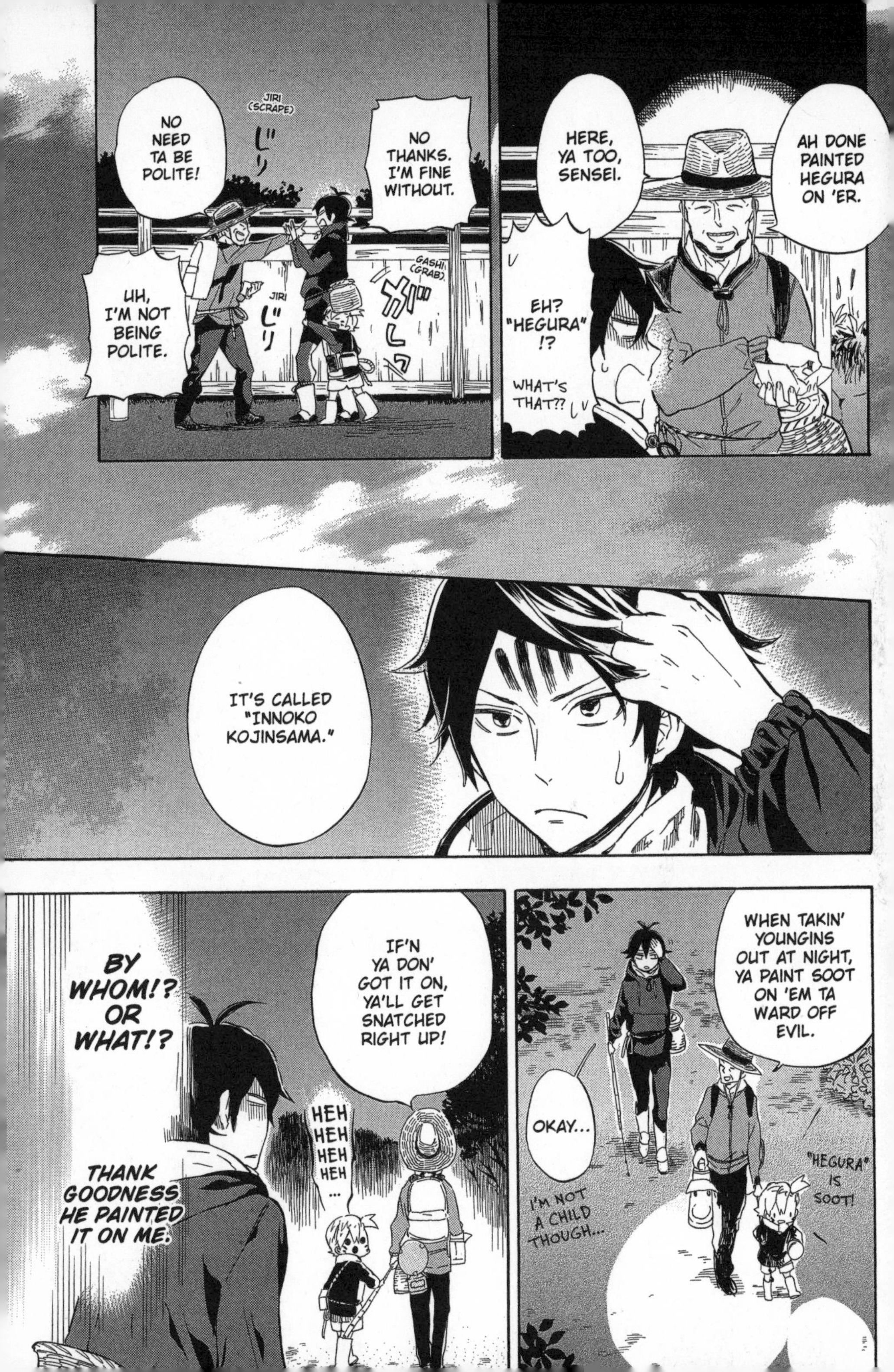
AH DONE PAINTED HEGURA ON 'ER.
HERE, YA TOO, SENSEI.
EH? "HEGURA" !?
WHAT'S THAT??
NO THANKS. I'M FINE WITHOUT.
JIRI (SCRAPE)
NO NEED TA BE POLITE!
GASHI (GRAB)
JIRI
UH, I'M NOT BEING POLITE.
IT'S CALLED "INNOKO KOJINSAMA."
WHEN TAKIN' YOUNGINS OUT AT NIGHT, YA PAINT SOOT ON 'EM TA WARD OFF EVIL.
OKAY...
"HEGURA" IS SOOT!
I'M NOT A CHILD THOUGH...
IF'N YA DON' GOT IT ON, YA'LL GET SNATCHED RIGHT UP!
HEH HEH HEH HEH ...
BY WHOM!? OR WHAT!?
THANK GOODNESS HE PAINTED IT ON ME.

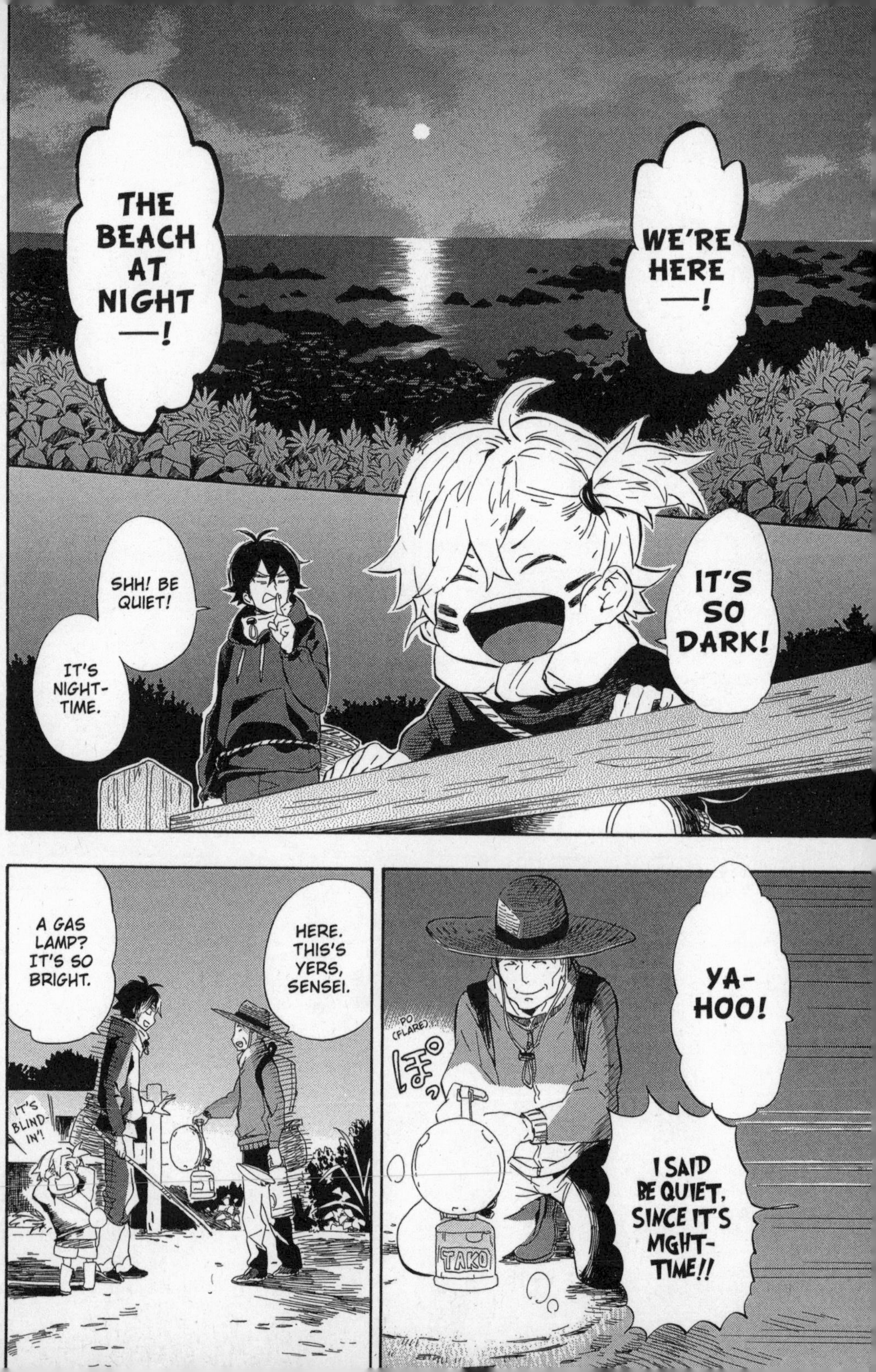

WE'RE HERE—!
THE BEACH AT NIGHT—!
IT'S SO DARK!
SHH! BE QUIET!
IT'S NIGHT-TIME.
YA-HOO!
PO (FLARE)
I SAID BE QUIET, SINCE IT'S NIGHT-TIME!!
TAKO
HERE. THIS'S YERS, SENSEI.
A GAS LAMP? IT'S SO BRIGHT.
IT'S BLIND-IN'!

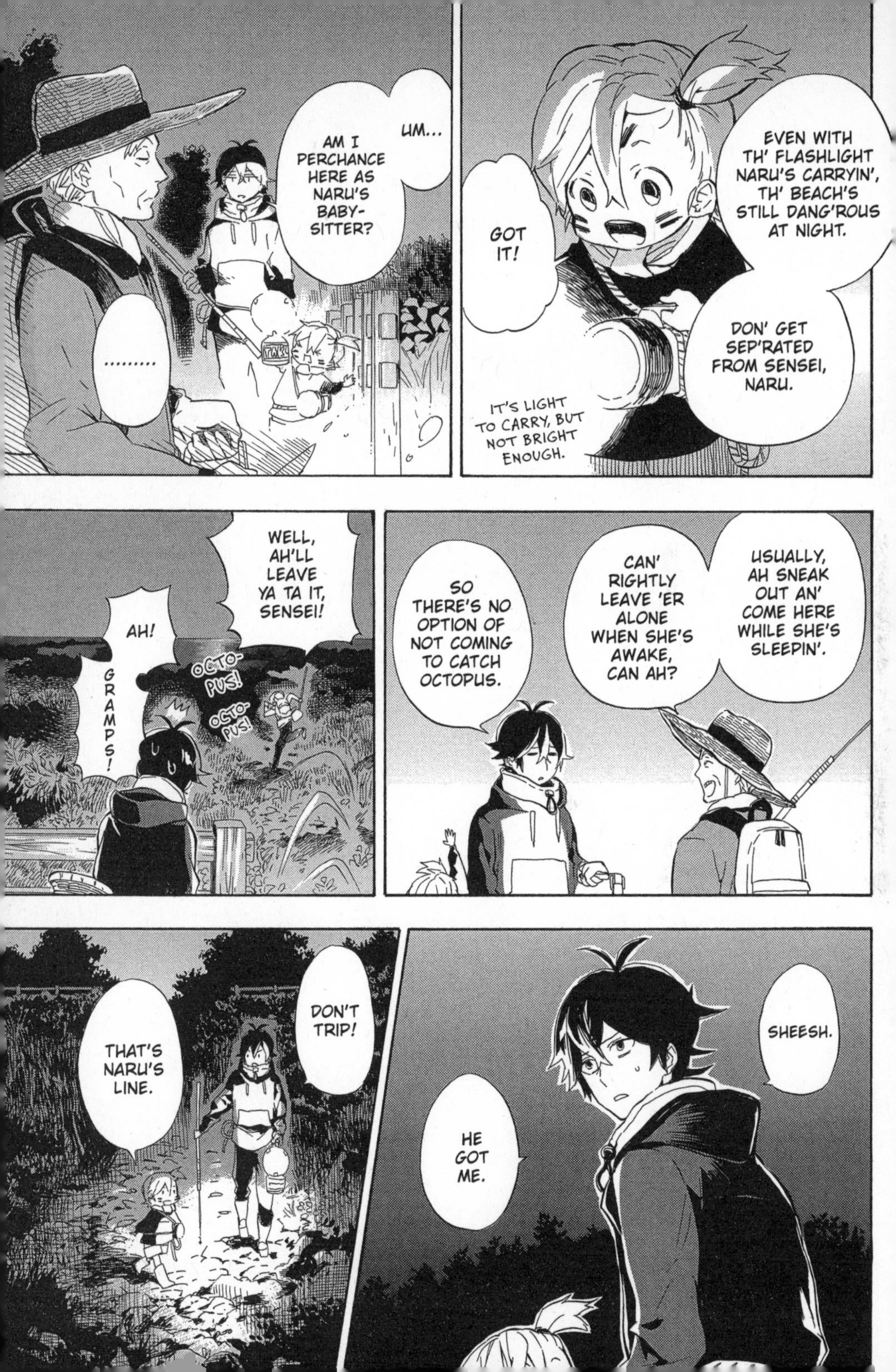
EVEN WITH TH' FLASHLIGHT NARU'S CARRYIN', TH' BEACH'S STILL DANG'ROUS AT NIGHT.
GOT IT!
DON' GET SEP'RATED FROM SENSEI, NARU.
IT'S LIGHT TO CARRY, BUT NOT BRIGHT ENOUGH.
UM...
AM I PERCHANCE HERE AS NARU'S BABY-SITTER?
....
TAKO
USUALLY, AH SNEAK OUT AN' COME HERE WHILE SHE'S SLEEPIN'.
CAN' RIGHTLY LEAVE 'ER ALONE WHEN SHE'S AWAKE, CAN AH?
SO THERE'S NO OPTION OF NOT COMING TO CATCH OCTOPUS.
WELL, AH'LL LEAVE YA TA IT, SENSEI!
AH!
GRAMPS!
OCTO-PUS!
OCTO-PUS!
SHEESH.
HE GOT ME.
DON'T TRIP!
THAT'S NARU'S LINE.

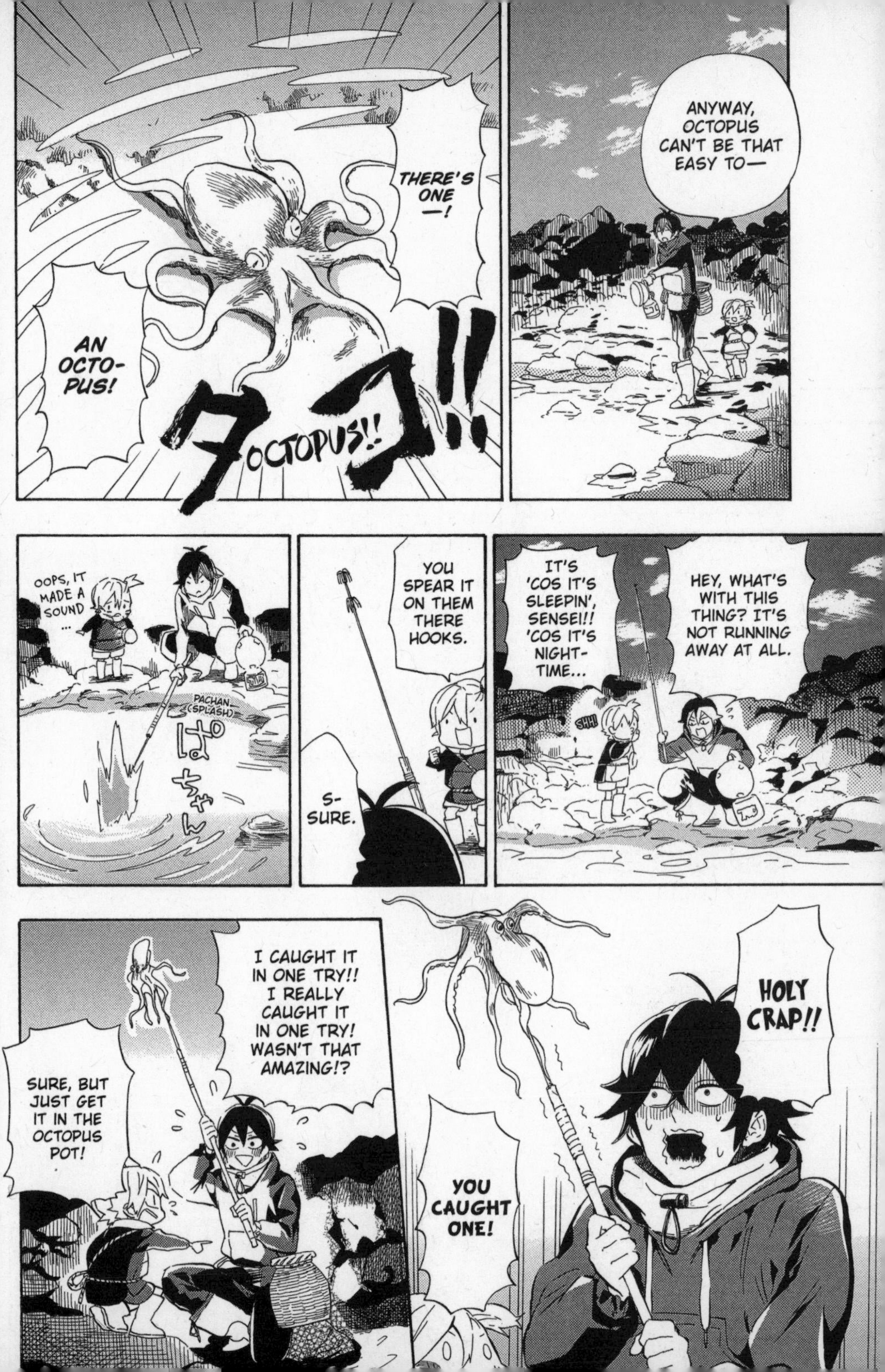
ANYWAY, OCTOPUS CAN'T BE THAT EASY TO—
THERE'S ONE—!
AN OCTO-PUS!
タコ!!
OCTOPUS!!
HEY, WHAT'S WITH THIS THING? IT'S NOT RUNNING AWAY AT ALL.
IT'S 'COS IT'S SLEEPIN', SENSEI!! 'COS IT'S NIGHT-TIME...
SHH!
YOU SPEAR IT ON THEM THERE HOOKS.
S-SURE.
OOPS, IT MADE A SOUND ...
PACHAN (SPLASH)
ぱちゃん
HOLY CRAP!!
YOU CAUGHT ONE!
I CAUGHT IT IN ONE TRY!! I REALLY CAUGHT IT IN ONE TRY! WASN'T THAT AMAZING!?
SURE, BUT JUST GET IT IN THE OCTOPUS POT!

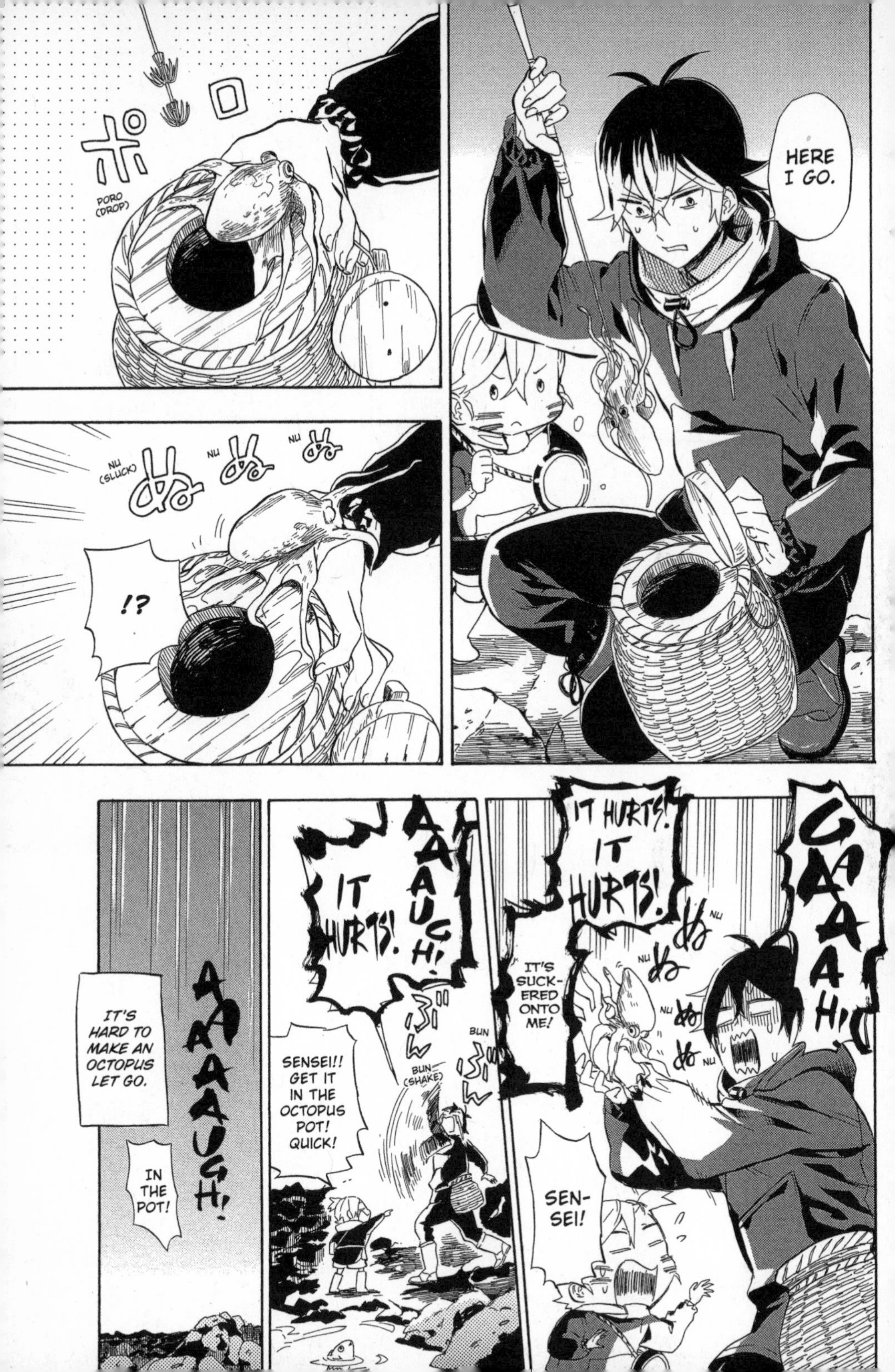
HERE I GO.
ポロ
PORO (DROP)
ぬぬぬ
NU (SLUCK)
NU
NU
!?
GAAAAAH!
IT HURTS! IT HURTS!
IT'S SUCKERED ONTO ME!
ぬ NU
ぬ NU
ぬ NU
ぬ NU
SEN-SEI!
AAAAUGH!
IT HURTS!
ぶん
BUN (SHAKE)
ぶん
BUN
SENSEI!! GET IT IN THE OCTOPUS POT! QUICK!
IT'S HARD TO MAKE AN OCTOPUS LET GO.
AAAAAUGH!
IN THE POT!

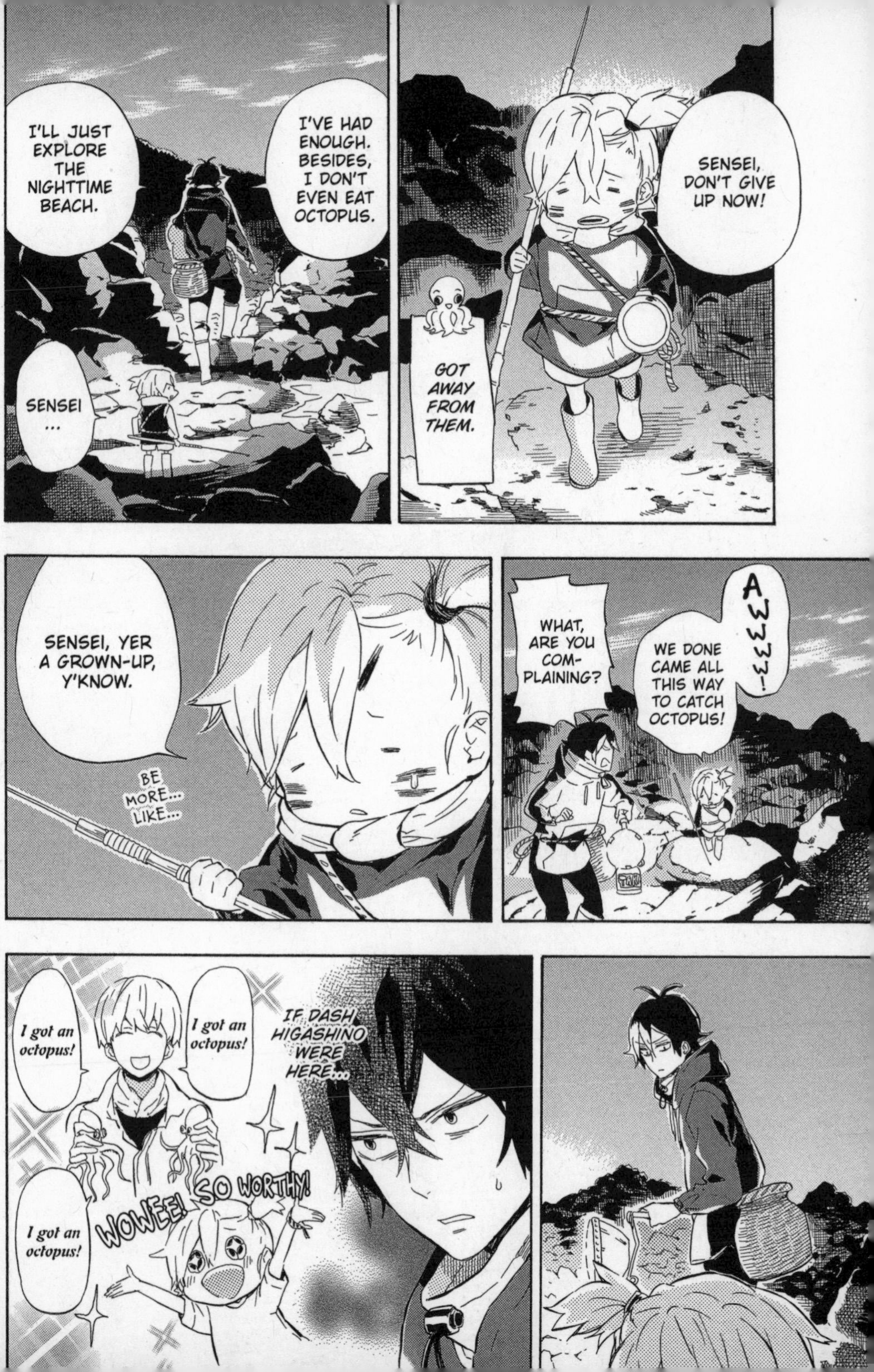
SENSEI, DON'T GIVE UP NOW!
GOT AWAY FROM THEM.
I'VE HAD ENOUGH. BESIDES, I DON'T EVEN EAT OCTOPUS.
I'LL JUST EXPLORE THE NIGHTTIME BEACH.
SENSEI ...
AWWWW!
WE DONE CAME ALL THIS WAY TO CATCH OCTOPUS!
WHAT, ARE YOU COM-PLAINING?
SENSEI, YER A GROWN-UP, Y'KNOW.
BE MORE... LIKE...
IF DASH HIGASHINO WERE HERE...
I got an octopus!
I got an octopus!
SO WORTHY!
WOWEE!
I got an octopus!

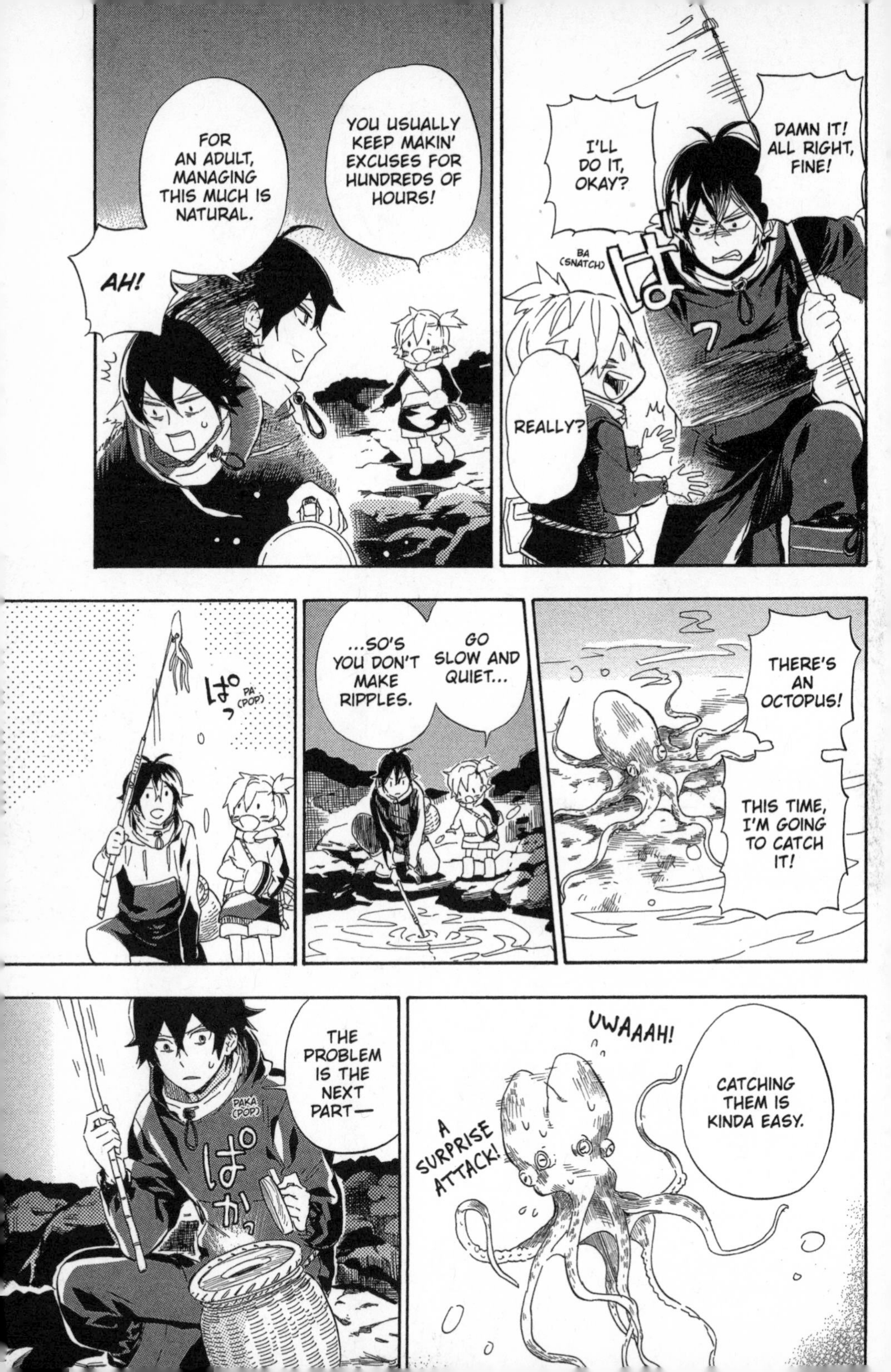
DAMN IT! ALL RIGHT, FINE!
I'LL DO IT, OKAY?
BA (SNATCH)
ば
REALLY?
YOU USUALLY KEEP MAKIN' EXCUSES FOR HUNDREDS OF HOURS!
FOR AN ADULT, MANAGING THIS MUCH IS NATURAL.
AH!
THERE'S AN OCTOPUS!
THIS TIME, I'M GOING TO CATCH IT!
GO SLOW AND QUIET...
...SO'S YOU DON'T MAKE RIPPLES.
ぱっ
PA (POP)
CATCHING THEM IS KINDA EASY.
UWAAAH!
A SURPRISE ATTACK!
THE PROBLEM IS THE NEXT PART—
PAKA (POP)
ぱかっ

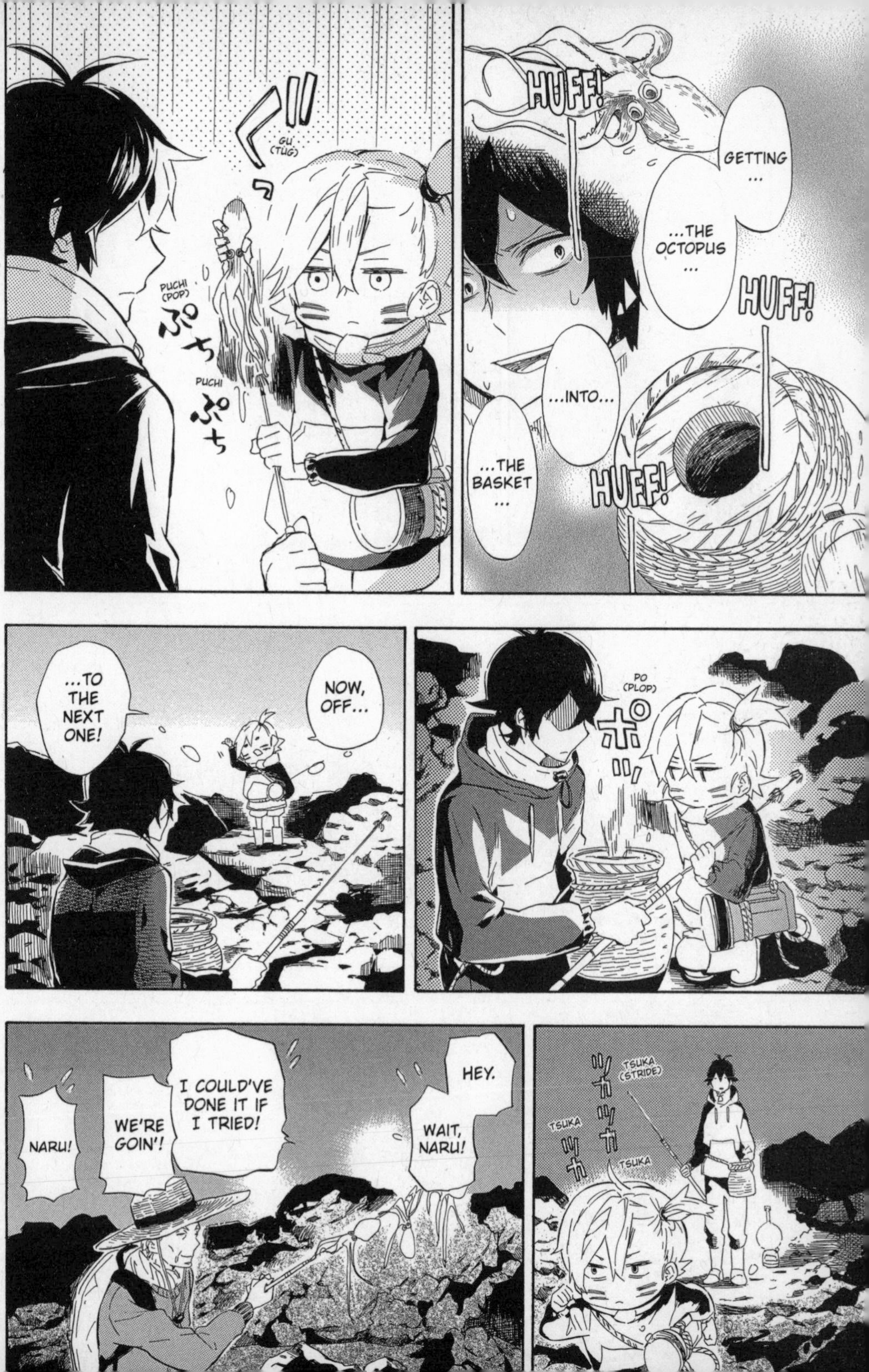
HUFF!
GETTING...
...THE OCTOPUS...
HUFF!
...INTO...
...THE BASKET...
HUFF!
GU (TUG)
PUCHI (POP)
ぷち
PUCHI
ぷち
PO (PLOP)
ポ
NOW, OFF...
...TO THE NEXT ONE!
TSUKA (STRIDE)
TSUKA
TSUKA
HEY.
WAIT, NARU!
I COULD'VE DONE IT IF I TRIED!
WE'RE GOIN'!
NARU!

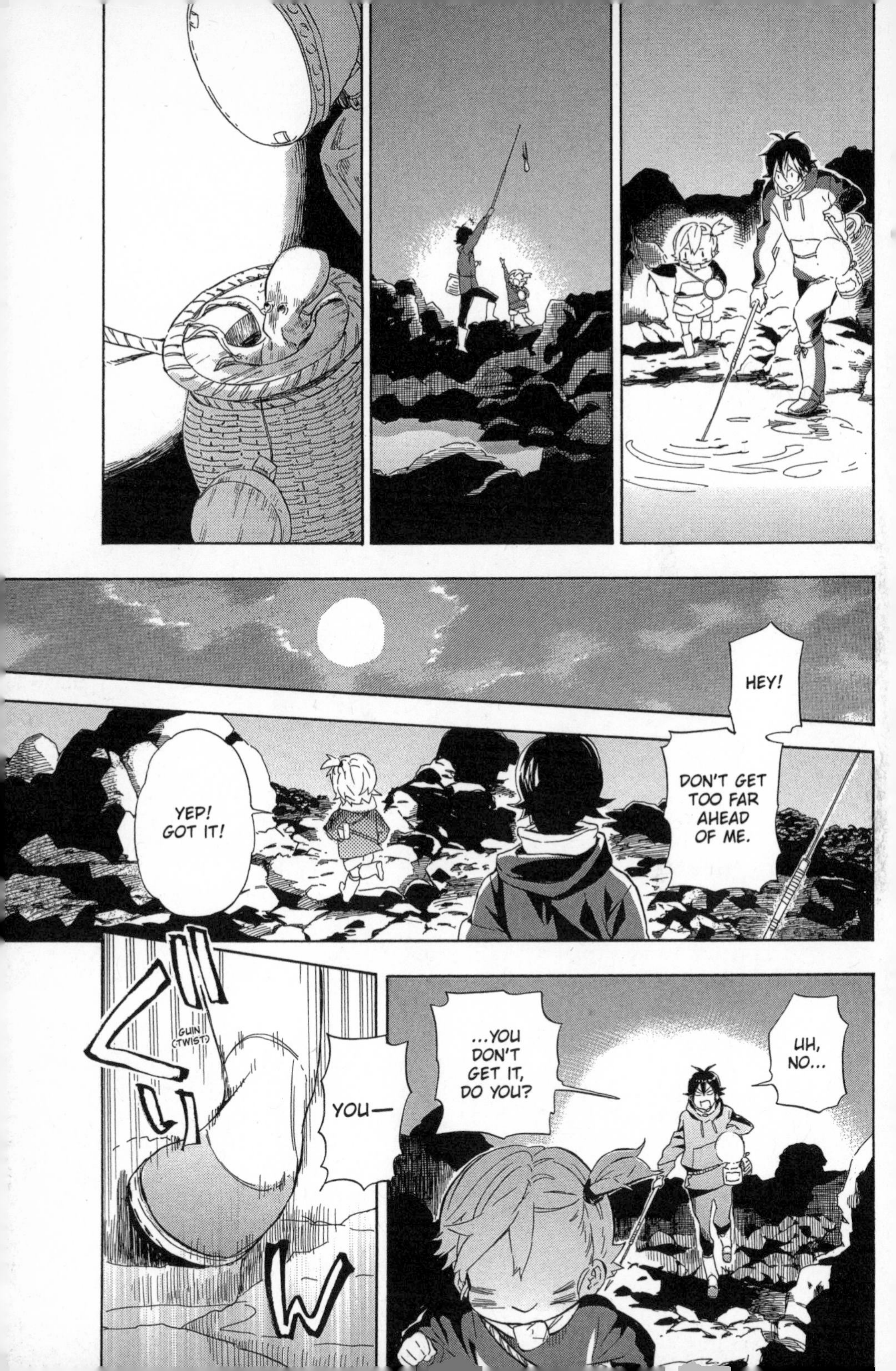
HEY!
DON'T GET TOO FAR AHEAD OF ME.
YEP! GOT IT!
UH, NO...
...YOU DON'T GET IT, DO YOU?
YOU—
GUIN (TWIST)

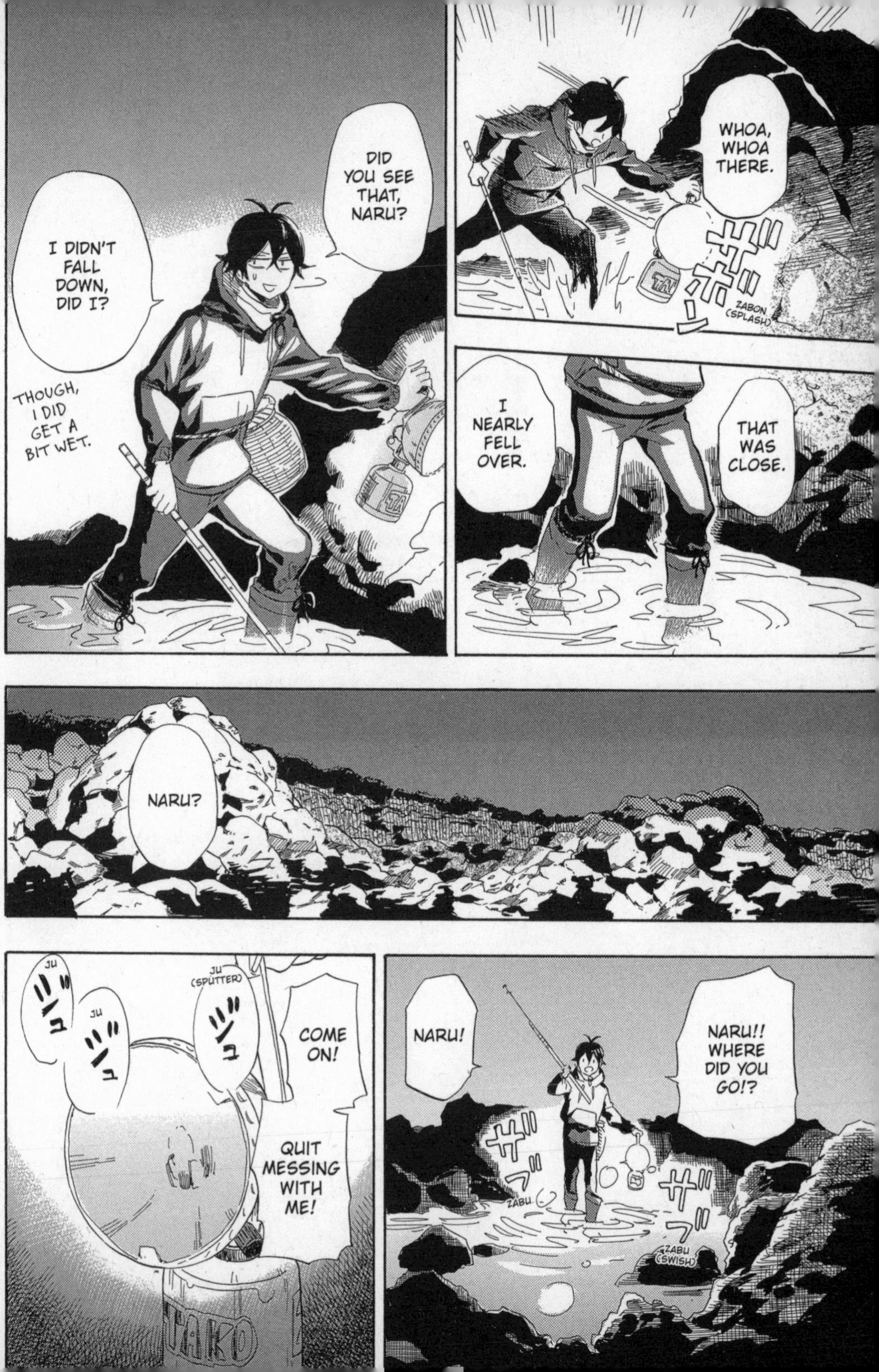
WHOA, WHOA THERE.
ZABON (SPLASH)
THAT WAS CLOSE.
I NEARLY FELL OVER.
DID YOU SEE THAT, NARU?
I DIDN'T FALL DOWN, DID I?
THOUGH, I DID GET A BIT WET.
NARU?
NARU!! WHERE DID YOU GO!?
NARU!
ZABU (SWISH)
ZABU
COME ON!
QUIT MESSING WITH ME!
JU (SPUTTER)
JU
JU
TAKO

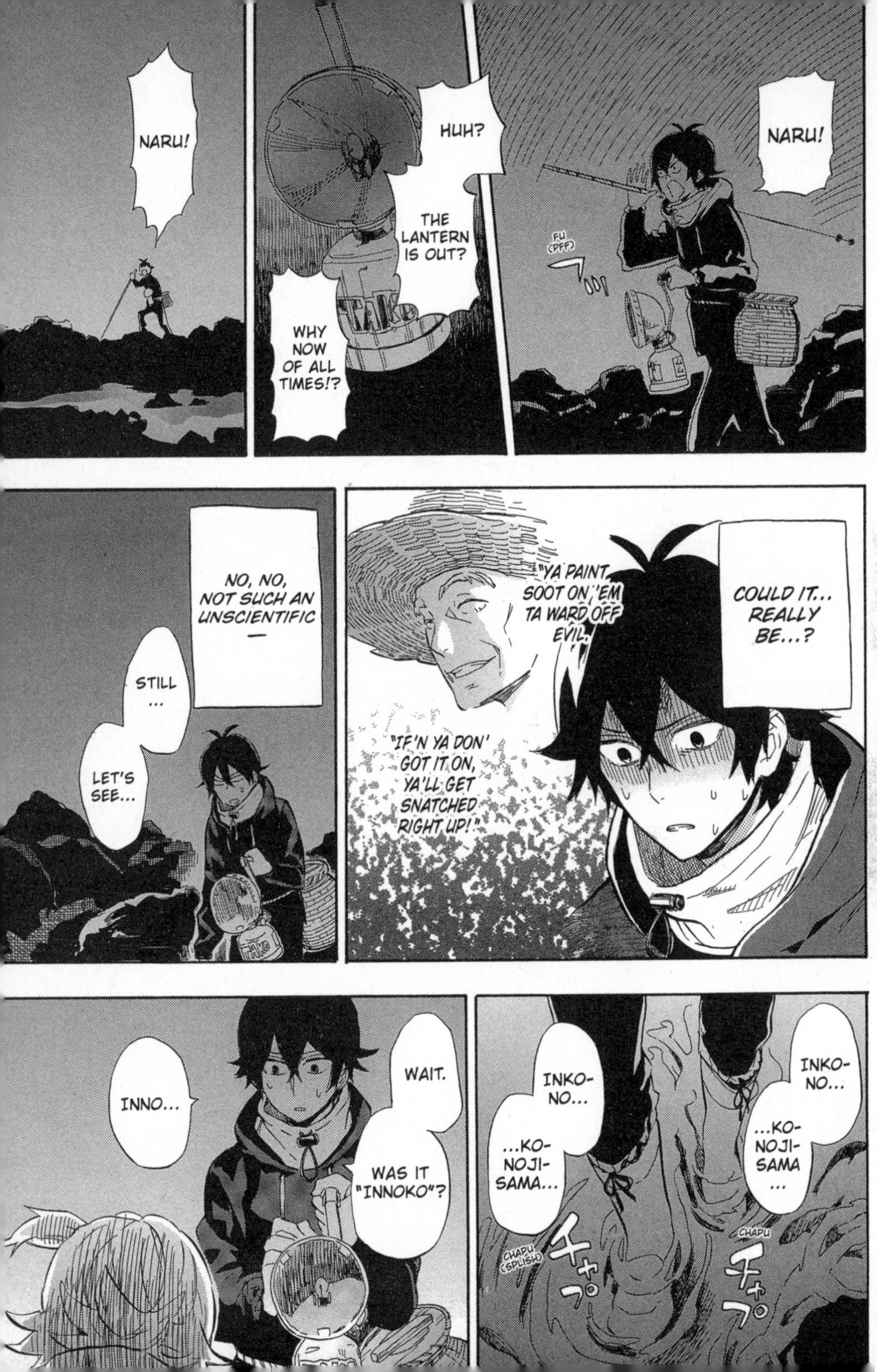

NARU!
FU (PFF)
HUH?
THE LANTERN IS OUT?
WHY NOW OF ALL TIMES!?
NARU!
COULD IT... REALLY BE...?
"YA PAINT SOOT ON 'EM TA WARD OFF EVIL."
"IF'N YA DON' GOT IT ON, YA'LL GET SNATCHED RIGHT UP!"
NO, NO, NOT SUCH AN UNSCIENTIFIC —
STILL...
LET'S SEE...
INKO-NO...
...KO-NOJI-SAMA...
CHAPU
チャプ
INKO-NO...
...KO-NOJI-SAMA...
CHAPU (SPLISH)
チャプ
WAIT.
WAS IT "INNOKO"?
INNO...

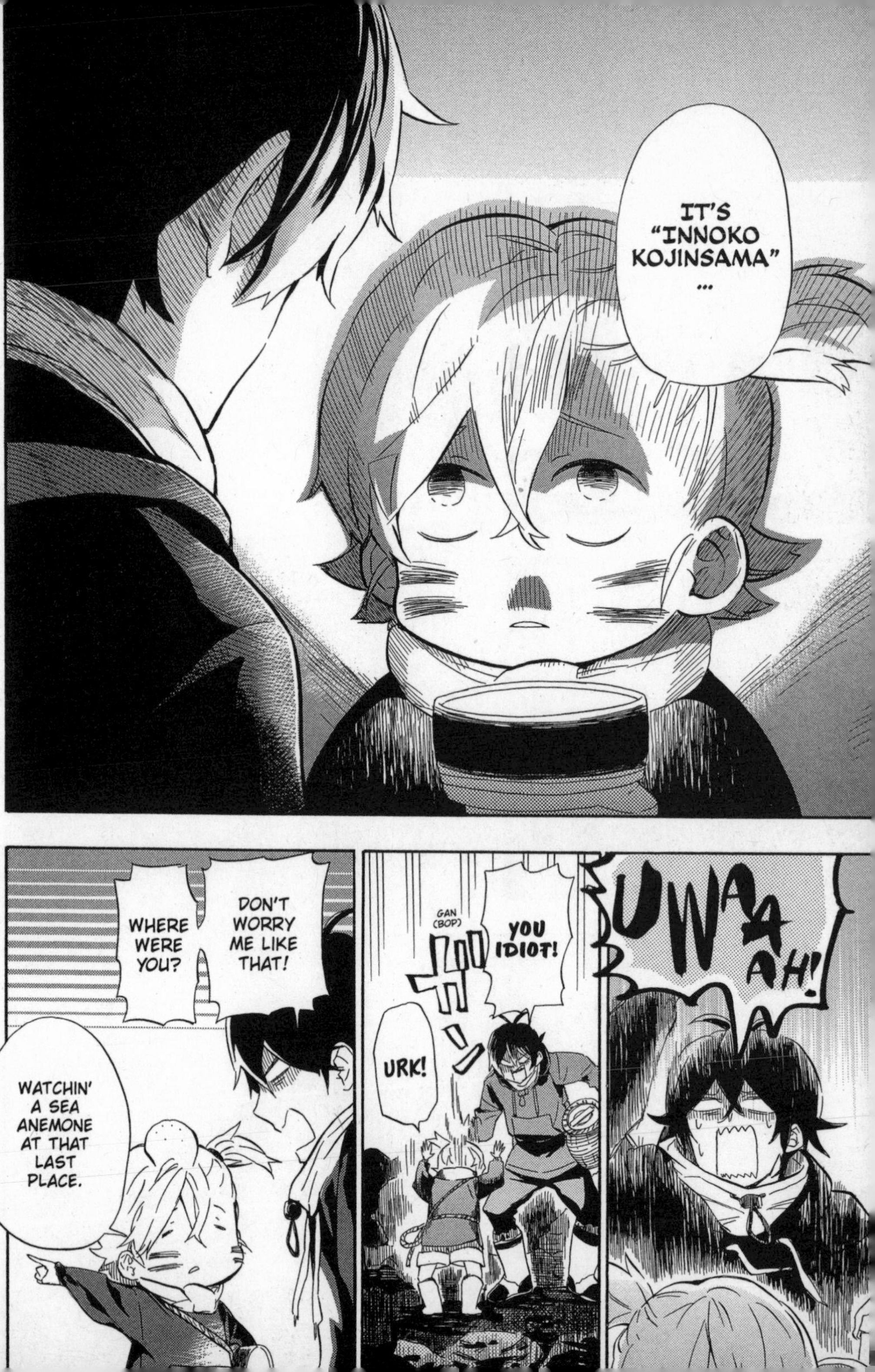
IT'S "INNOKO KOJINSAMA" ...
UWAAAAH!
YOU IDIOT!
GAN (BOP)
URK!
DON'T WORRY ME LIKE THAT!
WHERE WERE YOU?
WATCHIN' A SEA ANEMONE AT THAT LAST PLACE.

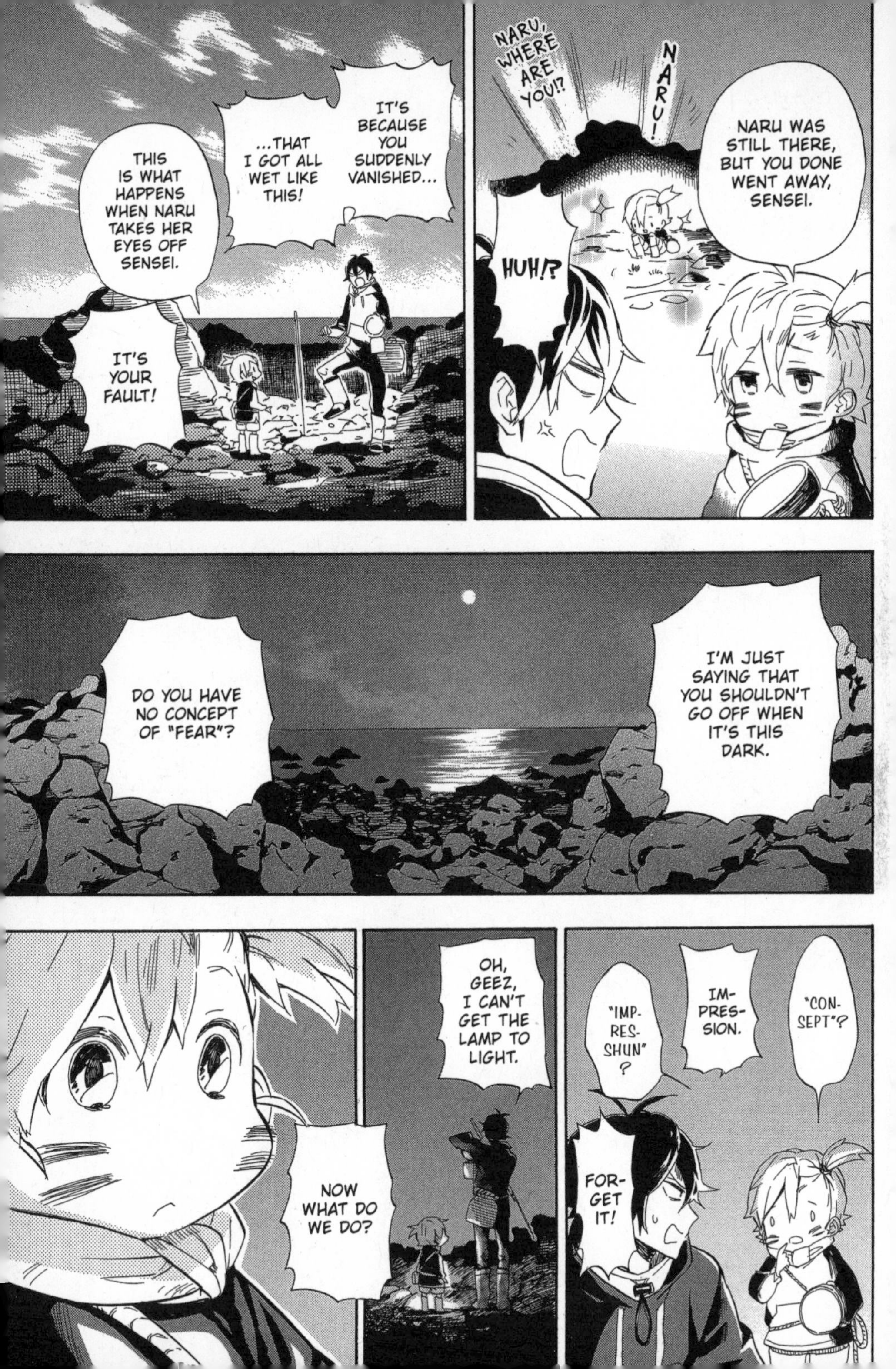
NARU!
NARU, WHERE ARE YOU!?
NARU WAS STILL THERE, BUT YOU DONE WENT AWAY, SENSEI.
HUH!?
IT'S BECAUSE YOU SUDDENLY VANISHED...
...THAT I GOT ALL WET LIKE THIS!
THIS IS WHAT HAPPENS WHEN NARU TAKES HER EYES OFF SENSEI.
IT'S YOUR FAULT!
I'M JUST SAYING THAT YOU SHOULDN'T GO OFF WHEN IT'S THIS DARK.
DO YOU HAVE NO CONCEPT OF "FEAR"?
"CON-SEPT"?
IM-PRES-SION.
"IMP-RES-SHUN"?
FOR-GET IT!
OH, GEEZ, I CAN'T GET THE LAMP TO LIGHT.
NOW WHAT DO WE DO?

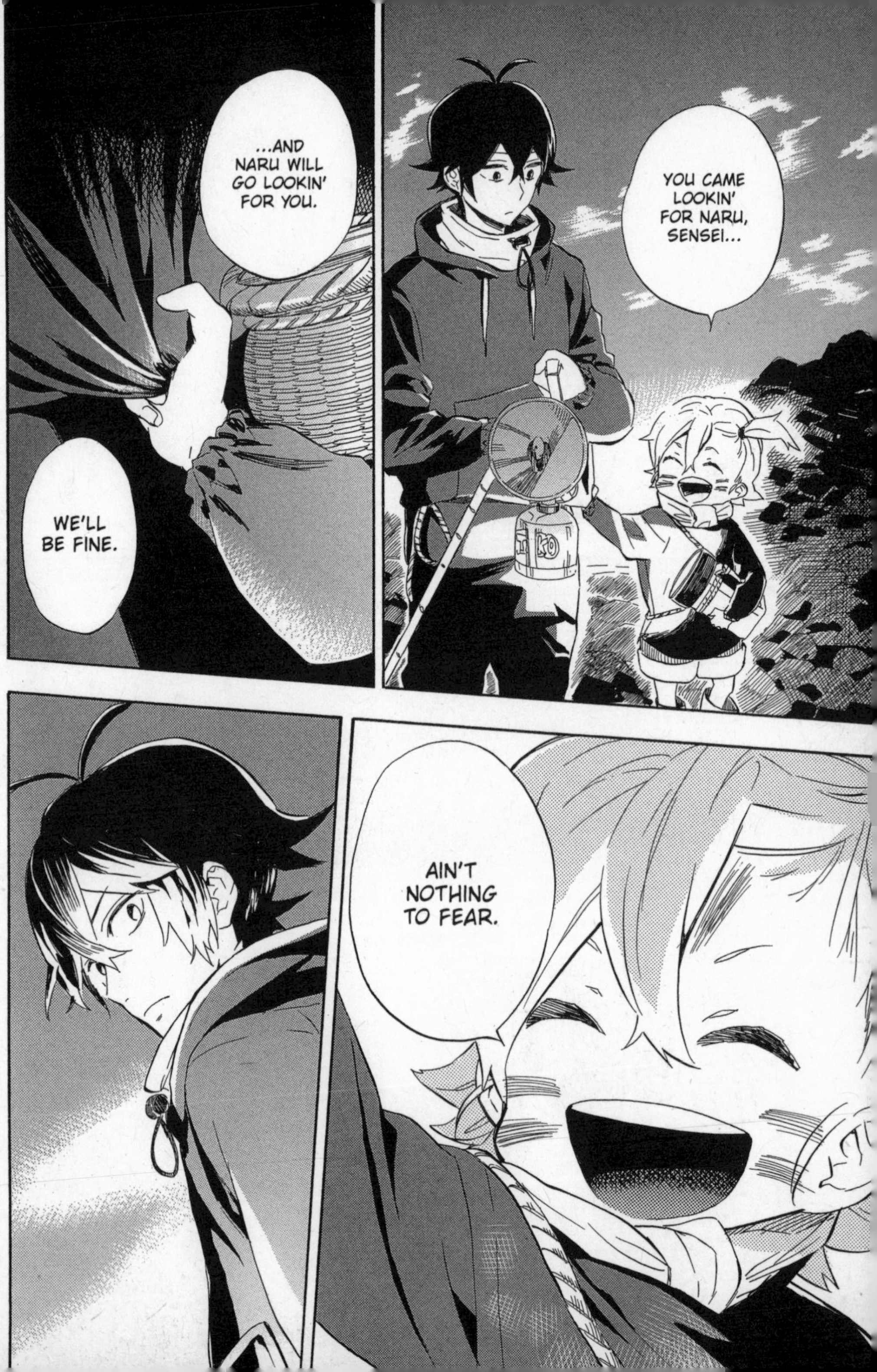
YOU CAME LOOKIN' FOR NARU, SENSEI...
...AND NARU WILL GO LOOKIN' FOR YOU.
WE'LL BE FINE.
AIN'T NOTHING TO FEAR.

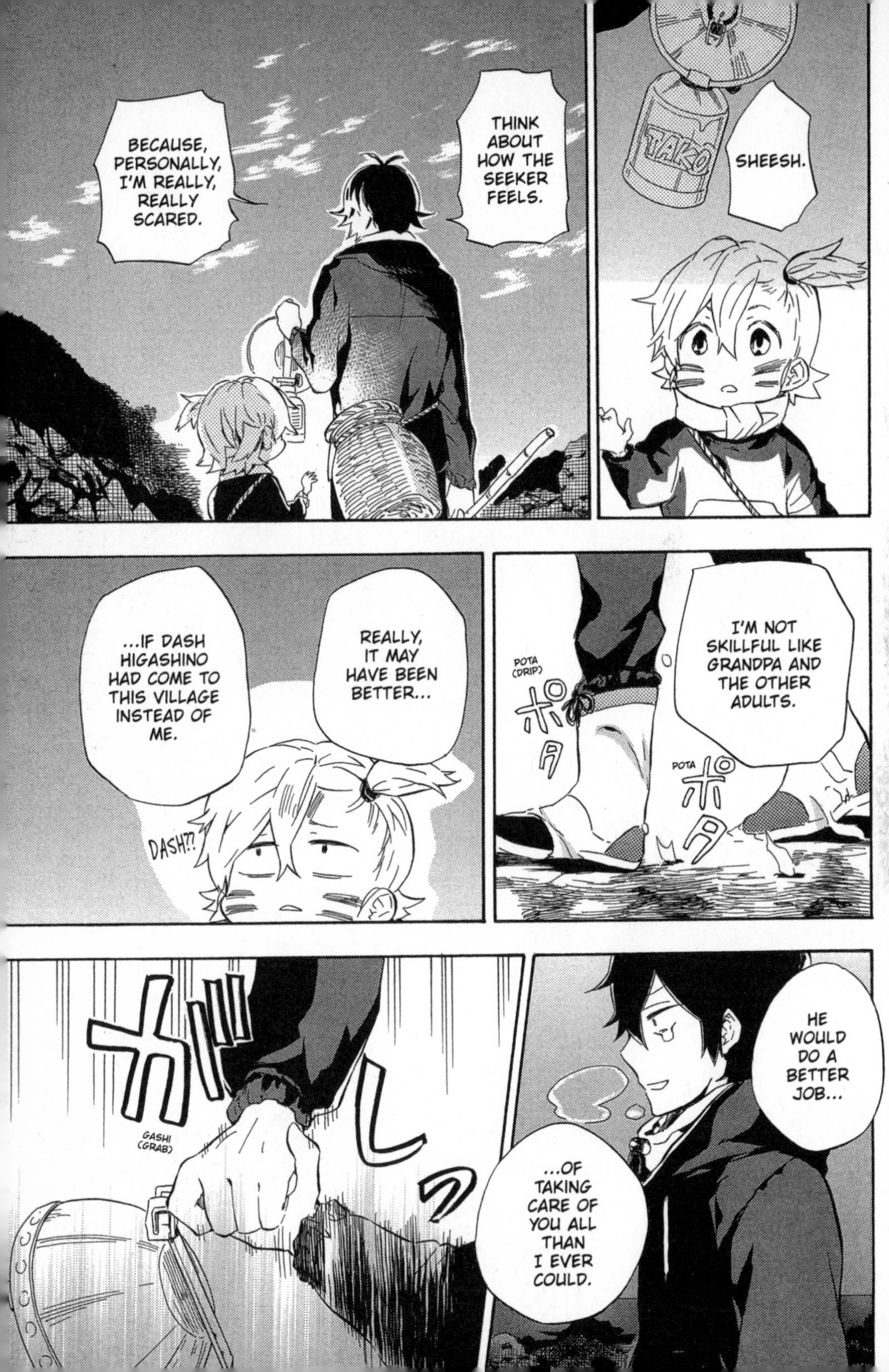

SHEESH.
THINK ABOUT HOW THE SEEKER FEELS.
BECAUSE, PERSONALLY, I'M REALLY, REALLY SCARED.
I'M NOT SKILLFUL LIKE GRANDPA AND THE OTHER ADULTS.
ポタ
POTA (DRIP)
ポタ
POTA
REALLY, IT MAY HAVE BEEN BETTER...
...IF DASH HIGASHINO HAD COME TO THIS VILLAGE INSTEAD OF ME.
DASH?!
HE WOULD DO A BETTER JOB...
...OF TAKING CARE OF YOU ALL THAN I EVER COULD.
ガシッ
GASHI (GRAB)

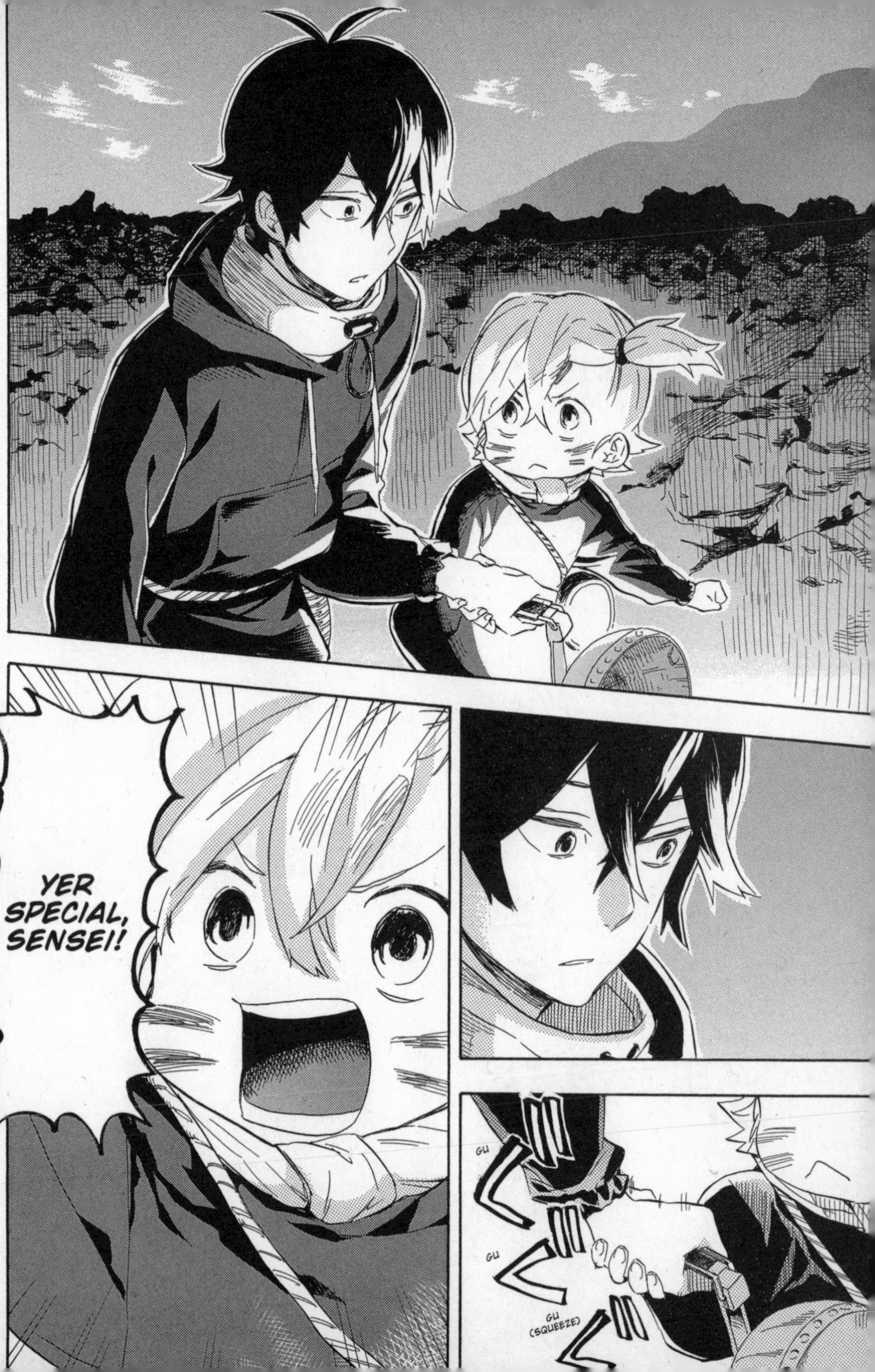
GU
GU
GU
(SQUEEZE)
YER SPECIAL, SENSEI!

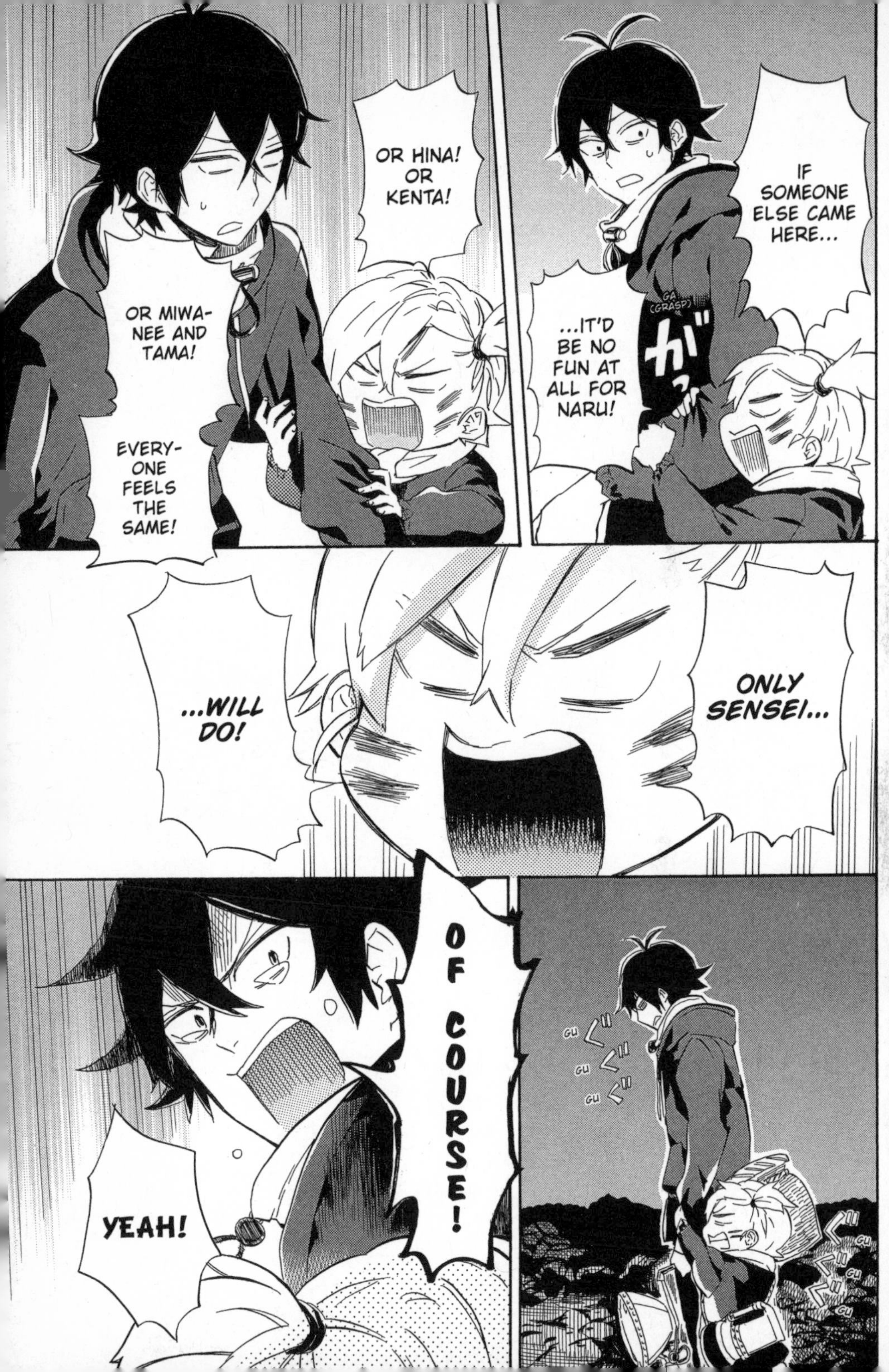
IF SOMEONE ELSE CAME HERE...
GA (GRASP)
がっ
...IT'D BE NO FUN AT ALL FOR NARU!
OR HINA! OR KENTA!
OR MIWA-NEE AND TAMA!
EVERY-ONE FEELS THE SAME!
ONLY SENSEI...
...WILL DO!
GU ぐ GU ぐ GU ぐ
GU ぐ GU ぐ GU ぐ
OF COURSE!
YEAH!

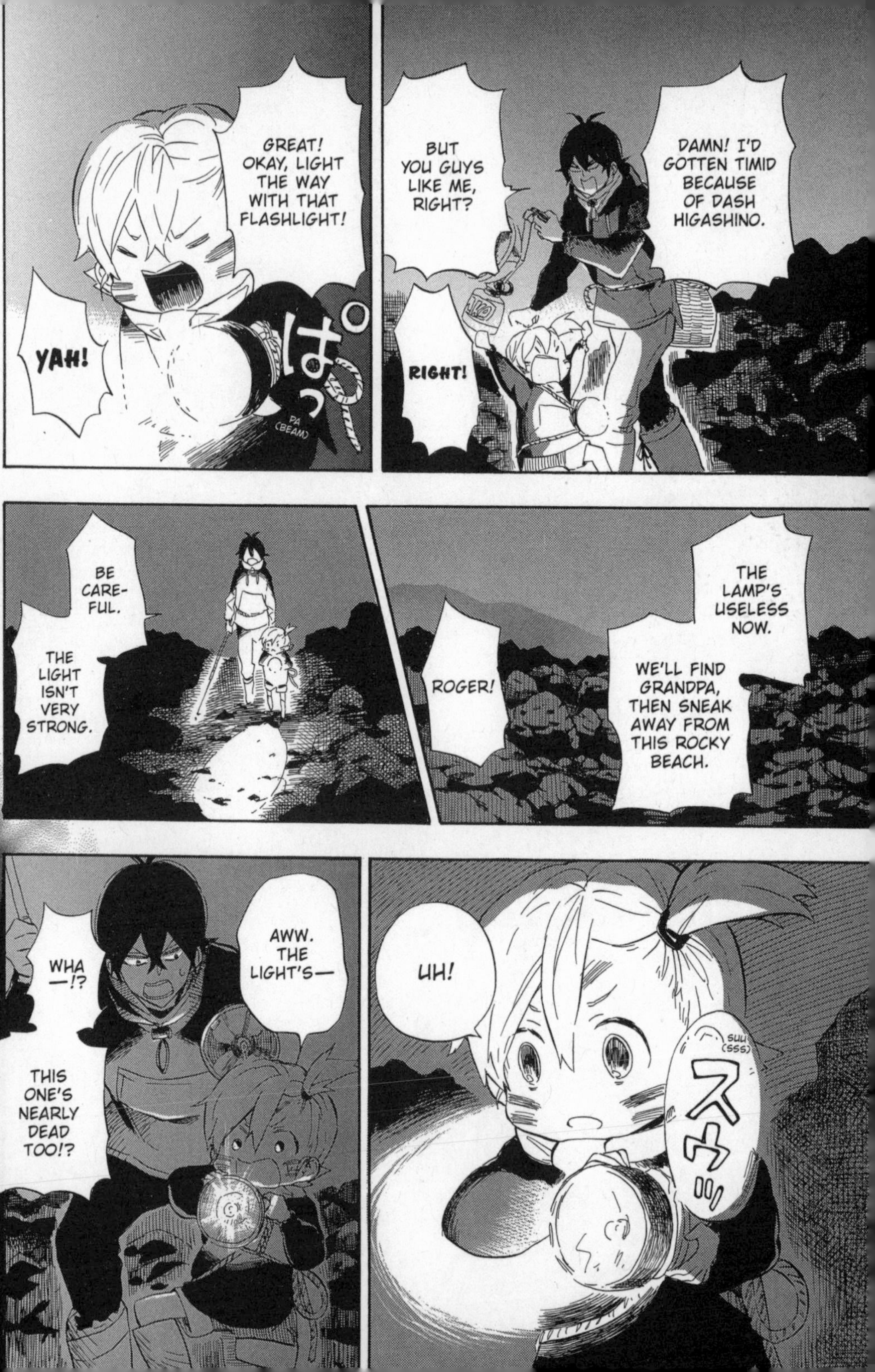
DAMN! I'D GOTTEN TIMID BECAUSE OF DASH HIGASHINO.
BUT YOU GUYS LIKE ME, RIGHT?
RIGHT!
GREAT! OKAY, LIGHT THE WAY WITH THAT FLASHLIGHT!
YAH!
ぱっ
PA (BEAM)
THE LAMP'S USELESS NOW.
WE'LL FIND GRANDPA, THEN SNEAK AWAY FROM THIS ROCKY BEACH.
ROGER!
BE CAREFUL.
THE LIGHT ISN'T VERY STRONG.
UH!
SUU (SSS)
スゥ
AWW. THE LIGHT'S—
WHA—!?
THIS ONE'S NEARLY DEAD TOO!?

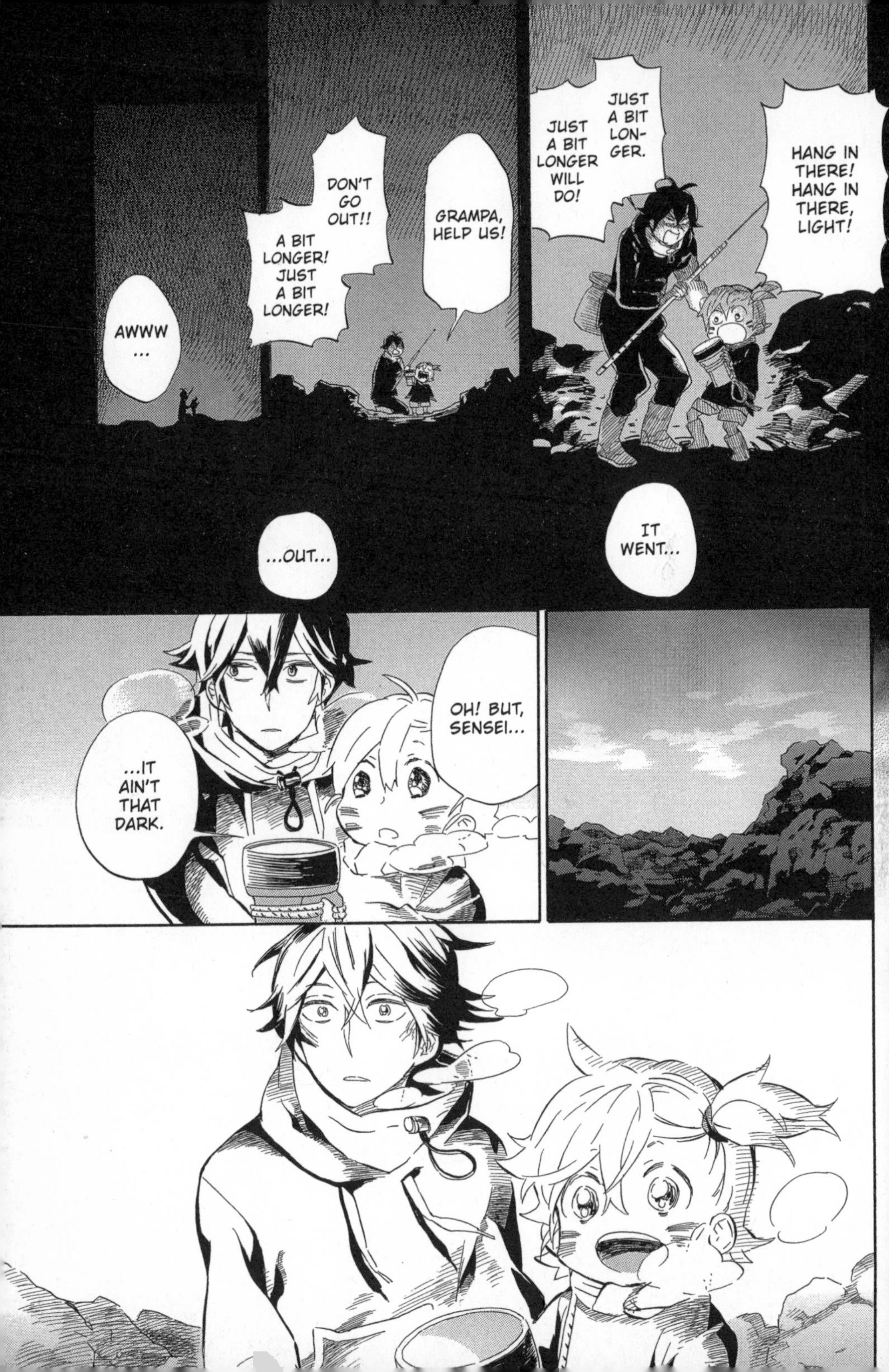
HANG IN THERE! HANG IN THERE, LIGHT!
JUST A BIT LON-GER.
JUST A BIT LONGER WILL DO!
GRAMPA, HELP US!
DON'T GO OUT!!
A BIT LONGER! JUST A BIT LONGER!
AWWW ...
IT WENT...
...OUT...
OH! BUT, SENSEI...
...IT AIN'T THAT DARK.

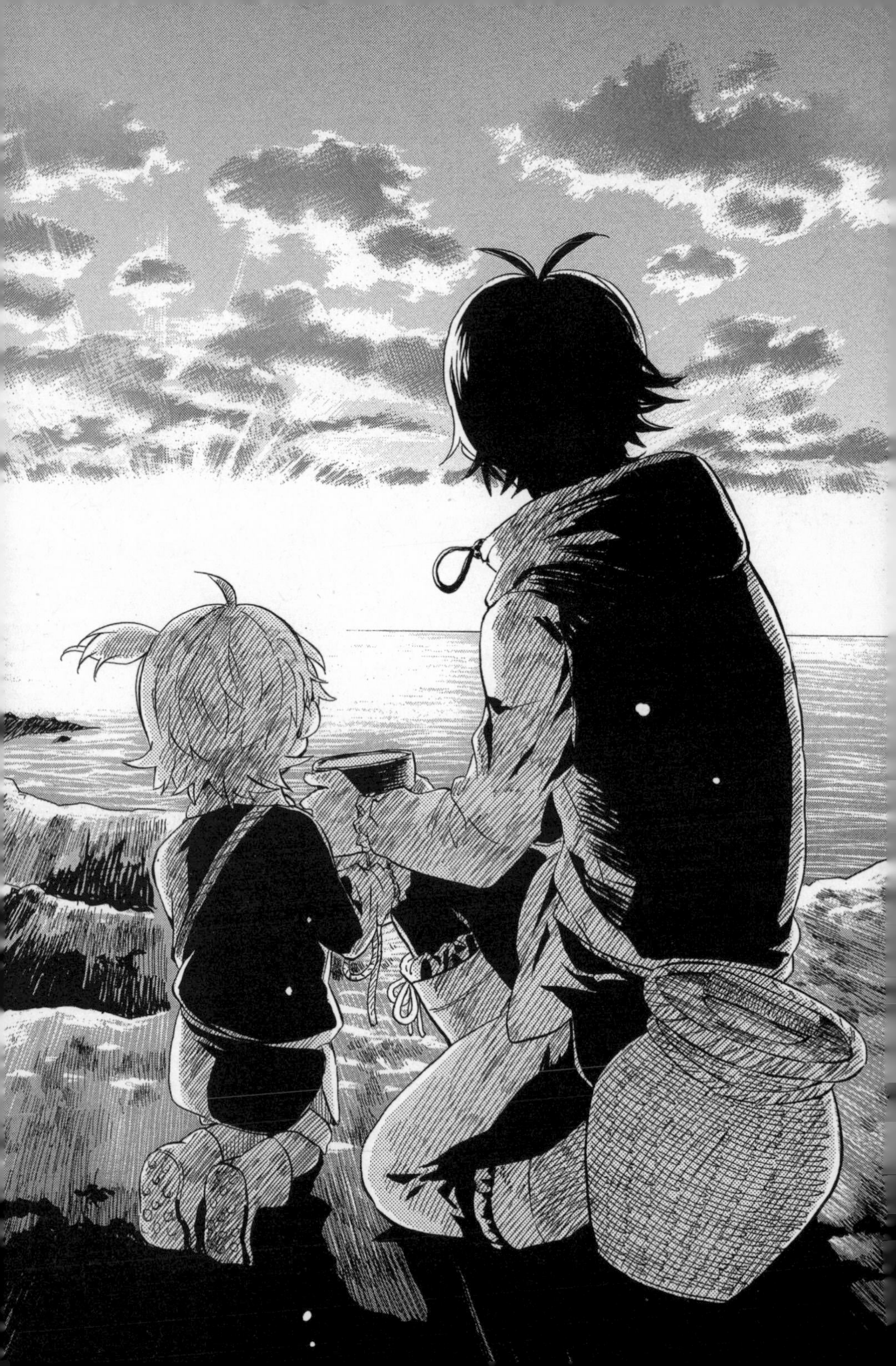

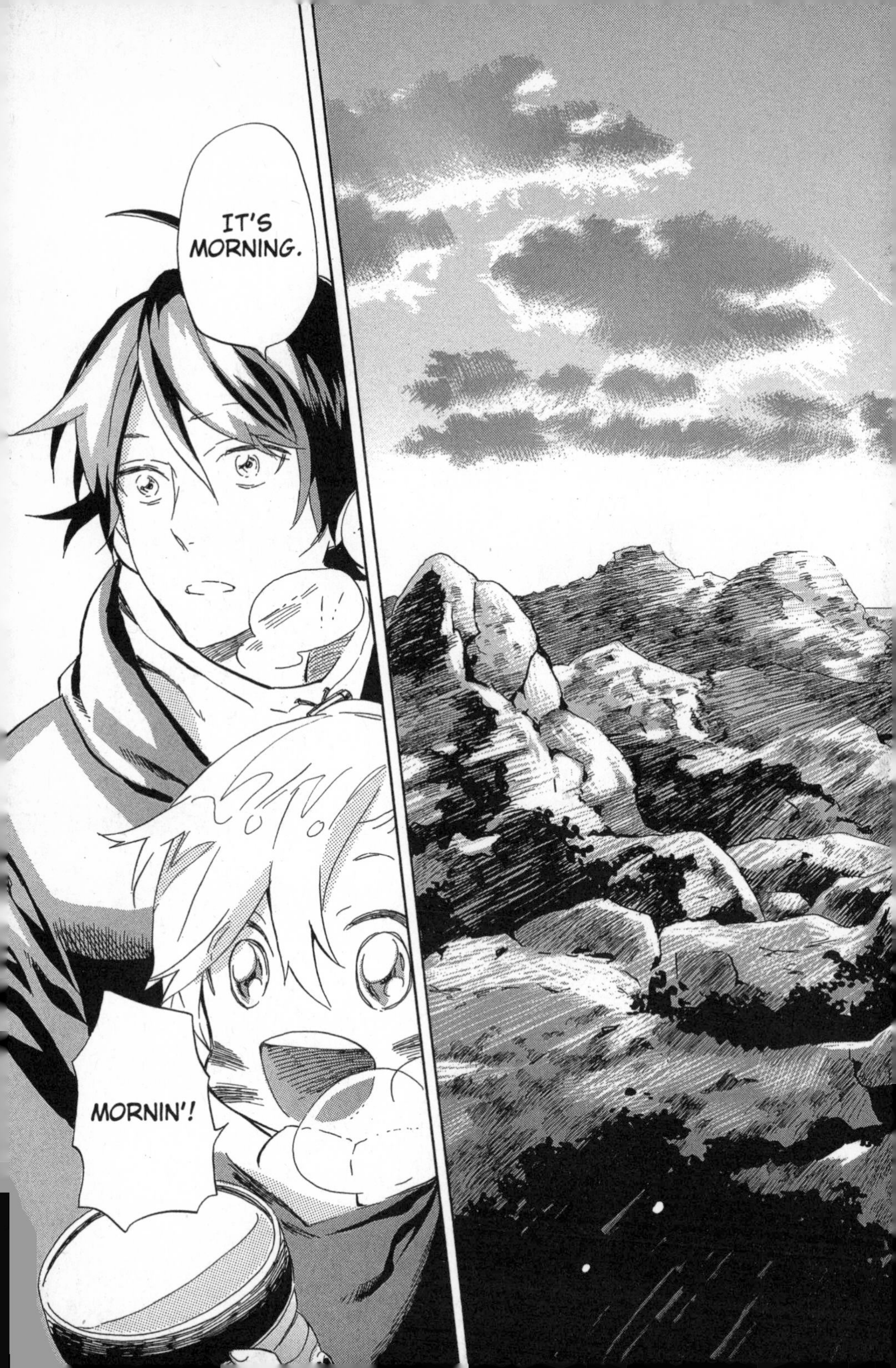
IT'S MORNING.
MORNIN'!

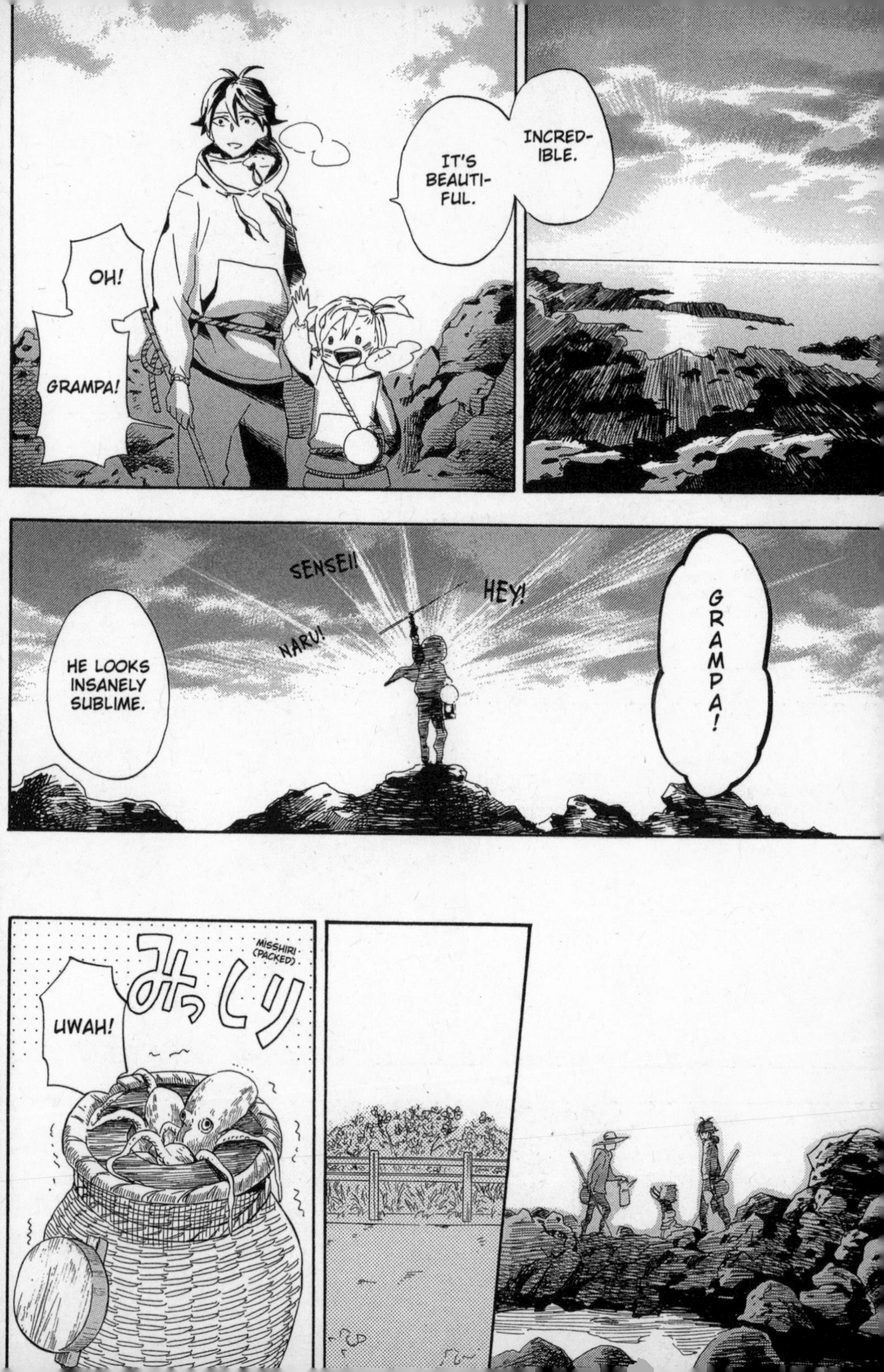
INCREDIBLE.
IT'S BEAUTIFUL.
OH!
GRAMPA!
GRAMPA!
HEY!
SENSEI!
NARU!
HE LOOKS INSANELY SUBLIME.
MISSHIRI (PACKED)
みっしり
UWAH!

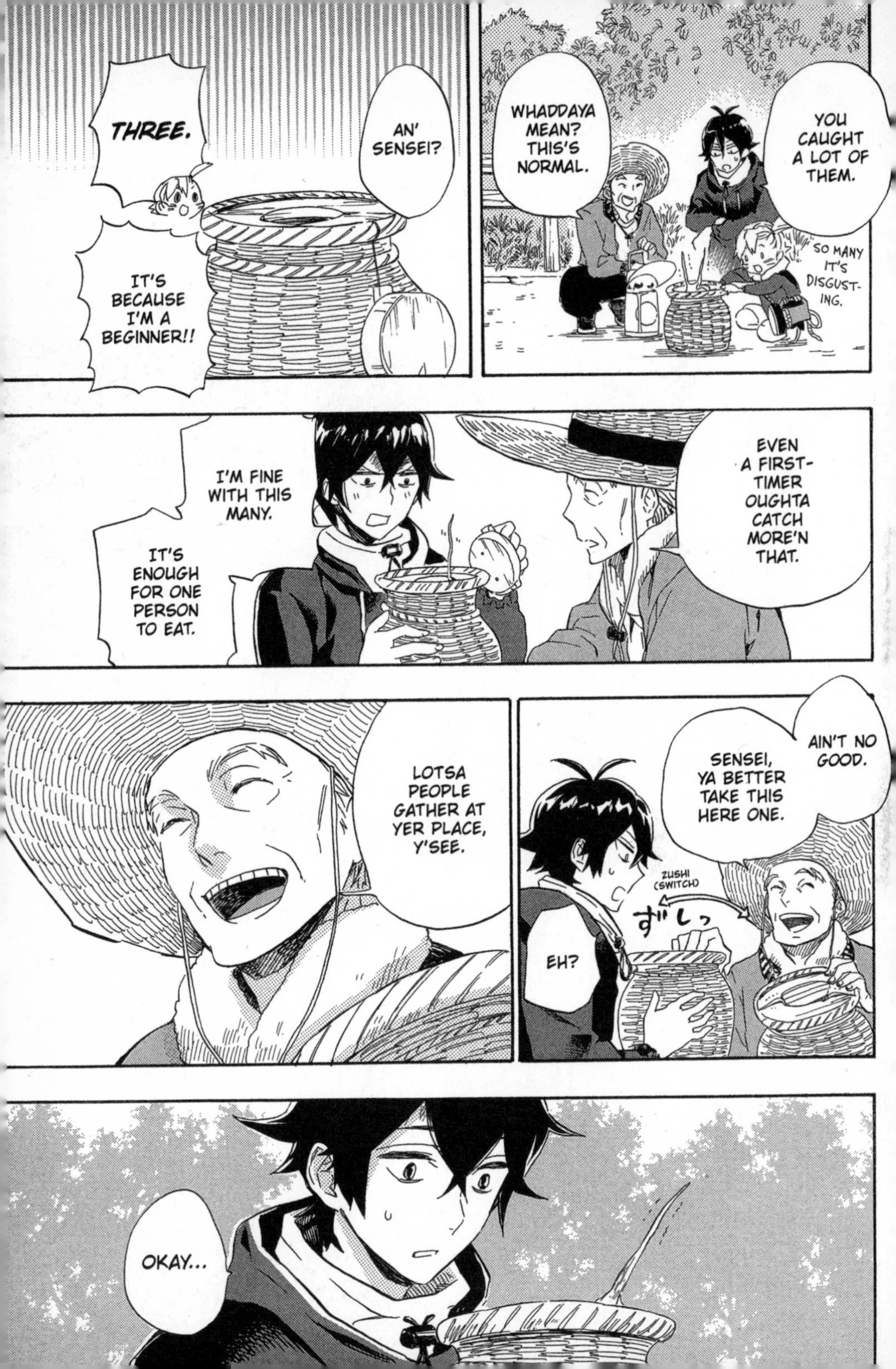
YOU CAUGHT A LOT OF THEM.
WHADDAYA MEAN? THIS'S NORMAL.
SO MANY IT'S DISGUSTING.
AN' SENSEI?
THREE.
IT'S BECAUSE I'M A BEGINNER!!
EVEN A FIRST-TIMER OUGHTA CATCH MORE'N THAT.
I'M FINE WITH THIS MANY.
IT'S ENOUGH FOR ONE PERSON TO EAT.
AIN'T NO GOOD.
SENSEI, YA BETTER TAKE THIS HERE ONE.
ZUSHI (SWITCH)
ずしっ
EH?
LOTSA PEOPLE GATHER AT YER PLACE, Y'SEE.
OKAY...

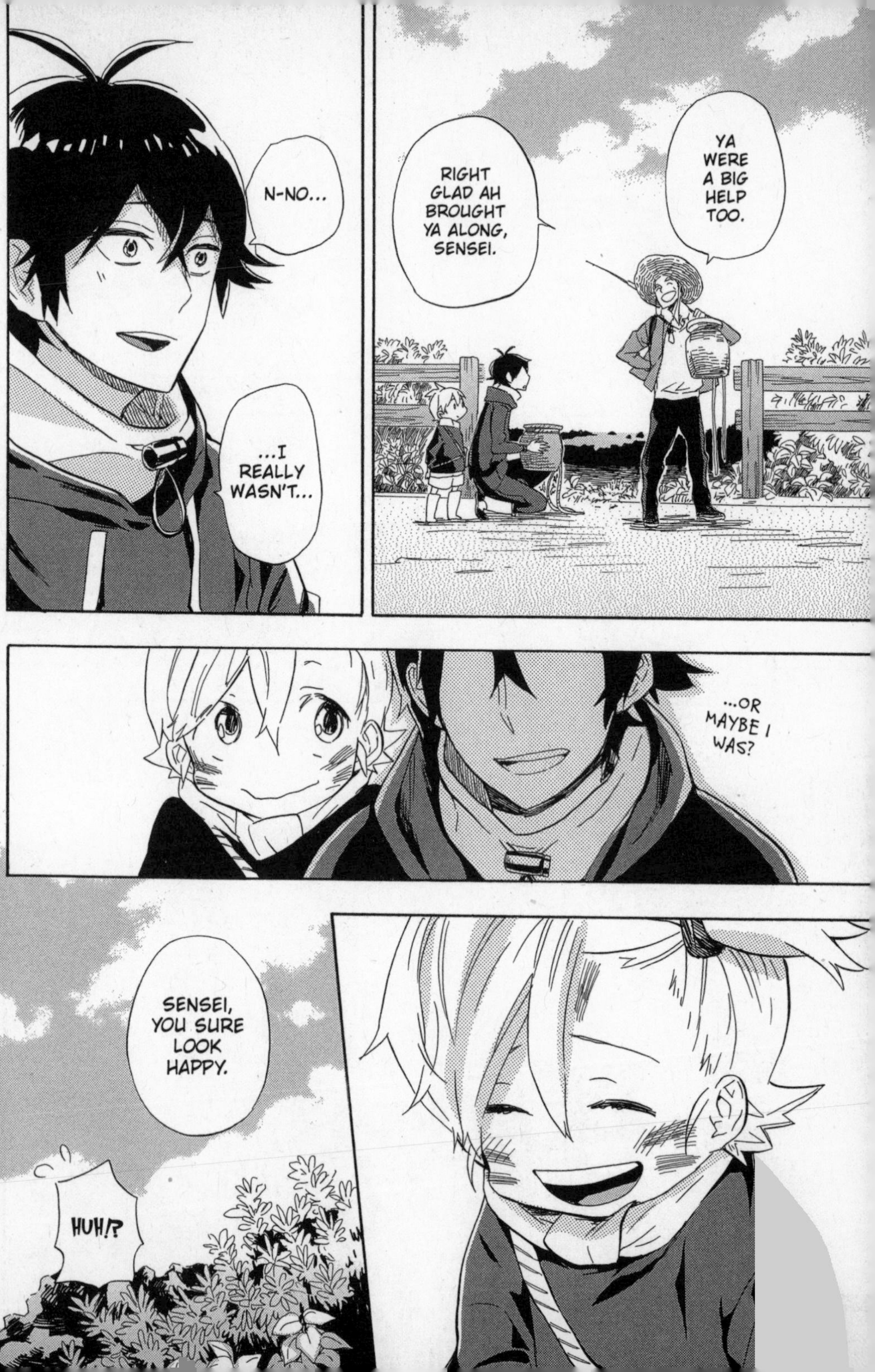
YA WERE A BIG HELP TOO.
RIGHT GLAD AH BROUGHT YA ALONG, SENSEI.
N-NO...
...I REALLY WASN'T...
...OR MAYBE I WAS?
SENSEI, YOU SURE LOOK HAPPY.
HUH!?

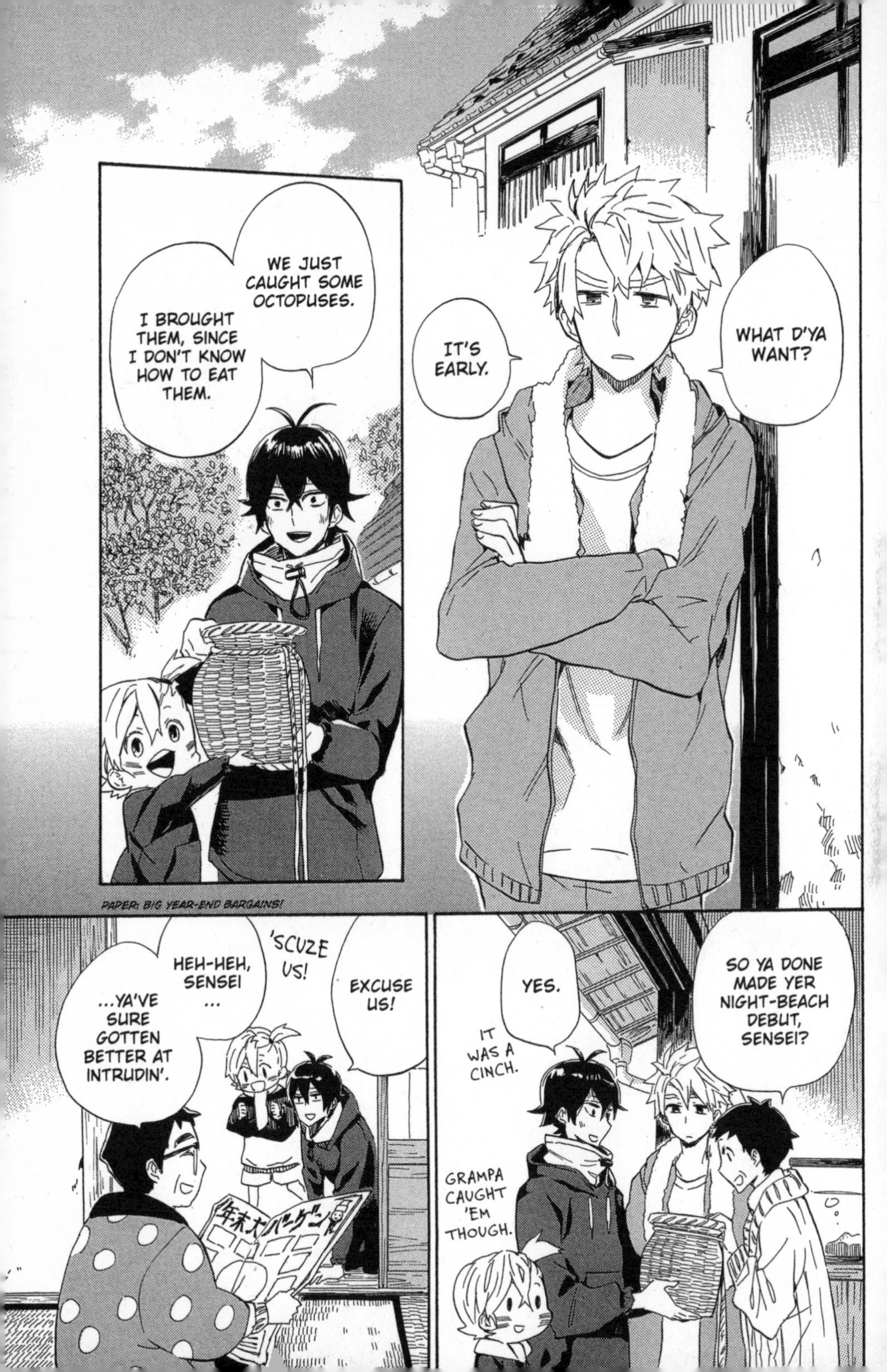
WHAT D'YA WANT?
IT'S EARLY.
WE JUST CAUGHT SOME OCTOPUSES.
I BROUGHT THEM, SINCE I DON'T KNOW HOW TO EAT THEM.
SO YA DONE MADE YER NIGHT-BEACH DEBUT, SENSEI?
YES.
IT WAS A CINCH.
GRAMPA CAUGHT 'EM THOUGH.
EXCUSE US!
'SCUZE US!
HEH-HEH, SENSEI ...
...YA'VE SURE GOTTEN BETTER AT INTRUDIN'.
年末大バーゲン
PAPER: BIG YEAR-END BARGAINS!

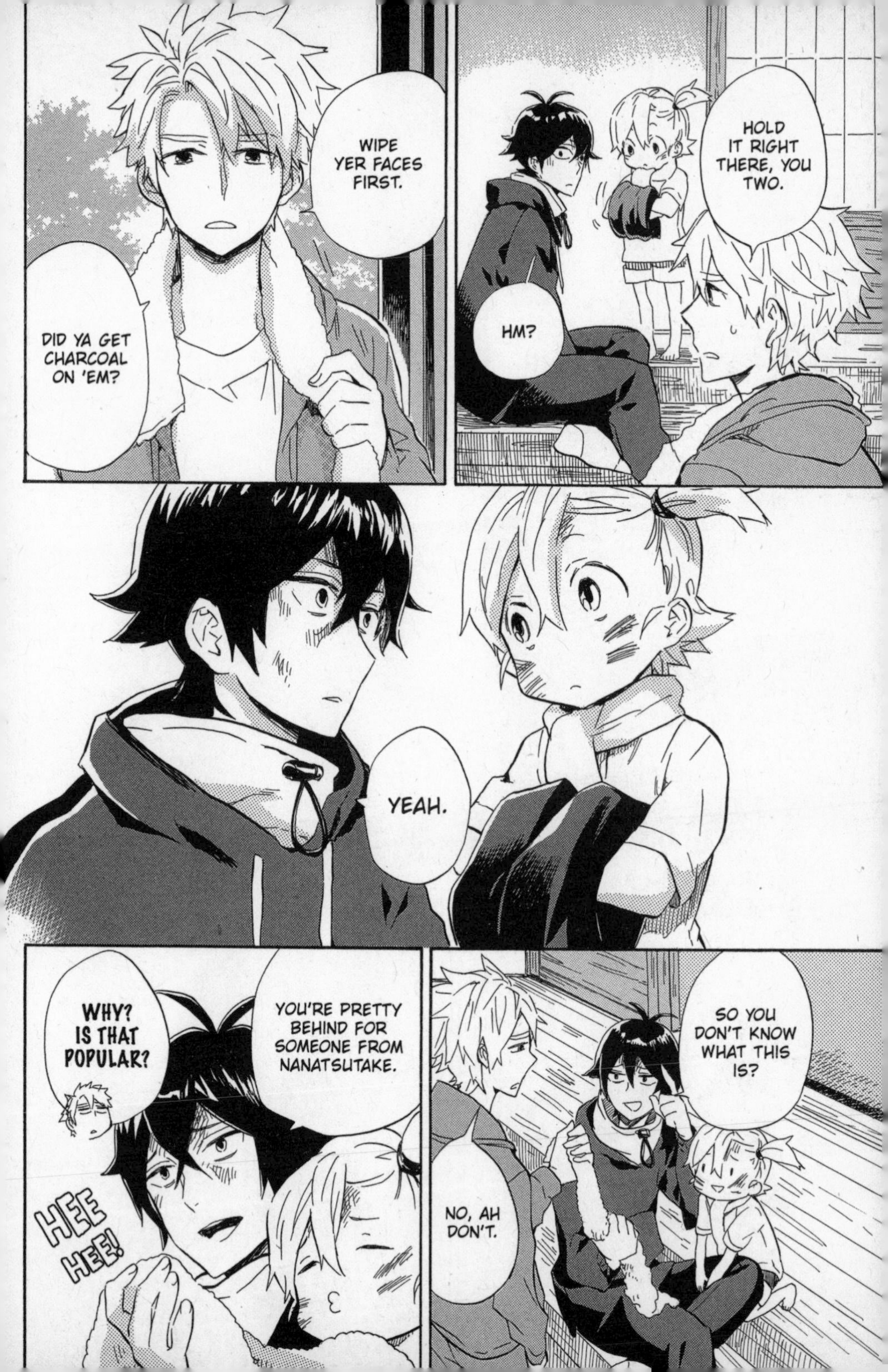
HOLD IT RIGHT THERE, YOU TWO.
HM?
WIPE YER FACES FIRST.
DID YA GET CHARCOAL ON 'EM?
YEAH.
SO YOU DON'T KNOW WHAT THIS IS?
NO, AH DON'T.
YOU'RE PRETTY BEHIND FOR SOMEONE FROM NANATSUTAKE.
WHY? IS THAT POPULAR?
HEE HEE!

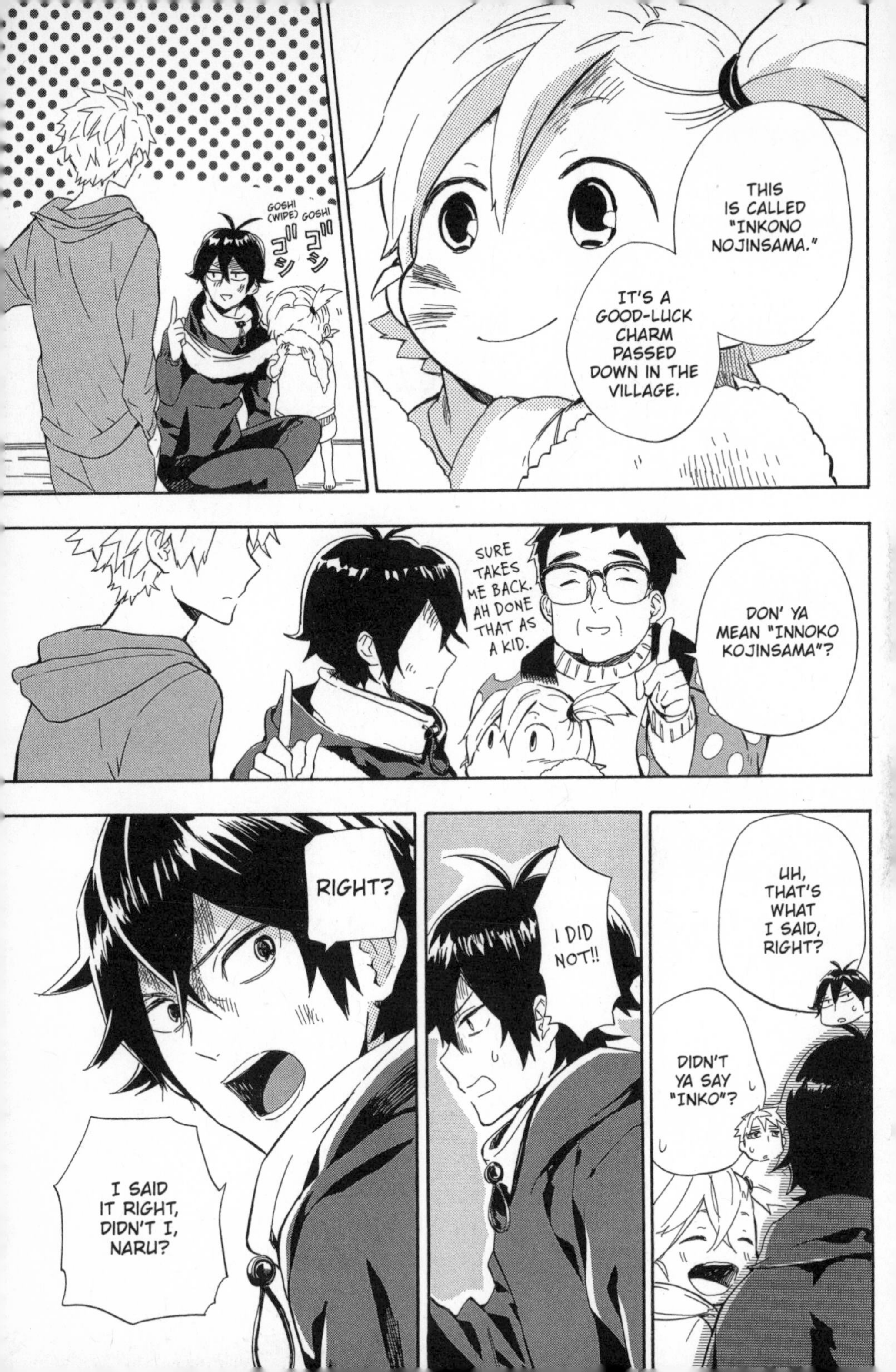
THIS IS CALLED "INKONO NOJINSAMA."
IT'S A GOOD-LUCK CHARM PASSED DOWN IN THE VILLAGE.
GOSHI (WIPE) GOSHI
ゴシ ゴシ
DON' YA MEAN "INNOKO KOJINSAMA"?
SURE TAKES ME BACK. AH DONE THAT AS A KID.
UH, THAT'S WHAT I SAID, RIGHT?
DIDN'T YA SAY "INKO"?
I DID NOT!!
RIGHT?
I SAID IT RIGHT, DIDN'T I, NARU?

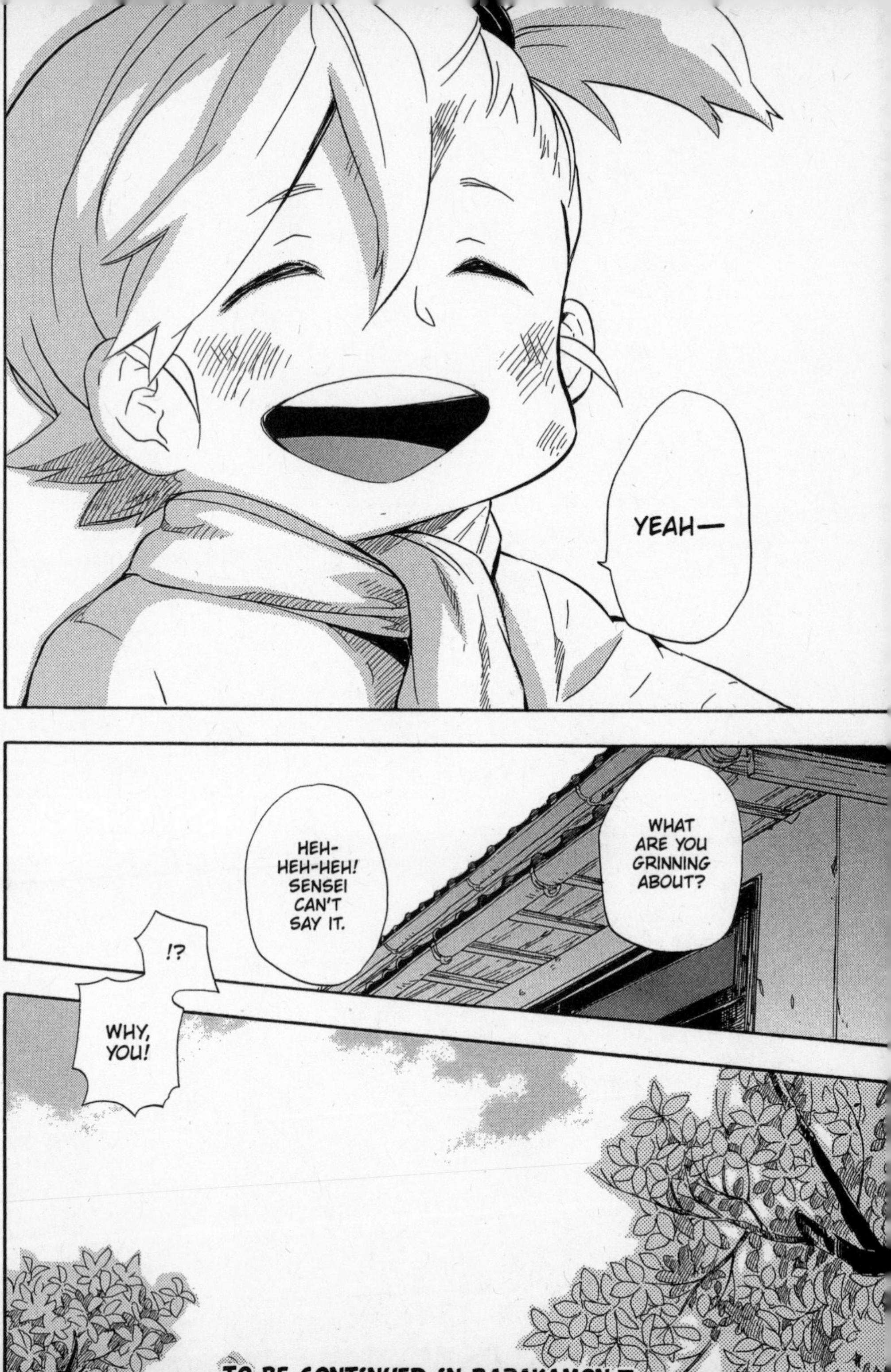
YEAH—
WHAT ARE YOU GRINNING ABOUT?
HEH-HEH-HEH! SENSEI CAN'T SAY IT.
!?
WHY, YOU!

TO BE CONTINUED IN BARAKAMON 12

BARAKAMON

BONUS: DANPO THE 11TH

(Translation: Pond)

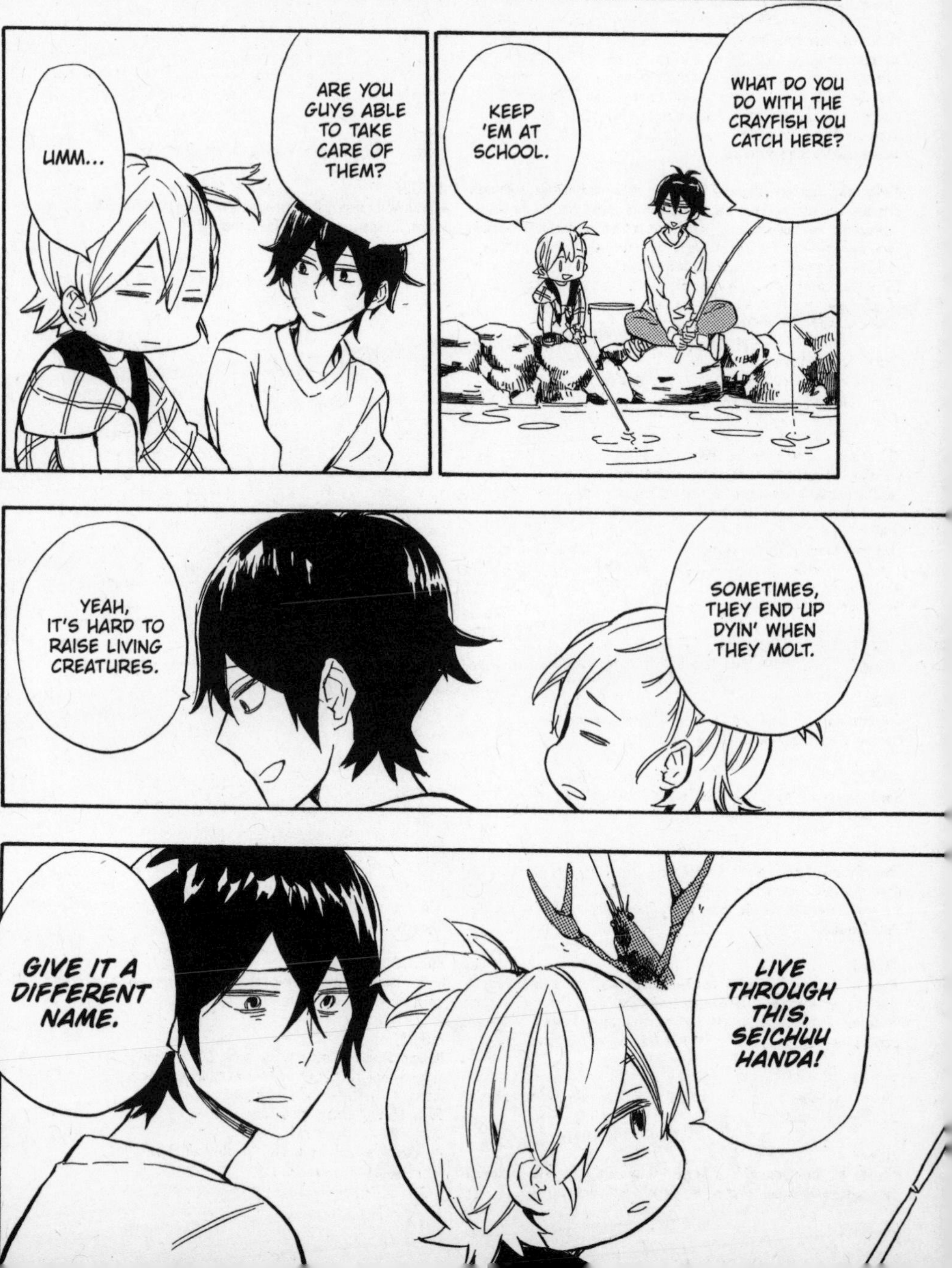
WHAT DO YOU DO WITH THE CRAYFISH YOU CATCH HERE?
KEEP 'EM AT SCHOOL.
ARE YOU GUYS ABLE TO TAKE CARE OF THEM?
UMM...
SOMETIMES, THEY END UP DYIN' WHEN THEY MOLT.
YEAH, IT'S HARD TO RAISE LIVING CREATURES.
LIVE THROUGH THIS, SEICHUU HANDA!
GIVE IT A DIFFERENT NAME.

TRANSLATION NOTES ···

COMMON HONORIFICS

no honorific: Indicates familiarity or closeness; if used without permission or reason, addressing someone in this manner would constitute an insult.

-san: The Japanese equivalent of Mr./Mrs./Miss. If a situation calls for politeness, this is the fail-safe honorific.

-sama: Conveys great respect; may also indicate that the social status of the speaker is lower than that of the addressee.

-kun: Used most often when referring to boys, this indicates affection or familiarity. Occasionally used by older men among their peers, but it may also be used by anyone referring to a person of lower standing.

-chan: An affectionate honorific indicating familiarity used mostly in reference to girls; also used in reference to cute persons or animals of either gender.

-sensei: A Japanese term of respect commonly used for teachers, but can also refer to doctors, writers, and artists. Hence, Village Chief is not implying that Handa is a teacher when he calls him "sensei."

Calligraphy: Japanese calligraphy has a long history and tradition, with roots stemming from ancient China. One of the traditions carried over was the Chinese expression of the "Four Treasures," which refers to the brush, ink, paper, and inkstone used in calligraphy. Traditionally, an inkstick—solidified ink—is ground against an inkstone filled with water in order to produce ink with which to write. This time-consuming process helped to teach patience, which is important in the art of calligraphy. However, modern advances have developed a bottled liquid ink, commonly used by beginners and within the Japanese school system.

Gotou Dialect: Many of the villagers, especially the elderly ones, are actually speaking the local Gotou dialect in the original Japanese. This dialect is reflected in the English translation with some of the grammar elements of older Southern American English to give it a more rustic, rural coastal feel without making it too hard to read (it's not meant to replicate any particular American accent exactly). This approach is similar to how dialect is made accessible in Japanese media, including *Barakamon*, because a complete dialect with all of its different vocabulary would be practically incomprehensible to most Tokyo residents.

PAGE 3
Marriage Meeting: Such meetings, known in Japan as "o-miai," are arranged between two people interested in marriage and often include their parents. Generally, it's meant as a starting point for courtship, rather than an actual arranged marriage, but sometimes there are exceptions...

PAGE 22
nikujaga: A beef and potato stew made using Japanese seasonings.

PAGE 35
kankoro mochi: A type of soft rice cake with lots of sweet potato mixed in, and a specialty of the Gotou Islands.

PAGE 39
gaze miso soup: Naru's favorite food, sea urchin miso soup. She sang this "song" in Act.31.

PAGE 48
Nobu Sanada: Possibly referring to Nobutsuna Sanada or Nobushige Sanada, two famous generals from the Warring States period of Japan. Might be significant to the conversation here that the "nobu" means "belief/faith" and the "sana" means "true/genuine."

PAGE 65
Ryou-tei: The word "ryoutei" is just a term for a traditional Japanese restaurant. The "-tei," as used in the Shinonome-tei Hiroshi interviewed at, has a fancy and traditional connotation. In contrast, the "-ya" on another of Hiroshi's restaurant names gives a folksier connotation while also indicating Japanese food.

PAGE 66
Choco-(Boo^)Bies: In Japanese, "pai" was added to the original katakana to turn it into "oppai" (boobs)."

PAGE 67
"Buttinsky Baker Brother": Eisuke was making a pun, since the Japanese word "sewayaki," which means "meddler," has the word for "bake/grill" in it.

PAGE 70
YuHi: Most likely a reference to ChuHI, a canned, flavored alcoholic drink whose name is a shortening of "shochu highball."

PAGE 96
Asakusa: A neighborhood on the eastern side of Tokyo, famous for being the city's historical entertainment district.

PAGE 102
green ticket window: Midori no madoguchi is a staffed ticket sales location at Japan Rail (JR) stations where guidance can be provided personally, as opposed to automatic ticket machines for those who already know where to go.

PAGE 118
oodles: The original Japanese dialect word was "bissha."

PAGE 124
Tokyo!: All the signs in that first panel have "Tokyo" written in either Japanese or English. The one exception has "Edo"...an old name for Tokyo.

PAGE 129
Chocolate Marbles: Maaburu Chokoreeto are M&M's-like candies sold by the Meiji Corporation.

"This ain't curry!": Chocolate is a common "secret seasoning" for Japanese-style curry, which tends to be sweeter and less spicy than Indian or Thai curries. It mixes in well with a rich curry roux but not so well with eggs...

PAGE 136
Shinjuku: A special ward in Tokyo that serves as the metropolitan center of government and also houses a variety of shopping and entertainment districts.

Tokyo Tower: A communications and observation tower in Tokyo with a design similar to the Eiffel Tower in Paris. It was the tallest structure in Japan until superseded by the Tokyo Skytree in 2010.

Trapple: Nickname for Triple Apple, the (human?) idol group that figured prominently in *Handa-kun*, Chapter 13. That group's got staying power, if it's still around six years later!

PAGE 137
youkan: Jellied bean jam, the same kind of traditional treat that Handa's mom brought as a souvenir in Volume 10.

PAGE 139
Ginza: An upscale neighborhood in central Tokyo, renowned for its luxurious shopping and dining.

PAGE 141
Kichijouji: A neighborhood west of the main wards of Tokyo, which is considered a highly desirable place to live and visit, especially for young people.

PAGE 152
illegible envelope: With context, it's possible to decipher Higashino's handwriting: "Kido-sama, the I.O.U. for the field is enclosed. Thank you very much. Kazuma Higashino."

PAGE 162
hooks: There are types of fishing hooks specially made for catching octopus and squid, with two sets of metal hooks each forming a circle.

PAGE 191
IC Card Stickers: Though the text on the cards is in English, or uses the Roman alphabet, they might be too hard to read on this page. So, here are transcripts of the Gotou dialect words and the matching English lines:
Daruca (tired): I wanna relax at home.
Unmaca (tasty): It tastes great!
Itaca (hurts/ouch): This is the DOJI ("blunder/clumsiness").
Mijyoca (pretty): How cute they are!

BARAKAMON NEWS

Vol.510

Running in two magazines concurrently, on the web and in print.

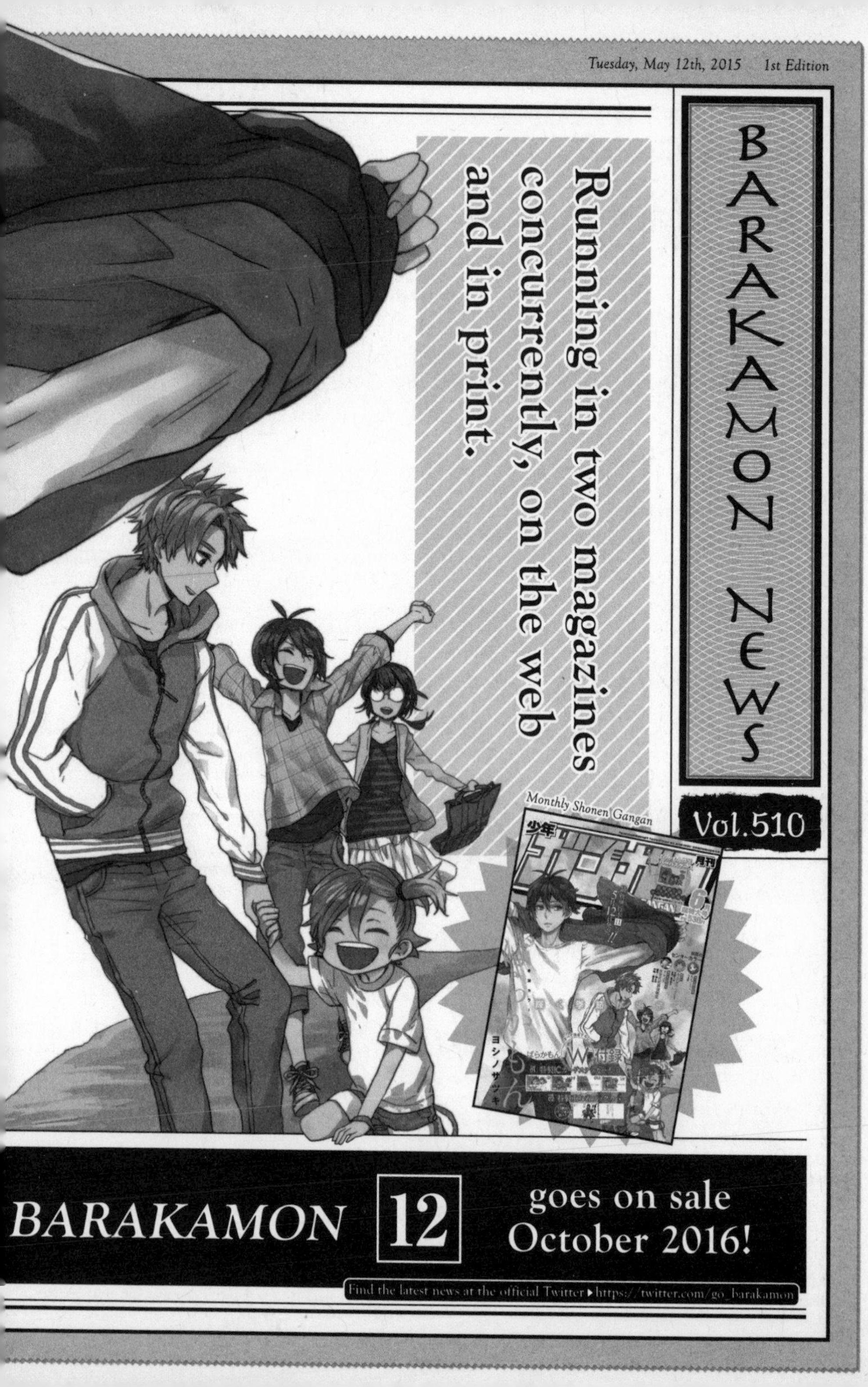
Monthly Shonen Gangan

BARAKAMON 12 goes on sale October 2016!

Find the latest news at the official Twitter ▸ https://twitter.com/go_barakamon

BARAKAMON 11

SATSUKI YOSHINO

Translation/Adaptation: Krista Shipley, Karie Shipley
Lettering: Lys Blakeslee

Barakamon vol. 11 © 2015 Satsuki Yoshino / SQUARE ENIX CO., LTD. First published in Japan in 2015 by SQUARE ENIX CO., LTD. English translation rights arranged with SQUARE ENIX CO., LTD. and Hachette Book Group through Tuttle-Mori Agency, Inc.

Translation © 2016 by SQUARE ENIX CO., LTD.

Yen Press
Hachette Book Group
1290 Avenue of the Americas
New York, NY 10104

www.HachetteBookGroup.com
www.YenPress.com

Yen Press is an imprint of Hachette Book Group, Inc. The Yen Press name and logo are trademarks of Hachette Book Group, Inc.

Library of Congress Control Number: 2016932686

First Yen Press Edition: June 2016

ISBN: 978-0-316-39352-2

10 9 8 7 6 5 4 3 2 1

BVG

Printed in the United States of America